THE BLAZING WORLD

THE BLAZING WORLD

A New History of
Revolutionary England, 1603–1689

Jonathan Healey

Alfred A. Knopf   New York 2023

THIS IS A BORZOI BOOK
PUBLISHED BY ALFRED A. KNOPF

Copyright © 2023 by Jonathan Healey

Maps copyright © 2023 by Michael Athanson

All rights reserved. Published in the United States by Alfred A. Knopf,
a division of Penguin Random House LLC, New York, and distributed in
Canada by Random House of Canada, a division of Penguin Random House
Ltd., Toronto. Originally published in hardcover in Great Britain
by Bloomsbury Publishing Plc, London, in 2023.

www.aaknopf.com

Knopf, Borzoi Books, and the colophon are registered
trademarks of Penguin Random House LLC.

Library of Congress Cataloging-in-Publication Data
Names: Healey, Jonathan, 1982– author.
Title: The blazing world : a new history of revolutionary England,
1603–1689 / Jonathan Healey.
Other titles: New history of revolutionary England, 1603–1689
Description: First American edition. | New York : Alfred A. Knopf, 2023. |
"This is a Borzoi book." | Includes bibliographical references and index.
Identifiers: LCCN 2022038721 (print) | LCCN 2022038722 (ebook) |
ISBN 9780593318355 (hardcover) | ISBN 9780593318362 (ebook)
Subjects: LCSH: Great Britain—History—Stuarts, 1603–1714. |
Great Britain—Politics and government—1603–1714.
Classification: LCC DA375 .H43 2023 (print) | LCC DA375 (ebook) |
DDC 941.06—dc23/eng/20220901
LC record available at https://lccn.loc.gov/2022038721
LC ebook record available at https://lccn.loc.gov/2022038722

Jacket images: Pictorial Press Ltd / Alamy
Jacket design by Linda Huang

Manufactured in the United States of America
First American Edition

For Alice, with love and curiosity.

Contents

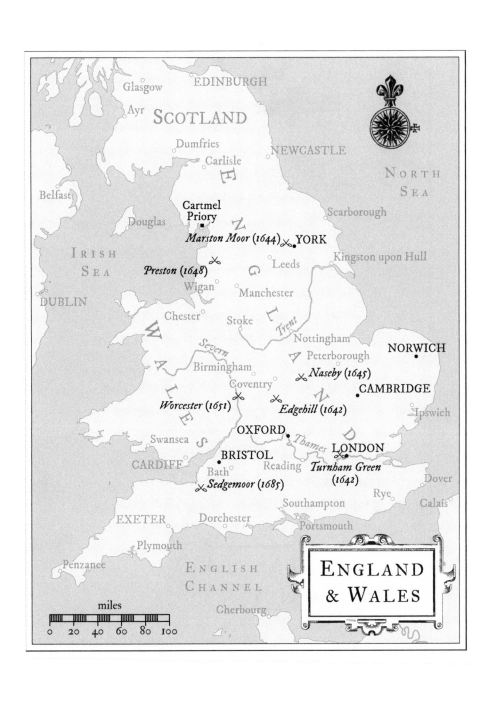

ENGLAND & WALES

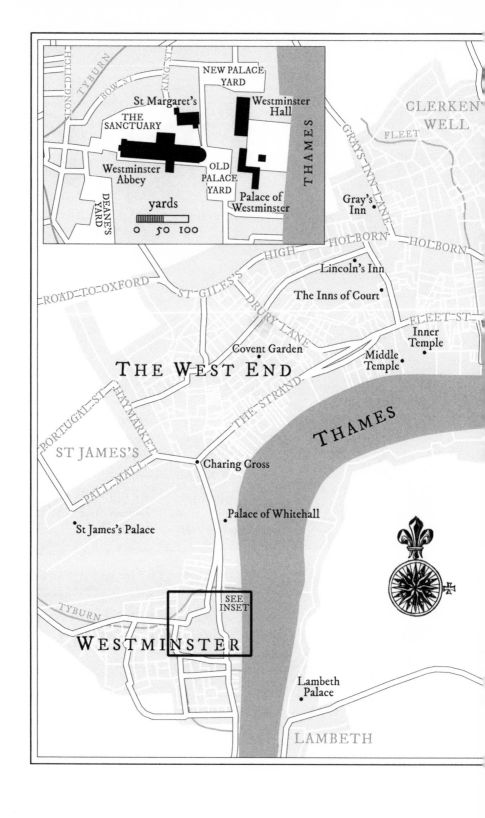

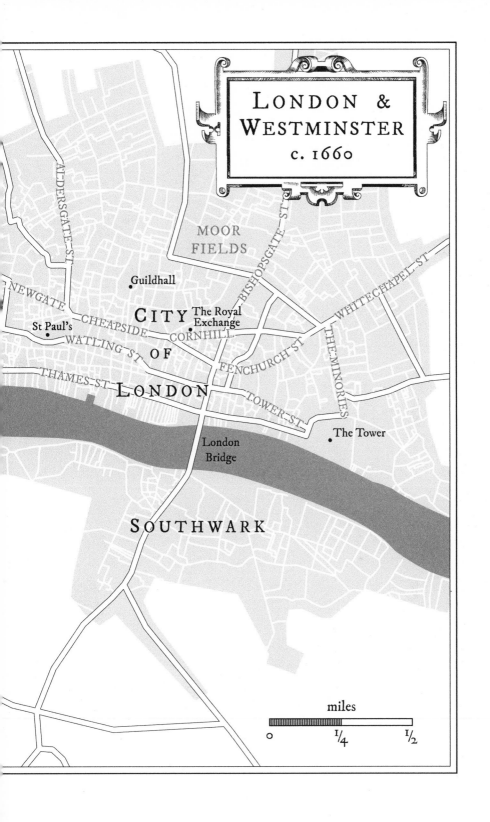

LONDON & WESTMINSTER
c. 1660

MOOR
FIELDS

·Guildhall

ALDERSGATE-ST

BISHOPSGATE-ST

WHITECHAPEL-ST

NEWGATE

CITY

The Royal
Exchange

CHEAPSIDE

CORNHILL

St Paul's·

OF

WATLING-ST

FENCHURCH-ST

THE-MINORIES

THAMES-ST

LONDON

TOWER-ST

·The Tower

London
Bridge

SOUTHWARK

miles

0   ¹/₄   ¹/₂

Introduction

The seventeenth century was a tough time to be alive. Not only was the weather unusually cold, but governments had an unhappy habit of collapsing. In China, India, Russia, France and elsewhere, countries self-immolated into civil war. Germany was ripped apart by 30 years of brutal conflict. In the Americas, European colonialism continued its expansion while the indigenous populations suffered. On the coasts of Africa, slave traders tore people away from their homes and subjected them to one of the vilest enormities of human history.

If you were a European peasant in 1600, you tended to find you were poorer and closer to starvation than you would have been a hundred years before. If you also happened to be female, then your prospects, your power and your voice were subject to even greater control and censure. Bubonic plague was a regular visitor, disease still badly understood and medical care rudimentary at best. Life was capricious and uncertain.

In 1603, the thirty-six-year-old James VI, king of Scotland, took the throne of England, as James I, the first Stuart monarch of the southern kingdom. He was cultured if rather uncouth, thoughtful but fundamentally lazy; an enigma wrapped in a velvet cloak. And his new realm was as unfathomable as he was. Despite the hardness of the times, it was wealthy, politically sophisticated and culturally rich. It was the land of Shakespeare, which had just defeated a mighty Spanish empire, and where sparkling new prodigy houses were announcing the power of the aristocracy and gentry. But it was also fragile and thoroughly traditional. A place still dominated by the land and the turn of the seasons.

Politics centred on the king, his Privy Council and the royal court. Government ministers were appointed and dismissed on a royal whim that owed more to court favour and faction than it did to competence. Nine out of ten of James's subjects lived in the countryside, mostly engaged in farming. The vast majority were illiterate. Thanks to recent advances in cartography, it was possible to get a sense of what England looked like, but no one had much idea of the size of the population, the wealth or the income of the country. Famine was a regular scourge, as was bubonic plague, and wattle and daub towns frequently burned to the ground. Population was growing, but the economy wasn't developing in such a way as to cope, leading to a serious poverty problem with unemployment, plummeting wages and rocketing rents. Fear about witchcraft was at its height, and executions for all kinds of crime, including fairly minor property offences, were peaking. You even had a pretty good chance of being prosecuted if you had extramarital sex.

By the end of the century, a new world had arisen. The great population rise had ended, but the economy kept growing: even labourers were earning more, and famine was now a thing of the past. There was a successful, if embryonic, welfare state. Towns were reborn as social hubs, rebuilt in brick and boasting coffee houses, theatres and concert halls. Trade was now the mainstay of economic life in a thriving market economy. Consumption was conspicuous and rampant, while motive power was increasingly coming from coal. Plague was gone; executions were far less frequent; the witch trials were all but over; and you were much less likely to be prosecuted for illicit sex. English Protestantism had simultaneously become firmly established while also fragmenting into a world of Church and Chapel: not just the official Anglican establishment, but also the widespread – and accepted – existence of Dissent.

In politics, too, so much had changed. James's son Charles I had been put on trial and executed for crimes against his own people, and although his grandsons Charles II and James II had both ruled – the first despite a youth spent in exile, the second despite serious attempts in Parliament to debar him from the throne for his Catholicism – both were forced to deal with a new political landscape. There were confident Parliaments, a vibrant and turbulent press, a split between two identifiable political parties and remarkable religious diversity. Both brothers were able to draw strength from a growing empire, but at home they had to contend with a newly confident public sphere and a politicised middle rank of people who enjoyed nothing more than discussing the latest news over a pipe of tobacco and a pot of coffee.

The elder of the royal brothers, Charles II, was able to navigate this world, although he ended up resting his rule on one of the two political parties, the Tories. James II, on the other hand, was not. In fact, in 1689 his Catholicism and his authoritarian streak would cost him his throne. The English monarchy – and its British successor – has never recovered the power it lost after this revolution, known to posterity as the 'Glorious'. Indeed, the new state that arose out of this was recognisably ancestral to our own: regular Parliaments, the National Debt and the Bank of England and – of course – in 1707 the Union between England and Scotland, all came soon afterwards.

Just as remarkable as all this, though, were the paths not taken. In the 1640s, England descended into civil war, part of a labyrinthine conflict that ripped apart the whole archipelago. The causes of this were complex. They included the failings of Charles I as a king, the long-term financial weakness of his monarchy and the challenges of ruling England, Scotland and Ireland simultaneously. Charles's personal authoritarianism clashed with a deep belief in an 'ancient constitution', and his monarchy – like that of his father, though in a more aggressive way – took a side in a simmering culture war between Puritans and their enemies. But the Civil Wars also arose out of social change: the rise of the literate 'middling sort' expanded the political nation at a time when a media revolution was producing a vast deluge of print, including newspapers. London was growing into a politically engaged and unruly metropolis, with whom the monarchy and Parliament would have to live cheek by jowl, especially as the built-up area spread west out of the City and into Westminster around the royal palace of Whitehall. As Charles and Parliament jockeyed for power in the crisis years of 1640 to 1642, it was the population of London which repeatedly made the decisive interventions that pushed England into Civil War.

The Civil Wars were conflicts about ideology: partly religious but also partly about the constitution. In the beginning, an absolutist monarchy faced off against an opposition that vested power in property rights, the traditional constitution and Parliament. By the time war broke out, it was the Parliamentarians who were starting to argue for radical change while the Royalists could claim that they, now, were the defenders of the traditional constitution. The shift had happened in the astonishingly fast-moving months between November 1640 and the summer of 1642. Gradually, the Parliamentarians went down a more radical path, the ultimate consequences of which were the abolition of the monarchy, the House of Lords and the bishops, followed by Oliver Cromwell's Protectorate based on a balanced, written constitution. Eventually all this would fail, but it remains the most radical political experiment in English history.

Meanwhile, the mid-century crisis also brought what is still one of the greatest explosions in political and social creativity the country has ever seen. New social and religious movements terrified the political classes, while more respectable voices suggested everything from legal aid to welfare reform to freedom of speech, divorce and a national health service. Even before the execution of the king, the political awakening of the Parliamentary army, a force of peasants and traders led by minor gentlemen, had generated astonishingly sophisticated debates over the country's future, including suggestions of giving the vote to all adult men. The Protectorate would turn its back on political radicalism, and after the Republic failed in 1660 the backlash against this, and the religious sects, would be forceful. This particular revolutionary moment passed, but it left a lasting legacy, and even today the story of people who transcended the confines of a reactionary culture to argue for genuinely transformative change remains an important one.

The echoes of seventeenth-century England are still with us, in our society, in the built environment and in the very landscape. We, too, are living through our own historical moment in which a media revolution, social fracturing and culture wars are redefining society and politics, creating issues that, dare we say it, not every leader has proved entirely adept at navigating. Comparisons between our own society and those that came before are often rather excitable and overblown, but it does seem worth thinking about what can happen when social change, cultural conflict and political mistakes combine. The answers are not always comforting, but neither are they uniformly negative. Crises can be creative as well as injurious.

More to the point, the seventeenth century also saw one fundamental change on the English political scene, which has consequences we're still working through now. When he sat down to write his own thoughts on why the Stuart monarchy had collapsed, the philosopher Thomas Hobbes observed that 'the power of the mighty hath no foundation but in the opinion and belief of the people'.[1] It was an idea that would have horrified the absolutist King James I. Through much of the century, ordinary people were derided by their betters as rascals, 'vulgar', a 'rabble'; they were 'giddy-headed' and 'fickle'. As one tutor to the future King Charles I put it in 1613 – translating an Italian historian – the people were a 'many-headed monster, which hath neither head for brains, nor brains for government'.[2] Such attitudes survive to this day, of course, in some quarters at least, but in the seventeenth century the people, including those outside the traditional elite, and *public opinion*, became decisive factors in politics.

The idea that power should, ultimately, reside in the people remains one of the cardinal slogans of the modern era. It is foundational to the United States constitution, beginning as it does with its stirring – if somewhat inaccurate – assertion to speak for the whole population: '*We the people* ...' Famously, also, it's there in the Gettysburg Address, with the call for 'government of the people, by the people, for the people'. And it's there in more recent times, too. In the 1960s, activists called and chanted for 'power to the people', while the belief that 'All Power Belongs to the People' was expressed at Tiananmen Square in 1989. Such is the power of the idea that even authoritarians have to appeal to the 'will of the people', and suchlike.

All of this had been anticipated in seventeenth-century England. In fact, a debate over sovereignty ran through the century. Even before the Civil War, the Parliamentarian propagandist Henry Parker had argued that 'Power is originally inherent in the people', while in 1650 one republican theorist – John Parker (no relation to Henry) – came remarkably close to anticipating President Lincoln's words during another great civil war, by arguing that government 'is in the people, from the people, and for the people'. As the century progressed, the theoretical notion that power ultimately resided in the people clashed with the absolutist argument that it lay with the monarchy.

Our story, though, is not really one of theories; it is one of grubby politics. Indeed, thanks to a major growth in the political literacy of those just outside the traditional political elite – namely the gentry and the newly confident 'middling sort' – English politics was, over the century, radically changed. It became essential for governments to present an ideological vision, and to try to sell this to the people. Central to this was Parliament, which was the institutional voice of the new political classes, and which by the end of the century had won control over taxation, the government and even the royal succession. The political world we live in today, with regular Parliaments and elections, ideologically defined parties, a vibrant press and mass campaigns centred on large protests and petitions, was born in the seventeenth century. For this, as well as so much else, the story told here remains fascinating and vital to this day.

It is also a story of detail and social depth, for in the seventeenth century, thanks to the astonishing variety of source materials available, from letters and diaries, to autobiographies, government and legal documentation, petitions and print, the lives of ordinary people can be accessed in vivid technicolour. The society they lived in and shaped can be seen in remarkable detail. So this book is about raw politics, but it is also about the social change that conditioned those politics. It is narrative history, and for this it makes no apologies, but it's also about how the forces that combined to create nearly a hundred years of turbulence, out of which arose a remarkable new world, one which – for better or worse – was blazing a path towards our own.

PART ONE

1603–29
The Hearts of Thy Subjects

I

St James's Day

When Hempe is Spun, England's done.
                    Late Tudor English Prophecy[1]

Probably the strangest way anyone celebrated the accession of King James I of England was when a gentlewoman in the far north of Lancashire organised a mock wedding in a country church, between two male servants.

The old priory of Cartmel was already, by then, a relic of a lost age. Before the Reformation it had been a monastic foundation, with around a dozen canons, working and praying within the cold stone walls. The nearby villagers welcomed the presence of such a great house, and when Henry VIII closed it down along with the rest of England's monasteries, several of them joined the great northern rebellion that became known as the Pilgrimage of Grace. At least ten of them, plus four of the canons, were hanged for doing so.

After the rebellion failed, the priory was shut. But the surviving villagers were savvy enough to organise a petition to the Tudor king, arguing that in such a poor corner of England they needed the building. Keeping it standing in the centre of the village would ensure, they hoped, that the light of God would continue to shine there. Henry's government had assented, and Cartmel Priory became Cartmel parish church, spared the destruction visited on most of England's old monasteries.

The poverty of the village didn't go away, though, and gradually the lack of investment was bringing the church to a parlous state. By 1600, much of the roof of the chancel was missing, so services were frequently interrupted by the characteristic local rain. Decay had set in.[2]

Around a mile to the north-east of Cartmel church, along a quiet country lane among pasture farms and crumbling stone buildings, lay the rather mediocre grey house of Hampsfell Hall. Crenelated against the Scottish raiders who still occasionally sallied south and took away cattle and sheep, it was the seat of the old gentry Thornborough family.

Thornboroughs had been in Cartmel for nearly two centuries, making fairly little impact, watching the religious makeup of the country change around them as England became Protestant. Around the time of James I's accession in 1603, they had welcomed a new daughter-in-law, married to Rowland Thornborough, one of the family's latest sons. Her name was Jane, and she hailed from another gentry family, the Daltons of Thurnham, near Lancaster. The Thornboroughs and the Daltons were locally influential families, possessed of significant farming estates. But they shared another thing, too. They were Catholics.

The day Jane Thornborough picked for her prank was the feast day of St James, 25 July 1604. It was exactly a year since the coronation of the new king at Westminster Abbey, nearly 300 miles away to the south, and to mark this occasion the villagers at Cartmel had organised a special sermon. They had invited one Mr Francis Fletcher, a travelling preacher, to speak. But as Jane Thornborough knew well, St James's Day was also an important marker in the parish's festival calendar. For it was the traditional day for the annual 'rushbearing' – a ritual in which youngsters garlanded themselves in greenery and carried rushes to strew across the church floor, followed by games and sports in a local field.

It was an unfortunate clash. The festivities would be boisterous, and hardly compatible with the solemnity of a commemorative sermon. Or, to put it another way, the gravity of the sermon was out of keeping with a traditional day of relaxation and sport. So the parish elders had suggested a compromise. Those wishing to bear rushes, they asked, should wait until Mr Fletcher had finished his sermon. Then they could let themselves loose, and the dancing and football could begin. Everyone would be happy.

When St James's Day came the villagers had gathered in the cool chancel of the church. With the summer morning light shining through the broken roof, Francis Fletcher began proceedings. He ascended the pulpit, opened his Bible and cleared his throat. His audience looked up at him: farmers in their best woollen coats, their wives in their bonnets, squirming children at their sides. As he spoke, 'dividing the text', some of the eager parishioners listened keenly. Others settled back and allowed their thoughts to wander, while Fletcher's words competed with the sounds of the cattle and sheep from the village pastures.

Then, something astonishing happened. Slowly, imperceptibly at first, a noise could be heard in the distance. Gradually, it grew into a deafening cacophony: the thud of drums, the shriek of fifes and the wail of bagpipes. Then came gunshots: loud cracks of powder followed by the fizzing of musket balls against the old stone walls. It was a procession, and soon it had entered the church.

Fletcher the preacher had stopped speaking. The heads of the congregation had turned away from the pulpit, and towards the company of young men, bedecked in greenery, carrying rushes, with many wearing masks over their faces. They were led by a man called William Dawson, farm steward at the Thornboroughs' Hampsfell Hall. He was carrying a truncheon, acting a role. He was a 'Lord of Misrule'.

Next, the men divided themselves up into two companies, then marched on through the church, casting their rushes onto the floor as they went. After this, they assembled again at the front. Now, two young lads emerged from their ranks. Of these, one was dressed in a woman's gown. His name was Oliver Staines and the gown – as at least one member of the congregation was able to recognise – belonged to Jane Thornborough herself.

Someone pushed to the front, carrying a copy of the Book of Common Prayer, one of the key texts of English Protestantism. With the Book open, he turned to the parishioners in the church and started reading. The tone he took was mocking, scornful, as he read the words of the official wedding ceremony, marrying the two men as if they had been husband and wife. Then he told the two men to sit down, inviting them to take the seats the parishioners normally reserved for newlyweds.

By now the pranksters were beginning to file back out of the church. As they left, they had one last hurrah. Coming out into the churchyard, Dawson the Lord of Misrule leapt up on a wall and called a 'Solemn Oyez' ('O-yay, o-yay, o-yay!'). Then, one of his fellows made a declaration, aping the formality of an official pronouncement, passing out paper copies to those watching. The days of Momus had gone, he announced. *Momus would tarry here no more.* And, with that, the men left, heading out onto a nearby hill, where they played football for the rest of the morning.

A change of leadership is always disorientating, but a change of ruling dynasty was all the more so. In March 1603, the last Tudor ruler of England, Queen Elizabeth I, died at Richmond Palace, the grand seat built by her grandfather Henry VII, on the winding banks of the Thames in the tree-shaded landscape of northern Surrey. With the country in a state of high alert, and watches placed on the coastal towns, the plan to bring in a peaceful succession was put into play. A messenger was sent north to Holyrood in Edinburgh, to King James VI of the Scots. Within a few days, the wily and coarse James was on his way south, following a grand procession down the eastern side of England as the great and good of his new southern realm flocked to give allegiance.

In Elizabeth's reign, a prophecy had circulated widely: 'When Hempe is spun, England's done.' 'Hempe' was an acronym for the Tudor monarchs since the break with Rome: Henry, Edward, Mary and Philip (II of Spain, Mary's husband), and Elizabeth. Prophecies were taken seriously, as signs of God's plan, and the belief was that once Elizabeth died, England would collapse into anarchy. But the peaceful accession of James allowed a more benign conclusion: now England and Scotland were under the same ruler. England was done: long live Britain.

There were other signs, though, that the older, more apocalyptic prophecy might still be the true one. Intellectuals and commentators of the day pored over cosmic events to assess whether the universe lay unbalanced and whether God's wrath was imminent. What they saw did not bring comfort. They looked at England and saw a land full of witches: 'They abound in all places,' fretted the Lord Chief Justice of the Common Pleas, Edmund Anderson.[3] People tried to divine signs of the future in meteorological phenomena like unusual tempests, and strange biological prodigies, such as 'monstrous' human births, and saw warnings from God.[4] For, as it was said, 'God doth premonish before he doth punish.'[5] There were blazing stars in the heavens, which were sure to be signs of cosmic disturbance. Comets, such as those of 1577 and 1580, foretold trouble, and most worrying of all, there were great new stars that shone bright enough to be seen in the daytime. One had appeared in 1572 and another would shine in 1604. No one remembered anything like this ever before.

The Cartmel wedding was a joke about the collapse of the universe. It was about the uprooting of the social order and the world turned upside down. Specifically, it was celebrating the fact that the world was about to be set the right way up again. Momus was a character who symbolised disorder; his expulsion brought balance.

Raucous processions like this, in which humour was made out of the world turned topsy-turvy, were part of the culture of the age. The most famous kind of procession was the *charivari*, what in England was called the 'riding', or 'skimmington'.[6] Here, some poor local folk would have offended the parish, perhaps two were living together unmarried, or perhaps a wife dominated her husband. The skimmington, which took its name from a kind of wooden ladle with which a wife might beat her henpecked spouse, was a way of ritually humiliating such transgressors. A procession of villagers would pass through the streets, banging pots and pans and making horn gestures with their fingers, symbolising cuckoldry, and leading an effigy of the couple seated backwards on an ass. The disorder, the noise and the inversion of the expected order all symbolised the way in which the subject of the skimmington had turned the world upside down. It betokens a world where the fabric of order is seen as fragile, where small deviations from social norms could take on a cosmic significance.

What Jane Thornborough organised at Cartmel was a skimmington against Protestantism. Momus, who was widely known from the bestselling *Aesop's Fables*, was the Greek god of satire. He represented a world turned upside down. He, the discordant music and the transgressive wedding were saying something straightforward enough: Protestantism had overturned the natural order, it had turned things topsy-turvy. After the procession had left the church (very symbolic), a mock-proclamation announced the end of Momus's time. The Protestants were being cast out of Cartmel church, fittingly enough a former priory. Their unnatural religion would reign here no more, and the old order could return. Such were the hopes of Catholics like Jane Thornborough when James I came to the English throne.

It was fashionable among some English churchmen to decry the irreligion of the age. It was said that ordinary English folk knew more about Robin Hood than they did the stories in the Bible.[7] In Cartmel, when a thorough-minded minister was appointed to the parish in the 1640s, the unfortunate cleric fell to discussing Jesus Christ with an aged local. 'Oh, sir,' the old man informed him, 'I think I heard of the man you speak of, once in a play at Kendal, called a Corpus Christi play, where there was a man on a tree, and blood ran down.'[8]

But clergy always bewail the lack of piety shown by their neighbours, and rural folk like the old man at Cartmel have always found ways of mocking over-earnest outsiders. The reality is that the English under James I were profoundly religious. The church remained the focus of life, the most durable building in most parishes and one which hosted not just baptisms, marriages and funerals, but parish meetings, and – of course – regular services which people were obliged to attend by law. The landscape was dotted with reminders of the Christian faith, from wayside crosses and holy wells to the very many features that were associated with the saints or with the devil. The very idioms with which people spoke were saturated with Scripture.

As the Stuart age began, England was entering a new phase of what was now an old battle. In the sixteenth century, the country had ripped itself away from Roman Catholicism, much to the shock and terror of her own people. Most of the old monasteries had been torn down in the 'fatal thunderclap' that followed Henry VIII's break with centuries of tradition, and despite a temporary swing back to Catholicism under his eldest child, Mary I (r. 1553–8), England had slowly clawed its way towards being a truly Protestant nation. Mary's younger sister Elizabeth had forged a new Church, backed by conformity enforced by law. In some ways it ploughed a middle path, the famous *via media* between the Catholicism of Rome and the hardline Protestantism practised in Geneva, but Elizabeth's Church was firmly Reformed, and although tradition claims she didn't wish to 'make windows into men's souls', the apparatus of her state was quite happy to do so, fining those who refused to come to Protestant church services and executing Jesuits and the roving Catholic priests who began coming into the country as European powers tried to win England back to Rome.

Within English Protestantism there was still considerable debate about church government, about the liturgy (ritual practice during worship) and about grace (how one got to heaven). The central texts, the English Bible, the Book of Common Prayer and the Thirty-Nine Articles (which stated the doctrine and practice of the Church of England), contained enough ambiguity for a range of viewpoints to have developed. Broadly speaking, most churchmen in 1603 were Calvinist, that is, they subscribed to a form of Protestantism rooted in the works of John Calvin, a Frenchman who had settled in Geneva and turned it into a beacon of the Reformed faith.[9] Calvinism held that man was inherently depraved, but God's grace had been made available to a small subset of humans, who were thus predestined to heaven, while the remainder of mankind were predestined for hell. Calvinists saw the word of God as especially important, and thus emphasised sermons, private prayer and the reading of Scripture. The elaborate ceremonies of pre-Reformation worship they viewed with suspicion.

Among the English Calvinists some of the trickiest debates were over the organisation of the Church and the faithful. One particularly difficult issue was the role of bishops. Were they sanctioned by divine law, or merely by established custom? Or should they be abolished outright, and churches ruled by elected assemblies of elders.

Those who subscribed to this last view were known as Presbyterians. Their movement, Presbyterianism, had enjoyed some significance under Elizabeth. A watershed had been reached in 1588–9, when a pamphlet war exploded in which scabrous publications under the pseudonym of Martin Marprelate ('Martin Bash-bishop') made noisy calls for the abolition of the episcopacy. In response, so-called 'anti-Martinist' pamphlets had attacked the call for Presbyterianism as dangerous, populist and damaging to the social order. The character of Martin himself was likened to Momus, not just a clownish figure, but also a sanctimonious one, the 'God of Fault-finding'.[10] It was a link that stuck, and Momus came to be used as shorthand for Martinists, for Presbyterians and for their most lasting group allies: those who came to be known by another name – an insulting one. Puritans.

The English Puritans under Elizabeth were Calvinists, and they differed from their fellows in temper and intensity rather than necessarily in actual belief. They placed even more emphasis on sermons, reading and private prayer, and were positively antagonistic towards many religious traditions. Their aims included the abolition of anything even vaguely reminiscent of Catholic ceremony, from decorated market crosses to graven images and stained-glass windows in the church, to the long surplices worn by ministers and even the wedding rings worn by those who married.

A central aspect of Puritans' lives was the sermon, and they might walk many miles on Sundays to market towns to enjoy outdoor preaching and huge communal 'fasts'.[11] Here, after listening to the often thrilling and theatrical sermons, they would gather in alehouses to end the fast and chew over the points made before travelling home with their bellies brimming with ale and hearty food, their souls full of the light of God. It was a sociable and lubricating experience very different from what we would expect from the modern stereotype.

Many Puritans had experienced a personal moment of conversion, not to Christianity, but to their own heightened understanding of it, to 'Godliness'. This brought a change of outlook, even of career. The theologian William Twisse had converted when bad fortune befell one of his classmates. Something of a libertine at Winchester College, he had been alarmed to be visited, when sitting on the toilet, by the ghost of one of his fellow rakehell schoolmates, whose message was clear: 'I am damned.'[12] Others, like the Cambridgeshire gentleman Oliver Cromwell, experienced this 'rebirth' after a period of bad luck and introspection: 'Oh, I lived in and loved darkness and hated the light; I was a chief, the chief of sinners,' he wrote, but God 'giveth me to see light in His light. One beam in a dark place hath exceeding much refreshment in it: blessed be His Name for shining upon so dark a heart as mine!'[13]

The culture of Puritans, so their detractors thought, could be dangerously irreverent towards accepted hierarchies and social norms.[14] Personal conversions were all very well, but they came from individual moments of revelation rather than participation in communal worship and ritual. And was it not suspiciously egalitarian for these people to go from place to place in search of sermons, critiquing them based on their own reading of Scripture, picking and choosing which preachers they listened to? Why not accept the minister they had been provided with in their own parish? Puritans believed that all members of the church were essentially equal, linked by their own personal conversion experience rather than deference to any worldly authority. They thought that ministers should be chosen by their congregations (though as one was at pains to point out, this meant that the 'chief fathers, ancients and governors of the parish' should do the choosing rather than the 'multitude').[15] If they accepted bishops at all – and not all of them did – they certainly did not accept that their position existed by divine sanction. To some, indeed, the Puritan suspicion of earthly hierarchies represented a dangerous, even a revolutionary, ideology. Just like Catholics, so one sceptic alleged, 'Puritans will have the King but an honourable member, not a chief governor in the churches of his own dominions.'[16]

A key goal for Puritans was to reform society more widely, to stamp out practices they felt were damaging to the commonwealth and offensive to God. Calvin himself had turned Geneva into a morally pure commonwealth by using secular authorities to crush sin. Puritans wanted to do the same in England. It would, they hoped, become a new Jerusalem, a shining city on a hill rid of vices such as illicit sex, excessive drinking and swearing. They wanted people to pray, read Scripture and give willingly to support the poor. A particular bugbear was therefore traditional festivities and pastimes, especially sport on the Sabbath but also festival days. Pancake day, Morris dancing, wrestling after church and, of course, rushbearings like that at Cartmel were all 'heathenish': the 'storehouse and nursery,' wrote one cynic, 'of bastardy'.[17] Traditional celebrations were both disorderly, and they had Catholic connotations, such as the marking of saints' days. They may have been exceedingly popular, especially with

younger folk, but they were an affront to God, and often themselves
brought drunkenness and illicit sex.

Naturally this was a campaign which ensured Puritans were seen
by their enemies simply as wretched miseries: cantankerous prigs
who instead of socialising sat 'moping always at their books'.[18] The
Puritan, someone quipped, was a person who loved God 'with all
his soul, but hates his neighbour with all his heart'.[19] Puritans were
therefore disruptive in ways that transcended fine points of theology.
They went about telling people the things they enjoyed were offensive to God and they caused bad blood between neighbours. They
put communities on edge, created cultural conflict that burrowed
deep into society.

It was this conflict, between the Godly and the merry, between
Puritan reformism and traditional beliefs, that was at play on St James's
Day 1604 in Cartmel. For Jane Thornborough's mock wedding wasn't
just a celebration hoping for better times for Catholics. It was also
a skimmington against a Puritan, one who was intruding a sermon
into a day traditionally given over to a festival. When she and William
Dawson, her Lord of Misrule, found themselves in court, their
defence alleged that the minister Francis Fletcher was 'a man given
to set dissensions & variance amongst neighbours and also between
man & wife'.[20] It was a coded innuendo, supposed to imply that he
was a Puritan. The fact Fletcher was mocked as 'Momus' was a reference people would have got. For Momus was a figure often used to
represent Puritans: the God of Fault-finding.

Under Elizabeth, Puritanism had initially flourished, but by the 1600s
it was in retreat. People had been arrested, imprisoned, mutilated and
in some cases killed. The dominant view, as expressed by the poet-
preacher John Donne, was that the radical Puritan sects were 'gangrened
limbs'.[21] Presbyterianism, the movement for a church without bishops,
had fallen to a low ebb. By 1603, therefore, Puritanism had evolved
into something rather amorphous: a tendency within the established
Church, a subset of a broad Calvinist consensus. Many Puritans now
accepted the existence of bishops, if not their divine sanction. Most of
the episcopal bench were now solid Calvinists anyway.

A hardline minority remained completely alienated, many breaking with the official Church altogether and forming illegal congregations of 'Separatists', such as the 'Brownists' (followers of Robert Browne), who came to be a byword for the movement. But those Puritans who remained within the Church still craved reform of the liturgy, and of society more generally, and when James came to the throne they thought their moment might have come. As representative of the thoroughly reformed Scottish Kirk, James was associated with an advanced breed of Calvinism. Scotland, after all, was considered by many English reformists as the next best place to Geneva. A huge petition – called the 'Millenary Petition' because it was said to have a thousand signatories – was passed to the new king on his journey south, and James agreed to a conference at Hampton Court on the future of the Church of England. In his first year, he issued a proclamation against plays, animal baiting and 'other like disordered or unlawful exercises' on the Sabbath.[22] It was a reformist agenda, that Puritans found encouraging.

Yet they were to be disappointed. Despite his own sympathies towards Calvinism, James's experience in Scotland, where the Kirk had proved politically volatile, had made him very suspicious of the more forward Protestants who made his country famous. So it didn't take much for him to transfer this prejudice to the English Puritans.

At the beginning of 1604, James's great conference convened at Hampton Court. He pleased everyone by ordering a new English Bible, which would eventually bear fruit in 1611 with the King James Version, but on pretty much everything else he took a strong anti-Presbyterian, anti-Puritan line. The Millenary Petitioners were told to stop their 'snivelling'. 'A turd for your argument!' James reasoned at one point to the reformist Bishop of Peterborough. 'No bishops, no king!' he famously declared.[23] Shortly after the Conference, a new version of the Prayer Book was issued, and this, too, was a disappointment to Puritans, for it was almost identical to the old one. And in 1604 the bad news kept coming, with new canons (church laws) issued which maintained plenty of traditional practices.[24] Even fasts, one of the mainstays of Puritan culture, were specifically banned unless licensed by a bishop. It was to be the first attack by the Stuart monarchy on English Puritanism, though it was not to be the last.

James probably never heard of the Cartmel wedding, though he would have liked the mocking of Puritans it entailed if not the overall anti-Protestant joke. But Jane Thornborough's prank did attract the attention of the authorities.

At first it was brought before the local criminal court at Lancaster, as a riotous disorder. But here the case was squashed by a local magistrate, James Anderton, whose family just happened to be full of Catholics. The argument Anderton made was, in effect, that this was a matter for the church courts not those of the secular law.

Anderton was stalling to protect his Catholic neighbours, but he did, in a technical sense, have a point. The church courts had a semi-separate jurisdiction in England, looking after canon law, including the moral failings of the people. Sitting in the shadows of England's great cathedrals, they punished people for moral lapses ranging from illicit sex to chatting and knitting in church, through to the unhappy case of one Edmund Booth of Holton, Suffolk, who was prosecuted because 'there was a fart let in the church in sermon time and he was vehemently suspected for the same'.[25] As poor Booth found out, irreverent behaviour in church was a major part of the courts' repertoire. Clearly, a raucous procession that interrupted a sermon, and which mocked the very institution of marriage itself, not to mention the Book of Common Prayer, was the very definition of the kind of offence that should end up in them.[26]

The trouble was that the sanctions they offered were minor – usually some form of public penance, such as having the offenders stand in a white sheet in church during divine service and forcing them to ask forgiveness of the congregation. Scarcely enough, therefore, for such an outrage as took place at Cartmel. And, more to the point, James Anderton himself had some local form. Shortly before the Cartmel wedding, he had conspicuously failed to investigate a violent burglary further south in the county, near Wigan. The sources we have are frustratingly vague, but it seems this may have been connected to the collection of fines on Catholics. Before this, when Queen Elizabeth died in 1603, Anderton had turned a blind eye as his associates involved themselves in a series of pranks directed against the church in his home parish of Leyland. During what was evidently a period of some disorder, Leyland's English Bible had been hidden away in an alehouse and – worse – some local schoolboys had clambered into the church and unlocked the door

allowing a herd of cattle in. The following Sunday the poor congregation of law-abiding Protestants had found themselves 'annoyed with
the dung'. With all this, plus now the tumultuous wedding at Cartmel,
James Anderton and his accomplices needed a stricter punishment than
that offered by the church courts. So their case was taken higher, to the
royal court of Star Chamber, at Westminster. It was a serious court for
what was evidently a serious business.[27]

Star Chamber was an important arm of the English state. So-called
because it convened in a room at Westminster with a star-spangled
ceiling, it was partly feared as an instrument of censorship and government terror, and partly respected as a useful tool by which rich provincial thugs could be brought to justice. It was increasingly choked
with business too. For this was a litigious age, and Star Chamber's
flexible approach to crime allowed it to hear many novel offences that
were much harder to prosecute in the main common-law courts. It
also dealt extensively with sedition, riot and particularly those cases
where malefactors were using their own influence in the localities
to evade justice. It was, therefore, the perfect place to prosecute the
magistrate James Anderton and the perpetrators of a riotous wedding
in a church that he was protecting.

The case against Anderton, and with him Jane Thornborough and
William Dawson, was brought by the victim of the burglary, one John
Roper, in the autumn of 1604. It is evident from it that he launched
his suit against James Anderton while he only knew of the Cartmel
wedding by rumour – in the first 'bill of complaint' it is described
rather vaguely as an 'outrage', and the date is wrong by nearly a
month. Clearly at some point shortly thereafter, Roper came into new
information about the specifics of the wedding, which was evidently
juicy enough for him to put together a second bill. In this, the full
glory of what happened at Cartmel is set out, and, from here, over
the coming months, the case proceeded. Interrogations took place,
witness statements were gathered, both in London and in Lancashire,
and the slow gears of the English law ground into action.

Roper vs Anderton, Thornborough, et al. has left a sprawling
bundle of fascinating documentation, the ageing paper and spindly

pen strokes revealing a vivid picture of a vast local controversy that would otherwise have been entirely lost to us. They include documents setting out the prosecution case, the answers of the defendants and depositions from dozens of local men and women: those who heard of the burglary, or the disorder in Leyland church, or the Cartmel wedding. The principal defendants, including Jane Thornborough and William Dawson, her Lord of Misrule, gave testimony, saying that the whole thing was just a bit of summertime fun – a rushbearing as was the tradition in the parish. Jane admitted lending one of her gowns to a servant lad, one Oliver Staines, so she accepted there was cross-dressing, but not a mock wedding or any gunfire. Congregants who had witnessed the whole thing were on hand to obfuscate and protect their Catholic neighbours. Whatever their thoughts of Jane Thornborough's joke, and whatever their thoughts about her Catholicism, it is clear that most of Cartmel's villagers had little desire to see prosecutions and the inevitable heavy fines for which Star Chamber was notorious.

But there is one element to the case that you would miss if you weren't looking very closely at the documents themselves, which links it to bigger things. It is a name. For at the bottom of the initial 'bill of complaint', the official document which stated the plaintiff's case, are three faint signatures, those of the attorneys who helped draft the case. One is an obscure lawyer named Robert Harte, about whom we know very little; another is the rising barrister Sir Ranulph Crewe, who would go on to be an MP and chief justice of the King's Bench. The third, though, is the most significant of all. It is that of Edward Coke, the Attorney General.

Edward Coke was England's richest lawyer, and one of the finest minds of the age. His life was to have many twists in the future, and like any good attorney he had plenty of enemies. But in 1604 he was close to the apogee of his career, basking in court favour and enjoying one of the highest legal offices in the land.

Coke was a man of principle: he didn't just practise law, he believed in it like a religion. To Coke, English law was based on precedent, the wisdom of ancient legal minds, and enshrined in reams of jurisprudence, statutes and Magna Carta. This wasn't top of Coke's mind in 1604, though. Not yet, at least. Instead, what was exercising James's Attorney General was Catholics, for Coke despised them. It was said he wanted to root them out, to prove 'that only being a Catholic is to be a traitor'.[28]

And the king was in broad support. Having wooed Catholics, disingenuously, from Scotland, once safely on the English throne James changed his approach. 'Na na, Good faith,' he joked, 'we'll not need the Papists now.'[29] In February 1604, the king had banished Catholic priests by royal proclamation. Come November, he increased fines for 'recusancy', for not attending communion in a Protestant church, something many Catholics still refused.* England's most prominent religious minority were therefore suddenly feeling the heat. And so, around this time, a group of them decided to hit back.

The conspirators had first met in May at an inn just off the Strand in London. Their leader was a charismatic Warwickshire gentleman called Robert Catesby. Among them was the aristocrat Thomas Percy, and a tall, rough-hewn Yorkshireman who'd fought for the Catholic armies in Europe, called Guy Fawkes.

The plan was to hit the Protestant state at its very heart, right at one of its moments of ritual triumphalism: at the reopening of Parliament after recess, with the king, queen, the heir Prince Henry, the House of Lords and those members of the Commons able to crowd into the chamber all in attendance. Burrowing under the building, the men planned to set off enough gunpowder to bring the room crashing down in an inferno of fire, splinters and falling stone. It would kill the leading figures of the nation in one go.

Percy rented a small house, with a cellar, next to the jumble of buildings that housed Parliament within the Palace of Westminster, and the men dug while Fawkes stood guard, pistol in hand. Then, an opportunity presented itself. A vault, once a kitchen, underneath the House of Lords became available: Fawkes snapped it up on the rental market, saying Percy his master needed it to store his winter fuel. The men started to fill the vault with barrels of gunpowder.

---

*I.e. for recusing oneself from church, as many Catholics still did.

Twice the day of Parliament's reopening was postponed, thanks to the threat of plague. Eventually it settled on 5 November 1605.

The planning continued. Catesby wanted to assemble a party of sympathetic gentlemen at Dunchurch in Warwickshire. Here, at a small timber-framed inn next to the major crossroads that cut through the ancient village, they were to be told it was a hunting party. But then the news of the blast would arrive, and so the plan would be to lead this expeditionary force to Coventry, where they would seize the king's nine-year-old daughter Elizabeth and proclaim her queen.

Catesby picked three gentlemen he knew to be secret Catholics and asked them to help fund the plot. Two of them, Sir Everard Digby and Ambrose Rookwood, recoiled in horror, not least because many good Catholics sat in the Lords. A third, though, promised £2,000. He was Francis Tresham.

The day neared. Late in October, Tresham's brother-in-law, Lord Monteagle, settled down for supper in Hoxton, on the outskirts of London. Sitting at his table, he was brought a letter. It was anonymous, undated and chilling. 'My Lord,' it said, 'Out of the love I bear to some of your friends, I have a care of your preservation.' It advised him to find some excuse, any excuse, to avoid the opening of Parliament. 'For God and man hath concurred to punish the wickedness of this time.' 'Retire yourself into your country,' it pleaded, 'for though there be no appearance of any stir, yet I say they shall receive a terrible blow this Parliament and yet they shall not see who hurts them.'[30]

They shall receive a terrible blow. Rather than burn the note after reading it, as it pleaded him to do, Monteagle took it to Robert Cecil, James's Machiavellian secretary of state. The king was hunting, but on Sunday he returned. 'I remember,' James mused on seeing the letter, 'that my father died by gunpowder', recalling stories of the violent dispatch of Henry, Lord Darnley, in 1567.* But the king's men shouldn't move too quickly. If they wanted to catch as many traitors as possible, they needed to wait, so the preparations for the Parliament continued.

Catesby found out about the letter and immediately suspected Tresham. But Tresham denied it, and Catesby kept on. It was only on Monday 4 November, the day before Parliament opened, that the plan came crashing down.

---

*He was actually smothered, though a gunpowder explosion did play a role in the conspiracy.

That day, the Lord Chamberlain, the Earl of Suffolk, went to search Parliament, with Lord Monteagle in tow. Reaching the cellar, they found a tall, tough-looking man with an auburn beard. He said he was a servant to Thomas Percy, who was using the cellar to store fuel. But Monteagle happened to be Percy's cousin. He knew him well, and he had never mentioned having a house in Westminster. There was something off, too, about the bearded man. He looked, the men thought, somehow desperate. Once their report reached Whitehall, James ordered another search, this time led by a magistrate, Sir Thomas Knyvet, under cover of looking for missing tapestries.

It was near midnight. The searchers came to the vault, where once more they found the bearded man. They ordered him to stand, and it was then that they saw the gunpowder beneath the wood and the coal. There was a scuffle, the bearded man was overpowered, his pockets searched. He had a fuse, kindling and a watch. Confronted, he declared his plan, to blast king and Parliament straight to hell. He was dragged to Whitehall and into the king's chamber. Still claiming to be Percy's servant, he calmly recounted his plan to the king, to send him to eternity, in the process murdering his family, his lords and his bishops. 'A dangerous disease,' the bearded man said, 'required a desperate remedy.'[31]

The conspiracy was blown and the plotters scattered to the winds. In London the atmosphere was surreal as the church bells rang and the sky glowed red to the blazing bonfires lit by the people in celebration. In the Midlands, Catesby and several others raided Warwick Castle on the 6th for weapons but were cornered by the Sheriff of Worcester and 200 men at Holbeche House in Staffordshire. The government's men attacked: Catesby and Percy were among the dead. Meanwhile, the bearded man had confessed. He'd finally given his real name: Guy Fawkes. Signing his confession with the tremulous hand of a tortured man, he used its Spanish form – *Guido*.

Parliament sat, its ears ringing to a stirring speech by the king. Led by Edward Montagu, a Northamptonshire MP with piercing eyes and a flame-red beard, Parliament ordered that 5 November would be set aside for a public, annual thanksgiving for England's deliverance from 'malignant and devilish Papists, Jesuits, and Seminary Priests'.

Legislation was passed against Catholics, acts that would underlie the whole century. They were forbidden from practising law or medicine, and a new oath of allegiance was passed. It came into law in the spring of 1606, requiring Catholics to swear that the Pope had no right to depose the king, nor 'to authorize any foreign prince to invade or annoy him'.[32] Meanwhile, recusants were to be harshly punished if they continued to avoid holy communion in their parish church: those who did not receive it at least once a year could lose up to two-thirds of their lands.

Coke was never able to convict the perpetrators of the Cartmel wedding. The recalcitrant magistrate James Anderton remained in office, and the Star Chamber suit against him and Jane Thornborough and the Lord of Misrule, William Dawson, stalled. The last we hear of it is in 1606, when Robert Cecil was being asked to get the case hurried up, though it never was. Instead, though, Jane and her husband Rowland were to suffer from the response to Catesby's gunpowder plot. As obstinate recusants, they lost two-thirds of their Hampsfell estate in 1608 and though the family remained in Cartmel for a couple of decades afterwards, their position was never quite the same.

But Coke got the Gunpowder Plotters. Eight were tried, with the Attorney General leading the prosecution and thoroughly relishing his opportunity to rid the commonwealth of the monster of rebellion. His victims were duly convicted and suffered the gruesome deaths of traitors. They were hanged to the brink of death, castrated, disembowelled, beheaded and cut into quarters, all before an expectant crowd of Londoners. Before this blood ritual, the plotters were drawn through the crowds facing backwards to the horse's tail. It was a symbol of disorder, of the world turned upside down. Their deaths would represent the return of order. It was an official skimmington.

2

The Smart of These Encroaching Tyrants

While the Gunpowder Plotters were meeting their grizzly fate, and while Jane Thornborough and her fellow Catholics were living with the consequences of the Plot, John Reynolds was simply trying to make ends meet.

All we know of Reynolds is that he was a pedlar or a tinker – one who either bought and sold small items or made and mended them – and that he lived somewhere in the Midlands, possibly in the tiny Northamptonshire market town of Desborough. A later source would describe him as 'base', meaning that he was poor, low-born.[1] He is one of the hundreds of thousands of ordinary English people who left little or no trail in the archives, yet who made up the majority of those alive in the reign of James I.

These were tough times for men like Reynolds, for England was in the midst of a great and long period of inflation. The reason for this lay in population growth. From 1500 to 1600, the number of people in England had nearly doubled, from just over two million people to somewhat over four million. This happened despite a death rate that remained punishingly high. Nearly half of all children died before their tenth birthday, and even if you survived childhood you could only expect to live until your late fifties. It also happened despite there being relatively little immigration. There were communities in England from Wales, Scotland and Ireland, from Europe, and even some from Africa, Asia and the Americas, but they were not large enough to drive population growth.[2] Instead, the main driver must therefore have been changes to the birth rate.

In pre-modern England, people tended to marry once they could afford a house: they knew children would be on the way soon in most cases, so wanted to wait until they could afford it. The upshot was that, when times were good, people could afford to marry earlier. Since the vast majority of children were born in wedlock (indeed, sex outside marriage was technically illegal thanks to the work of the church courts), this meant that the birth rate was largely determined by the timing and prevalence of marriage. If people generally married earlier, or if a lower proportion of people never married, both of which had been the case in the second half of the sixteenth century, then the birth rate would increase.

We don't know whether John Reynolds married, or even how old he was. He probably grew up, as most people did, in a small nuclear household with just the parents and their children. Like many, he may have left his parents' house in his early teens. He would go to another small household, probably one slightly higher up the social scale, to work as an apprentice or a 'servant-in-husbandry', where he would learn, respectively, a trade or the basics of running a farm. If this was his path then he would leave his new master in his early twenties, at which point he was likely to begin courtship, attending festivals, weddings and market days hoping to meet a compatible future spouse. If he did marry, statistically he was likely to have done so in his mid-to-late twenties, to a woman aged about twenty-three to twenty-five. Those who married among Reynolds's class did so for love, and though the approval of one's living parents was desirable, it was not considered entirely necessary. But a proportion of people never married, and it seems entirely possible that this was the case with John.

By the 1630s, England's population would reach 5.5 million. But the whole demographic system had an inbuilt braking mechanism, the consequences of which will have been painfully evident to people like John Reynolds. In a world of limited technology, rising population meant land hunger, falling wages and rising rents. The prices of food and shelter were rising, those of wages were dropping. Eventually, inevitably, this crisis in the cost of living would make it harder for young couples to find houses. Thus they would marry later and thus the birth rate would fall. Population growth would slow, stop and even start to reverse. Meanwhile, more people would be entirely unable to marry. If we are correct in our assumption that John Reynolds was one such person, then rising population growth and the associated inflation would create more people like him, and thus gradually the birth rate would start to slow.

[handwritten margin note: Oscillations → the world's own natural solution]

In 1600, this slowdown lay in the future, but the full impact of population growth was being felt. The landless, the wage labourers, the smallholders were all finding their livelihoods badly squeezed. Wages were probably as low in the 1590s as they ever had been. Famine had struck as recently as 1597 and threatened again whenever food prices rose.[3] In fact, the evidence is that, at this time, England was in the grip of a major social crisis.

We can see evidence of this pretty much anywhere we look. It was a great record-keeping age, and many of those records still survive. Records exist relating to the land, the law, poor relief and to births, marriages and deaths. From this cacophony of archival voices, historians have shown that levels of reported crime, especially property crime, were exceedingly high.[4] They have worked out that more English men and women would be hanged in the hard years between 1580 and 1630 than between 1630 and the abolition of capital punishment in 1967, and many of them died for property crimes. Civil lawsuits were astonishingly common, too, and it's been calculated that there was an average of around one lawsuit per household every year.

For those wishing to see signs of moral crisis, as plenty at the time did, the number of children born out of wedlock was peaking between around 1590 and 1610, at around 5 per cent of births. There is even some evidence that gender relations were becoming particularly fraught. At the theatre, audiences will have recoiled in horror at the cosmic disturbances represented by Lady Macbeth and the Duchess of Malfi, and a large proportion of them will presumably have laughed heartily as Shakespeare's shrew was savagely tamed.* The last decades of Queen Elizabeth's reign had seen an increase in the number of witch prosecutions, and while there were some men convicted of witchcraft, the vast majority were, as usual, women. Meanwhile, many villages

---

*Although not everyone was impressed, for one of Shakespeare's contemporaries hit back with a comedy entitled *The Woman's Prize: or, The Tamer Tamed*, in which Petruchio was widowed, remarried, and then was himself 'tamed' by his second wife.

around this time invested in 'ducking stools' to punish 'scolds' (i.e. women deemed troublesome – *not*, as the popular myth for some reason has it, witches).

Ducking stools could be at the centre of nasty community violence against, and between, women, all of which suggests a society ill at ease, in which local conflicts could be pretty ugly. In one village in the Wiltshire Cotswolds, for example, two women were prosecuted as 'scolds' for having a public falling-out, and one of them was sentenced to a ducking while the other was let off. So, to get revenge, on Christmas night allies of the first woman – including several local officials – entered the other's house, 'suddenly devoured' her minced pies, found a pot full of pottage for the servants and children and 'in a brutish and uncivil fashion did piss into the said pot', finally dragging her out of bed to the ducking stool, where they plunged her into the river.[5] *eye for an eye*

Ultimately, the root of this social crisis lay in population growth. It was putting pressure on land and wages, pushing people into poverty, generally straining the sinews of society. It had also left a large and growing population of unmarried young folk, whose wages were falling, who couldn't buy houses and were technically banned from having sex. For young men who had expected to become fathers and husbands – householding patriarchs – the failure to do so generated frustration, resentment, and anger.[6]

personal matters *less personal* ↓ *than*

Many of this volatile group of people gravitated to the towns, especially London, where life for the poor was very precarious indeed. Perhaps John Reynolds thought of migrating to London. He will have known people who did make the decision to do so, and – especially if it is true that he grew up in the town of Desborough – he will have met travellers to the capital, tramping south on the great trunk road that passed through the town on its way towards London from the north-west. For the capital was growing rapidly, to around 200,000 in 1600 and then doubling to 400,000 by the 1640s. The old Square Mile was filling up, as more and more people crammed into the timber-framed alleyways of the City. But most growth was in the suburbs: the Tower Hamlets in the East End, where life ebbed and flowed with the maritime economy, where men were frequently absent and their wives ruled the roost, and where the name of the main market, Billingsgate, became a byword for foul language. Or Southwark, south of the river, where the watermen dropped off customers from the north who decanted into the taverns and theatres, and where life was under the shadow of the heads of executed traitors that poked out from London Bridge. Or, increasingly, in the West End, where parishes were growing quickly, with hovels and rookeries within a few minutes' walk from the grand palaces of Whitehall, which housed the royal court, and Westminster, in which sat the main law courts and Parliament.

The countryside was changing, too. Most of the good land was already under crop or grass, so in the early seventeenth century, growing demand for land and food was met by great projects for draining the fens or enclosing the old forests. The fens supported an amphibious economy of fishing, grazing and gathering, the forests a mixture of wood collecting, pasture and pig farming and berry picking. The forests were medieval hunting areas: pasture and heath with clumps of trees rather than the deep greenwood we so often assume. Here workers and their families enjoyed common rights which helped support them. In addition, they often devoted themselves to industrial work. Most important was textile manufacture, specifically the processes of spinning, weaving and fulling (this was the method by which cloth was cleansed and thickened by being doused in urine and pounded with hammers operated by watermills). When the enclosers came, whether Crown or great aristocratic projectors, these economies came under direct threat: if manufacturing survived, labourers would now be without traditional common rights and much more dependent on wages.

In time, the enclosure of the forests and the draining of the fens would cause considerable opposition. But this was not what was troubling the Midlands where John Reynolds grew up. The problem here was a different type of enclosure. The great 'open fields', farmed co-operatively between the main tenants of the village, were being fenced off by the landlords and replaced with individual plots. Under the old regime, the landlord had shared the pasture with their tenants, and been prevented by complex systems of by-laws from overexploiting it. Once enclosed, this co-operative system of farming was expunged, the courts that managed it and protected neighbours from exploitation were hollowed out. Now it would be every tenant for themselves.

Meanwhile, the growth of London had created specific market conditions in the Midlands that favoured pasture farming, particularly for raising great herds of cattle and sheep which would then be marched to the capital and slaughtered for meat and hides. Trouble therefore arose between wealthy landowners who wanted to enclose the land and turn it to pasture, and the small farmers and labourers who knew this would not only squeeze them out of the land but also decrease their wages, for farming animals required less labour than growing cereals – and lower labour requirements inevitably meant lower wages for all the local farmworkers. So people like John Reynolds suffered a vicelike grip on their livelihoods, with wages falling at a time when other prices were rising. It was a recipe for class conflict.

Tension had simmered in the region in 1596 when a young lad called Bartholomew Steere from the gentle Cherwell Valley north of Oxford briefly terrified Elizabeth's government into savage repression.[7] Unmarried and faced with falling wages and prospects, Steere dreamed of a world of easier working conditions, in which peasants would 'work one day and play another'. He allowed his thoughts to drift into plotting an uprising, telling people that since the Spanish commons 'did rise and cut down all the gentlemen in Spain', they had 'lived merrily there'.[8] An old revolutionary refrain, an echo of the Peasants' Revolt of 1381, was overheard in alehouses and muttered in hushed conversations in the fields: 'When Adam delved and Eve span, who was then the gentleman?' Such was its currency in the 1590s that, writing *Hamlet* a few years later, William Shakespeare had the gravediggers make an absurdist joke about it: Was Adam a gentleman? asked the second gravedigger. 'He was the first that ever bore arms,' said the first. 'The Scripture says, "Adam digged": could he dig without arms?'

But Bartholomew Steere's rising was a dud. Only a handful turned up at the meeting place on a sloping hillside on the banks of the Cherwell, and Steere and his gang were arrested, tortured and killed. Enclosure and depopulation continued. Food prices remained high. In the 1604 Parliament, Edward Montagu, the Northamptonshire MP who would sponsor the bill to commemorate Powder Treason Day, reported the 'cry of the country' against 'depopulation' and the 'conversion of tillage', in other words the replacement of arable farms with pasture.[9] By 1607, it was reported that some 340 villages in the region had been depopulated.[10] That winter, ice and floods had brought great hardship everywhere. It served to remind people, wrote a pamphleteer, that God could choose to drown mankind again, as he had done so once before.[11]

It was in the spring that the Midlands erupted. A series of riots fanned out across the countryside of Northamptonshire, Warwickshire and beyond. Finally, John Reynolds had his moment to change things.

Reynolds was a charismatic man, and he was to become the symbolic leader of an enclosure protest that swept the region. Passing from village to village as the rioters tore down hedges and fences, Reynolds's most distinguishing feature became his large leather satchel. Its contents, he told his followers, would protect them against 'all comers'. And it gave him his *nom de guerre.* Now, he was 'Captain Pouch'.

He goaded his followers – men, women and children, calling themselves 'Levellers' and 'Diggers' – to throw down the hated enclosures. He told them he had authority from the king to do just that, and that he was 'sent of God to satisfy all degrees whatsoever, and that in this present work he was directed by the Lord of Heaven'. As rebellion gripped the countryside, a group of protestors, some thousand-strong, set up a camp at Newton, Northamptonshire. An evocative, poetic exhortation 'from the Diggers of Warwickshire to all other Diggers' gives a sense of what was at stake. 'We, as members of the whole, do feel the smart of these encroaching tyrants, which would grind our flesh upon the whetstone of poverty.'[12]

Workers slipped out of towns to join in. Local people brought food and drink, and ferried protestors about in carts. There was an atmosphere of celebration as men played pipes and drummed on tabors. They went about their work pulling down field boundaries with mattock and shovel. Hedges were removed and burned: plumes of smoke and the smell of burning hawthorn rose out of the fields, as the air rang to church bells. Protests were orderly, generally. A later account, not necessarily from a sympathetic observer, notes that they 'bent all their strength to level and lay open enclosures, without exercising any manner of theft, or violence upon any man's person'.[13] But this didn't stop them being frightening to some. One rich farmer, William Burton of Ladbroke, a recent encloser, saw rioters attack his house. They threatened to 'cut him in pieces and bury him quick [alive]', in his own ditches.[14]

By now, the realisation dawned on the king's Privy Council that the revolt was serious and spreading fast, so by the end of May the government was beginning to mobilise. The king issued a general proclamation calling out the county militias and ordered the young Earl of Huntingdon, newly appointed Lord Lieutenant of Leicestershire, to take personal charge of a situation that was rapidly sliding out of control.

Huntingdon had only just turned twenty-one, but he was determined to make his authority felt. He arrived in Leicester on 5 June, a Friday, after a long journey that had taken him through some of the worst affected parts of Northamptonshire. Here he made what he thought would be a powerful statement to the people of Leicester, by setting up a gibbet in the marketplace. But it was pulled down a few days later by a group of town officers, a prisoner and 'divers boys'.[15] Leicester wasn't loyal yet.

The young earl needed good news, and soon he got it, for he was informed that Captain Pouch had been captured, near Withybrook in Warwickshire. With its charismatic leader neutralised, the rebellion might now stall, but the camp at Newton remained. Come 8 June, though, there was a force ready to strike back. With the county militia slow to act, indeed with some of them clearly in sympathy with the protest, the local gentry had assembled a vigilante force of their own retainers, furnished with horses and arms. It was led by the local MP, Edward Montagu.

Appearing before the camp, they read a formal proclamation against the riots, then charged, but resistance was stouter than expected. Regrouping, a second attack was made and this time the gentry force made their superiority count. Around 40 or 50 protesters were killed then and there, and countless others were captured, two promptly hanged under martial law at Kettering. Some more met the grisly fate of traitors: they were hanged, drawn and quartered, and their dismembered body parts displayed in local market towns. It was a warning that the wages of rebellion were death.

Little could save Captain Pouch from a similar fate. Sent to London for interrogation and denounced by the Privy Council as a 'turbulent varlet', John Reynolds was 'made exemplary', said a later account, almost certainly meaning that he too was hanged, drawn and quartered.[16] The country was quieted, helped by a royal offer of pardon to those who submitted, though Montagu noted how there was still 'much muttering and murmuring' about the fight at Newton and the Kettering hangings, 'especially by women'.[17] Of the fate of John Reynolds's pouch, we know nothing, save that when he was captured it was searched, and 'therein', said a later observer, 'was only a piece of green cheese'.[18]

why more savage graphic back then?

There is a remarkable document that still survives in the Northamptonshire Record Office.[19] In faded ink, it records the names, signatures and (more usually) marks – for those who couldn't write – of some of the protesters who accepted the king's pardon. Specifically, it recorded those who travelled to the great manor house of Boughton, home of Edward Montagu. Boughton was just a couple of miles down a country lane from Newton, where the camp had met, so most of the 144 names (142 men, 2 women) would have been actual campers. The names start with John Meadows, a baker from Kettering, and run through shepherds, butchers, millwrights and tailors from the local villages and towns. In total, there are 62 labourers in the list, plus 21 husbandmen, i.e. small peasant farmers. The rest were artisans.

Strikingly absent is anyone described as a 'yeoman'. The yeomanry (not to be confused with the military uses of the term) were a class of affluent countryfolk with good farms and decent landholdings, but below the level of the gentry. They had a reputation for honesty, plain-speaking and credit. 'The yeoman wears russet clothes, but makes golden payment, having tin in his buttons and silver in his pocket', it was said. He was the 'main man' on juries and though he seldom went far, 'his credit stretches further than his travel'.[20] The yeomanry thought of themselves, not completely without good reason, as the backbone of rural society.

In previous peasant uprisings, like those of Wat Tyler (1381), Jack Cade (1450) and Robert Kett (1549), many yeomen had joined forces with their poorer neighbours to oppose the very rich. But this group was now becoming very prosperous. Yeomen were able to benefit from the rising prices, rising land values and falling wages that came with population growth. In other words, they did well out of exactly the things that were harming their poorer neighbours like John Reynolds. Between the mid-sixteenth century and the second quarter of the seventeenth, yeomen saw their wealth rise *fourteenfold*.[21] They were rebuilding their houses and investing in their farms, thousands of which still survive today.[22]

Of course, in theory, England remained a strictly hierarchical society, with a 'great chain of being' from the king down through the 60 or so temporal lords, the rest of the nobility, the roughly 15,000 members of landowning gentry (accounting, with their families, for about 2 per cent of the population, but owning 50 per cent of the land), to the farmers, tradespeople and labourers who made up the rest of society. This had never been entirely static, but the changes of the sixteenth century were notably destabilising. The rise of the yeomanry was part of a more general improvement in the position of those in the middle of the hierarchy, whom historians call the 'middling sort'. This included many small-town traders and manufacturers – like, say, Shakespeare's father John, who died in 1601, a prosperous glovemaker at Stratford, living in the impressive rebuilt timbered town house on Henry Street.

Shakespeare himself would ascend from his 'middling' background and, as he became rich later in life through landholding, grain trading and a successful literary career, would purchase the coat of arms that allowed him to present as a gentleman. In this, he was like many members of the rising middle sort, buying their way into the next rung of the landed class. Indeed, many of gentry were doing very well, too. On average, their wealth increased sevenfold between about the 1550s and 1620s. Like the yeomen, they were able benefit from rising food and land prices.

These newly wealthy classes enjoyed richer lives. They bought more consumer goods, invested in businesses and farms and rebuilt their houses. Curtains, chimneys, glass windows, furniture and fashionable clothes all became markers of the newfound status of the gentry and middling sort. Reading and book ownership became much more common. Spurred by this growing wealth and by the ballooning of the population of London, ready markets developed for almanacs, pamphlets, polemics, plays, penny ballads, true crime, foreign treatises and books about everything from how to run an efficient farm to how to play chess, or even how to be a dutiful wife. Most of all, there was a torrent of books about faith: how to be a good Protestant, and on the finer points of the liturgy, not to mention Bibles, *Foxe's Book of Martyrs*, England's Book of Common Prayer and catechisms.

There were more schools now than ever before, and more children of the gentry and yeomanry attended Oxford and Cambridge or the Inns of Court. The Inns, in which young men learned the basics of the legal trade, were in fact more socially prestigious than the universities. And London offered just as much of a lively student experience as old Oxford and Cambridge. Students at the Inns could sample the delights of the City, its drinking holes and theatres. Here, student antics could go down in legend, such as when the future poet, playwright and politician John Denham got stupendously drunk one night as a law student and decided as a prank to blot out all the street signs between Charing Cross and Temple Bar with a plasterer's brush and a pot of ink, causing utter confusion when people woke up the following day and visiting litigants tried to navigate the warren of roads and alleys.[23]

As they experienced the world of education, culture, print and the bright lights of London, members of the middling sort were able to dream, quite literally, about future prosperity for themselves and their children. When Alice Abbot, wife of a modest Guildford clothworker, was pregnant with what would turn out to be her fourth child, she had a dream that if she could fish a pike or carp out of the nearby River Wey and eat it, then her child would grow to be a great eminence. She did so, and the story took hold. When young George was born in 1562 his baptism was attended by many of the town's leading inhabitants. Sure enough, he rose through the Church, and in 1611 became James I's Archbishop of Canterbury.[24]

There were other success stories: Shakespeare was one; John Selden, one of the greatest lawyers of the age, was another, for he was born in a humble cottage on the Sussex downs. All the while, wealth and literacy brought these groups the belief they had a stake in the nation. '[H]e that hath done well for himself,' wrote one pamphleteer, 'will know how to do well for the public good.'[25] Members of the wealthy middle saw themselves as among the 'better sort', the 'principal sort', as distinct from the 'ruder' or 'vulgar' sort.[26]

Perhaps naturally, many members of the gentry and middling sort were drawn to Calvinism, taking their growing wealth as evidence of their predestined salvation. Not all Puritans were middling folk, nor were all middling folk Puritans – far from it – but their worldviews had many points of similarity. Many believed, quite naturally, that God favoured the saved with success in this life. Health and wealth were therefore easy to take as signs of one's own salvation. While middling folk needn't agree with the (unlicensed) schoolteacher Grace Coates, of Nottinghamshire, who claimed that 'all such as cannot read are damned',[27] they did nonetheless tend to accept that their acquisition of letters brought them closer to the Word of God. Even lightning was believed never to strike the righteous. Their stake in the social order, meanwhile, led many successful folk to look askance at their neighbours who engaged in disorderly drinking, cursing and damning in alehouses and having illicit sex.

The growing wealth of those in society's middle attracted comment, mostly negative, from their social superiors. The Earl of Northampton, for one, worried about the proliferation of schools aimed at those outside the traditional elite: there was nothing, he said, 'so hurtful to the commonwealth as the multitude of free schools', which turned people away from soldiery and apprenticeships and instead led them to 'go up and down breeding new opinions'.[28] Covetousness, too, was seen a great sin, especially when it was committed by upstart crows outside the proper elite. Comfort was to be had in predicting the future misery of such irritants with their ill-gotten gains. 'Look high,' went one proverb, 'and fall into a cow-turd.'[29]

But however annoying it might have been for society's traditional aristocratic ruling class, the lesser gentry and middling sort were increasingly critical to the operation of the English state. Many could vote in Parliamentary elections, but more important than this was office holding. Because the English state had no standing army, no professional police force and precious few bureaucrats, it depended for its functioning on householders willing to serve office. The gentry would supply the magistrates and grand jurymen, the middling sort the constables, petty jurymen, overseers of the poor, churchwardens and the various urban offices. All told, around one in ten male householders would hold office at any one point, making this the most important form of political activity. Women took part, too: a very small number held office, although fewer than a hundred years previously. More likely, they would be active as litigants and witnesses in lawsuits, as midwives – at this point a semi-official role – or as part of a 'jury of matrons', empanelled when a married woman became pregnant in order to find out who the father was.

Essentially what was happening was that gentry and middling sort were becoming more engaged with law, politics and government. It meant that any ruler, or administration, that wanted to succeed in governing England would have to work with and through these groups. And as they got more literate, more educated, and especially as they partook in the growing world of print, the gentry and middling sort were becoming more opinionated. *Middle class on the MAP*

King James had little time for listening to his people, though. In any case, his Scottish childhood had taught him that obedience, not opinions, made for a happy rule. His father had been murdered, his mother deposed; he'd been beaten, held hostage, seen executions and political assassinations, all before his sixteenth birthday. His mother, when he was just twenty, had been executed by the English. In 1600, he was almost tricked into being kidnapped (or worse) at Gowrie House in Perth. His first year in England saw two plots against him by disillusioned aristocrats that ended with executions and the imprisonment of one of his predecessor's favourites, Walter Raleigh.

All around him was the discord that had been brought by the Reformation, from the Protestant Dutch revolt against Spain, to the French Wars of Religion, to England's own recent brush with Catholic terrorism. Indeed, the religious turmoil had prompted some writers to countenance active resistance to monarchs. If, went the argument, one's ruler was a heretic, then it might actually be your duty to resist them. According to one Jesuit, who happened to be a correspondent of the Gunpowder Plotter Robert Catesby, a king who governed badly could be removed 'by the authority of the assembly of the people'.[30] Religious imperatives were encouraging some to suggest that monarchs, ultimately, were accountable to those they ruled.

In reaction, others among the European political class began to advocate for the opposite, for royal absolutism. To absolutists, royal authority came directly from God not the people.* They accepted that kings were supposed to rule according to God's law, but ultimately, if they didn't, the people had no recourse to any human restraint. They must content themselves with 'prayers and tears'.

King James himself subscribed entirely to claims of his own absolute power. His was the 'prayers and tears' view: these were the people's only remedy against a bad ruler (which, anyway, he wasn't). In 1598 he had written a book setting forth a full theory of royal absolutism. Then, after the Gunpowder Plot, when the 1606 Oath of Allegiance was imposed on Catholics, he wrote a series of tracts, which were then printed, arguing that his powers derived from God, and so he was accountable to neither the Pope nor his own people.[31]

The bishops tended to accept absolutism, too, as did most of the clergy – thus giving a huge audience to absolutist ideas through the pulpit and press (the licensing of which was partly controlled by the bishops). There was no contradiction – for now at least – among the clergy between being Calvinist and full-throated support for royal absolutism. Quite the opposite in fact, for many argued that opposition

---

*In some cases, they argued that it came from an irreversible grant from the people, or from the Norman Conquest. The point was that, however monarchs had got the power, the people had lost all oversight of it.

to royal power was suspiciously popish: was not the deposing of kings the way of the Pope, of the Jesuits and of the Gunpowder Plotters?

Playwrights often helped reinforce the absolutist message, too. One play about the Tudor rebel Perkin Warbeck rhymed (badly): 'But Kings are earthly gods, there is no meddling / With their anointed bodies, for their actions / They only are accountable to heaven.' Shakespeare, of course, dwelt at length on the consequences of the deposition of Richard II. By all accounts he was a bad king who deserved what was coming, but – so Shakespeare was making clear – the remedy was worse than the disease, for the consequences were decades of civil war and political turmoil: 'The blood of English shall manure the ground.'[32]

Laymen with legal training, however, often felt very differently. Among the legally minded, royal power was not just accountable to God, it was also restricted by human institutions. One such institution was England's unusual legal code, based on jurisprudence and ancient practice, embodied partly in various statutes and Magna Carta (which generally people understood to have been a statute). The Common Law, as it was called, was part of the warp and weft of English society, but it was particularly important to the gentry. Their youth, if they were male, often took them to the Inns of Court. After this, whether they were men or women, their lives as owners of landed estates would have been punctuated by regular bouts of litigation.

Here, social change was having a significant impact on the way people thought. As the economy became more complicated and prosperous, the law became more thoroughly embedded in life. One of the most basics facts of the age, for example, was that in the last hundred years, economic growth had rapidly outpaced the supply of coins. So more and more transactions were undertaken using credit, meaning this was fertile territory for battles over who owed what to whom.[33] Local court records abound with seemingly trivial debts being called in: a few pence for a peck of malt here, a shilling for unpaid wages there. All this meant more time spent at law, learning the various writs one needed, all with exotic-sounding Latin names like *certiorari*, *replevin*, *nisi prius* or *habeas corpus*, or the different types of tenure. 'Where be his quiddities now, his quillets, his cases, his tenures, and his tricks?' asked Hamlet by the grave of a putative dead lawyer, speaking a language his audience would have found intelligible.

In a culture so saturated with lawyers and litigants, legal ideas inevitably seeped over into politics. Many, indeed, saw law and politics as two sides of the same coin. Importantly, the Common Law had at its core not only precedent, but a series of maxims: the idea that 'an Englishman's home is his castle' remains one of the most famous, but they also included the dictum that one could not be a judge in one's own case, and that one couldn't be imprisoned without cause shown. One particularly important pair, because they would lie at the heart of future political conflict, held that people couldn't be bound to a new law, or deprived of their property, without first consenting to it. This consent was given by a second key human institution, which acted as the representative of the people. This was Parliament.

In the Middle Ages, Parliament had evolved as a body to represent the English aristocracy, through the Lords, and everyone else through the House of Commons. Its normal place of sitting was the royal Palace of Westminster, on the River Thames, a few miles upriver from London, and under the shadow of the great Westminster Abbey. Medieval kings used the Palace of Westminster as a residence, and it also housed – notably in the great medieval hall – the epicentre of the legal system. King, Church, law and people met together in the same collection of buildings.

It was the fall of Cardinal Wolsey that changed this. Since the thirteenth century, the Archbishops of York had maintained a residence in Westminster, a place called York House just to the north of the abbey and the royal palace. Henry VIII's great minister had built it up into a complex of grand buildings, so when he fell, the greedy monarch eagerly made it his own. At this point, York House was gaining a new name, from the gleaming white stone used to construct it. It was called Whitehall.

From the 1530s, therefore, the royal household moved out of the Palace of Westminster and settled in a short distance north in the Palace of Whitehall. It meant they were physically separated from the law and from Parliament, for the first time.

Meanwhile, Parliament had evolved into a regular, if not permanent, fixture of the political landscape. Within the great complex of yards, buildings and cloisters that made up the Palace of Westminster, the House of Commons sat in the large chapel of St Stephen. Members of the Commons – of whom by the middle of the seventeenth century, there were well over 500 – were elected to represent the English people, although 'election' was a rather complex concept. In the majority of cases, the successful candidate was decided before the election day, and simply presented to voters who dutifully assented: *selected* rather than elected. In a minority of constituencies, albeit a growing one, there was a formal contest. In such cases, the electorate really mattered. Some 90 Members of Parliament, known as 'knights of the shire', represented counties, where voters comprised all freeholders whose land was worth more than 40 shillings (£2) a year. The vast majority of MPs, though, were burgesses or citizens, representing boroughs and cities respectively, and here the franchise might range from all male residents of the town in question to a tiny number of landowners.

All told, however, and partly because elections were only one part of a consultative process which included lobbying and petitioning MPs, the Commons existed as a powerful voice for ordinary Englishmen and (to a point) women, especially those of the literate gentry and middling sort. Parliament was therefore of real significance. Indeed, English government was held to be balanced, between monarchy, aristocracy (broadly represented by the House of Lords) and democracy (represented by the House of Commons).

Yet these were not equally poised. Parliament only sat at the behest of the monarch, and existed to pass laws and grant taxes, not to have any direct control of the actual government. Absolutists, meanwhile, believed that, in times of necessity, the king could override the law (and Parliament). Neither was the Common Law the only system in play. The church courts, for example, administered canon law, while there were also courts of 'equity' which based judgements not on precedent but on conscience. Star Chamber, meanwhile, was a criminal court whose jurisdiction came entirely from the royal prerogative. Such institutions could, in the wrong hands, act as bulwarks to royal power, even to royal tyranny. One maxim, drawn from the Roman scholar Cicero, had it that *salus populi suprema lex esto*: the health of the people was the supreme law. Taken to its logical end, this meant that, if necessity demanded it, the king could tax his English subjects without getting consent from Parliament. He could even imprison them without recourse to the Common Law. Ultimately the king might have an absolute right to his subjects' property, if he needed it.

And James did need it. One of the first things that will have impressed him as he came to England will have been its wealth. On his way south he stopped at Newcastle, its stone buildings home to a growing and extremely lucrative trade shipping locally mined coal to London. From there he visited the great cathedrals of Durham and York, passing through the verdant arable fields of eastern England, skirting around East Anglia, the great breadbasket of the country. He passed thriving market towns, great new prodigy houses built by the landed rich, and hunted on great deer parks shaded by leafy oaks. As he travelled, aristocrats, townspeople, landed gentry and the dons of Cambridge University all came out to see him in their finest clothes. When he reached London he was welcomed by the richest men of the City. James could be forgiven for thinking, as he did, that it was just like Christmas.

The trouble was, while England was one of the wealthiest countries in the world, its monarchy remained chronically short of money. When James came to the throne, finance was being badly affected by population growth. Because it caused inflation, rising population increased the cost of basic government functions, most importantly warfare and defence. War was becoming more expensive anyway, thanks to the growing size of armies, to gunpowder weapons, elaborate fortifications and to the increased need for great warships with three enormous masts and broadside-mounted copper and iron cannons. In 1603, England was at war with Spain and in Ireland. Both conflicts James brought hastily to a close, but while this was a major saving, it was offset by the cost of his family and entourage, which was much larger than that of his unmarried predecessor. James also had the rather unfortunate habit of paying off his courtiers' debts for them. Worst of all was in 1606, when he blew an astonishing £44,000 by paying off the debts of two Scots and an Englishman of the royal bedchamber. The consequence was to make much needed financial reform politically very difficult. People blamed the parlous state of the royal coffers not on long-term structural issues like inflation, but on the king's own profligacy.

Nor was James helped by the infamously raucous nature of court life. When the king of Denmark stayed at James's Hertfordshire mansion of Theobalds in 1606, it seems that neither of the two men experienced so much as a day of sobriety between them, with masques and dances accompanied by courtiers stumbling about and vomiting around the grounds of the great prodigy house. In the daytime, the parties spent their time hunting – one of James's foremost pleasures – in such an unruly manner that one of the late queen's godsons Sir John Harrington thought the world was being turned upside down, 'the beasts pursuing the sober creation'.[34] Within a few years of riotous spending, the annual shortfall had risen to £81,000, and the total royal debts had ballooned to £735,000, even in what was now peacetime.

The upshot was that, by the early seventeenth century, the monarchy was faced with very difficult choices as to how to increase its revenue. Borrowing was one option, but it was expensive and left the monarchy in debt. Indirect tax was another, but it was controversial and unreliable, particularly as international trade remained underdeveloped. Yet another option was the sale of Crown estates, which raised immediate cash but obviously also reduced the monarchy's capacity in the longer term. So the most promising solution was to increase direct taxation, which to all but the most ardent absolutists still meant asking Parliament.

With reform so urgently needed Robert Cecil, now Lord Salisbury, set about to gain some semblance of solvency. He was a smart operator, and exactly the sort of person who was likely to make progress on this thorniest of issues. Within a few years he had done just that: management of the Crown lands was improved, and in 1606 there was a helpful legal judgement in a dispute (*Bate's Case*) over taxes on currants, that created the precedent for placing levies on luxuries. Salisbury (who had masterminded the whole business) seized the moment and in 1608 drew up a new list of royal duties on various imports, ignoring merchants who claimed this would harm trade and lawyers who said it was an unconstitutional use of the royal prerogative.

These 'Impositions' were controversial not just because they were a new tax, but because of *how* they were imposed. By getting a favourable judgement in *Bate's Case*, Salisbury had created a strong precedent for extra-Parliamentary taxes on international trade. In the course of the lawsuit, one judge, Chief Baron Fleming, had deployed the classic absolutist argument that the king could act in the common good, and 'the wisdom and providence of the king is not to be disputed by the subject'.[35] It was all very concerning, not least because it showed – in a manner that did not bode well – that the judiciary were much more pliable to the royal will than Parliament might be.

When Parliament sat again in 1610, another cause célèbre appeared, this time over a dictionary of legal terms. The author, John Cowell, was a law professor (and former Cambridge choirboy), and with the book he called the *Interpreter* he hoped to tap the huge demand for a decent law primer that explained key terms. But it was not a neutral text, and it caused a considerable stir with its apparent irreverence towards the Common Law. More troublingly, it claimed the king was 'above the law by his absolute power'.[36] The liberties of the subject were not rights, but privileges at the king's discretion.

Many in the House of Commons were outraged, and MPs began proceedings against Cowell's book. Such was their anger that some, it seems, even hoped to have the author hanged. Eventually the king agreed to suppress the *Interpreter*, ordering anyone who owned a copy to hand it over to the authorities, though his issue was not that the book's views were wrong as such, but that his own prerogative shouldn't be up for discussion at all. 'It was dangerous,' James said, 'to submit the power of a king to discussion.' More to the point, James thought, the Commons had much better things to do.

In particular, they needed to deal with a new plan hatched by Salisbury, which aimed to put the king's finances on a much stronger footing. He called it the 'Great Contract', and it involved Parliament, in return for the reform of certain royal annoyances such as 'purveyance',*

---

* This was a system in which officials could demand goods to be provided for the royal household at below-market prices. It was particularly irksome in those areas unlucky enough to have a royal palace nearby.

giving James a one-off grant of £600,000 to clear his debts, followed by £200,000 every year. It was a sensible scheme, but it was also expensive, and it would, by giving the king a regular income, potentially have sidelined Parliament. So the Commons stood resolutely in its way. Perhaps if James had not been so obviously profligate it would all have been different, but while he was lavishing cash on his Scottish entourage, while 'the royal cistern had a leak', as one MP put it, Parliament wasn't interested.[37]

So things were at an impasse, and James dissolved Parliament. When it returned, briefly, in 1614, similar issues reared their heads, although Salisbury himself was now dead. James was still short of money, and MPs still thought he was wasting it and that his taxes on trade goods were illegal. He, for his part, thought their bargaining with him was thoroughly disrespectful. Soon the Parliament was sent away again, to be known to history as the 'Addled', and James still had no money. In fact, he was now so desperate that he was putting peerages up for sale. The money business hadn't been solved, nor had the limits of royal power.

In 1612, tragedy hit the royal family. Prince Henry was just eighteen when he died, a popular figure of martial temperament, and he was widely mourned. The solemn atmosphere was hardly helped, either, by an incident later the same year when a young lad ran into St James's Palace claiming to be the prince's ghost.[38] But at least James's subjects were reassured that there was a surviving younger brother, Charles, who still promised a male succession.

Then the court was hit by a major scandal. It centred on the death in 1613 of the poet Sir Thomas Overbury. The unfortunate Overbury had opposed an affair between the Scottish royal favourite Robert Carr and Frances Howard, partly because he hated her rich and influential family. Carr was thoroughly handsome, and James, who had same-sex desires from his youth, would do anything for him. Frances Howard, meanwhile, was the wife the young Robert Devereux, 3rd Earl of Essex. Lady Frances managed to get Essex declared impotent, the marriage thus annulled, and so cleared the way for her to wed Carr. King James obliged the young couple by offering the bothersome Overbury an ambassadorship to Russia to get him out of the way, but

Sir Thomas rather unwisely refused, and the angry king threw him in the Tower. Thus, when Overbury was then found dead in his cell, suspicion inevitably fell on Carr and Lady Frances. With Carr himself finally falling out of favour (the French ambassador thought because his good looks were ageing and because he'd developed '*beaucoup de barbe*'), he and Frances suddenly found themselves on trial and thrown in prison. Their accomplices, meanwhile, were hanged, notably one Mrs Turner who was known to go about in masculine dress and who had allegedly practised sorcery.[39]

Despite all this, the 1610s were mostly peaceful. Harvests were better and religious and political controversies were in fact somewhat calmed.

The Puritans' defeat in 1604, with the Hampton Court Conference, the new canons, and the failure to significantly update the Book of Common Prayer, had led some of their number away from the official Church. Some embraced 'Independency' or Congregationalism, the belief that people should come together to worship in the manner they see fit, though not wholly separated from the formal parish. The basic tenets of this movement were set out in a series of pamphlets written by Henry Jacob and William Bradshaw, two men of the middling sort – one the son of a yeoman from the bracing coasts of Kent, the other from a formerly prominent but now declining family in Market Bosworth, Leicestershire. They held that people could legitimately gather together to worship in a manner of their choosing, without the need for top-down structures like bishops, or formal Presbyterianism with its system of elders and synods. To Bradshaw, 'every Company, Congregation or Assembly of men, ordinarily joining together in the true worship of God, is a true *visible church* of Christ'. It was very much a minority view, for now, but it was a foundation for a grassroots, even democratic, approach to religion.[40]

James's government actually burned two Protestant heretics in 1612, though they were exceptional – and, indeed, to prove the last such cases in England. The first was Bartholomew Legate, the wealthy son of an Essex clothier. He reached a series of eccentric conclusions about faith, including a denial of the divinity of Christ, leading him to be summoned for a dispute with the king himself. Despite his own not inconsiderable powers of theological argument, James was unable to show Legate the error of his ways. So the exasperated king reached for one of the most persuasive devices in his arsenal and had Legate sent for trial, found guilty and eventually burned to death.[41]

The other sorry victim was Edward Wightman, a draper from Burton-on-Trent, who had also espoused anti-Trinitarian views, specifically that Jesus was 'only a man and a mere creature, and not both God and man in one person'. Tried at Lichfield Cathedral, he was sentenced to be burned in a public space outside the city. As the flames seared his skin, he panicked and said he would recant, but – having been shuffled back to prison – he continued to blaspheme 'more audaciously than before', so after a few weeks he was dragged back out to the stake, and there the grim deed was finally done.[42]

Wightman's son, himself also a radical, would understandably tire of the country that had treated his father so savagely, and would eventually move to the growing colonies of New England. This was a generation in the future, but emigration was already becoming an option for religious dissidents, particularly Separatists. Many at first went to the Netherlands, where they found a more tolerant welcome, but some would take the next step and migrate across the Atlantic. The American colonies were as yet in their earliest days. Virginia, settled in 1607, struggled at first, and only took hold with the development of tobacco plantations in the 1620s. Further north, in what would become New England, a decisive step would be taken in 1620 when a group of Separatists based in the Netherlands, though originating in eastern England, left for the New World, via the old country on the *Mayflower*.

The new colonies could also serve as an outlet for the rough old sea dogs who had served in Elizabeth's navy and could now carve out a life fighting indigenous Americans on the frontier. Or they might enlist in the new East India Company, founded in 1600 with the aim of trading lucrative spices from Asia and resisting the challenge of the Dutch beyond the Cape of Good Hope. At home, though, the opportunities for the violently inclined were fewer and further between. Some even worried that the English were going soft. We are

'effeminated', complained one writer, 'our martial exercises and dis-
ciplines are turned into womanish pleasures and delights'.[43]

There were, indeed, plenty who decried the state of the nation. On
a cold winter's day in 1613, Londoners huddled at St Paul's Cross to
hear a sermon from Thomas Sutton, the son of a Westmorland farmer
now turned Oxford academic and clergyman. '[W]e have dared our
God to his face,' he chastised. ['O]ur whole land begins to swarm
with sins, as thick as Egypt did with frogs.' Usury, adultery, corrupt
lawyers and the theatre were to blame.[44] Others lamented the death of
good neighbourhood, and the frailty of social relations. 'Witness,' the
Calvinist minister John Day told his audience on Easter Day 1615,
'those many quarrels now afoot between neighbour and neighbour,
especially in the country. Witness that multiplying of lawyers in our
age more than ever in former times.'[45]

Wherever one looked, one could find signs of sin, depravity and
social strain, and not just in the profusion of lawyers. 'Never was the
world so wicked as it is now,' explained the reporter of a monstrous
birth discovered in Lancashire in 1613.[46] Every parishioner will have
been able to see that the costs of poor relief were rising, the numbers
of prosecutions for theft, too. In a speech given in 1616, King James
complained of the abundance of alehouses, ordering that 'to avoid
the giving occasion of evil, and to take away the root, and punish
the example of vice', he 'would have the infamous Alehouses pulled
down'. Beggars, too, 'so swarm in every place, that a man cannot go in
the streets, nor in the highways, nor anywhere for them'.[47] Everywhere
people seemed to swear, blaspheme and drink too much. One only had
to see the aftermath of the town fair, it was suggested, and it looked
as if some battle had been fought: 'here lies one man, there another'.[48]

Parliament, for its part, had passed laws in 1606 against swearing
and drunkenness (it was helpfully defined by a leading legal commentator as the condition 'where the same legs which carry a man into
the house cannot bring him out again').[49] In 1610, a statute had been
passed ordering Houses of Correction – institutions that combined
the functions of both prisons and workhouses – to be set up in every
county.

Thus, despite the peace, and despite the prosperity of some, this
had become a time of serious moral unease. Ministers fumed at the
iniquity of it all, and intoned dire warnings of God's wrath. Local

responses to lapses could be stunningly disproportionate. In 1615, Joan Thorne, a married woman of Ely, was hauled before the church courts for what to us seems like an astonishingly tame piece of public indecency: while out dressing turves she caused a stir 'by stripping off herself into her smock being a thing very unseemly before men, & very much offensible unto women that did see the same'.⁵⁰ Even more extreme was the unofficial justice meted out to William and Margaret Cripple of Burton-on-Trent, who claimed to be married, but were thought by the town to be unmarried and possibly even brother and sister. Found in bed together of a Sunday, they were dragged through the streets in a bizarre skimmington, to a 'great noise and with ringing of cow bells, basins, candlesticks, frying pans and with the sound of a drum'. There were cries of 'a whore and a knave, a whore!' as they were mercilessly pelted with ordure and put in the stocks, where the crowd flung yet more muck at them, while some of their number 'pissed on their heads'.⁵¹

It was the kind of world where Puritanism was always likely to thrive. But while most people believed society was decaying, not everyone agreed the remedy was deep Godly reform. Indeed, there were many who thought the Puritan remedy might be worse than the disease, that burying themselves in books and grumbling about fun might be harmful to the community; that the best hopes of healing a fractured society lay with the old ways of tradition, festivities and deference to the established hierarchies.

So anti-Puritans set out their stall in the defence of 'Merry England': of Sunday sports, Morris dancing and rushbearings, like that at Cartmel, and other such traditional forms of fun. These were celebrated with vigour, with moping Puritans mocked as enemies of the community. In Wells in 1607, for example, the elaborate festival of May Games drew some 3,000 spectators and included 'morris dancers, loving dancers, men in women's apparel, new-devised lords and ladies'. It also involved vicious satire against local Puritans who had opposed the revelries, especially a rich clothier with the regrettable name of John Hole, and the wife of John Yard, whose name, again unfortunately, was a common euphemism for a penis.⁵²

Sensing an opportunity to recruit the young and to drive wedges between different types of Protestant, some Catholics became enthusiastic sponsors to local festivities, just as Jane Thornborough had at Cartmel. The most spectacular example came around 1612, when an enterprising Catholic lawyer called Robert Dover created the rambunctious Cotswold 'Olympick Games' during Whitsun week, in the Gloucestershire market town of Chipping Campden. It was a calculated way to irk the Puritans, and of course Dover ensured that, unlike the religious zealots, his games respected traditional hierarchies: the men of quality would enjoy fencing and horse racing, with everyone else left to more plebeian entertainments like wrestling and shin-kicking.

In 1617, the time came for James to make a royal progress to Scotland. His began his journey in March, travelling north up the east of England. In early August, he was ready to return back to England and this time he took the western route: via Carlisle. The wild moorland and rugged pastures of the west side of the country will have given James a very different view of England's wealth than his previous journey south, in 1603, though he was still lavishly entertained.

For three days in August, James stayed at Hoghton Tower, in Lancashire, the house of Richard Hoghton, now a conformist but from a family streaked with Catholicism. Many of the county's great and good were there, as were several members of James's court. Here, James received a petition from local folk, complaining about attempts by Puritan magistrates to stamp out their traditional festivals and Sunday sports. James was even treated to some entertainment, fitting for the season: this was to be a traditional summer recreation, common in the area. A rushbearing.

As the rush-carriers processed through Hoghton Hall with their greenery and their masks, James was duly impressed, and he agreed to put out an official declaration: 'Honest mirth is not only tolerable but praise-worthy and the prohibition of it likely to breed discontent.' This 'Declaration of Sports' of 1617 gave royal backing to certain pastimes and festivities for Sundays and holidays. At first, it was issued for Lancashire, but in 1618 it was applied to the whole country as the 'Book of Sports'.[53]

Although it was never fully enforced, the 1618 Book of Sports was a clear statement that the Stuart monarchy was increasingly positioning itself as anti-Puritan. It was stoking a culture war. In fact, it even carried the potential to link up high political debates about absolutism with parish controversies over Puritanism and festivals. For what was one to do if a king ordered you to commit blasphemy? It was an issue tackled by writers like the Puritan schoolmaster Thomas Beard. It was 'law and reason', Beard wrote, that subjects honour their lords, princes and kings, just as children bore reverence to their parents. But this was only so long as that deference was 'not derogatory to the Glory of God'.⁵⁴ Among Beard's students at his small grammar school in Huntingdon was a young gentleman's son called Oliver Cromwell.

Around the same time, a new trend was taking hold in the Church, and again it was – in part at least – a reaction to Puritanism. There were those, like the eloquent Bishop of Ely Lancelot Andrewes, whose theology led them to put much more emphasis on ceremony, on the 'beauty of holiness', in direct contrast to the austerity of the Puritans and even many of the more moderate Calvinists. In some cases, parishioners were themselves leading the way, and taking it upon themselves to renovate their churches with new, elaborate decorations. One such church was Cartmel parish church, where, from 1616, and with funding from the church rates, the local gentleman George Preston (who had almost certainly been present at the 1604 skimmington) began adding lavishly carved woodwork depicting the Passion, as well as elaborate fret plasterwork and a new pair of organs, not to mention a much-needed new roof. Services would now resound to the sound of music, under the shadow of exquisite images.⁵⁵

A rising star of this movement was the new Dean of Gloucester, appointed by the king in 1616. He was an Oxford academic named William Laud. Five foot tall, plagued by anxious dreams, Laud was podgy, shy, difficult and donnish: a perpetual bachelor more comfortable with his cats than with other humans. He was also an arch ceremonialist, advocating a sumptuous liturgy, ordered but thoroughly elaborate. Thus in early 1617, only a few months into his new post at

Gloucester, Laud caused a stir by moving the communion table from the centre of the choir to the east end of the cathedral, where it had stood like the old altars had in Catholic times.

In 1618, a series of astronomical phenomena appeared, all of which portended ill. The summer saw a total eclipse of the sun, followed in the late autumn by three blazing comets in quick succession.

But even before these tokens of cosmic disturbance appeared, news had come from the Continent of a massive Protestant uprising against a Catholic power. It was to bring the relative calm of James's second decade to a shuddering halt, and it was to set England on a path towards political crisis, towards war, and ultimately towards revolution.

3

A Strange Humming or Buzz

One evening in December 1620, two men approached the door of John Harris's alehouse in Bridgwater.

It was a winter's night: the smell of woodsmoke scented the crisp air of the Somerset coast, accompanied by the clattering percussion of the masts from the town's dock. In the windows of the town houses, candlelight flickered against the warm smoulder of the log fires. The short winter day had given over to a cold, dark night. It was around 5 p.m.

Entering the house, Alexander Whilligg, a farmer from nearby North Petherton, sat down to drink with his companion, Edward Cadwallider. They were expecting another man, but in the meantime Cadwallider ordered two pots of beer, paying on the spot. The two men drank and, as they did, the conversation turned to the news.

Whilligg had just returned from London. Cadwallider wanted to know what he had heard. He particularly wanted news from the Continent: from Bohemia, where a revolt had put the Protestant Frederick V on the throne, in defiance of the Holy Roman Emperor; and from the Palatinate on the Rhine, where Frederick's ancestral lands had just been invaded by Spain. The talk of London, replied Whilligg, was that the generals of both the Spanish and imperial forces – the two Catholic armies that were pushing hard against the Elector – were dead.

Talk turned to the Catholics at home. Cadwallider hoped that the new Parliament, due to meet in just weeks, would clamp down on them hard. Whilligg replied that if it did, then 'you shall see as much stir in England as is now in Bohemia'. Evidently earwigging, the landlord Harris cut in: 'I hope we shall see these papists driven out of England,' he said, 'or hanged up.' Clearly the conversation had become heated. Cadwallider agreed with Harris the landlord, but Whilligg immediately retorted that neither Cadwallider, nor his children, nor even his children's children, would see Catholics driven from England. Cadwallider came back, saying that a search should be made of the Parliament House, 'that the king may safely go and safely come'. It was an obvious reference to the Gunpowder Plot.

Then, Whilligg said something he would later regret.

The exact words are disputed. 'God defend the man who shall do the king harm' was what landlord Harris heard. Or was it 'do the king wrong'? Whilligg, though, claimed he'd said something different: 'God defend *that* any man should do the king wrong.' Either way, Harris replied – with heavy irony – that 'this is a very good prayer indeed', repeating (twice) the words 'God defend the man that shall do the king wrong.' And Harris's wife, her presence unrecorded until now, chimed in: 'this is a pretty fellow,' she said, before adding with obvious menace, 'if he were examined, 'tis pity'.

The conversation turned back to Parliament. 'I think the Papists will be cut,' said Whilligg, 'but they must suddenly rise.' 'I think there will be as many of the one side as of the other,' he continued, 'for,' he added cryptically, 'there are great birds above.'

At some point, having said his piece, Whilligg decided to leave. But according to Harris the landlord, when he did, he hung around out-side, 'harkening at the window', listening to the conversation inside. He heard Harris, Cadwallider and another man discuss what they'd just seen and heard. Clearly worried, Whilligg re-entered, confronted the men and told them he would stand by his words. This was enough for Harris. He 'immediately' (so he later said) complained to the mayor of Bridgwater, and Whilligg was arrested.[1]

For these were dangerous times. In 1618, the powder keg of European politics exploded. The touchpaper was Bohemia. In 1617, the Holy Roman Emperor Matthias had succeeded in getting his cousin Ferdinand chosen as crown prince of the strategically vital Czech territory, but his Catholicism made him unacceptable to the many Protestants there. In May 1618, two imperial envoys were unceremo-niously (though not fatally) thrown out of a top-floor window in what would come to be called the 'Defenestration of Prague'. The crown of Bohemia was offered by the rebels to the Elector Palatine, Frederick V, who accepted in November.* Although the Bohemian crown was itself 'elective', this was still a dangerous act of mutiny against Matthias and Ferdinand (who would become Holy Roman Emperor the following year). War was inevitable, and in the tangled geopolitics of the age, it threatened to pull in the major powers with frightening speed.

For England, the thread that pulled her towards war was one of marriage, for Elector Frederick, the man now at the centre of European politics, was James's son-in-law. He had married Princess Elizabeth Stuart in 1613, on St Valentine's Day at the royal chapel in Whitehall, before returning with the Scottish teen bride to his capital at Heidelberg. So family honour was at stake, but this was not all. Elector Frederick was also a good Calvinist and therefore the darling of the English clergy. His cause, standing like David against the Austrian Goliath, stirred the hearts of the English people.

For James, though, the reasons for staying out were considerably stronger. He liked to present himself as Europe's peacemaker, the *Rex Pacificus*, but an intervention would also inevitably cost money – something James didn't have. Quite the opposite in fact: he was £700,000 in debt. There was another complication, too, and again it related to the marriage of the royal children. James's son Charles, who had become his heir after Henry's death, still needed a bride. From 1614, James had been negotiating with the Spanish king Philip III to marry Charles to his daughter, the Infanta Maria Anna. The potential dowry was more than James's entire annual income. But it was a deeply unpopular match. Not only was she a Catholic, but the Armada was still within living memory, and the sheer power of the Spanish monarchy, with its territories from the Americas to the Philippines and its vast silver mines in Peru, inspired fear and loathing among the English.[†]

With the Bohemian crisis, the international situation could only get worse for James. The Spanish and Austrian monarchies were linked by ties of blood and faith. Both were branches of the House

---

*There were seven 'Electors', rulers of territories within the Holy Roman Empire who had the right to cast their vote for the new emperor. In reality, they always elected a Habsburg.
†To make matters worse, since 1580 the Spanish Crown had been united with the Portuguese, meaning that the Habsburgs also controlled the extensive territorial network of the Portuguese East Indies.

of Habsburg, and both were leading a Catholic resurgence on the Continent. In August 1620, a huge Spanish deployment from its Flanders army marched out of Brussels. It invaded, and overran, the lower Palatinate. Then, in November 1620, in the bloody Battle of White Mountain, near Prague, the imperial army obliterated the Elector's forces in Bohemia and ended the revolt there. The cause of Elector Frederick, and by extension also of European Protestantism, had fallen to a desperate ebb. James knew that he had little hope of changing the course of the war, and the last thing he wanted to do was to antagonise his prospective new in-laws. But English public opinion demanded action.

As the new decade began, a new statue of King James had been cut to adorn the new quadrangle of the library of Oxford University, which had been recently fortified with a huge donation from the diplomat Sir Thomas Bodley. Crowned and resplendent, James is depicted handing two books to figures representing Fame and the University. Above him, inscribed in bold letters, is James's motto, *Beati Pacifici*, 'Blessed are the Peacemakers'.

To the apocalyptic mind of the age, though, the spiralling conflict was one of Good versus Evil, and in such cases the blessedness of the peacemakers might not be clear-cut. Since the Reformation, the wide availability of printed Bibles had changed people's understanding of Scripture. Now that the Word of God was available in their own language, the English fell into the temptation to read it literally. Especially important was the wider access to the Books of Daniel and Revelation, with their compelling and vivid foretelling of the end times. These chimed with what people saw going on around them in Europe, as the Muslim Ottoman Empire pushed its way through the Balkans and threatened Vienna itself, and as Christendom was torn asunder between Catholic and Protestant. '[T]he last hour is now running,' wrote a Puritan clergyman, and 'we are those on whom the end of the world has fallen.'[2]

Many Calvinists therefore now took the Pope not simply to be some misguided and overweening bishop, but, rather, to be the actual Antichrist, as foretold in biblical prophecy.[3] It was a point of view that encouraged people to see the world in binaries: disagreement was no longer just that. Rather, one's opponents were in league with the Antichrist. Neutrals were suspect: 'Art thou for us, or for our adversaries', as Joshua asked outside Jericho. Or in the words of Jesus himself: 'He that is not with me is against me; and he that gathereth not with me scattereth abroad.'[4]

There was, therefore, much pressure on James to intervene in the European war, and much of this – in a way that was new, even radical – was coming from public opinion. The print trade was already thriving, as reflected in what survives today. Around 150 titles per year survive for the 1550s, but this rises to around 500 in the 1620s, and this must only be a fraction of what was actually produced. Literacy was rising, too: in 1500, only 10 per cent of adult men and 1 per cent of women could sign their names. By the second quarter of the seventeenth century this had risen to somewhere near 30 per cent and 10 per cent, respectively.[5] Literacy depended on where you lived, and where in the social scale you were. Almost all male gentlemen were literate; in the West Country and East Anglia, around two-thirds of yeomen were, though rates were lower in the north among this group. In general, literacy was highest in London.

What added particular energy to all this in the 1620s was the rapid spread of political news. With the outbreak of the war, suddenly it was everywhere, and not just in print. One could not pass through the streets of the capital, wrote one observer, without being 'continually stayed by one or other, to know what news' from Bohemia. In rapidly growing London, two locations were key. One was the walks around the great medieval cathedral of St Paul's, where bookstalls and hawkers vied with street preachers and where promenaders brushed off beggars and clutched their purses against the unwelcome hands of pickpockets. It was said of Paul's walk that '[t]he noise in it is like that of bees, a strange humming or buzz, mixed of walking, tongues and feet'; it was 'the great exchange of all discourse', but also (rather less positively) the 'general mint of all famous lies'.[6] Another centre was the Royal Exchange, the great Elizabethan shopping centre and commercial hub, where men about town would meet to chat business while aristocratic women clambered out of coaches, gathering up their coats against the mud of the streets and scurrying into the shops. All around St Paul's and the Exchange, the streets and taverns chattered with news, especially on Cheapside, Fleet Street and the Strand. Watermen would talk politics as they ferried people across the Thames between Paul's Wharf and Southwark Bankside. Once they left the capital, news and rumours would be carried by traders, peddlers, chapmen and animal drovers from town to village, and alehouse to alehouse.

Printed domestic news was, in theory, tightly controlled, but there were plenty of ways to avoid the censors. Some material was produced abroad and smuggled in. Some news remained in hand-written form. By the early seventeenth century, news-hungry punters could even subscribe to professional journalists. In Herefordshire, Sir John Scudamore employed at least eight correspondents in the 1620s and 1630s, while the Suffolk gentleman and MP Sir Martin Stuteville employed a Cambridge don, Joseph Mead, to send him regular news.

Perhaps most revolutionary of all was the new type of publication that appeared on the bookstalls of London in 1620. Published in Amsterdam by a Dutchman, it was a folio broadsheet, untitled, bearing news – in English – from the Continent. This was the first of the English 'corantoes': news serials. Ironically, the earliest sur-viving edition, dated 2 December that year, opened with the rather uninspiring admission that 'The new tidings out of Italy are not yet come.'[7] The first line in the first surviving English news periodical, then, was an admission that there wasn't any news. Nonetheless, the idea stuck, and in 1621 a number of competing publications started to appear. As early as February that year the first London-printed periodical appeared, carrying news translated from Dutch into English.

Some news was reliable, much was not. The trick was knowing which was which. Careful readers compared reports, probing for inconsistencies and gaps in logic. In 1621, for example, the Devonshire gentleman Walter Yonge recorded in his diary reports of a Turkish invasion of Spain but it was, he noted, a 'false report'. Then, a few pages later, he notes that it 'is reported that the Emperor put twenty-four nobles of Bohemia to death – True'.[8] In a world in which repu-tation and honour counted for so much, the position of the teller was critical – were they gentry, merchant or vagrant? Neighbour or stranger? Man or woman? Adult or child? It was easy for news to be concocted in bad faith and then fed to eager and indiscriminate consumers.

Indeed, the circulation of news had the potential to open up political discourse beyond the ruling class, and there was a clear danger that the people would develop the wrong opinions. The poorer sort, grumbled one magistrate in 1601, 'are carried more by rumours without a head, than by the truth of things'.[9] To Francis Bacon, political songs and 'false news' were 'amongst the Signs of *Trouble*', and as early as 1610 King James had complained about 'the common printing and dispersing of traitorous and seditious books and of profane and scurrilous pamphlets and libels'.[10] There was a ready market, it was said, for 'such trash as infatuates the foolish vulgar'.[11] Such was the concern in elite circles that it was seriously suggested that the government should set up its own gazette to counter bad news, giving 'the ploughman and the artisan' access to the official story, so they needn't rely on 'rumours amongst the vulgar'.[12]

Whether the government could ever hope to control the views of the people is highly doubtful. Nor were they helped by the fact the early seventeenth century also saw a torrent of satire. At the more sophisticated end this included, in the early 1620s, the first true political cartoons. But the bigger part of this new flood came in the form of vitriolic ballads, songs and verses known as 'libels'. These were circulated by word of mouth and in manuscript – often placed in prominent public places. In 1623, a verse libel addressed to Queen Elizabeth was even left in the hand of her statue in Westminster Abbey. So concerned was King James about libels that he penned a poetic response, urging the people to leave off matters of state beyond their ken: 'Hold your prattling, spare your pen,' it urged, 'be honest and obedient men.'[13]

But obedience was clearly being strained. Preachers would use their Sunday sermons to expound on the cosmic significance of the latest events, and their conclusions were not always supportive of the government. Many mainstream Calvinists felt the king was being too pacific, so for the first time one of the groups most supportive of royal absolutism, the Calvinist clergy, were finding themselves at odds with the king's policy. Meanwhile the Spanish ambassador to James, Count Gondomar, found his lodgings at the centre of frequent demonstrations by angry Londoners. One pamphlet, *Vox Populi* – the 'voice of the people' – published in 1620 and written by one Thomas Scott, was a particularly brutal attack on royal policy. It caused a sensation, went into multiple editions and led its author to go into hiding abroad. It all contributed to an increasingly febrile atmosphere. 'Audacious language, offensive pictures, calumnious pamphlets, these usual forerunners of civil war, are common here,' wrote the French ambassador.[14] A way out of the crisis was needed, fast.

Hoping to force a diplomatic solution, James decided to rattle some sabres. His plan was to summon Parliament, a body whose member-ship, he knew, would take the first opportunity to vent their hatred of Spain. He hoped that this would focus the Spanish king's mind on agreeing to a peaceful solution, but if that didn't work, then James would need money for war. And the only way to raise enough money, without setting off a constitutional crisis, was to call Parliament.

Sittings of Parliament had become a rarity. The previous decade had only seen one, the infamously ineffective 'Addled Parliament' of 1614. Parliament largely existed to do the king's bidding, and its sittings were expected to be, and in many cases still were, occasions of happy co-operation in which sensible men sat for the good of the common-wealth, to get things done.

When the new Parliament assembled on 30 January 1621, James was said to be 'very cheerful all the way', as he left the Palace of Whitehall, sandwiched between the Thames and St James's Park, where a great new Italianate building, a Banqueting House, was gradually emerging under scaffolding and cranes, and headed down King Street towards Westminster.[15]

James opened proceedings with an hour-long speech, explaining to Parliament that he had summoned them because he needed money, specifically for his military. He hoped not to fight, he said, and would try to obtain a 'happy peace'. But it was still better 'to intreat of peace with a sword in my hand'.[16]

The Parliament's first session was fairly harmonious, but if there was calm at Westminster, elsewhere the atmosphere had become very tense. London's youthful population showed signs of growing discontent, often aimed at Catholics and foreigners. On Easter Day (1 April), the Spanish ambassador Gondomar's horse litter was attacked on Fenchurch Street by a group of apprentices crying, 'There goeth the devil in a dung-cart.'[17] An attempt by the authorities to make an example by having the worst instigators whipped then went badly wrong when a crowd assembled and rescued them. James ordered the Lord Mayor to keep control of his city, else he would deploy troops.

Parliament agreed to grant James two subsidies, totalling £140,000. It was an impressive amount, not least because England's all-important textile industry was entering a serious crisis. There was a shortage of coin and problems in the export market, partly thanks to an unnecessary policy debacle the previous decade that had seen English cloth cut off from continental markets. 'When was it seen a land so distressed without war?' asked one observer.[18] In one part of Wiltshire it was reported that over 2,500 textile workers were unemployed.

Yet the MPs' attention was focused on something else – monopolies. This was the controversial practice of giving royal grants to individual projectors allowing them to take total control of a particular trade or industry. In the face of a deepening economic crisis, monopolies did relatively little harm; in fact, they had a certain logic at times. However, they did cause prices to rise, and denied competitors access to markets. Thus, to the common-law mind, they contravened what many saw as a natural right to follow a trade. They were therefore an issue of principle, in which a royal grant had been used to give away the rights of Englishmen without their consent.

More to the point, monopolies had the happy benefit of providing obvious scapegoats. So, to deal with the most obnoxious monopolists, Parliament resurrected a long-discarded tool called 'impeachment' (last used in 1459) – whereby selected villains would be charged by the Commons and judged by the Lords. Impeachment was a specific tool to deal with a specific issue, but as the monopolists had been appointed by the Crown, it had a wider significance: ultimately, it had the potential to be a way in which Parliament could put pressure on the Crown and its officers. Among the victims was the Lord Chancellor, Francis Bacon, himself. Described by a rather predictable libel as 'a hog well fed with bribery', he was fined £40,000 and ordered to be imprisoned at the king's pleasure, though he was promptly released and the fine never collected.[19]

As the session wore on, some problems began to appear, notably over a bill to crack down on Catholics, which James understandably thought would complicate his negotiations with Spain. Once Parliament had finally adjourned an irritated James had the most disruptive MP, Sir Edwin Sandys, arrested, along with the Earl of Southampton from the Lords – the latter, who was something of veteran troublemaker, for 'mischievous intrigues with members of the Commons'.[20]

Parliament then reassembled on 20 November and if the last session had ended on something of a sour note, the new one was nothing short of a disaster. Although another subsidy was promptly voted, Parliament – so the king saw it – dramatically overstepped its constitutional position by drafting a petition urging war on Spain and arguing that Prince Charles should marry a Protestant. Livid, James wrote to the Speaker on 3 December ordering him to stop debates on matters of government or the Spanish Match. In a further rebuke, James ordered Parliament not 'to trench upon the prerogative of the Crown', else it forced him 'to retrench them of their privileges'.[21]

On 18 December, the Commons responded with a 'Protestation', defending the privileges of Parliament – including freedom of speech – as the 'birthright and inheritance of the subjects of England'.[22] Drafted by the lawyer and MP Edward Coke, it was a clear statement that they believed they had rights beyond those given them by the king, arising out of the English Common Law and its ancient constitution. James was furious. In his view, all the rights enjoyed by Parliament had originally been granted to them by the monarchy. The Protestation thus revealed a critical fracture in English political ideology and James could not let it stand. He swiftly had Parliament adjourned, and physically ripped the Protestation from the Commons Journal with his own hands. He took the unusual step of making a public justification of his conduct, and had the ringleaders arrested. Edward Coke was sent to the Tower. Then, on 6 January, the feast of the Epiphany, Parliament was dissolved.

With Parliament gone, the centre of political gravity shifted back to the court and the Privy Council. These were still, at this point, the places where political fame was made and one could win appointment to the government. And by 1622, both had come to be dominated by a bright new star.

George Villiers of Leicestershire had been about as minor as a minor gentleman could be. The second son of the second marriage of a second-rate provincial knight, he was nonetheless charming, good-looking and an exquisite dancer. 'From the nails of his fingers, nay, from the sole of his foot, to the crown of his head, there was no blemish in him', one of James's chaplains was to write.[23] Villiers caught James's eye on a hunt at Apethorpe, Northamptonshire, in 1614, and was seized upon by opponents of the then-favourite Robert Carr, Earl of Somerset. They bought him a new wardrobe and managed to secure him the position of royal cup-bearer. This gave direct access to the king, who was duly smitten and Villiers was promoted, his rise coinciding with the fallout from the Overbury scandal and Somerset's eclipse. In 1617, with Somerset now in the Tower, Villiers was made Earl of Buckingham; then Marquess in 1618. In 1619, he was made Lord Admiral, in charge of England's navy, still only in his mid-twenties. He even had the honour of having a ship named for him, *Buckingham's Entrance*, though the name was hastily changed for fairly obvious reasons.

In 1620 Buckingham married a bride of impeccable noble lineage, Katherine Manners, daughter to the Earl of Rutland, although within a couple of years he was also having an affair with the vivacious Lucy Hay (née Percy), Countess of Carlisle. He would eventually rise to the dukedom of Buckingham in 1623, one of only two dukes in James's realms. Buckingham's mother and sister became countesses and his brothers got peerages. Buckingham's ambition soared like a comet, though his talent would stutter like a damp sparkler. Advancement at court now went through him: those who sought office, wrote a contemporary sourly, 'can obtain no grace except they vow and beseech at the shrine of the great one'.[24] And the 'Great One' also became fabulously rich. By 1625 his property portfolio included two great country houses and a mansion by the Thames. His art collection was enough to enflame the jealousy of even the most refined connoisseur.

Such a rise inevitably made enemies. Twice his opponents at court tried to catch James's eye with another handsome young 'darling'. Twice they failed. For the street balladeers, Buckingham was a deliciously tempting target. Some harpooned Villiers's obvious attempts at advancing his family: 'George shall cap his brother Jack.' Others were scurrilously sexual: 'The King loves you, you him', went one popular epigram, 'Both love the same / You love the King, hee you / Both buck-in-game.'[25]

'Buck-in-game' was not just a poor quality pun: it was also a fairly explicit reference to anal sex. For it was widely held that Buckingham and James were lovers. By the early 1620s, some rhymers even dared refer to Buckingham as 'Ganymede': the Trojan boy with whom Zeus fell in love, and whose name in Latinised form (*Catamitus*) had given the English the word 'catamite'. The allusion will have been immediately obvious, especially as in one version of the story Zeus even gave Ganymede the role – like Villiers – of cup-bearer. It was too perfect. One scandalous poem, rich in classical allusions, sang of moral and political disorder while 'Jove with Ganymede lies playing'. 'Bacchus quaffs,' it rhymed, 'Momus laughed.'[26]

Whichever way you look at it, their friendship was an astonishingly close one. They shared a love of the hunt and spent hours together in the field. They had affectionate nicknames for each other. After Queen Anne died in 1619, more than once James would go on to refer to Buckingham as 'my sweet child and wife'. When the duke wrote to the king, he called him 'Dad and Gossip': father and god-father. James called the duke his 'sweet heart', or 'Steenie' in reference to the younger man's likeness to a painting of the beautiful St Stephen. Buckingham referred to himself as the king's 'most humble slave and dog'. On one occasion, James even likened his friendship with Buckingham to that between Jesus and St John, telling the Privy Council 'Christ had his John, and I have my George.'[27]

Perhaps surprisingly, James was also deeply affectionate to the duke's wife Kate, whom he called 'my daughter', though this didn't stop James also referring to her and Buckingham's mother and sister as 'the cunts'. The mother and sister were countesses, so it was a pun, of sorts. The duke himself clearly considered it just banter, though we don't know how the three women felt. Certainly Kate sometimes stood her ground against the king, and relations between the Buckingham women and James occasionally became fairly icy. So much so, in fact, that before coming to visit the king in 1625, Buckingham wrote to ask 'whether it would offend you or not, if I brought the cunts with me'.[28]

The two men definitely shared beds, though this was some-thing close male friends did at the time. Nonetheless, the language of Buckingham's letters is clearly very intimate indeed. He writes of getting hold of the royal bedpost and never letting go, of 'having my dear Dad and master's leg soon in my arms'. And he wrote of 'the time which I shall never forget at Farnham, where the bed's head could not be found between the master and his dog'.[29] The belief that James and Buckingham were lovers was not mere tattle, either. It was political electricity: an open secret in England, widely talked about abroad. In 1622, the Puritan diarist Simonds D'Ewes worried that 'the sin of sodomy' had become 'a sin in the prince as well as the people'.[30]

In a world of print and news, therefore, the duke's relationship with the king ran the gauntlet of public opinion. Some thought this explained James's reluctance to join the war in the Palatinate. The nation was going soft, people said, a stark contrast to the martial glories of Queen Elizabeth. 'There was in England, a King Elizabeth', so it was said. '[T]here is now a Queen James.'[31]

As 1622 dragged on, and still with no official English involvement, Elector Frederick's cause continued to deteriorate, and by the summer his capital at Heidelberg was under siege. It finally fell on 9 September, despite the efforts of a garrison of English volunteers. Reports grad-ually filtered home. When they reached James, one newswriter wrote, he 'went a hunting presently'.[32] It was said that the debacle caused a 'cooling' of the people's 'affections towards their sovereign'.[33] There was a crackdown on preaching: 'No man can now mutter a word in the Pulpit,' bragged Buckingham to Gondomar, 'but he is presently catched and set in straight prison.'[34]

By now the economic situation was going from bad to positively frightening. The harvest of 1621 had been poor, leading the govern-ment to halt grain exports. The food supply had strained without yet breaking, but in the summer of 1622, as Heidelberg fought for its life, in England it just didn't stop raining. The grain crop mildewed, and the harvest was a disaster. There were food shortages across the country, worsening as winter approached. In North Wales, 'a number die in this country for hunger, which is a lamentable thing to see; and the rest have the impression of hunger in their faces'.[35] Evidence from farm accounts suggests a catastrophic collapse in food production. In Lincolnshire, there were reports of 2,000 poor people rising in protest. 'Dog's flesh', wrote a landlord there in April 1623, was considered 'a dainty dish', to be 'found upon search in many houses'.[36]

The north was hit especially hard. Here, where the land was poor and, where markets hadn't developed enough to provide a regular supply of cereal from outside, food was so scarce that people died.[37] With little comment, around the autumn of 1622 the names of the buried started to multiply in the parish registers. Cartmel was one example: here the burials more than doubled. One of those who would die, in August 1623, was a William Staines, five-year-old son of Mabel Swainson of Yorfulyate and of Oliver Staines, one-time servant of Jane Thornborough and one-time wearer of one of her gowns.[38] We don't know whether poor William starved, but one village, Greystoke in Cumberland, did make a sad note of the dozens of poor who pined to death from hunger: 'a poor fellow destitute of succour', found in the street and brought into the house of the constable, 'where he died'; 'a poor hungerstarven beggar child'; and James Irwen 'a poor beggar stripling born upon the borders of England' who died 'in great misery'.[39] Many poor unfortunate souls left their homes to tramp the highways, and they rarely found much welcome. Communities tried to close their borders against migrant beggars. The village court at Dilston, Northumberland, ordered a watch of the streets coming into the village for 'all such travelling people … especially the poor'.[40] In Lowick in northern Lancashire, the manor court fined millers if they allowed the poor to linger at their mills, and even threatened penalties to those 'who shall give any alms to any poor folks'.[41] In places like this, charity ran as cold as the winter.

In such conditions, it was hard to see much prospect of James's kingdoms fighting a war. But, as tragedy unfolded in the north, a farce was playing out on the Continent that would eventually send his monarchy stumbling towards conflict.

Having dissolved Parliament, and despite doubling the duty on wine, James remained seriously short of money, leaving little choice but to push the Spanish Match, and hopefully collect the large dowry on offer. The trouble was, there was next to no chance that either the king of Spain or the Pope would agree to it unless Prince Charles turned Catholic, and of course this was a red line for James.

In response, Charles and Buckingham, who were growing to be close friends, tried something dramatic. In February 1623, hoping that their sudden appearance at the Spanish court might speed things up, they slipped away to France en route to Madrid. As England suffered under biting winter food shortages, the Prince of Wales and the country's leading politician were gallivanting through France in false beards. James was distraught at Buckingham's absence. Buckingham himself was viciously attacked in rhyme, while the Spanish ambassador claimed to be 'besieged', quite literally.[42] There was fighting on the Strand between the embassy entourage and angry Londoners, and in September a brawl in Drury Lane left a baker dead. Protestants were miserable: left, it was said, in 'a dead dump'.[43] Catholics, though, took heart. A later writer recalled 1623 as the year when 'the Romish foxes came out of their holes'.[44] Buckingham's wife and mother converted, coming hot on the heels of a scandal the previous year in which his brother had punched through a window at Wallingford House near Whitehall, shaking his bloody fist at passers-by and shouting that he was a Catholic 'and would spend his blood in the cause'.[45]

Predictably, Charles and Buckingham got nowhere. James and Philip did manage to thrash out terms, but in a delicious irony English Protestants were saved by the Pope, who disliked the whole enterprise. Frustrated with the delay, Charles decided to call the whole thing off and return to England. Come October he and Buckingham were back in London, without the Infanta and without much diplomatic dignity (though Charles now had a real beard).[46] At least the English were happy. Despite the drizzle on the Thames as the prince approached London on the 5th, he was met with jubilant bells and a thunderous salute of cannons from the Tower. Celebrations swept the country. '[O]n the 5th day of October / it will be treason to be sober' went a rhyme. It was, wrote William Laud, now Bishop of St David's, 'the greatest expression of joy by all sorts of people that I ever saw'.[47] Such was the anti-papist fervour that when, later that month, a collapsing upper floor killed around a hundred Catholic worshippers next to the French ambassador's house at Blackfriars, many Londoners responded with cheers and gloats. Others pelted victims with mud and stones as the bodies were pulled out of the debris, and the so-called 'Fatal Vespers' became a favoured topic of gleeful Protestant satire (although Catholics scoffed at the idea that the tragedy was a judgement of God, instead placing the blame on some mouldy floorboards).

By now, the humiliated Prince Charles had rather drastically changed his mind about Spain. Now he wanted revenge, and so he joined the clamour for a new Parliament and a war. The prince was suddenly riding a wave of popularity, the duke was now the 'darling of the multitude'.[48] Between them, Charles and Buckingham pestered and manipulated the king. Their relationships with him started to strain, but there was little James could do.

Writs went out, and Parliament met on 19 February 1624 to a speech by James asking – with little sense of irony – for the House to give him advice on how to proceed with the Spanish Match and the crisis in the Palatinate. It was to be a busy, indeed successful, session: some 73 statutes were passed in the space of just three months. After some haggling, Parliament agreed to fund James's military to the tune of £300,000, with extra cash should it become necessary (as it inevitably would). At this point, there was little else the king could ask for, and on 23 March, James – the *Rex Pacificus* – finally committed to war. London celebrated, and the Spanish embassy was duly bombarded with stones. The next casualties were England's Catholics, who were to be disarmed and barred from attending services at foreign embassies (which, until now, had been a way around the ban on Catholic mass). Then fell the Crown's chief finance officer, Lionel Cranfield, who could see what the whole escapade would cost and so had to go. Charles and Buckingham had him impeached for bribery: he was removed from office, banished from court, fined and thrown in the Tower, although the king dutifully had him released after a few days and gave him a face-saving role at court. The wider implication was that Parliament was being used to impeach ministers, for the first time since the Middle Ages, and thus effectively claiming a say in the personnel of government. The king, for his part, thought young Charles might one day live to regret his role in reviving the process.

Now with battles to fight, a reluctant James – ageing and increasingly sick with severe arthritis – turned his attention once more to diplomacy, trying to build a coalition. He managed to gain the support of Louis XIII, king of France, in return for which Prince Charles was now to marry Louis's sister, Henrietta Maria. The young French princess – who, of course, was Catholic – would come with a £120,000 dowry, and in return she would be allowed to keep her faith, and indeed to maintain 28 religious attendants who could publicly wear the habit. Privately, James also agreed to release any Catholic prisoners of conscience. The treaty was signed in November, though the marriage itself – the first between a Catholic princess and a Protestant prince – would have to wait.

By this point, an army was being raised in England and Scotland led by the German mercenary Ernst von Mansfeld. Their contribution to British military history was to be short and inglorious. Starved of money as the Parliamentary subsidy only trickled in, an English army of 12,000 mostly conscripted men sucked the Kent countryside dry as they waited to embark at Dover. Meanwhile, James and Louis clashed over the aims of the war. The French king wanted to thrust the troops straight into the Spanish Netherlands (roughly modern-day Belgium); James, on the other hand, didn't. Rather, he wanted the focus to be on the Palatinate, where technically the Spanish were fighting for the Holy Roman Empire and therefore perhaps a full-scale Anglo-Spanish war could be avoided. Louis, for his part, was understandably wary of Mansfeld's ill-disciplined troops, so he refused them permission to land at Calais. Instead, they headed for the Dutch coast, but Buckingham neglected to warn the Dutch. Without proper supplies, and in a bitingly cold winter, many starved or deserted.

As his army withered, the aged king himself grew sicker. With winter turning to spring, a fever had him confined to bed at Theobalds in Hertfordshire, his favourite country retreat. Here, on 27 March 1625, he died. He was fifty-eight, and his had been an eventful life, in which two warring Crowns had been united. But his wider dream of a peaceful Europe lay in ruins.

The army James never wanted would last out a few more weeks. By the time it came to do any fighting, trying to lift the siege of Breda as part of a ramshackle international coalition, it was but a pale shadow. When Breda eventually fell to the Spanish in June 1625, only something like 600 English soldiers survived.

It was a harsh epitaph to a king who had tried his utmost to keep his realms at peace, even faced with a contested religious settlement and some of the toughest social conditions in the whole of English history. Ultimately, the external shock of what would become the Thirty Years War, beginning with the Bohemian Revolt of 1618, was starting to expose some of the cracks in England's heart.

4

If Parliaments Live or Die

King Charles I succeeded to the throne aged just twenty-four. Thoughtful, sensitive and emotionally rather delicate, the new king was short of stature and suffered a pronounced stammer from a young age, of which he was more conscious than anyone else. The difference in style to James was very quickly apparent. Most obviously, he placed great emphasis on decorum and order in every aspect of his life. Within weeks of James's death, Charles issued a proclamation noting how 'in the late reign of our dear father', there had been 'much disorder in and about his household', and so he 'resolved the reformation thereof'.[1] He was a perceptive man in religious matters. His father had reckoned Charles could 'manage a point in controversy with the best studied Divine of them all'.[2] Indeed, while James had mostly enjoyed theology for the arguments it allowed him to have, his son and successor was genuinely pious. It was to be a defining characteristic of his life, and – for that matter – his death.

Charles's immediate problem was money. His father had left the Crown £1 million in debt, and there was a war to pay for, expected to cost another million. Parliament remained the obvious solution, not least with Charles enjoying a bout of popularity as an anti-Spanish hardliner. He was also a parliamentarian of no little experience: he'd first attended aged just thirteen and had since served on several committees.[3] His Parliamentary orations were popular, mostly because, unlike those of his father, they were brief. As the Cornish MP John Eliot later recalled, 'with the new king a new spirit of life and comfort possessed all men'.[4]

But it was not to be. Wary of continuing costs, Parliament proved reluctant to reopen its purse. The irony was that Parliament had pushed England towards a war it was ill-equipped to pay for, but was now chafing at royal attempts to raise enough money to put up a decent fight. Recalling how James had allegedly misused the traditional life grant of 'Tonnage and Poundage' (import and export duties), Parliament decided that Charles's grant should first be carefully scrutinised, so it was sent to committee. By this point, though, Parliament was in a hurry, for over the spring and into the summer a deadly outbreak of plague had taken hold in London. Come summer it was claiming several thousand lives a week. It meant Parliament didn't have time to get Tonnage and Poundage right, so they stalled, granting the tax to Charles for one year, rather than for his lifetime. They would return to it when the plague had lifted, such was the theory, but in the meantime Charles was deeply offended.

The other area of controversy was religion. A critical fracture was beginning to open up in the Church, one whose consequences would be enormous. Calvinism remained dominant among the English clergy, but abroad there had emerged a countervailing set of ideas within Protestantism, known as Arminianism. Inspired by a Dutch theologian called Jakob Hermanszoon (1560–1609, Latinised to 'Arminius'), this strand held that God had gifted his free grace to all mankind, and that everyone had the free will to gain salvation. In many ways, the issue cut right to the heart of Protestant theology: one crucial difference between Catholicism and Protestantism lay in the fact that the latter believed in divine determinism, the former in human free will. Arminianism tried to be a form of Protestantism that accepted free will. It was theological dynamite.

The crunch came in 1618–19, in the sleepy Dutch town of Dordrecht (known to the English as Dort). Here, an international synod assembled to settle the dispute between Arminians and Calvinists. James sent an English delegation to back the Calvinists, and, ultimately, that Calvinist side carried the day. In England, though, Arminian ideas about grace proved highly attractive to those who had embraced ceremonialism. James himself helped prepare the ground for such developments, partly because he wanted a counterpoint to the Puritans, whom he hated. Already, by 1617, seven

English bishoprics were held by those sympathetic to the Arminians. Meanwhile, Lancelot Andrewes, who leaned strongly towards ceremonialism, became Bishop of Winchester, the richest episcopate, and Dean of the Chapel Royal in 1618.

The Bohemian crisis proved another significant staging point. It was James's Calvinist clergy who led demands for intervention, so his pacifism drew him towards their theological rivals. Even Archbishop Abbot of Canterbury, a staunchly pro-war Calvinist, fell from favour and gradually lost influence, not helped by an incident in the hot summer months of 1621 in which, while hunting in Hampshire, he accidentally shot a park keeper with a crossbow. The poor man died from the wound, and Abbot was never the same again, the misfortune having 'pierced' him 'in the very marrow of his bones'. Catholics rejoiced, and despite sympathy from the hunt-loving king, no fewer than three bishops-elect, including both William Laud and the Calvinist John Williams, refused to be consecrated by Abbot since he was a 'man of blood'.[5]

Come 1625, 12 of the 24 English bishoprics were in the hands of committed Arminians or ceremonialists, while the Calvinist Archbishop of Canterbury was increasingly shunned, partly through politics and partly through sheer bad luck. Just as important, in 1619 when James had lain dangerously sick at Royston, Andrewes approached him and told him he was worried about the tutelage of the young Prince Charles, whose religious instruction was thus far solidly Calvinist. James promised to make amends, and was true to his word, adding anti-Calvinists to the prince's entourage, none more significant than the Andrewes protégé and ceremonialist hardliner Matthew Wren, from 1622.

By now, though, Parliament's ears had pricked. In 1624, a rather caustic archdeacon named Richard Montagu had published a long tract entitled *A New Gagg for an Old Goose*, supposedly in response to a Catholic pamphlet. It argued that Calvinist predestination was not a true component of the English Church.[6] In May, Parliament received a petition asking it to suppress Montagu's book, containing as it did the 'dangerous opinions of Arminius'.[7] To Calvinists, views like these veered way too close to Catholicism, and at a time when the European war was going badly, this was a worrisome business indeed.

The Commons appointed a committee to investigate, headed by
an earnest Westcountryman called John Pym. For all the outrage,
though, all that came of the controversy was a royal request that
Montagu explain his views by writing yet another book: hardly
Parliament's desired outcome. By the early months of the new reign,
MPs were on Montagu's case again. Having alleged – in print – that
his views had the support of the late king, Montagu was accused
by Parliament of insulting James's memory and bringing discord
between king and people, and so he was arrested. At this point,
though, Charles intervened, revealing to considerable shock that
the beleaguered clergyman was now a royal chaplain, and was
thus protected. More alarmingly still, Charles's own views on the
Church were beginning to look suspect. His choice for the sermon
that opened Parliament was none other than William Laud, who was
known to be a keen ceremonialist and was suspected of Arminianism.
Calvinists, meanwhile, were being shut out. One of the men who
lost out was the Godly Yorkshireman Henry Burton, who had been
acting clerk of the closet to Prince Henry and then Prince Charles.
When his master became king, Burton made the mistake of attacking
the allegedly popish inclinations of Bishop Richard Neile of Durham
and William Laud, and he was promptly dismissed.

By the summer of 1625, plague had become a daily reality in London,
so Parliament was adjourned to Oxford. But pestilence followed
here, too, and as rancorous debates continued with little prospect of
supplying funds to the king, the assembly was dissolved. The bill for
Tonnage and Poundage fell by the wayside.

Charles knew he couldn't do without Parliament for long, so
in order to ensure a smoother sitting he moved against those he
considered particular troublemakers. The Calvinist bishop John
Williams was fired from his secular role as Lord Keeper and replaced
with the pliable Sir Thomas Coventry. Charles also, rather cleverly,
had six members of the Commons appointed as sheriffs, including
Edward Coke and a talented young Yorkshireman called Sir Thomas
Wentworth. The point was that sheriffs retained the role of organising
county elections, meaning they couldn't personally stand as MPs.

It was a neat way of 'pricking' out potential opponents, though it generated considerable annoyance among the pricked.*

Meanwhile, the war on the Continent continued. In September Charles formally allied with the Dutch against Spain. A naval expedition was prepared against Cadiz, and over 10,000 soldiers, more than 80 ships and nearly 6,000 seamen were mobilised. It was to be a mortifying fiasco. Landing without provisions, the commander Sir Edward Cecil allowed his men to drink the local wine. The outcome was predictable, and by the time Cecil could order a retreat around 2,000 Englishmen were so inebriated that the enemy simply moved in and killed them. Not for the last time, an English expedition to the Continent had ended in drunken humiliation.

Back at home, in January 1626, a conference of bishops was summoned to put the Montagu issue to bed, but as the panel comprised five ceremonialists they predictably decided that Montagu's views were perfectly fine. The response came from two Calvinist peers, Robert Rich, the Earl of Warwick, and William Fiennes, Lord Saye. Between them Warwick and Saye pushed for a conference on the doctrinal issues that were starting to split the Church, and one was convened at the Duke of Buckingham's grandiose residency at York House on the Strand. Senior Privy Councillors were in attendance and the duke himself was in the chair. By now, though, Buckingham seems to have become a convinced Arminian, presumably to help him retain Charles's favour. As a result, the Calvinists were unable to get the conference to agree to an outright condemnation of Montagu or to give the decrees of the Synod of Dort force in the Church of England.

Parliament was in session again, with Bishop Laud once more giving the opening sermon: a rather aggressive diatribe in which he evoked an imagined conspiracy by Presbyterians (who in fact were currently only a small subset of Calvinists) against Church and monarchy.[8] Lord Keeper Coventry, meanwhile, blandly announced that the king had called Parliament to 'advise of provident and good laws, profitable for the public and fitting for the present times and occasions'.[9] The Commons had their own agenda, though, and Buckingham was

---

*The word originated in the practice whereby the monarch would 'prick' names from a list using a pin. Of course, the quaintness of the process didn't make the outcome any less annoying for the 'pricked', especially if they had political ambitions at Westminster.

now in their sights. The Cadiz disaster, his Arminian sympathies, the open Catholicism of his family, and of course the overbearing nature of his power and influence at court made the duke an obvious target.

On 10 February, John Eliot, who had seen the bloodied and diseased soldiers and sailors disembarking at Plymouth from the catastrophe at Cadiz and was emerging as a rather sharp thorn in the king's side, began the assault. Then, nearly a month later, when the government made its awaited request for supply, the Commons agreed in principle (to the tune of £300,000) but demanded redress of grievances first. The attack on Buckingham intensified, and now there were even sensational allegations that he had not only used enchantments and had 'frequent consultations with the ringleaders of witches', but he had actually murdered the late King James, using a poisoned treacle posset provided by the duke's Catholic mother.[10]

Charles was furious, and demanded the House back off Buckingham immediately. On 29 March, he summoned the two Houses to Whitehall where, in the majestic Great Hall, he rebuked the Commons specifically. '[C]ease this unparliamentary inquisition,' he demanded (ventriloquised by Lord Keeper Coventry), telling them that if they didn't give supply without conditions, then the sitting would be ended. 'Remember,' Charles warned, 'that Parliaments are altogether in my power for the calling, sitting and continuance of them. Therefore as I find the fruits either good or evil, they are to continue or not to be.'[11]

But while the Commons did continue to discuss supply, they doggedly pursued other issues. In May, they finally laid articles of impeachment against Buckingham. Not holding back, the MP Sir Dudley Digges charged on the 8th that the duke was like a comet 'drawn out of the dross of the earth'. He was a modern-day Sejanus, said Sir John Eliot on the 10th, incidentally setting off a surge in demand for Roman histories from the booksellers.[12] On the 11th, Charles sent Digges and Eliot to the Tower. The Commons responded by suspending business. After a few days, Charles pulled back: the two MPs were released, though he still refused to have Buckingham arrested. On 8 June, the duke put his defence before the Lords in some detail, and the following day Charles warned the Commons once more to leave off his favourite and turn back to the matter of supply. Otherwise, he said ominously, he would need 'to take other resolutions'.[13]

Yet the Commons persisted. Now they prepared a 'remonstrance' against Buckingham, effectively a formal denunciation to the king, and copies were available to buy in Westminster before Charles had even seen it.[14] For those who wanted it, divine vindication was shown by a violent storm on the 12th that – according to reports – tore the dead bodies of last year's plague victims out of the ground and culminated in a terrifying whirlwind, a 'tempest whirling and ghoulish', on the Thames. It crashed – providentially – into Buckingham's residence at York House.[15] But Charles stuck by his man, and on the 15th he finally dissolved Parliament.

By now Charles's young queen, Henrietta Maria, was proving quite the liability. On St James's Day (25 July) there were rumours that she'd made a pilgrimage to Tyburn and prayed for Catholic martyrs. With Arminianism on the rise and with Catholicism so close to the royal person, the fears of Calvinists were growing by the day. But the main problem for Charles remained the lack of money he needed for the war. That summer, the Privy Council announced that Charles may collect Tonnage and Poundage, despite its lack of Parliamentary sanction. Charles even ordered the deputy lieutenants in each county to raise troops and 'to lead them against public enemies, rebels and traitors', giving them power to impose martial law, 'sparing and putting to death according to discretion'.[16] This was partly to keep control of the soldiers returned from Cadiz, who were underpaid and potentially unruly, but such a force might also be used against any civilian dissidents. Then, in late summer, there was more bad news from Germany. After the fall of the Elector Palatine, the Protestant cudgels had been picked up by the armies of Denmark, whose king was Charles's uncle. But on 17 August, their troops had been badly mauled at Lutter in Lower Saxony. Who now would keep up the Protestant cause in Europe?

For the time being at least, Charles was sworn off Parliaments, even saying in council that he 'did abominate that name'. Instead, to raise much-needed cash he decided to impose a 'forced loan' on the country. It was hardly likely to be popular, not least because it was asked of those of modest means as well as the wealthy, and because the promises of repayment were ominously vague. But the government encouraged the people to give 'willingly and cheerfully', while warning that those who refused would suffer the king's 'high displeasure'.[17] Subjects who spoke against the loan, declared Charles, could not be allowed to go unpunished. The clergy were told to ring forth the cry of unity from the pulpits. Disharmony, they were to proclaim, had recently 'grown too great and common among all sorts of men'. It was time for the country to come together again.

And so the cash came in: £243,000 in the first year, but at what cost? In November the Privy Council, with Charles present, narrowly decided not to imprison those lords who refused to pay, though it decided that their names were to be 'put into the black book'.[18] The next month it was still anticipated that 15 or 16 peers would refuse. These included the anti-Arminians Warwick and Saye, but also Robert Devereux, Earl of Essex. A flamboyant courtier, Essex was a hero of Germany and a former playmate of the king, even though his father had been a notorious rebel against Elizabeth. But he was also a wronged man, having been declared impotent by his own wife during the Overbury scandal, and he was a Calvinist.

While peers like Essex, Warwick and Saye allowed their opposition to be known, so too did many of those down the ranks of society, for whom the consequences were more severe. Desperate for money, Charles allowed his government to engage in bullying tactics. A hundred leading gentry were thrown in prison, while ordinary folk who didn't pay were threatened with being pressed to the forces or worse: the Privy Council menaced defaulters in Essex with hanging from 'the next tree to their dwellings' as 'an example and terror unto others'.[19] The Lord Chief Justice of King's Bench, Sir Ranulph Crewe, was fired for refusing to testify that the loan was legal. One MP from Kent later recalled paying the loan, but only, he said, 'to escape imprisonment and death'.[20] Mobilising the propaganda of the pulpit, the government was forced into arguing that the king ruled by divine right and resistance was sacrilege. One of the most hardline sermons was delivered by Dr Robert Sibthorpe at Northampton Assizes in February 1627. Taking a classic absolutist line, he attacked those who, he claimed, would 'make the Law above the king, and the people above the law, and so depose Princes by their tumults and insurrections'. Instead, he argued, the king was above the law.[21]

Sibthorpe's sermon was so controversial that it brought Charles into dispute with his own Archbishop of Canterbury, the unfortunate George Abbot, who when asked to license publication of the text, refused (it technically wasn't his job), and was finally sequestered from his office. His duties were handed over to a commission made up entirely of Arminians, including Laud, who had been promoted once more, to the bishopric of Bath and Wells. Nor was Sibthorpe the only one. Another cleric, Roger Maynwaring, gave two sermons extolling royal absolutism in the summer of 1627 Charles agreed wholesomely with the content and soon the sermons were published, 'by his majesty's special command'.[22] Even Laud thought this was likely to stir up trouble, and tried to put the king off publishing, saying, 'there were many things therein which would be very distasteful to the people'.[23] But Charles went ahead anyway.

The Forced Loan was creating a crisis, and it was one centred on issues of principle. The increasingly absolutist tendencies of Charles's rule were running headlong into opposition. The Loan, in essence, was ordering his subjects to lend him money that they would probably never see again. It cut against the old maxim that subjects could not be deprived of their property without consenting to it in Parliament. Worse, in response to opposition, Charles was throwing people in prison, and because he didn't want any legal proceedings to end up as a test case of the Loan itself, he was doing so without allowing them a trial. Thus arbitrary imprisonment became another grievance. It was all, quite frankly, a terrible mess.

The cause célèbre came in November 1627, when five knights who had been imprisoned for refusing to pay the loan sued out a writ of habeas corpus. The knights pleaded Magna Carta, but the Attorney General argued that the king could imprison for 'state matters' without showing cause (though it was, of course, to be assumed that he had one). In the end, the judges sided with the Crown, helped by the fact that they had been carefully interviewed beforehand by Charles, who made his expectations clear. The knights were sent back to prison, though the judges did at least record their judgement as an 'interlocutory order', so it didn't set a potentially dangerous precedent. There were accusations, from John Selden, that the Attorney General Sir Robert Heath attempted to tamper with the record of the judgement, so as to make it precedent-setting. The thought of the Attorney

General manipulating legal records to support royal absolutism was worrying indeed, though the matter was eventually allowed to drop.

That summer, England had suffered yet another military humiliation. Relations with France had cooled since it emerged that Louis XIII was using loaned English ships to wage war on his own Protestant subjects, and in the winter of 1626–7 the two countries finally slid into war. The English plan was to relieve the Protestant stronghold of La Rochelle, but the expedition, led by Buckingham, lurched into catastrophe. The lowest point came in October, when Buckingham decided to attack a citadel on the Île de Ré, in the driving rain, only for his men to find their ladders were too short. The whole shambolic escapade cost around 5,000 English lives. Buckingham was forced to return home, his defeated and demoralised men billeted in the southern port towns, seething with anger. '[S]ince England was England,' the Godly young Denzil Holles wrote to his brother-in-law Thomas Wentworth, 'she received not so dishonourable a blow.'[24] Charles was determined to avenge the catastrophe, so once more he needed money. The reality was that this meant Parliament had to be called. Charles's decision to do so was to be one of the most fateful of his reign.

The elections to the Parliament of 1628 went against the king, notably so. Critics of his government were returned; worse, so were 27 loan refusers, only recently allowed out of prison: men like Thomas Wentworth of Yorkshire. It met on 17 March. 'These times,' came the royal announcement, 'are for action.'[25] But MPs were nervous. Conscious of Charles's growing dislike of Parliament, many were aware of the trend in European politics – not least in neighbouring France – for kings to look past representative bodies and to take 'new counsels'. To embrace absolutism, in other words, raising taxes and making laws without Parliaments. For England, said one MP, this was 'the crisis of Parliaments'. 'We shall know by this if Parliaments live or die,' he continued. 'If the king draws one way and the people another, we must all sink.'[26]

Buckingham was under scrutiny again, though for now Parliament was content to grant the king some supply. In April, to Charles's delight, they agreed in principle to no fewer than five subsidies, totalling some £300,000. 'I love Parliaments,' Charles announced, 'I shall rejoice to meet with my people often.'[27] But MPs remained cautious and delayed finally passing the subsidies until a statement could be made of what they considered to be the main liberties of the people. Imprisonment without cause shown, in particular, had grown into a major grievance as a result of the Forced Loan crisis.

For his part, Charles was happy to confirm that he intended to 'govern according to the laws and statutes of this realm', including Magna Carta.[28] But this wasn't enough. MPs also wanted to add some formal 'explanations' to existing laws, that would protect them from arbitrary royal power. Edward Coke, seventy-eight years old and enjoying a late stint as an MP, told Parliament that the question was 'what is the law of the land', and suggested an unusual course: a 'petition of right' to be made to the king.[29] By 8 May, this petition existed in draft.

It centred on four grievances: the Forced Loan, 'free quarter' (i.e. the billeting of troops), martial law and imprisonment without cause shown. Charles was prepared to yield on all of these except the last. As May progressed, his room for manoeuvre was limited by the failure of another attack on La Rochelle, and the eventual decision of a majority of the Lords to align with the Commons. He formally received the Petition of Right from both Lords and Commons at the new Banqueting House on the afternoon of the 28th.

Soon, though, the king was busy trying to undermine the Petition. Rather than grant formal royal assent, which would have given the Petition unambiguous legal force, he agreed instead that 'right be done according to the laws and customs of the realm': he was merely affirming existing law rather than giving additional protections to his subjects.[30] MPs were furious, and turned back to other grievances, thus again threatening Charles's precious subsidies. And so the king retreated. On 7 June he gave formal assent to the Petition of Right, and Londoners celebrated with bonfires and the ringing of bells: the greatest celebration, said Coke, since the king's return from Spain in 1623. This time, though, Charles wasn't basking in popular favour: now the bonfires were celebrating his opponents.

Charles agreed the Petition should be entered as a formal statute and printed; the Commons duly passed the subsidy bill. But then the Commons pushed things too far. On 14 June, they drew up another remonstrance against Buckingham. By now the duke was grievously unpopular. The day before the remonstrance, his personal adviser Dr John Lambe, an astrologer and quack, an alleged practitioner of the black arts and convicted child rapist,* was killed on the streets of London. Leaving a playhouse, he was 'pelted with stones and trash' by 'boys and mariners'.[31] His pockets were rifled, to reveal in his possession a crystal ball. A rhyme suggested that this was not the end to the bloodshed: 'Let Charles and George [Villiers] do what they can / Yet George shall die like Doctor Lambe.' That summer, a chronogram doing the rounds managed to get the number 1628 from the letters in 'GEORGIVS DVX BVCKINGHAMIAE', concluding that 'Thy numerous name with this year doth agree / But twenty-nine, Heaven grant thou never see!'† 'Hath no witch poison?' asked another rhyme, '[N]ot one man a dagger?'[32]

To his enemies in Parliament, Buckingham's malign power was the source of England's ills: Tonnage and Poundage was being collected without Parliamentary authority, and there were the disasters at Cadiz and Île de Ré to be accounted for. Another charge against the duke was religion. The English Church was dividing on binary lines and the debate was getting increasingly polarised. The Arminians tried to tar all Calvinists as Puritans, while Calvinists, for their part, painted Arminians as crypto-Catholics. With royal support, though, the Arminians were winning. In 1626 Buckingham was given the chancellorship of Cambridge University, and the teaching of predestination there was banned. A royal proclamation, meanwhile, proscribed any divergence from official doctrine, effectively putting Calvinists under formal disapproval. Then, in 1627, Laud became a Privy Councillor. The attack on Buckingham was part of the response. His power, MPs said, brought a 'general fear' of a Catholic plot. In the Protestant mind of the age, Catholicism was associated with tyranny and arbitrary government. The duke's Arminianism was directly linked, it was thought, to his support for the Forced Loan, imprisonment without trial and the use of soldiers to cow English civilians.

But Charles still publicly backed the duke. By late June, the critical issue once more was Tonnage and Poundage. Parliament was by now

---

*Although sentenced to hang, he had been pardoned by James Ley, Lord Chief Justice, who considered the evidence unsound.

†The method, such as it was, involved taking those letters in the phrase which corresponded with Roman numerals, and totting them up to reach the Duke's year of ultimate doom. So, georg*IV*s *DVX bVCkInghaMIae* = I V D V X V C I M I = M (1000) + D (500) + C (100) + X (10) + V (5) + V (5) + V (5) + I (1) + I (1) + I (1) = 1628.

arguing for more time to finalise its passage into statute, but there was little chance of finishing things off before summer recess. Provocatively, the Commons issued a remonstrance reminding Charles that if he continued to collect it, then he would be in violation of the Petition of Right. Charles, furious, prorogued Parliament until October.

Charles spent the summer heaping new favours on the Arminians. In July, Laud became Bishop of London, giving him control (in theory) of the printing press. The king also struck back at the Petition of Right: recalling all copies printed with his second answer, 'to be made waste paper', then republishing it with his first response, appended with a list of qualifications and the text of his upbraiding speech at the prorogation of Parliament.[33] It was a devious move, and one that hardly augured well for the next session. In Suffolk that summer there was 'secret whispering' that Charles would be deposed, and replaced with his popular sister, Elizabeth of Bohemia.[34] And before Parliament returned, English politics had already taken a shocking turn.

In August 1628, John Felton bid farewell to his family in London. He had lived in a lodging house in Fleet Street for some nine months. Fallen on difficult times, Felton was troubled with recurrent bad dreams, of fighting and war. For he was a survivor of both Cadiz and Île de Ré. He was, his brother later said, a man 'sad and heavy and of few words'.[35] Elizabeth Josselyn, with whom he shared lodgings, agreed that he had few words, but noted that he did like reading. More to the point, Felton was overdue wages, and, he said, he should have been promoted. To push his cause, in July he had visited a scrivener in Holborn to procure petitions for the Privy Council. In the shop, he saw copies of the Commons's remonstrance against Buckingham. He took one away and pored over it in the Windmill Inn on Shoe Lane. He had heard rhymes and gossip about the duke, a man whose incompetence he had experienced first-hand. Some of those rhymes predicted Buckingham would shortly be dead.

Heading south, Felton made his way to Portsmouth. There, Buckingham was lodging at the Greyhound Inn, a timber-framed hostelry in the town's ancient High Street. He was preparing his navy for another expedition, and was engaged in intense negotiations with Huguenot military men. On Friday 22 August, he had been faced with a minor mutiny. A sailor who had insulted the duke was about to be hanged, but some of his fellow men tried to break him free: Buckingham and a group of troops fought back, driving the sailors back onto a ship, killing two, and proceeded with the hanging.

The next morning, after breakfast, Buckingham made to leave the Greyhound, en route to see the king, who reposed at nearby Southwick. In the parlour, a press of people had gathered and as the duke approached a doorway one of his colonels stopped him to discuss business. The conversation ended, and the two men bowed to each other, but as they did, there was Felton. Leaning over the colonel, he stabbed Buckingham hard through the chest. With one blow, and with a cold dagger worth just a shilling (he'd borrowed the money from his mother), Felton had achieved what Parliament had failed to do for years. The Duke of Buckingham was dead.

Charles was inconsolable, and Felton ended his life at the end of a Tyburn rope. To loyalists the assassin was the spawn of the many-headed monster. Matthew Wren, the ceremonialist Master of Peterhouse College, Cambridge, suggested that Felton's case proved Puritans – whose cause Wren thought he represented – were potential regicides: they were 'that most pernicious sect', 'dangerous to a monarch'.[36] For many, though, Felton was a hero. In the eyes of one rhymer, he was an 'immortal man of glory', who had saved 'ancient English liberty'.[37] Buckingham's funeral even had to be held at night, to save it from jeering crowds. At Felton's trial, he claimed he'd acted 'to rid the Commonwealth of a monster'.[38] And with the monster gone, the old cosmic order could return and the body politic could start to heal. 'The Duke is dead, and we are rid of strife', went one verse. 'A rotten member, that can have no cure / Must be cut off to save the body sure.'[39]

With its leading star gone, there were inevitable changes at court. Charles grew much closer to his young queen, whose own father, Henri IV, had died by an assassin's knife, and a prominent role was now played at court by the pro-Spanish Richard Weston. One of Weston's early successes, even before Buckingham was killed, had been bringing the talented Thomas Wentworth into the peerage as a baron.

Wentworth had opposed the Forced Loan and been imprisoned in 1627, and while Buckingham was alive his career was always stalled. He had been a vocal supporter of the Petition of Right. But in December, with Buckingham dead, Wentworth was appointed Lord President of the Council of the North. His was a career now firmly on the up.

But talk of the ending of strife was premature, and it was in the old palace at Westminster that England's political crisis finally ignited.

Reassembling on 20 January 1629, MPs, led by Johns Eliot and Selden, were incensed by Charles's attempt to undermine the Petition of Right, not least since the Privy Council were trying to force merchants to pay Tonnage and Poundage by seizing their goods and sometimes their persons. Refusing to allow the reading of the government's bill for Tonnage and Poundage, the Commons instead debated religion. They went after the Arminians. The doctrine was, said the MP Francis Rous, 'the spawn of a Papist'.[40] Debate meandered, but on 24 February the Parliamentary subcommittee for religion agreed to a series of explosive resolutions. These attacked the 'extraordinary growth of Popery' and the 'subtle and pernicious spreading of the Arminian faction'.[41] They intended to present them to the Commons the next day. For Charles, it was the final straw.

On the 25th, a Wednesday, instead of the committee's report Parliament received a message from the king ordering them to adjourn until the following Monday. That Monday – 2 March – prayers were said as normal. Then the Speaker, Sir John Finch, rose from his chair. The House, he said, was to adjourn again, until the following Tuesday, by order of the king. The packed chapel of St Stephen went into uproar. Eliot rose and asked to read a declaration stating the case of the House, and with a dramatic flourish threw the paper copy on the floor in front of him. As the Speaker tried to leave, two MPs, Denzil Holles and Benjamin Valentine, pulled him back and held him in his chair. Another, Sir Miles Hobart, locked the door. Repeated messengers from the king were refused entry. There were blows, it was reported, between 'Patriots' and 'Royalists'. Angry hands grabbed the hilts of swords, threatening to draw.

With the Speaker held firm, the House continued for two hours. It passed a protestation, to the effect that anyone who pushed for popish or Arminian innovations, or who supported Tonnage and Poundage, was to be considered 'a capital enemy to this kingdom and common-wealth'. Even those who paid Tonnage and Poundage voluntarily 'shall likewise be reported a betrayer of the liberties of England, and an enemy to the same'.[42] Then, at last, the Speaker was released, and the House adjourned.

Immediately, Charles fired off a royal proclamation dissolving Parliament. Eliot, Holles, Valentine and six other men were arrested. On the 10th, Charles went through the formal process of dissolution in the Lords, performing the final act of this unhappy Parliament. He did not blame the Lords, he said, nor all of the Commons, just 'some few vipers amongst them'.[43] A declaration a few days later set out Charles's case to the news-hungry public. 'Princes are not bound to give account of their actions but to God alone,' he averred, but he went ahead anyway and gave his side to the people.[44]

If he hoped to forestall criticism, though, it was in vain. Discussions of the news continued in parlours, in markets, in fields and in alehouses. A group of servants in Northamptonshire chewed over the dissol-ution and agreed that the queen was to blame. When two men met on a Shropshire highway, one reported to the other that Parliament was dissolved and some gentlemen had been imprisoned, to which the reply came that 'the king would lose the hearts of his subjects' by his loans and taxes.[45] There was even a rumour that the king was about to mortgage the Isle of Wight to the Dutch.

In the middle of May, a scrap of paper was found at St Paul's. It addressed Charles himself. 'Oh king,' it said, 'or rather *no* king, for thou hast lost the hearts of thy subjects, and therefore no king, nor they any longer thy subjects.' 'That relationship now ceaseth,' it continued, 'violated on thy part.'[46]

To Charles it was his unruly people who had poisoned that rela-tionship. They had opposed his taxes, questioned his religious pol-icies and celebrated when his beloved favourite had been killed by a cold dagger. For Charles, who was starting to prefer the company of his dogs to that of his subjects, it suggested a new approach to gov-ernment was needed. One that would do away with Parliament for as long as he could.

PART TWO

1629–42
Paper Combats

5

The Arch of Order and Government

Each year, the most important event in the calendar was nothing to do with the king, his court or Parliament, or even the law courts. It was the harvest. And the harvest of 1628 was very bad indeed.

The weather was dreadful, crops failed and food was scarce. Prices rose, and, as people spent a greater proportion of their income on putting bread on the table, they had less left over to spend on other things like clothes. Demand therefore collapsed in the textile industry, so industrial workers were doubly hit. The result was that, in the early months of 1629, as Westminster descended into acrimony, tension was mounting steadily in the country.

The flashpoint was Maldon, in Essex. Here, in March, a crowd of hungry women and children seized a grain ship moored in the town's harbour, about to leave for the Continent. The sailors were forced to hand over the grain and pour it into the women's bonnets and aprons. Eventually order was restored, but the shortages remained. So, in May, Ann Carter, a poor butcher's wife who styled herself a 'Captain', raised another crowd of several hundred and boarded another grain ship. 'Come, my brave lads of Maldon,' she cried, 'I will be your leader, for we will not starve.'[1] She was arrested and hanged.

Disorder continued. In late 1630, a rhyme was found on the curate's porch in Wye, discovered by the maid who came to sweep in the morning, threatening those in power with a rising of the poor.[2] Around Christmas there was dangerous talk in Rutland about a plot among the poor and the tradesmen of Oakham, Liddington and Uppingham to seize arms and throw down enclosures.[3] If a hundred folk could be raised, declared a Somerset stonemason that year, 'they would kill some of those rich men [so] that the rest might sell corn cheaper'.[4] In the West Country, meanwhile, there were riots in the old forests against attempts by the king's government to remove common rights for the local peasantry. These were often led by men calling themselves 'Lady Skimmington', a reference to the way, so they believed, Crown policies were turning the world upside down.[5]

It was hardly an auspicious beginning to Charles's rule without Parliament, his 'Personal Rule'. But gradually things calmed. The rioting, as the harvests improved, petered out.

Charles was helped by the diplomatic situation. In 1629 England signed a treaty with France, followed the next year by peace with Spain. For the next few years, England's friendship would tread a delicate line between France and Spain. The recovery of the Palatinate for the Protestant cause remained a key goal, but it was less pressing after May 1630, when a new son was born, leaving Elector Frederick's wife Elizabeth no longer next in line to the English, Scottish and Irish thrones. Then, in 1632, both the unhappy Frederick and his greatest Protestant champion, Gustavus Adolphus of Sweden, died. A military intervention was no longer plausible, so for now Charles pursued diplomacy and rapprochement with Spain. His son, who was given his father's name, Charles, survived.

So England remained at peace even as conflict raged in Europe. The port of Dover, now a haven of calm compared to a troubled Continent, emerged as a significant international entrepôt. Peace took some of the fire out of the religious debate, too, while the death of Buckingham had brought back the old rhythms of court. No longer did everything go through the 'Great One'. Members of the old nobility found themselves basking in the glow of royal favour (although not the earls of Essex or Warwick, both of whom Charles rather disliked).

The court was now where politics happened. In fact, with Parliament gone, its doors expected to be closed 'for many years', so, too, was much of the divisive politics of the 1620s.[6] Enthusiasts for the 'ancient constitution' considered Charles's Personal Rule to be illegal, but their voices were quiet. Most were happy to accept the new approach to government as long as it brought much-needed stability. It was to be a period that later writers – and some contemporaries – would see as 'halcyon days'.[7] As early as August 1629, the painter Peter Paul Rubens was duly impressed. This was, he chirped, 'a people rich and happy in the lap of peace'.[8]

The image Charles cultivated was one of quiet decorum: slightly set apart; unobtainable, unassailable. If the assassination of Buckingham had taught him to distrust his people, it also reinforced his desire to associate his rule with order and hierarchy. His monarchy was to be one of dignity and propriety, standing tall above the commotion of contemporary life and politics. He saw himself as a kind, loving patriarch charged with keeping his people in order, for their own good. Unlike so many of his contemporaries he never took a mistress. To the conservative mind of the age, it made a welcome change. Even the Puritan Lucy Hutchinson much later recalled that Charles 'was temperate, chaste and serious', and so 'the fools, and bawds, mimics and catamites of the former court grew out of fashion'.[9]

Nonetheless, the court remained a world of luscious art, music, poetry and pleasure. The clothes and jewels were fine and beautiful. Chambers at the royal palaces sang to the sounds of viols, lutes, harpsicords, virginals and the increasingly fashionable guitars; corridors echoed to haunting madrigals. The king and queen, like their predecessors, acted starring roles in the court masques: great fusions of art, music and dance. The theme, often, was the conflict between disorder and order and the eventual triumph of the latter. One masque, performed in 1627, included the use of imitation dogs' heads with gaping mouths to represent the constant barking of the common people.[10] They were powerful propaganda, at least for anyone who happened to be in the room.

Charles was a genuine aesthete: Rubens, in London as a foreign ambassador, described him as 'le plus grand amateur de peinture du monde', and once Anthony van Dyck had been tempted over to England Charles would regularly visit his studio at Blackfriars to watch him at work.[11] Indeed, there are few greater expressions of Charles's ideology than his art collection. Portraits of Charles emphasise the twin virtues of order and a happy family life. Painters used informal poses and touch to show genuine affection between a father, mother and their happy children (and pets); and Charles adored it – he had one of Van Dyck's paintings of his family hung over his breakfast table so he could gaze upon it as he began the day.[12] Meanwhile, the ceiling to the Banqueting House, which ambassador Rubens would paint, extolled a divinely ordained monarchy centred on the figure of James I.

So with art, also with life. Charles's household was to be a bastion of good order: a defender of refined beauty against ugliness. Nothing discordant. Nothing out of place. There were plans in 1629 to restore an imagined medieval respect for proper hierarchy: 'every distance and degree being then well known and strictly observed'.[13] The sale of titles for money was stopped, and English aristocrats were decreed to take priority over Scottish and Irish. Later orders made sure that only barons and above (except Privy Councillors and gentlemen of the bedchamber) were allowed in Whitehall's Inner Closet, while in the presence chamber, where the king gave audiences, only 'persons of quality' were to be admitted.[14] Charles made a point of dividing his day into ordered sections, and uniquely among his fellow western monarchs, he expected to be served on bended knee.[15]

New efforts were made to keep the bedraggled poor out of the palaces. The porters at Whitehall, with its lodge facing out to the noise of King Street, were to make sure that 'no ragged boys nor unseemly persons be suffered to make a stay in any of the courts', and that no 'uncivil, unclean and rude people' were allowed to gain entry.[16] Charles also took a hard line on sexual scandal. During the infamous Castlehaven affair, an 'obscene tragedy' in which an Irish earl was convicted for rape and sodomy committed at his Wiltshire country house, and ultimately beheaded, Charles prohibited all women from attending the trial in Westminster Hall, on 'pain of ever after being reputed to have forfeited their modesty'.[17]

The queen was starting to be a great asset, at least to those who were lucky enough to meet her. Her political views were clearly close to those of her husband. Still only twenty in 1629, she recognised the danger monarchs could be in from their unruly subjects: for her father, Henri IV, had been assassinated when she was a baby. She would eventually prove the more zealous of the two, but for the moment it didn't matter because those views were hardly tested. In any case, it was said that Charles 'neither gives nor allows her any part in affairs'.[18] But it was her youthful *joie de vivre* that made her very popular at court. She threw herself into the art, the music and the masques with sparkling enthusiasm. So much so that when in 1632 she had an eye infection, it nearly ruined Christmas.

By contrast, the king himself could sometimes be emotionally very cold. When Francis Cottington's wife died in childbirth in 1633, Charles ignored the mourning period and summoned him to court, without even acknowledging the loss.[19] Charles had an overwhelming belief in the suppression of private interest in the name of the public good. It was a set of principles that, for example, allowed him to countenance projects like vast schemes to drain the eastern fens because, despite the hardship they obviously caused to many poor families, they not only brought public gains in the shape of improved food production, but also brought order to a previously unruly, untamed landscape. 'It is better the subject suffer a little', ran one of his maxims, 'than all lie out of order.'[20] *the masses in mind*

In London, Charles tried to remodel the mucky, messy old town into a glimmering capital, fit for a great empire. It was 'our royal city, the imperial seat and chamber of this our kingdom', so it should look the part, with raised and levelled streets with central passages for coaches and horses.[21] His government ordered a new fleet of fire engines – a recent German invention – and, in 1636, decreed that no hackney carriages be taken for journeys shorter than three miles, the point being to reduce congestion. He set up a commission for the regulation of buildings, and fined subjects who built where they shouldn't.

Beyond London, a postal system was created to connect the country and an attempt was made to standardise the grammar taught in schools. Charles tried to discourage people from taking tobacco, because it led them to drink and to the 'depraving of their manners'. He issued a proclamation ordering the enforcement of the 1624 statute against swearing (although at least one individual had to be prosecuted because he said he didn't care a fart for it).[22] He went after those who depopulated the land through enclosures, with rather overblown claims made that some 2,000 farms had reopened, even while Charles himself allowed enclosures on his own estates.[23] He also tried, as his father had, to get the landed elites to leave London and to tend to their affairs in the country. Unlike his father, though, he backed proclamations with actual enforcement, and in the process caused some irritation. Simonds D'Ewes, peeved at having to leave Islington for the sticks, complained that the policy 'took away men's liberties at one blow', though he was being rather dramatic. Some, indeed, took a more positive view. A report in 1632 claimed that in the countryside 'more chimneys are likely to smoke this Christmas than have been seen many years before'.[24] In the bleak winter, the presence of landed families in their country homes was supposed to bring warm hospitality to their poorer neighbours.

Charles was very much in charge. 'Everything is but discourse until His Majesty give his consent,' wrote the diplomat Thomas Roe.[25] His approach was not about the kind of drastic, forward-looking administrative reform that was then taking place in France. Instead, it was about making old ways work better: staffing the government with reliable men, making sure people obeyed commands. Giving order and direction. Being *thorough*.

If anyone defined Charles's government, save the king himself, it was the Yorkshireman Thomas Wentworth. Although born in London, Wentworth was from a wealthy West Riding family, and his early years were spent there. Then, like so many of his class, he studied at the Inns of Court and Cambridge. With short, dark, curly hair and a face of stony determination, he was now a man of some experience, having been first elected as a knight of the shire for Yorkshire in 1614 aged just twenty. He had opposed the Forced Loan, but had been returned to favour in 1628 by a government that clearly recognised his talent. In 1632, having made a success of his time as Lord President of the Council of the North, he was promoted again, this time to Lord Deputy of Ireland.

Wentworth was not always a likeable man. His role was to be that of the trusted administrator, sent to the difficult corners of Charles's realms to keep them in line. It suited his temperament well, for he wasn't a natural court charmer. He had the hard stare of the zealot and the busy diligence of a particularly determined accountant. His aptitude was for government, not politics. 'Nature hath not given him generally a personal affability,' wrote one observer, something of an understatement.[26] Even his friends admitted he was 'severe' in business, though they did allege he was 'sweet in private conversation'.[27] Yet he was a public servant par excellence and a man whose political outlook aligned closely with Charles's. Princes, Wentworth had declared in a famous speech at York, 'are to be indulgent, nursing fathers to their people'. 'The authority of a king,' he continued, 'is the keystone which closeth up the arch of order and government.'[28]

To Charles, closing the arch of government meant quieting the restless spirits of those below. Parliament, that 'hydra' as the king called it, was already gone, but political discussion by the people more generally also had to stop. Loyal clergymen, of whom there remained very many, reminded the people of the requirement to know their place. It was quite wrong, preached Francis Rogers in 1632, for the king's rule to be appraised by 'goodman the cobbler, by master the mercer', by those with 'clouted shoes and russet coats'.[29] Print was restricted. Already, as of early 1629, all 'matter of news, relations, histories, or other things in prose or in verse that have reference to matters and affairs of state' had to be signed off by the authorities.[30] The government even worried about what people were keeping in their private collections. It closed the treasure-house medieval library of Robert Cotton in 1630, suspecting that it had been used to help push for the Petition of Right. Cotton himself was locked up, and died the following year (of grief, it was said). In 1634, the voluminous legal and historical papers of Sir Edward Coke were impounded as the great lawyer lay dying. There were rumours that the government was opening people's letters.[31]

Charles could certainly be vindictive to those he considered disloyal. The MP John Eliot, architect of the 1629 troubles in Parliament, was left to rot in prison, where he died in 1632, and in an act of fairly petty cruelty on Charles's part, his family were refused permission to take his body home. Meanwhile, the court of Star Chamber ramped up its attempts to control sedition, printed and otherwise. One sensational trial involved Alexander Leighton, a personable if acidic Scottish Presbyterian, pamphleteer and physician (unlicensed). He had published a tract in which he called bishops 'men of blood' and the canons of 1604 'nonsense'. He also attacked the royal supremacy, Charles's foreign policy and (for good measure) the queen. So in 1630 he was prosecuted and thrown in 'a nasty doghole full of rats and mice' in Newgate prison. The experience left Leighton so ill that he had to be represented in court by his wife, and he was sentenced to be degraded, fined, pilloried, whipped, have his ears cut off, his nose slit and be branded on the cheeks with the letters 'SS', for 'sower of sedition'. Most of this was carried out, despite him briefly escaping and having to be recaptured. He was then imprisoned for life.[32]

Another victim was William Prynne, a firebrand Puritan. Prynne was a pompous prude with a poisonous pen, among whose literary output was a broadside against men wearing long hair, entitled *The Unloveliness of Lovelocks* (1628). In 1634, his *Histriomastix* launched an extended tirade against the theatre world, containing an attack on women who acted in plays (index entry: 'Woman actors, notorious whores').[33] This was taken as, and indeed probably was, another slingshot aimed at the queen, so Prynne won little sympathy as Star Chamber tossed him in prison and snipped off the top of his ears. It was said that Attorney General William Noy laughed so hard at the punishment that he bled from his penis.[34]

And yet, if the state wished to control what people thought and wrote, it faced a fairly thankless task. Puritan sermons were still published, and religious issues were still debated. Despite the increased regulation, there are just over 600 titles surviving per year of Charles's 'Personal Rule', actually slightly more than during the turbulent 1620s. And there were other options available than print, too. 'Manuscripts,' wrote one Puritan, 'are now the best help God's people have to vindicate the truth, printing being nowadays prohibited to them.'[35] Indeed, we should not exaggerate the picture of a fearful government, breaking into people's studies and mutilating its enemies. There were no political executions, and one lucky individual was even pardoned because, when he publicly slandered the government, he'd been drunk.

The social problems caused by population growth hadn't gone away, and fear of disorderly and wandering paupers remained feverish. The beggars who tramped the wide country tracks were, sniffed an Oxfordshire clergyman, the 'very scum of all the land', a 'dishonour to the king' and a 'confusion to the kingdom'.[36] Meanwhile, hardship in Ireland had brought immigrants over to Britain, where they received a cold welcome.[37]

Emigration might provide some relief. Having come near to collapse in the early 1620s, the new colony in Virginia was starting to take root as an economy of tobacco plantations. It tried to draw poor Englishmen and women, though soon it would depend on exploiting enslaved Africans, indeed some of the earliest victims of the English branch of this trade had already been brought to Virginia in 1619. Thousands of English migrants crossed the Atlantic in the 1630s, mostly in search of economic opportunities unavailable in the overpopulated old country. Some went to the Caribbean, while an increasing number gravitated to New England. Here, settlement brought conflict with the indigenous American populations. In 1637 the English launched a series of brutal attacks on the Pequots, culminating in a massacre near the Mystic River, after which the remaining Pequots were rounded up, the men murdered, and the women and children enslaved.

But however much land was taken from Native Americans, and however many plantations were created in the Caribbean to draw in migrants from England, the home country remained under severe population pressure. An active social policy, so those in power thought, was ever more essential.

Here the government's chief weapon was to issue a series of 'Books of Orders' in 1630 and 1631.[38] These tackled plague and food shortages, and directed local magistrates to enforce formal poor relief, put youngsters into apprenticeships, round up 'rogues' and suppress unnecessary alehouses, reporting back on their efforts to the Council.

Broadly speaking, magistrates in the counties were supportive of a programme that tackled poverty and addressed what they considered fairly obvious social problems. In the 37 counties that returned reports, at least 26,000 vagrants were reported as being arrested. In Essex, over a thousand young people were put into apprenticeships over the decade. In fact, counties were becoming more active in their own government anyway, regardless of orders from Whitehall.* But central direction made some impression at least: in Lancashire in 1632, when one old man, Hugh Winstanley of Wigan, asked for poor relief, his appeal was supported by a handwritten note from a local gentleman. It noted that 'his Majesty hath lately called upon us to be careful in the relief of the poor'.[39]

But there were limits to the success of central intervention. Many magistrates simply gave soothing but noncommittal reports to the Council. *Omnia bene*, they said. All is well. What such reports conceal is anybody's guess. Alehouses, for one thing, always had an unhappy

---

*In Cheshire, for example, the number of orders by the county Quarter Sessions had risen from just over 40 a year in the 1610s to 75 by the 1630s.

tendency to spring up again whenever they were closed down. Nor did everyone welcome the drive to apprentice children. In the Chippenham and Calne areas of Wiltshire, centres of the struggling cloth industry, magistrates complained that the best employers were unwilling to take apprentices because the youths were 'untrusty & thievish and therefore dangerous for them to keep', while the 'foolish poor parents' proved unwilling to part with their children. The exasperated magistrates were finding the whole thing 'a very troublesome & difficult business'.[40]

Another of Charles's great projects was to bring the English state to financial solvency. After decades of rotting finances and now several years of expensive war, the debt stood at a daunting £2 million, and prospects were not helped by the fact that between 1625 and 1630 Charles had sold £640,000 worth of Crown lands. Even his happy family life came with a cost. His marriage was fruitful, and thus expensive: five children in ten years, each needing their own establishments. The costs were worth it given that two of the children were much-wished-for sons, with the heir Prince Charles (1630) followed by James (1633), who became Duke of York. But this didn't make it any easier on the purse.

There was certainly a belief that the people could afford to contribute more. All that wealth accruing to the gentry and middling sort was still not going to the monarchy. '[T]here is blood enough in the king's subjects,' thought Secretary of State Francis Windebank, 'if the right vein be opened.'[41] Sometime in 1627, the keeper of the Tower's records, Sir John Borough, had been sent to dig around in the archives and find old ways that the Crown drew. He filed his report the next January and it listed everything from the exploitation of the forests to maximising profits from the king's fish. Even fines on Jews were included as a medieval precedent, although officially the country had none.[42] Not everything Borough found was tried, but much was. There were, for example, fines for those whose lands were on the old medieval forests. This was combined with a dubiously large view of what lands constituted 'forest' and proved very controversial for little gain: the Crown, it was said, had 'abused its dignity for a mess of pottage'.[43] There were even fines for the roughly 9,000 landowners who had lands worth £40 a year but had not, as they were supposed to, yet presented themselves to the king to be knighted. It was hardly a policy likely to win friends among the gentry.

Monopolies were back, too. The statute of 1624 had banned the granting of monopolies to individuals, so instead the government sold them to corporations. There were many, relating to commodities ranging from spectacles to beaver hats, but the most notorious was a monopoly for the production of soap. This was granted in 1632, to a group of investors strongly tainted with Catholicism. Their soap was terrible: it neither washed 'so white nor so sweet' as the older soap it replaced, nor lasted as long.[44] Worse, it burned people's hands. Unbowed, the government went to the lengths of staging a public contest, in which two laundresses faced off tubs of the old soap against the new, finding that the results weren't too different and, in any case, the new one lathered much better. The government also used Star Chamber to prosecute manufacturers of illicit soap. Eventually, in 1637, the old manufacturers managed to buy their way back into the market, but not before five years of complaints against the monopolists and their 'Papist soap'.

Meanwhile, other money-raising schemes were being suggested. A tax on lawyers, perhaps? (probably popular). Or a death duty? (probably not). Or even a tax on beer? (least popular of all). One idea was for an income tax of 2 per cent on anyone earning more than £125 a year. Another was to follow the French practice and to sell government offices. Ultimately, though, for all the political costs, Charles's government was able to stay just about within the confines of precedent, and gradually the state finances were improving. In 1636, the crown jewels – which had been pawned in the Netherlands – were redeemed. In particular, the Crown drew benefit from the major increase in international trade brought by peace at home in a time of war abroad. Those 'new impositions', the taxes on imports brought in by Salisbury in 1608, were pulling in around £54,000 a year by the mid-1630s, and this had topped £140,000 by 1640. It was estimated in July 1635 that, per year, the customs brought in £358,000, more than half of the total revenue of the exchequer. And receipts continued to rise. The English state was becoming one that depended more on the health of its international trade, and less on direct taxes voted for by Parliament.

This meant, therefore, that investment in the royal navy was an urgent priority. Under Buckingham, for all his faults, England's navy had more than doubled in size from 26 to 53 vessels, and he had ensured repairs at the key dockyards at Deptford, Portsmouth and Chatham. But in the hazardous waters of the 1630s this was not enough. 'Christendom is full of war, and there is nothing but rumours of war,' said Lord Keeper Coventry in 1635, correctly. The best defence, he argued, was the navy, for 'wooden walls are the best walls of this kingdom'.[45] Yet England's shores were weak, beset by pirates and raiders. In 1633, Sir John Borough was once again sent scurrying away to the historical records to find precedents for English sovereignty of the narrow seas, and in 1635 John Selden's *Mare Clausum* (having been written during the previous reign) was published, pushing the idea that the English Channel was entirely the dominion of the king of England.

Building a navy to make good such claims, of course, required yet more cash, so the government turned to a device called 'Ship Money'. Technically this was not a tax but a levy of service (in this case the service was the provision of ships), and legally it could be taken when the king deemed there to be an emergency. But it had always been limited to the coastal towns and counties. Thus it was at first, but when a second round of writs went out, people were concerned to discover that they applied to the whole country. There was confusion and some opposition, for Ship Money depended on the idea that when necessity demanded it, the king could bend the law. The diarist D'Ewes claimed that by the extension 'the liberty of the subjects of England received the most deadly and fatal blow it had been sensible of in five hundred years last past', though he was admittedly once again being dramatic.[46] Government supporters took a different view. As one of Charles's judiciary put it, there was 'a rule of law and a rule of government, and many things which might not be done by the rule of law might be done by the rule of government'.[47] It was a classically absolutist argument.

On the surface at least, Ship Money can look like a considerable success. Between 1634 and 1638 over 90 per cent of the assessed value came in. Communities dug deep to fit out the king's fleets. Some even said it was the fairest tax the realm had seen, though others like William Prynne complained of how much it burdened the 'middle and poor sort of people'.[48] And in reality the high level of eventual compliance conceals considerable sluggishness and local resistance: the records of the government, for example, show numerous instances of people refusing to pay and fighting constables when they came to impound goods in lieu. Eventually the majority paid, but such was the resistance that many did so very late.

Nonetheless, in the end Ship Money did raise enough money to overhaul the king's navy. The first fleet built with the levy saw 42 vessels unfurl their great sails and clear the docks. Nineteen of them were over 500 tons. By 1640, the levy had brought in nearly £800,000 – more than thrice the amount of the Forced Loan – and Charles's navy carried nearly 1,200 heavy guns. The Ship Money fleet was a forceful statement of England's international prestige. 'Nothing,' wrote Sir Kenelm Digby during the negotiations with France in 1637, 'could have buoyed the reputation of England so much as this has done.'[49] It was a nice nautical metaphor.

Naturally, though, the most significant of Charles's campaigns to bring order to his English realm was in the field of religion. Charles was personally devout, but religion was also intertwined with his wider project for social order. Charles wanted 'peace and quiet' in his Church just as he did in society as a whole. He wanted a ministry that was 'peaceable, orderly, and conformable', and subjects who would 'demean themselves with all Christian reverence and devout obedience'.[50] He didn't want debate. Predestination, in particular, shouldn't be 'meddled withal', since it was 'too high for the people's understanding'.[51] His own preference was for a rich liturgy, with strong emphasis on the 'beauty of holiness' so beloved of the ceremonialists. Critically, these were not to be days of latitude. Direction from the top, from the king, the Archbishop of Canterbury and the rest of the episcopacy, were to be followed. The Book of Common Prayer and the canons of 1604 were to be enforced in full. Parishioners would stand for the Creed and the *Gloria Patri*, kneel at the sacrament and bow at the name of Jesus. Those who, like Londoner and aspiring poet

John Milton, preferred a 'homely and yeomanly religion' without a 'deluge of ceremonies', were deeply worried.[52]

Charles promoted ceremonialists and Arminians. By the middle of the 1630s, Charles had created what was effectively an anti-Calvinist church establishment, particularly among his bishops, and not least when Richard Neile became Archbishop of York in 1631 and William Laud, finally, was appointed Archbishop of Canterbury in 1633 on the death of Abbot. The losers were men like John Williams, the Calvinist Bishop of Lincoln and sometime Lord Keeper. He fell out with Laud, was pursued in the courts and found himself fined by Star Chamber and imprisoned in the Tower.

The Church itself was suffering under long-standing economic problems, partly caused by inflation. Most visible were its crumbling buildings: indeed, much of Charles's campaign for the beauty of holiness was really about stamping out the ugliness of neglect. The great London cathedral of St Paul's was a case in point. Its spire had fallen down after a fire in 1561, and it was so overgrown with stalls and hawkers that it resembled a marketplace as much as a house of God. So unlike a church was it that one old Warwickshire farmer who was visiting London accidentally ('in a beastly manner') defiled St Paul's 'with his excrements'. He claimed that he did this 'merely through ignorance & necessity being not able to go any further through his weakness & age', and he found his explanation was accepted and was let off with a fine.[53]

Charles and Laud's aim was to bring back order and dignity to the Church. It was a programme that had real rationale, though some ministers took it to extremes, such as an Essex vicar who refused communion to menstruating women or those who had had sex the previous night, all in the name of decorum.[54] The most prominent policy related to the condition and positioning of church communion tables, a critical element to Christian worship. According to the existing rules, they could be kept in the centre of the church, physically accessible to the parishioners, but where they might fall to all kinds of profane uses. Some tables were used as storage, or as a desk, or even as somewhere to put squirming babies. To Laudians, the obvious solution was to rail them off. This would help encourage people to treat the tables with more respect, but it would also symbolically set them apart from the congregation. Indeed, Charles and Laud wanted to go even further. They also pushed for tables to be moved permanently to the east end of the church – placed 'altarwise', i.e. like a Catholic altar, and at much greater physical distance from the congregation. It was a fundamental point of disagreement with Calvinists, and especially with Puritans. To Laud, the altar was the 'greatest place of God's residence upon earth', much more so than the pulpit: 'yea, greater than the pulpit, for there 'tis *Hoc est corpus meum*, "This is my body", but in the pulpit 'tis at most but *Hoc est verbum meum*, "This is my word".' Laudianism *versus* Puritanism was, to an extent, altars *versus* pulpit, ceremony *versus* sermons.[55]

From 1633, placing tables altarwise became national policy, while a debate raged about it in the press, despite the shadow of censorship. Some bishops went even further and ordered that congregants must come up to the rail and kneel to receive communion. In Essex, one minister denied communion to 'at least a hundred' parishioners who refused to come to the rail. To some, these changes were veering way too close to Catholicism. Opponents referred to rails as 'pillars of popery'.[56] The minister of Ware, Hertfordshire, wrote in 1637 that the Church 'will have priests not ministers, altars not communion tables, sacrifices not sacraments; ... will bow and cringe to and before their altars'. '[W]hat,' he asked, 'is this but the mass itself?' So disgusted was he that the same year he migrated to New England.[57]

It didn't help either that all this coincided with a high point for Catholicism abroad. The German war, now well into its second decade, was going badly for Europe's Protestants. And there was the very visible Catholicism of the queen. She maintained a chapel at Somerset House, designed by a reluctant Inigo Jones, with a hundred candles adorning the high altar to which very many of the capital's Catholics could be seen going for mass. As the decade progressed, there were rumours that Charles himself was leaning towards Rome, that he shared mass with the queen, and that Laud was aiming to be made a cardinal. The Pope even sent a stunning Bernini bust of Charles's head as a gift – for which the now famous triple portrait of him by Van Dyck was a model.

Both Laud and Charles were keen to elevate the social position of the clergy, setting them apart from, and above, the laity. Laud in particular was a staunch defender of the bishops, without whom, he thought, all 'shall be democratical'.[58] Indeed, the new Archbishop of Canterbury was quite the authoritarian. 'Fear,' he once said, 'is the beginning of wisdom.'[59] Ministers would be appointed from above, without any need for acclamation by their congregations. The government tried to reduce the scope for laymen to appoint ministers, a right that many members of the gentry held and which allowed rich patrons to support Puritans. The policy made sense in terms of ensuring greater uniformity, but they offended many members of the same gentry the regime was simultaneously asking for money.

Another notorious controversy took place in Salisbury, where an eminent local Puritan, Henry Sherfield, had taken down and smashed some stained-glass windows in the parish church of St Edmund's. He had permission from the vestry – the body of laymen who governed the parish – but not from the bishop, so Sherfield was prosecuted in Star Chamber and subject to a swingeing £500 fine, partly on the instigation of Laud himself. In fact, Laud accepted the windows should have come down, for they portrayed God as a doddery old man. The problem was that Sherfield didn't use the proper channels, and publicly undermined the bishop, something Laud felt quite unacceptable for a layperson to do.

Laud also thought the elaborate rituals associated with ceremonialism were wonderfully good at getting people to show their obedience. Attempts to get parishioners to kneel and bow at the right times were about order, and they were also about subordination: these were 'gestures and behaviours of humility', a 'clear demonstration of our subjection'.[60] Nor was it just symbolism, for the prescribed ceremonies were orderly and controllable; crucially, they lacked the potential for discord inherent in the private revelation and public preaching so dear to the Puritans.

To some, this drive for uniformity was a rude awakening, but attitudes were undoubtedly complex. People disagreed with some aspects but wholeheartedly endorsed others. Some people simply didn't care, or they preferred communal harmony over dissension. Sometimes reluctance to 'beautify' churches was based on Puritan principles, sometimes it was simply unwillingness to pay. Plenty of people could accept the railing of communion tables on grounds of simple decorum. Not all of them necessarily also accepted that they should be placed 'altarwise' or that communion should be taken at the rail.

And there *was* opposition. Indeed, this was a serious problem, for the whole programme of reform was based on the idea of uniformity. As one ceremonialist put it to his Kentish congregation, 'Where *disorder* is, there's *confusion*, where confusion, there's *dissention*, where dissention, there's *tumult*.'[61] Nonconformity, said another, was like a 'gangrene'. So Laud made use of the notorious Court of High Commission, a prerogative court, to enforce control. Among its most notorious defendants was the man who printed the so-called 'Wicked Bible' in 1632, so named because it (mis?)printed the seventh commandment as 'Thou shalt commit adultery', and Deuteronomy 5:24 as 'the Lord hath shewed us his glory and his great ass'.[62] But the court could also be used to terrify Puritans. Men such as Nathaniel Barnard of Emmanuel College, Cambridge, who urged resistance to Charles's religious policy and was excommunicated, fined and locked up for his pains. For the Laudian establishment *hated* Puritans: they were 'black toads, spotted toads, venomous toads', said one minister, who also likened them to popular rebels Jack Straw and Wat Tyler.[63] Thomas Vahan of Chatham, Kent, meanwhile, informed those who refused to bow at the name of Jesus that he hoped their 'bowels might drop out'.[64] Puritans gave as good as they got, of course. One London minister harangued his congregation as 'knaves, villains, rascals, queans, she-devils, and pillory whores', while another suggested that those rebuilding St Paul's were merely 'making a seat for a priest's arse'.[65] But the crucial thing was that Charles and Laud had the coercive mechanisms of the state on their side.

As part of his anti-Puritan drive, in 1633 Charles made the decision to reissue his father's Book of Sports. The aim was to link royal policy, and the Laudian church, to older notions of good neighbourhood and the traditional social hierarchy, explicitly allowing pastimes after divine service as well as festivities such as May Games and rushbearings.

Charles's rule was seeing something of a revival of the old festival culture of 'Merry England', and it was taking a more clearly Laudian, even Catholic, hue. The Cotswold Olympics were in their heyday, sponsored by the Catholic Robert Dover and the Catholic-sympathiser and courtier Endymion Porter, celebrated in poetry by the reliably anti-Puritan Ben Jonson. As part of this revival, it seems that the old northern tradition of rushbearing – the centre of the Cartmel wedding, of course – became even more elaborate than before. One rushbearing, recorded in Hornby, Lancashire, in 1633, involved 'Morris dances & great fooleries', a Lord of Misrule, and 'Clowns, Picklers like Giants' and 'Ugly shapes'. The processors marched like warriors with staves and pikes, 'shooting with guns and muskets', but they had also put 'Crosses & Crucifixes upon their rushes'.[66] It was a distinctly provocative move against Puritans.

By reissuing the Book of Sports, Charles was explicitly helping to encourage this revival and set himself up as an anti-Puritan.[67] Like his father he was taking sides in a culture war, but he was doing so in a considerably more aggressive way, for this time the reading of the Book was to be enforced. Dubbed the 'Morris Book' by opponents, Charles's Book of Sports was thus hugely divisive. Despite Charles and Laud's promotion of ceremonialists, there remained plenty of moderate Calvinists among the lower clergy, and even some Puritans. Together they were appalled by the Book of Sports, and many clergymen refused outright to read it. One troublesome London Puritan even told his congregation, having read the Book followed by the Ten Commandments, 'Dearly beloved, you have heard now the Commandments of God and Man, obey which you please.'[68] The king, many thought, was going directly against the law of God, which ordered the sabbath to be kept holy. Local conflicts flared up, with parishioners taking directly opposing views. In Buckinghamshire, one minister was suspended for refusing to read the Book and for asking the constables to prevent people dancing after evensong, while another church official found himself 'cursed to the pit of hell by the women of Buckinghamshire' for supporting it.[69]

Such local broils were not themselves likely to bring down Charles's government any time soon, though almost 30 years later one minister would even claim that it was the Book of Sports that 'was the cause of all the war and blood shed in this nation'. Yet the controversy was a timely reminder of something important, and dangerous. In what remained a deep cultural conflict, Charles's monarchy was actively taking a side.

6

Black Ribbons

By 1637 the outcry over the Book of Sports had calmed. In fact, that year had started with a victory for Charles. In February he had written to his 12 judges of the Common Law to shore up the legal case behind Ship Money. He asked two questions, clearly expecting a positive answer. The first question was whether, when the 'good and safety of the kingdom' required it, could he demand ships from his people. The second was whether it was he, as king, who was to decide what constituted a threat to that 'good and safety'. Two of the judges were uncertain, but eventually all 12 fell behind the king and gave him the answer he wanted.

But then, in spring, the government committed a needless and damaging blunder. It was decided to make an example of three of the most clamorous Puritan writers. One was William Prynne, whose confinement in the Tower had done nothing to stall his literary career. The other two were the physician John Bastwick and Henry Burton, former clerk of the closet to Princes Henry and Charles, now a radical and thoroughly disgruntled Puritan. In early 1637, they were tried before Star Chamber for seditious libel and sentenced to pillorying, whipping and having their ears – in Prynne's case the remaining parts of his ears – cut off. The three were then to be detained in far-flung corners of the realm: Jersey (Prynne), the Isles of Scilly (Bastwick) and Lancaster (Burton). The punishments were harsh, and their infliction on members of the social elite particularly offensive. More to the point, the men behaved like martyrs. Three times, shocked crowds watched as the blood poured down from the pillory, and the victims were cheered and garlanded as they progressed to their places of imprisonment. Far from instilling fear and respect, the government had managed to make themselves look like vicious tyrants.

What brought the king's peace to a juddering halt, though, was not the prosecution of Prynne, Burton and Bastwick, but events in Scotland.

Charles was born a Scot, but he'd left as a toddler and was seen there as thoroughly Anglicised. He didn't help his reputation much in 1625 when he pushed a radical plan, known as the 'Revocation', to reclaim all lands granted by the Scottish crown since 1540, plus any properties owned by the pre-Reformation Kirk. It was a serious threat to the Scottish nobility, who had been the main beneficiaries of the land transfers, although the following year it was announced that they'd at least be adequately compensated. Charles had then waited nearly eight years before coming to Scotland to be crowned as their king, and when he did so – in 1633 – it had been a disaster.

The Scottish Kirk maintained a much stronger Presbyterian tradition than the Church of England. In 1618, James had pushed back against this, bolstering the power of the Scottish bishops and trying to enforce such traditional practices as kneeling at communion and the celebration of Christmas and Easter. Charles wanted to go further. He wanted to draw Scotland closer to conformity with England and its now increasingly ceremonialist Church. It was a project that quickly provoked serious disquiet.

During his visit, in which he was accompanied to Edinburgh by Bishop Laud, Charles also held a meeting of the Scottish Parliament. From this, he wanted higher taxes and the ratification of both the Revocation of 1625 and his father's reforms of the Kirk. There was considerable opposition, despite Charles attending personally, intervening with a 'great deal of spleen' and threatening to write the names of his opponents down on a list.[1] Afterwards, a petition circulated claiming that James's reforms had brought little but trouble, and noting a general fear of innovation that might harm the Kirk. Charles refused even to hear it, and when a manuscript copy ended up in the hands of the Archbishop of St Andrews, one of the promoters, Lord Balmeniro, was put on trial for treason and convicted (though later pardoned). Before leaving for England,

Charles made the archbishop chancellor of Scotland, and put five more bishops on the Scottish Privy Council. And, he bolstered the Scottish bishops further by creating a new cathedral out of the grand Edinburgh kirk of St Giles.

Soon afterwards he had a Scottish version of the English Book of Common Prayer published. The Scottish bishops, as supportive as they were, informed Charles that it couldn't simply be forced on the Kirk, so the government changed tack. Now Scotland would get its own prayer book and new canons. Two years later, these were nearly ready, with Charles himself having kept a close eye on the writing process. The canons were finished in January 1636; they banned extempore prayer – which to Laudians was disorderly but to Calvinists was a practice of fundamental importance – and they ordered communion tables to be placed altarwise. One Scottish bishop, punning horrifically, warned that the new canons would 'make more noise than all the cannons in Edinburgh castle'.[2]

The new Scottish Prayer Book was ready soon after, still based heavily on the English, and both it and the new canons were to be imposed by royal order. Time was needed for printing and dissemination, though, so Easter 1637 was set for the date at which the new rules would kick in. But implementation was delayed thanks to problems at the printers. Come 16 July, Charles was losing patience, so the Bishop of Edinburgh was ordered to use the new service in and around the capital the following Sunday: 23 July.

Come the day, everything was in place. The Scottish Privy Council processed through Edinburgh, to St Giles, where the dean rose to conduct the service while the congregation murmured. Within minutes, a riot began, led by Edinburgh's women. Chair stools and insults were thrown: 'Woe! Woe!' some shouted. 'Sorrow, sorrow for this doleful day.' According to one minister, when a congregant was seen nodding approval to the dean's words, a 'she-Zealot' started shouting at him: 'traitor, says she, does thou say Mass at my ear, and with that struck him in the face with her Bible in great agitation and fury'.[3] Terrified, the bishop fled the city: rumours had it that he literally shat himself on the way.

Frozen by panic, it took three days for the Council to write to the king to tell him what had happened. Everyone wanted to blame someone else. All the while, the disorder spread. On 29 July, the Council backed down and suspended the new services. Charles was livid, and he ordered the bishops to return to their pulpits. But resistance continued through the summer and beyond. By late September, Scotland had produced 68 petitions against the new Prayer Book. On 19 September, a committee of nobles consolidated the local petitions into a national one, but the king was unmoved. He meant to be obeyed.

Through autumn and beyond there were hundreds of petitions, and opposition meetings gathered up and down Scotland. Then, into the winter, the influential men of Scotland began organising themselves into more formal political bodies, to represent their nation. Clearly something very serious was taking place.

In February 1638, Charles issued a proclamation. The Prayer Book was his own responsibility, he stood by it and it was here to stay. Those who had gathered to present petitions must return home, else be considered traitors. That same month, another royal proclamation, this time in England, told subjects of the 'odious' example set by the rebellious Scots. The matter was not really about some prayer book, nor even about the role of bishops, 'but whether we are their king or not'.[4] If a king's direct order could be so roundly disobeyed, Charles thought, what kind of a king was he?

But still Scottish opposition refused to back down. Now organised as the 'Tables', they summoned their supporters to Edinburgh for 'the most important business that ever concerned this nation'. On 23 February with the Tables setting themselves up as a rebel administration, they composed 'a band [i.e. a bond] of mutual association for offence and defence'.[5] Five days later, this became the Scottish National Covenant, first signed by the leading opponents in Greyfriars kirk in Edinburgh. Then, in the coming weeks, copies were sent around Scotland, where it received wide popular support throughout most of the country. One minister described the Covenant as 'a mutual combination for resistance'. 'There is nothing expected here,' he said, 'but civil war.'[6]

Meanwhile, in England, Charles's Ship Money project was entering a critical juncture. The harvest had been poor and the levy was biting hard at a time of high food prices. '[I]f it be so, that the king must have all,' declared a Cotswolds man, very dangerously, 'I would the king were dead.'[7] By now, opposition had focused on the refusal to pay by John Hampden, for his lands in Stoke Mandeville, beneath the Buckinghamshire Chilterns. Hampden's hearing at Westminster Hall dragged on into the next year, drawing a great throng of people. His lawyer, the fiercely astute Oliver St John, argued that, given England was at peace, the levy could only continue if a Parliament were called. The counter-argument, though, was that while there was no war, the situation at sea was still very dangerous. More controversially, the king's side claimed that there was no legal basis to the idea that he couldn't take taxes without Parliamentary consent. In effect this meant that one of the key maxims of the Common Law itself was on trial: that the Englishman couldn't be divested of his property without his consent.

In June the king won. The rulings were complicated and technical, but ultimately the judges came down seven to five in favour of the king. It was a major victory for Charles, finally putting to bed an issue that had plagued the levy. But it did come at a cost. If Ship Money was legal without agreement from Parliament, the king's rule was more absolute than people thought. More absolute than they were necessarily comfortable with. In fact, the Crown's victory in *R vs Hampden* actually led to more determined, indeed occasionally violent, resistance to Ship Money.[8] Sometimes collectors were physically attacked. Sometimes, when they came to impound the goods of those who didn't pay, the goods were simply taken back again by their owners.

Now, though, the government could at least turn its full attention to Scotland, where the prospects of a peaceful solution were fading fast. Charles had sent his trusted servant and friend the Marquess of Hamilton to take control. Hamilton, who was at least Scottish (though he'd left as a young adult to join the royal court), found things much worse than Charles imagined. He urged engagement with the supporters of the Covenant, or the 'Covenanters' as they came to be known, but Charles refused. 'So long as the Covenant is in force,' Charles spat, 'I have no more power in Scotland than as a Duke of Venice; which I will rather die than suffer.'[9] 'My heart is broke,' wrote

Hamilton in July, 'since I can see no possibility to save our master's honour ... or the country from ruin.'[10]

By this point, Charles had decided to use force. The Scottish Covenanters, meanwhile, were buying arms from abroad. In August, Hamilton was instructed to offer enough concessions to keep the Covenanters distracted while Charles prepared an invasion. Charles then agreed to a revocation of the new Scottish Prayer Book, the new canons, and even James's 1618 reforms, and to summon both an Assembly of the Kirk and a Scottish Parliament. But he did so in bad faith, stalling for time.

The Assembly met first, in Glasgow in November, in a cathedral packed with onlookers. Hamilton was unable to wrest control from the Covenanters, so he tried to dissolve it. The Assembly ignored him and kept sitting and, on 8 December, it raised the stakes dramatically by formally abolishing the Scottish episcopacy. Charles's attempt to enforce his church reforms on Scotland had led to a popular uprising that jolted the Kirk in exactly the opposite direction, towards Presbyterianism. Now, if he wanted to reimpose bishops on Scotland, let alone the new Prayer Book, he would have to tread the path of war.

Charles's strategy was for a three-pronged assault on his northern kingdom. Irish troops would land from the west, Hamilton would take eight warships and 5,000 men, blockade Scottish trade and land in the east, while Charles himself would lead the main English force of 30,000 troops from the south. To this end, he summoned his nobility to appear at York on 1 April 1639 with as many men as they could muster.

But the Covenanters had already struck the first blow. In March, the main royal strongholds in Scotland, including Edinburgh Castle, had been taken without so much as a shot being fired. Even the Scottish crown and sceptre had been surrendered to the rebels. Meanwhile, Hamilton's harrying of the coast was also going dreadfully. Charles had sent him to the Firth of Forth where he found stout opposition onshore, including from his own mother who – brandishing a pistol – announced that she'd shoot him herself if he ever dared land.

The Scots benefited from sympathisers in England, too. In February, pro-Scottish books had been scattered in the streets of Newcastle, and a similar incident seems to have occurred at Carlisle. Some Londoners were maintaining suspicious correspondence with Edinburgh, and the Scots 'blue bonnets' were seen by many in England not as rebels but as justly aggrieved subjects, resisting a papist plot emanating from the court. The king's cause was not helped by the fact that the queen was urging London's Catholics to give generously to support the war effort, nor by the very visible presence of his Catholic mother-in-law, Marie de Medici, who publicly hoped for Charles's conversion to Rome. Once more the conflict took on an apocalyptic significance. As the Puritan gentlewoman Brilliana Harley wrote from Herefordshire to her eldest son, 'this year 1639 is the year in which many are of the opinion that the antichrist must begin to fall. The Lord say amen to it.'[11]

In May there was trouble at York. Charles had ordered the nobility and gentry to gather there and to take an oath of allegiance. The Puritan Lord Saye and his ally Lord Brooke both refused, claiming that the government's forcing an oath without Parliamentary sanction was unconstitutional. They were briefly detained.

There were rumours that the gathering Covenanter army was large and well organised. Their ranks were swelled with battle-hardened men recalled from the Continent, stirred to the cause by effective preachers. The English army, meanwhile, was made up of unhappy conscripts and untrained substitutes; their ministers were either clandestine Catholics or tobacco-puffing nonentities. The Covenanters' commander was Alexander Leslie, who had served under the Swedish warrior-king Gustavus Adolphus. The English, by contrast, were led by the fifty-four-year-old Earl of Arundel, who, though he possessed an important chivalric title as Earl Marshall, had no actual military experience.

The English soldiers were poorly paid, too. The City of London had wisely refused to send their good cash after a bad cause, and Ship Money collection was stalling, not least because people were being told to pay an additional, equally resented, levy known as 'Coat and Conduct Money'. Charles had managed to bring a force of 18,000 men to the border – no mean feat. Loyal courtiers helped: Sir John Suckling, a flame-haired, drink-swilling poet famed for his wit and his skill at both cards and bowls, had managed to put together a gallant force of a hundred young gentlemen, flamboyantly dressed in white doublets, scarlet breeches and coats, with hats, feathers, and strong horses and plenty of weapons. But in the main Charles's men were tired, demoralised and reluctant to fight: 'as like,' wrote one gentleman, 'to kill their fellows as the enemy'.[12] Perhaps a joker at Christchurch, Hampshire, said it best, when he announced that the king had taken men 'more fit to use such weapons as these', grabbing his crotch.

In early June, having sighted a well-drilled Scottish force readying its artillery at Kelso, the English commanders wavered. On the 18th, the king thought it prudent to agree to a truce, at the Border town of Berwick. What has come rather grandly to be known as the 'First Bishops' War', had thus ended with hardly a shot fired. The Scots agreed to disband and return the king's castles, the king to call another Assembly of the Kirk, and a meeting of the Scottish Parliament. The treaty said nothing about the reinstatement of the Scottish bishops, nor did it commit Charles to accepting the decisions of the Assembly or Parliament. Peace seemed unlikely to last.

The new Assembly met in Edinburgh in August, and it confirmed the resolutions of Glasgow, including that against bishops. The Scottish Parliament met soon after. It, too, proved recalcitrant, and when the king's representative tried to dissolve it, the Parliament formally refused, instead appointing a committee – effectively a continuation of the Tables – to sit until the next meeting and look after Scottish affairs in the meantime. It was a radical experiment: an executive government appointed by a legislature.

Charles was back in London. He even blundered by arriving in Marie de Medici's coach, again making it seem he might be in the thrall to a Catholic plot. By this point, a second Scottish war was already inevitable. The plan, eventually, would be similar to that of the first; but before that the king needed money. One option was a treaty with Spain, which might bring cash, but risked only confirming fears of a Catholic conspiracy even further. The project, though, took a body blow when a Spanish fleet taking shelter in the Downs off the Kent coast was mauled by the Dutch, while the English fleet watched on impotently, and a crowd of spectators gathered to gloat. Not surprisingly, the Spanish were unimpressed.

Another plan was to look across the Straits of Moyle. Irish society was beset with tensions, and Charles himself retained the colonialist mindset of the English of his day, particularly towards the Gaelic majority: 'It appears that oftentimes force and terror do more to restrain such people than law or religion,' he once said of them.[13] For the English government, the Scottish rebellion meant Ireland was both a threat and an opportunity. The threat came from the Protestants, especially those of Scottish origin, who had moved over to Ulster since the beginning of the century. To keep them quiet, the government ordered Scots in Ireland (and in London) to swear a widely despised oath of loyalty, known as the 'Black Oath'. But Ireland also offered an opportunity. Early in 1640, the Lord Deputy Thomas Wentworth called a Parliament to Dublin, which voted enough money – together with support from the Irish clergy – to raise 9,000 men, the basis of a potentially powerful force. In April, with this success behind him, Wentworth, now raised to the earldom of Strafford, set sail for England.

By this time the mood in London had changed drastically. Charles had bowed to the inevitable. In February, the writs had gone out for a new English Parliament, after an 11-year gap, to meet on 13 April. It was a decision that 'begot much joy amongst all country people'.[14]

The elections took place in the spring. Somewhat less than a quarter were contested – though this was an unusually high proportion. There was, it was written, 'much bandying for places'. By March, there were rumours that the elections had gone badly for the government. 'Such as have dependence upon the court,' wrote Northumberland, 'are in divers places refused.'[15]

If Charles wanted a pliant assembly, then he seemed likely to be disappointed.

Charles's opening speech to the new Parliament was just a few lines, almost insultingly short, and it was left to the new Lord Keeper, John Finch (the ill-fated Speaker of the last meeting), to outline the king's aims. Charles wanted Parliament to offer supply first (the war was expected to cost £1 million), then he would discuss grievances. But the opposition MPs wouldn't budge. On the 16th, the fiery Harbottle Grimston gave a speech that argued that while the Scottish issue was important, there was 'a case here at home of as great a danger'. It is impossible, he said 'to cure an ulcerous body unless you first cleanse the veins'.[16] The ulcerous body whose veins needed cleansing was England.

The next day, John Pym stood up to give a two-hour speech to the MPs crammed into St Stephen's Chapel. A Puritan of fierce intelligence, Pym had been a thorn in Whitehall's side since the 1620s. Raised in a world of Elizabethan Protestant heroes like his fellow Westcountrymen Francis Drake and Walter Raleigh, Pym carried with him a pathological fear of popish plots. Notably mirthless, he had nonetheless scored the biggest laugh of the 1628 Parliament by ending his speech on a bill against adultery with the procedural motion 'that we commit it'.[17] The humour, no doubt, was unintended.

He now spoke – as he preferred – from a prepared script, which would be circulated in handwritten copies to avoid the censors. There was a plot, Pym said, 'to reduce our land to the Pope'.[18] The government was a threat to property and to true religion. Only Parliament, he said, was 'able to apprehend and understand the symptoms of all such diseases which threaten the body politic'. Parliament, he argued, was 'the soul of the commonwealth', and should be sitting every year. There followed seven constituency petitions, from contiguous areas, all of which mirrored Pym's arguments. To conservative observers it all seemed dangerously similar to the populist tactics of the Scottish Covenanters. Oliver St John, common lawyer and master rhetorician, argued with sincere conviction that Parliament couldn't be dissolved without its consent. Meanwhile, the judicial records relating to Ship Money were sent for: Parliament was reopening the case.

The king's programme was listing badly, so the next day Charles summoned Lords and Commons to the Banqueting House and sat, glowering in silence, while Lord Keeper Finch urged them to come into line and vote funds. Charles also instructed the Lords to push for supply, telling them their brothers in the Lower House had 'put the cart before the horse' by trying to redress grievances first.[19] The Commons were incensed, and on the 29th went back to discussing grievances.

It was all too much, and on 5 May the king dissolved this unhappy, 'Short Parliament'. He made it clear that he didn't blame his Lords, nor even the whole House of Commons, but only 'some cunning and ill-affectionate men'.[20] The return of Parliament had been sadly brief.

That same evening, a critical meeting of the eight-man Committee for Scottish Affairs took place at Whitehall. Notes were taken by Sir Henry Vane, a pragmatic former diplomat newly made secretary of state.[21] The debate was whether to negotiate with the Scots or to go on the offensive, and the decisive intervention came from Wentworth, now Earl of Strafford. His chilling contribution survives to us only in Vane's notes, but there is no mistaking the intensity of his speech.

> Go vigorously or let them alone, no defensive war … Go on with a vigorous war, as you first designed; loose and absolved from all rules of government, being reduced to extreme necessity, everything is to be done that power might admit … They refusing, you are acquitted towards God and man, you have an army in Ireland, you may employ here to reduce this kingdom. Confident as anything under heaven Scotland shall not hold out five months. One summer well employed will do it.

It was a deeply significant moment, not just for Charles's kingdoms, but also – as would be clear within the year – for Strafford himself.

Preparations for war continued. Strafford had finally negotiated a treaty with Spain by which England agreed to an alliance against the Dutch and to allow the Spanish to recruit 3,000 men in Ireland. All for £300,000. The earl tried to keep it quiet, but the secret got out. Meanwhile, the government worked to gather evidence on the opposition peers and MPs, spying on known Covenanter sympathisers, opening letters. The people were not to be trusted. '[T]hey have neither constancy nor gratitude,' lamented Viscount Conway, one of the commanders of the royal army, in May 1640.[22] Rumours spread that Strafford was planning to use his Irish troops against England. Leading opposition MPs and peers including Warwick, Saye, Pym and Hampden had their London houses, lodgings and even their pockets searched for evidence of collusion with the Scots, though nothing was found. The City once more refused money.

The discontent in London's busy streets was mounting rapidly. Placards, bills and libels were posted on gates, doors and in 'public remarkable places'.[23] Papers were scattered in streets and markets, graffiti appeared on walls. There would be a hunt for 'William the Fox' (Archbishop Laud), and the apprentices would gather to 'kill the bishops, who would fain kill us, our wives, and children'.[24] Laud, waiting in the South Bank palace of Lambeth, was terrified. At his behest, cannons were placed on the roof, easily seen from the other side of the river and from the surrounding fields. But it wasn't enough: on Sunday night (10 May), he threw on a cloak and crossed the river in a boat, to safety at Whitehall. He was just in time, for the following morning a crowd of Londoners marched on Lambeth to the beat of a drum. Learning their target had gone, they smashed up his garden. Arrests were made, but, three days later, the four prisons holding detainees were attacked. The crowd now had pseudonymous leaders: Captain Club and Captain Mend-all. Whitehall Palace was reinforced, as was St James's. Even in the country idyll of Richmond, several miles up the Thames, an extra guard was felt to be necessary for the royal children, who were staying in the palace there.

A tense calm returned by the end of the month, but the placards continued to appear and rumours were discussed on streets and in shops, and carried across town by scurrying water bearers. People started to hide their money.[25] Threats were aimed at Hamilton and Strafford. A libel was found in London alleging that Catholics were plotting to detonate gunpowder in the City.[26] There were also, to top it all, a few ominous cases of the plague.

Evidently spooked, the government's response was brutal. The drummer who'd led the march to Lambeth was tortured on the rack, the warrant made out in Charles's own hand. Another protester, Thomas Benstead, was convicted and hanged, drawn and quartered, his body parts set up on London Bridge. He was a teenager.

The dissolution of the Short Parliament, meanwhile, had left a critical constitutional anomaly. As was usual, the sitting of Parliament was accompanied by a meeting of Convocation, the governing body of the Church of England. Helpfully, indeed, it had agreed to give Charles money. But when Parliament was dissolved, Convocation was allowed to continue sitting, which was unusual. In fact, the meeting was tasked with updating the canons: not to overturn anything that was already there, but to set down new laws to aid the battle against both papists and Puritans. Seventeen new canons were introduced on 29 May, including provocative orders to affirm the divine right of kings and that all communion tables be placed altarwise and railed. The bishops ordered 17,500 copies to be printed and distributed around the country, so everyone knew about them.[27] Most controversial of all, canon six ordered that the clergy swear to the doctrine, discipline and government of the Church of England, and not attempt to alter 'the government of this church by archbishops, bishops, deans and archdeacons etc'. Puritans naturally balked at this, but even many moderates worried about what the 'etc' might come to mean. It seemed to open the door to strict enforcement of a hierarchical Laudian church, so the 'Etcetera Oath' was fiercely opposed. At least one author allowed their thinking to lead down a potentially radical path. If a king were controlled by an oppressive and anti-religious faction, it argued:

> ... is it not now high time for the whole state either to labour to heal the breach, or if necessary, when there is no other remedy, to stand up as one man to defend themselves and their country until the faction shall be utterly cashiered, and so the king reform himself and renew the covenant and conditions of the kingdom to the good and just satisfaction of the people?[28]

The author stayed (wisely) anonymous, and published in Amsterdam (also wise); but the tract found its way to London, where it was widely read. The idea that the people might rise to force the king's hand was out there.

In June, meanwhile, the Scottish Parliament met once more, against Charles's explicit order. In just ten days it passed 60 acts, including a 'Triennial Act', ordering that it sit at least once every three years. In London, the violence of May had passed, but in the country as a whole, discontent continued. The common people were sick, wrote one newswriter. They 'are struck in the head' so that they 'rave and utter' against the king and his government.[29]

A new royal army was being assembled, but it was once again beset with disorder and mutiny. In Lincolnshire, able-bodied men were reported to have hidden in the woods armed with pitchforks rather than join.[30] Viscount Conway wrote that his troops at Newcastle were more 'fit for Bedlam and Bridewell' – the lunatic asylum and the work-house – than for war.[31] After a minor mutiny, Conway had the leaders throw dice to decide which of them would be shot. Another mutiny, in Warminster, Wiltshire, saw a company dismiss their Catholic cap-tain when he refused to take communion with them.[32] The alehouses thronged with unruly and libidinous soldiers. When not busy drinking, many took action against recent grievances. Altar rails were smashed in at least five counties, enclosures were thrown down and prisons thrown open. By the autumn, at least four officers had been killed by their men. In August, a soldier in Ashford, Kent, was set upon and stuck in the pillory simply because he had the misfortune to bear the surname 'Bishop'. Had, perhaps, the Scottish crisis reawakened a popular animus against English bishops, last seen under Elizabeth?

In London, the few isolated cases of plague were now developing into a serious outbreak. Opposition to the government, meanwhile, was starting to crystallise, centring on the Earl of Warwick and a clique of aristocrats, gentlemen and lawyers who met regularly at his grand mansion on Holborn. The group included his cousin the Earl of Essex and his son-in-law, Edward Montague Viscount Mandeville.* One cover was their involvement in the Providence Island Company, a Puritan venture aimed at colonising a small tropical island in Central America, in which Warwick was the leading figure. Investors also included Lord Saye, Oliver St John and John Pym – the last two employed by the Company as (respectively) lawyer and treasurer. Another knot developed around the more moderate Earl of Bedford. He was a plutocrat whose property portfolio included the newly developed square at Covent Garden, designed with Inigo Jones, and a huge fen drainage project in Cambridgeshire (which still, as the Bedford Levels, bears his name). He had also employed Pym and St John, the latter as in-house lawyer for the drainage project.

---

*He was the nephew of Edward Montagu of Boughton.

Across town, alehouses and taverns hummed with political gossip and argument. Some ordinary folk were even taking it upon themselves to preach in the street. In the summer, a cobbler, Samuel How, was drawing a great crowd as he preached at the Nag's Head near the tightly packed overhanging timber houses of Coleman Street. A Kentish farmer, James Hunt, preached in St Paul's churchyard.[33] 'People,' wrote the courtier Sir Kenelm Digby, 'are strangely disaffected and untoward.'[34] And the weather was foul, too.

Still, Charles's government managed to put a large army into the field: no small achievement, even if one rather tempered by the fact that a third of the men didn't have weapons. The Scots, though, were themselves showing signs of division: some wanted an aggressive strategy against England, others thought this too risky. Some thought the great Covenanter leader Archibald Campbell, the Marquess of Argyll, had ambitions to depose Charles. In England, people still hoped that a treaty could be reached. Perhaps Charles might abandon the Scottish bishops and make a deal? But there were also fears the Scots might launch a pre-emptive strike. The Covenanter army was going hungry; would they march south simply to make sure their soldiers and horses were fed?

There is a letter – printed much later but quite possibly genuine – to the Scots, signed by seven English peers, including Warwick, Essex and Bedford. It offered support should they invade (though stopping short of offering actually to join the Scots army). Crucially, it seems from a second letter, the peers' plan was to present a public petition to the king. Specifically, Oliver St John had alerted the peers to a discovery he had made in the historical archives, namely that the Oxford Parliament of 1258 had decreed that 12 barons (i.e. peers) could summon a Parliament, even without the king. If the support of 12 peers could be gathered, maybe Charles's hand could be forced. Maybe a new Parliament could be summoned. A two-pronged strategy, with a Scottish army rolling over the border to the north, and a petition from 12 peers in the south calling for a new Parliament, seemed to give Charles's opponents, Scots and English alike, the best hope of success.

At the end of July, the royal governor of Berwick received intelligence from across the border. It showed that preparations for a Scottish attack were advancing rapidly.[35]

The invasion began on 17 August, as the vanguard of Scottish cavalry crossed the River Tweed. Three days later the rest of the army followed, their pikes trailing black ribbons and their trumpeters dressed solemnly in mourning clothes. As soon as news reached London, the king set off for York to rally his force. Strafford, too, rushed north, leaving the loyal but flappable Francis Cottington in charge of the Tower. By this point, the financial situation was utterly desperate. Ship Money was all but collapsing, and news was coming through of a major rebellion in Catalonia, destroying any hopes of relief by Spanish gold. The East India Company was asked for a loan, but they refused. Indeed, relations between the government and the spice barons became so fraught that Cottington even threatened to turn the Tower's guns on the Company's ships.

In the north, the king's army was split in two. One part was gathering at York; another was close by Newcastle. The Scots encountered the latter on 28 August, at Newburn Ford on the River Tyne. The day was won by the 40 Scottish cannon, supported by snipers, that cut down the ranks of the English soldiers. The brunt was mostly borne by Somerset men, fighting far from home. Their commander was a Sussex gentleman and 'swaggering ruffian', Thomas Lunsford.[36] By 1640 he'd already been convicted of attempted murder, escaped prison, fought for the French in Picardy, been fined £8,000 and outlawed by Star Chamber, and been pardoned. Joining the king's army, he'd shot two mutineers as he led his English company across the countryside to Newcastle. He fought with characteristic ferocity at Newburn, but it was not enough. More than 300 lay dead by the end of the day. With the English in retreat, and the Scots now south of the Tyne, Newcastle was abandoned. The Scots now controlled the major city north of York: the source of London's coal. And winter was coming.

London already was in near panic even before news of the Newburn Fight arrived. On 30 August, the kingless court withdrew from Whitehall to Hampton Court, with a plan to retreat further upcountry to Windsor if necessary, 'a place of more safety'.[37] There were hurried military preparations as the government feared an uprising or a coup. On the other side of London, on 1 September a dangerous sermon preached before the City's Honourable Artillery Company muster at Moorfield had set out a case for resistance to the king's government. The Company was a citizen militia for London, and something of a hotbed of Puritanism, led by the tough Norfolk-born soldier Philip Skippon. Another veteran of the European wars, Skippon had found someone in his home parish in east London to give the sermon. His name was Calybute Downing, the son of a Warwickshire gentleman and a graduate of the Puritan Emmanuel College, Cambridge. Addressing the amassed London citizens who made up the Company, Downing argued that the king bore ultimate responsibility for the state of the nation, indeed, 'when a party in power breaks the laws of the land', subjects must 'make a stand'.[38] Ultimately, the safety of the people was the supreme law: '*salus populi* should be *sola, & suprema lex*' – it had been a maxim to justify kings ruling beyond the laws when necessity required. Now it was being used to justify resistance to the monarchy. The same night, news of Newburn reached the capital, and Scots and their sympathisers celebrated brazenly with feasts, as the church bells rang to celebrate the king's defeat.[39]

On 3 September, the peers' petition was presented to the king at York, complete with the necessary 12 signatures, and to considerable shock in the royal camp.[40] Copies found their way to the streets of London. Using a medical metaphor, appropriate for an attempt to heal the body politic, the petition set out the 'great distempers' that now threatened Church and state. The only remedy was another Parliament. And this Parliament would try and punish the key royal advisers behind the country's malaise. These were unnamed, but the petitioners meant Strafford, and probably Laud. The English dissidents, meanwhile, were writing to the Scots assuring them that there were nine regiments of the English army that were ready to defect and form what would be called the 'Armies for the Commonwealth'.[41]

The king's response was to undercut the petitioners' claims to speak for the nobility by calling a Great Council of Peers to meet at York on the 24th. This was another old medieval body (although last summoned less than a century previously under Mary I), and it included the *whole* of the nobility. It was, in many ways, a smart move, though whether anyone – nobility or otherwise – would accept a Great Council in lieu of a Parliament remained uncertain to say the least.

In London, though, the situation was still getting worse. The Privy Council worried that any move against the earls of Warwick or Essex would set off a popular fury even worse than the Lambeth Riots in May.[42] Placards appeared in the City telling apprentices to rise 'for the reformation of Religion'. There were reports of a man hanging around Gray's Inn with a 'cloak bag full of books' of Scottish propaganda.[43] By 10 September, promoted by two leading citizens (and members of the Honourable Artillery Company), a second, more populist petition was circulating, calling for peace and a new Parliament. It was said to have gained 10,000 signatures, 'of every condition'.[44]

It reached Charles on the 22nd. The same day, he received the terrible news that his last redoubt in Scotland, Edinburgh Castle, had fallen once more to the Covenanters. By this time, more than 20 great aristocrats, signatories of the peers' petition, were converging outside York. Then, with all the pomp they could muster, they rode in procession – coach following coach – into the northern capital. It was a remarkable show of strength by the peerage, aimed at their own king. They would, they said, not 'recede from one tittle of the petition'.[45] According to government intelligence, no fewer than 37 peers now supported the Scots. As the appointed Council sat on the 24th in the Deanery at York, Charles addressed them. He had decided, he said, of his own choosing, to summon a Parliament.

Even the Great Council went badly for Charles. It ordered cessation of military action against the Scots, and the opening of treaty negotiations. Worse, the negotiations were entrusted to those peers friendly to the Scots, with 11 of the 16 appointed commissioners among the signatories to the peers' petition.

The negotiations took place in the tiny town of Ripon, just a few miles from York. The agreement reached was not in Charles's favour. It ordered that England would subsidise the Scots army that was now occupying Northumberland and County Durham to the tune of £850 a day. There was only one way that this was going to be paid for. Money would have to come from the new Parliament, the elections for which were now proceeding apace. It would be this Parliament that changed everything.

7

To Knock Foxes and Wolves on the Head

At the beginning of November 1640, London had come alive. More than 500 MPs had taken up lodgings in the City, in Westminster, and nearby. Boats skimmed along and across the river. Coaches clogged the narrow streets. Pulpits rang with sermons; tobacco-fumed taverns and alehouses hummed to news and political chatter. Politicians walked purposely through Hyde Park and St James's, or the bowling greens of Piccadilly, exchanging gossip and planning tactics. The doors and stables of the great houses of the Earl of Bedford on the Strand and the Earl of Warwick on Holborn welcomed allies and scurrying messengers. In the Guildhall, the governors of the City spoke earnestly about how to keep order. Upriver, politicians gathered in the rooms of Lord Mandeville's lodgings at Chelsea, plotting by candlelight with claret glasses in hand. At Whitehall, courtiers, officers of state and Privy Councillors conferred with the king and queen, not quite knowing where this latest burst of political energy would lead. In the country, local communities had prepared petitions to send up to Westminster, calling for reform and the peeling back of the Laudian innovations in the Church.

But amid the anticipation all was far from well. Trade was stalling. The cost of coal coming to London out of Scottish-occupied Newcastle was unusually high, just as the winter closed in. In the autumn, London had been convulsed by the worst disorders since May. A recent 'visitation' of the diocese of London* organised by the bishop, William Juxon, and led by his chancellor Dr Arthur Duck had been a disaster. Parishioners, apprentices, even 'amazons' jeered and jostled Duck and

---

*The diocese of London included not just the City, but also the largely rural counties of Middlesex and Essex, and part of Hertfordshire.

his officials all the way, chanting against the infamous 'Etcetera Oath'
from the recent canons. On one occasion, the unfortunate Duck was
chased across the Thames to the safety of Lambeth Palace by boats
full of people throwing stones, jeering and making quacking sounds.
In October, when the protesters were prosecuted at the Convocation
House at St Paul's,* a crowd assembled and chased Duck out through
a window, quacking and 'hooting as birds at an owl'. It was a sign
that, whatever transpired at Westminster and Whitehall, whatever the
future held, the London crowd would play their part.

people

Parliament convened on Tuesday the 3rd, not with the usual triumphant royal procession, but with a much smaller affair in which
Charles (who had only arrived at Whitehall from the north a few
days ago) approached by barge, ascended Westminster Stairs and
went through the motions of a small parade with some of his Lords
to the Abbey. It had, one observer later remembered, a 'sad and mel-
ancholic aspect'.[1] But many spoke of the new meeting of Parliament
with feelings of hope and expectation. The elections had gone well for
opponents of the court – the House of Commons that assembled that
November was a body of men ready to start the work of dismant-
ling the worst excesses of Charles's government. '[W]e dream now of
nothing more than of a golden age,' wrote one commentator.[2]

With the Speaker, William Lenthall, installed, the first day in earnest
was the Friday 6 November. In the Lords, the key players were the
earls of Bedford and Warwick, together with others, including Lord
Mandeville, Lord Saye and the radical Lord Brooke. These were the
core of the men who had signed the petition in the late summer. They
were widely suspected, at least by those close to Charles, of collusion
with the Scots. Critically, their actions the previous year, which at the
very least had skirted close to treasonous plotting against the king,
meant it was in their personal interest to place as many checks and
balances on royal power as possible. An unbridled monarch was a
personal threat to their safety. For this group, it was never just about
religion. The king needed to be constitutionally restrained.

---

*It was a meeting of the High Commission.

In the Commons, opposition was led by the now veteran Parliamentarian John Pym. He had become a thoroughly skilful operator in the House, though he managed to get laughed at when his bigotries got the better of him and he supported a petition from Londoners asking that Catholics be forced to wear distinctive dress (perhaps, thought the French ambassador, like Jews in other countries).[3] In any case, what he lacked in charisma and occasionally in guile he more than made up for with hard work, an obsessive knowledge of Parliamentary procedure and a critical willingness to stay on the right side of whomsoever happened to be Speaker.

Charles, for his part, was working behind the scenes. One of his first acts had been to summon Strafford from Yorkshire, where he was commanding the royal army. Stopping briefly at his family seat near Rotherham, Strafford hastened south, entering the capital on the 9th, Monday. In him was the king's best hope of heading off the opposition, for Strafford was a canny operator and a bluntly effective Parliamentary manager, as his track record in Dublin proved. He was also convinced that members of the opposition had been collaborating with the Scots, and if the rumours were true he was actively preparing formal accusations of treason against them. In short, he was a huge threat to Pym, Bedford, Warwick and their allies.

Ominously, Londoners could see gathering activity at the Tower, the royal fortress that loomed over the City. New heavy artillery was being installed: the garrison was performing manoeuvres. At Deptford, battleships from the royal navy were testing their guns, the thud of the cannons shuddering the windows upriver in the eastern suburbs. Was this the preparation for a Royalist coup? Was the Tower being fortified against the City and Londoners, who might stand ready to resist any attempt to arrest the leading Parliamentarians?

Wednesday 11 November was to be one of those days where political events suddenly moved at a lightning pace. The opposition needed to neutralise Strafford before he could strike at them. To do so, they planned an impeachment. This was an ancient procedure, but it had lain dormant since the Middle Ages before being brought back in the 1620s. The process was not entirely clear or settled yet, but in the

Strafford trial, the approach was the most widely accepted one. An accusation was made by members of the Commons, and then put before the Lords, where – eventually – any trial would be conducted.

On the morning of the 11th, as Strafford took his seat for the first time in the Lords, the Commons were discussing alarming reports about the military build-up, delivered by the Puritan merchant–MP Matthew Craddock. Guns, said Craddock, were being mounted 'this day'. His suggestion that the Tower was being armed with 'mortars planted to shoot wild' was terrifying.[4] With Strafford ready in the Lords chamber, he could launch accusations of treason at a time of his choosing, while the military forces in the Tower were used to cow and subdue the people of London.

For now, though, Strafford kept his powder dry, and by the afternoon he had slipped out of the Lords and headed up to the royal palace at Whitehall, no doubt for a meeting with Charles. But this brought more danger for his enemies. If the Commons moved for an impeachment, but were unable to put their motion before the Lords before the peers adjourned, then Strafford would have a window – when he returned the next day – in which he could launch a counter-attack. So Pym asked leave to visit the Lords. Here, it seems, he conferred with his allies and asked them to keep the Upper House in session.[5] They had to keep talking to give Pym his chance to strike.

Back in the Commons, the debate continued – focusing not on Strafford but on the alleged misdemeanours of Secretary Windebank. Then, as the debate wound down, the Commons finally moved. First they appointed a committee of six, to prepare for a conference with the Lords. The terms of the committee seem to have been quite wide, but crucially it was filled with Strafford's enemies, and these men steered it towards a more direct path. Returning to the packed Commons chamber, they presented a charge against Strafford. The House, ringing with fears of a coup, of popish plots and of the guns of the Tower and Deptford, accepted the charge without needing a vote.

As the late autumn light faded outside, Pym led a delegation to the Lords, to accuse Strafford of high treason and ask for his immediate detention. This latter was critical: if the Lords refused then Strafford might still be able to sit while the formal charge was prepared. The Lords took this into consideration, but as they debated, Strafford returned. He made to take his seat, but was met with cries from his fellow peers of 'Withdraw! Withdraw!' Strafford conceded the point and withdrew. His next appearance, some while later, was humiliating. Called back to the Lords chamber, he was forced to kneel. He was told the peers' decision. He was to be sequestered from his seat, and to be committed to custody.

Charles's military preparations stopped. If he had been planning a coup against Parliament, then it had been outflanked. With his chief adviser under guard, the king was drastically weakened.

Now that Strafford was out of the way, and on the 25th had been moved to the Tower through a jeering crowd, Parliament could turn to business. Top of the agenda was the staging of huge public rehabilitations for those who had suffered during the king's Personal Rule.

On the 16th, Bishop John Williams was released from the Tower by the Lords. Even before that, after an emotional speech by a rather scruffy East Anglian MP called Oliver Cromwell, orders had been made for the release of Alexander Leighton and a spirited young polemicist named John Lilburne – imprisoned in 1638 for importing 'scandalous' books from the Netherlands. The biggest celebration, though, came on the 28th, when – on a crisp sunny Saturday – Henry Burton and William Prynne returned from imprisonment to the capital. Church bells chimed amid a chorus of cheers as the men processed slowly through town. There were so many followers, throwing flowers and herbs from their gardens, that it took the procession a reported three hours to pass Charing Cross.

Now, as winter approached, the work of unpicking Charles's government could begin. '[T]here was never, I dare say, so busy a time in England,' wrote one correspondent.[6] Soon, though, Londoners staged a stunning intervention which threatened to disturb the whole project. On 11 December, braving the icy cold, a delegation of some 1,500 citizens crowded into Westminster Hall bringing with them a printed petition, signed by 10,000. It blamed the bishops for everything from problems in the cloth industry, to 'whoredoms and adulteries', to the 'swarming of lascivious, idle and unprofitable books'. It asked not just for reform of religious abuses, but that the episcopacy itself be abolished, 'with all its dependencies, roots and branches'.[7] Here was the potential for a complete radicalisation of the reform agenda. More to the point, the sight of so many ordinary Londoners, petitioning publicly for the uprooting of the ecclesiastical order was staggering.

For now, Parliament carried on, confining itself to attacking the worst excesses of Archbishop Laud. Just five days after the London petition, the Canons of 1640 were declared illegal; Laud himself was impeached two days after that, and detained. The most far-reaching proposal in Parliament, though, was not a religious one. It came in the last week of December when, on Christmas Eve, the Devonian MP William Strode introduced a bill mandating annual Parliaments: if passed, it would ensure Parliament's permanent sitting. The gauntlet had been thrown.

Charles was evidently weak, not least as the Scottish army was still sitting in camps across the north-east and was still demanding its £850 a day. But, early in January 1641, an opportunity arose for him to stage a fightback, albeit one on moderate terms. The key developments were in Charles's court. Here, the Scot Hamilton had become fearful of meeting the same fate as Strafford, so he allied himself with the group around the Earl of Bedford in the Privy Council. Happily, the ageing Dutch Stadtholder Frederick Henry also chose this moment to suggest a marriage alliance between Princess Mary (then nine years old) and his own heir, Prince William of Orange (then fourteen). Thus a shift at court matched with a new foreign alignment might possibly have allowed the creation of a moderate administration, led by Bedford, with a popular anti-Spanish, pro-Orangist diplomatic posture. As if to signal the possibilities of this new settlement, on the 19th Charles agreed to appoint a new Solicitor General from Bedford's circle: the lawyer Oliver St John, the very man who had led John Hampden's defence in the great Ship Money trial.[8]

In the Commons, meanwhile, Strode's bill had now been modified into one in which Parliament must sit at least once every three years (i.e. triennial Parliaments). It passed the Commons on the 20th and went up to the Lords. To Bedford's group it was crucial, because while they expected Charles to appoint them to positions in the government, they also needed to be sure he wouldn't simply dissolve Parliament and remove them. For his part, Charles seemed to be opening the door to a settlement. On 23 January, he summoned both the Commons and the Lords to the Banqueting House, where he conceded a moderate reformist agenda: the 'reformation' of his Church and state, returning the Church to the 'best and purest times' of Elizabeth, and renouncing any revenue found to be illegal.[9] That same day, the Commons received a petition and 'remonstrance' from over 700 parish ministers, criticising the actions of the bishops, but failing to call outright for their removal.

Between Charles's speech and the ministers' remonstrance, it seemed possible that a compromise could be reached, whereby the Church returned to its (alleged) Elizabethan heyday, shorn of its ceremonialist excesses. Such a settlement would appeal to moderates, for whom the gathering debate over Root and Branch, i.e. the complete abolition of the bishops, was generating significant unease. Sir John Strangways, a former Forced Loan refuser, worried that tearing down the bishops would lead to an uprooting of other social hierarchies: 'if we make a parity in the church, we must come to a parity in the commonwealth'.[10] At the same time, Charles's treaty with the Dutch was proceeding well, with marriage expected between William of the House of Orange and the young Princess Mary Stuart. And, most important of all, Charles finally assented to the Triennial Bill, although not without serious soul-searching. The evening after he signed, bonfires roared and the bells rang through London and beyond. Peace, moderate reform and regular Parliaments seemed to beckon.

The situation in the country as a whole, however, was worrying, for disorder was growing again. Many Laudian innovations were being pulled down by parishioners: unofficially, but partly in response to what was happening in Parliament. Altars, Ann Temple of Warwickshire wrote triumphantly, 'begin to go down apace, and rails in many places'.[11] New, independent, illicit religious meetings were starting to emerge, often on hills and heaths, in suburban lanes or by owl-light. In Norwich, daytime sermons competed with night-time conventicles,* and the latter were said to be better attended.[12]

---

*Unofficial religious gatherings.

Three days after the king agreed to the Triennial Act, he appointed seven opposition peers to the Privy Council, including Bedford, Saye, Essex and Mandeville. Apparently he hated doing so, and had to be persuaded by Hamilton, but it was in many ways a smart move. The Council had little power these days anyway, and it helped pull Bedford's power base away from the more radical group around Warwick. The plan, no doubt, was to split the opposition. In particular, the hope was that it would allow Charles to save the Earl of Strafford, whose trial was planned for the spring and was now fast approaching.

Nervous about these moves to save the earl, Warwick's hardliners responded by drawing on their Scottish allies. On 24 February, the Scots treaty commissioners duly presented a demand to their English counterparts that Strafford be brought to speedy justice. This was promptly printed as a short 'handbill', ready for distribution around the capital to the people. It was a critical day, for it was then that Strafford gave his initial defence to the Lords. The king, unexpectedly, took his throne, smiling at the earl and pointedly removing his hat to honour him.[13] The coming trial was to be the biggest test of strength yet. Any hope of compromise would depend on its outcome.

The case brought against Strafford was deeply flawed. Treason, by definition, was against the king, but by all accounts Strafford had been a devotedly loyal servant. His enemies thus settled on the dubious idea of 'cumulative treason'. This, essentially, was the allegation that Strafford's acts, when considered together as a whole, were so heinous as to have brought the king himself into disrepute. The prosecution compiled 28 articles that, they argued, built up to a summative proof of treason. But that, in the end, was all they had.

The earl's enemies were in a dangerous position. If he were acquitted, then he was free to resume his place at the king's side, and he would be burning for revenge. So they toyed with another plan: to use another ancient and little-used process, called 'attainder', by which Parliament simply passed an act *declaring* the earl guilty of treason without the need for a trial. Yet this seemed even less promising: as with any Act of Parliament, it not only needed to be passed by the Lords, but it also needed the assent of the king. The chances of Charles's agreeing to Strafford's death were slim indeed.

Nor was this all. Through March, as the date of Strafford's trial crept nearer, there were signs that the royal army, still stationed in the north, might present a serious threat. After suffering defeat, arrears of pay and a cold northern winter, the royal army was ripe for discontent. In the shadows, a plot took shape to bring the army south, intimidate Parliament and break Strafford out from the Tower. Perhaps, as winter turned to spring, Charles might gain the opportunity to use his army raised to fight the Scots against his enemies in England.

Strafford's trial finally began on 22 March. The earl was brought by river from the Tower to Westminster. Wearing all black, he looked physically weak. Now 47 years old, his body toiling under the strain of kidney stones. His ordeal would take place not in the Lords, but in Westminster Hall, the very heart of the English legal system. The assembled Lords would sit at the centre, in their ermine-trimmed crimson finery, hats on their heads. On their sides were the hatless Commons, on specially built stands; in their midst were the clerks of the court, kneeling as they scribbled the notes that would become the formal record. Opposite Strafford's dock was the throne, but it lay empty, for – after his performance on 24 February – the king had been specifically told not to use it. Instead, Charles was forced to watch from a latticed box behind the throne and to the right (as viewed by the earl). His first act was to tear out the lattice covering so his presence was there for all to see.

Behind Strafford's dock was a gallery with space for some 1,000 spectators. For this was to be a very public trial, attended by an audience of Londoners, huddling together, scoffing food and swigging from bottles of beer and wine. The hope was that it would broadcast Strafford's crimes to the country. But it had a more radical edge than this, for the trial also presented an opportunity for Charles's opponents to shine a beacon on his government. To invite his people to judge it. '[E]veryone is engaged, and that passionately, either for my lord Strafford's preservation or his ruin', it was said.[14] Yet it wasn't just Strafford on trial, it was the whole edifice of Charles's previous rule. By dealing with Strafford so publicly, the trial would underscore the tyranny of rule without Parliament, and the return to the glorious old days under the new, post-Triennial Act administration.

The trouble was, as Charles watched on from his box, '*incognito*, though conspicuous enough', the trial went very badly.[15] The prosecution's arguments were weak, Strafford's rebuttals hit the mark. '[W]hen a thousand misdemeanours will not make one felony,' he scoffed, 'shall twenty-eight misdemeanours heighten it to a treason.' 'Almost every article sets forth a new treason that I never heard of before.'[16] Just as bad, by appearing humble, intelligent, witty, he began to claw back some of his public image. Such growing sympathy was aided by the prosecution themselves, who 'so banged and worried his lordship as it begets pity in many of the auditors'.[17] The trial had been intended to show Strafford to the public as a monster. But instead of the 'Black Tom Tyrant' he was supposed to be, he just looked like a frail old man, battered and bullied by a clique of politicians who hadn't properly done their homework.

Even the prosecution's star witness was a disaster. Henry Vane was supposed to provide evidence that Strafford, in that meeting when the Short Parliament had been dissolved, had called for the Irish army to be used against England. But he had to be reminded three times before he was able to remember what he was meant to say: 'My Earl of Strafford did say in a discourse, "Your Majesty ... you have an army in Ireland, which you may employ here to reduce this Kingdom", or some such words to this effect.'[18] Even then, the attendant Lords were sceptical as to whether 'this Kingdom' *really* meant England. In any case, Vane was just one witness: in general, proof of treason required *two* witnesses. Prosecuting counsel argued that there was a second witness: 'vox populi', the voice of the people. But this was rather desperate.*

On Saturday 10 April, the prosecution tried one last manoeuvre. They had a copy of Vane's notes on that fateful meeting. They'd been reluctant to use it, perhaps because it would be painfully obvious that Vane himself had leaked them. But now, with the case in pieces, they had little choice. They revealed to Westminster Hall that they had new, damning evidence against the earl.

---

*This is a rather startling statement, but it is perhaps not totally without precedent. Church courts, for example, used 'common fame' to convict offenders, and equity courts might listen to the 'voice of the country'. The difference is that these related to minor sexual infractions and debated pastures, not trials of blood.

Strafford's response was simple. If the prosecution could bring new evidence, then so, surely, could his defence, something which threatened to stall the trial even further. The only way forward was an adjournment while the Lords considered the request. They shuffled out of the Hall and, after an interminable debate, returned with the news that they had decided to grant Strafford's request. The prosecution team was outraged, but after another half an hour's debate the Lords stuck by their original decision. The Hall erupted; shouts of 'withdraw', aimed at the prosecution counsel from their own side, were misheard as 'draw!', so some of the 1,000 spectators drew their blades. The king, who was watching the debacle with the queen from the comfort of his box, was delighted. Strafford, too, 'could not hide his joy'.[19] For the opposition, the ramifications were gloomy indeed. For this was not just a tactical defeat. It was more ominous. It showed they were losing their grip on the Lords.

But that same day another plan was already in motion. There was always a group who believed, perhaps correctly, that Strafford was inherently dangerous: men like the earls of Essex and Warwick for whom the only way of safety was for Strafford to be neutralised, permanently. The Warwick group was more radical, more tied to Root and Branch, and had less to gain by the Bedfordian compromise. Late in the day, with the House thinning out for the evening, a debate began about a new, more drastic strategy against the earl, a bill of attainder. As the debate rolled on, a Leicestershire MP, Arthur Haselrig dramatically produced a ready-drafted bill. Haselrig was to prove an impressive figure in the years to come, but he was also married to the sister of Lord Brooke, giving him a family tie to the Warwick circle. At this stage, one suspects, Haselrig was working on Warwick's orders. The bill proposed Strafford should be declared guilty of treason, of introducing 'an arbitrary and tyrannical government against law', and that he should suffer hanging, drawing and quartering.[20]

On Tuesday, the trial resumed in Westminster Hall. Here, Pym – who remained an ally of Bedford rather than Warwick – gave a rambling speech for the prosecution which even his friends thought was a catastrophe. Strafford then responded with a measured and powerful defence.

The next day, the Commons voted to give the attainder bill a second reading. In two separate chambers in the Palace of Westminster, two separate attacks on Strafford, driven by two separate groups, were under way, the one – the trial in Westminster Hall led by Bedford – stuttering; the other – the attainder in the Commons driven by the Warwick circle – gaining momentum by the hour.

There were ill portents, too. Bedford, by now, knew something of the developing plots within the royal army, and there were reports of smallpox in the capital. On Monday 19 April, the Commons received unsettling news. They were notified that army officers had been told over the weekend to return to their men. It came by the command of the king.

What could this be if not the prelude to a coup? On the Wednesday, the Commons took up the third reading of the attainder bill. It now had a groundswell of support. As the afternoon light faded, some several thousand Londoners had gathered outside Parliament. They brought a petition calling for Strafford's death, but they also had a more direct aim. The fear was that Charles would suddenly decide to dissolve Parliament by sending royal commissioners out from Whitehall, down King Street, to Westminster. The crowd's aim, should this happen, was to block them.

In the Commons, debate continued. By around 6 p.m., the House was ready to vote. The attainder passed, 204 to 59. This was, in fact, a House but half full. Many of those who might have opposed the bill appear not to have sat. Even John Hampden, the hero opponent of Ship Money, stayed away, believing that killing Strafford without a proper conviction was dubious: morally wrong, in fact.

There were still hurdles. Now the attainder bill had to go through the Lords, and there remained, even now, a chance of compromise. By the 23rd, Charles had accepted that Strafford would have to fall – though not into the hands of an executioner. Over the weekend, negotiations continued between Bedford and the king. Strafford would suffer exile, but not death; Charles would make more irksome appointments of members of the opposition to positions of trust, few more galling than that of Warwick himself, called to the Privy Council on the Sunday. Bedford, the moderate, also reached out to Essex, the hardliner. If the flamboyant military hero Essex could be won over to the cause of compromise, then a moderate settlement was within grasp.

Bedford's intermediary was a Wiltshireman called Edward Hyde, who approached Essex while he was walking in the shaded gravel walks and bowling greens below Piccadilly, a favoured haunt of English aristocrats. But Hyde found Essex immovable. The only way Strafford could be permanently removed from the picture, a tired Essex said, was through death. For, as the proverb had it, 'stone dead hath no fellow'.[21]

But there was something else.

Bedford didn't know it yet, but he was dying. Sometime in the last days of April, he developed a fever. Around the 30th, his daughter found spots on his body. His physician told him there was nothing to worry about, but his physician was wrong. For it was smallpox.

On the 29th, there was a conference between the two Houses about the attainder. It began at 9 a.m. Strafford was present, as were the king, queen and the young Prince Charles, now approaching his eleventh birthday. The Lords didn't wear their robes, nor did they sit separately from their colleagues in the Commons: they were all Parliamentarians together.[22] Oliver St John stood to speak. He was, as everyone knew, a long-standing Bedford ally, so the expectation was presumably that he would argue for compromise. But he came not to foster conciliation. He came to bury Strafford. One of the most brilliant legal minds of his generation, he had come down strongly in favour of attainder.

The speech lasted three hours, with St John deploying a mastery of the law and of rhetoric. The king had two bodies, he noted: the body natural and the body politic. By subverting the laws of the realm, Strafford had committed treason against the king's body politic. St John appealed to the Upper House's natural social conservatism. 'My Lords, take away law, and there is no peerage, but every swain is equal.' He appealed to their self-importance, citing a medieval judge's dictum that he could not judge a treason in Westminster Hall, but he could in *Parliament*.* And he appealed to a rustic common sense that pleased those whose power rested on broad acres. 'It was never accounted either cruelty or foul play to knock foxes and wolves on the head ... because they are beasts of prey.'

The speech thrust the knife into Strafford. The Hall thundered with applause. The Lords were turning. As a German observer put it, '[T]he whole scene seemed changed.'[23]

But in the face of the gathering momentum in Parliament against Strafford, the king still seemed resolute. Two days later after St John's virtuoso performance, Charles attended the Lords. The Commons were summoned to crowd into the chamber to attend him as he spoke from the throne. He accepted that Strafford was not fit to serve, 'not so much as to be a high constable'.[24] But Charles's conscience dictated that he must save Strafford's life, and it was as simple as that. Just as bad, he implied the Irish army would stay in arms until all three armies, royal, Scots and Irish, could be disbanded together. The implications were shocking – it showed he was not willing to listen to his Parliament on this matter – on *any* matter – that impinged on his conscience. And it showed Charles was at least thinking in terms of a military confrontation. Here, in England.

Charles, having given the speech, waited for the applause, but was met with stunned silence. After a few awkward moments, he turned and left.

The next day, Sunday 2 May, Whitehall Palace finally marked the wedding of the nine-year-old Princess Mary to the fourteen-year-old William of Orange. Celebration was in the air as the groom was carried by a fleet of 16 coaches from Arundel House at the eastern end of the Strand to Whitehall. Members of Lords and Commons were invited; and London traffic was at gridlock.

As the Dutch prince made his ponderous way down the Strand, a group of men was gathering at the White Horse Tavern on Bread

---

*A pleasing irony, of course, given that the Lords were sitting as part of a Parliament, but physically in Westminster Hall.

Street, just east of St Paul's. They were led by the loyalist poet Sir John
Suckling, the swashbuckling veteran of Newburn. By the afternoon
they numbered about 60, wearing their buff coats and carrying swords
and pistols. News of this ominous assembly spread quickly. By the
evening another crowd was starting to gather, 1,000-strong, on Tower
Hill. If the men at the White Horse Tavern made a move against the
Tower, attempting to free Strafford, then they would meet resistance.
Abandoning the plan, the men at the tavern slid away into the night.*

But the damage was done. As Parliament reassembled the next morning,
the courtyards of Westminster were filled with angry Londoners. 'In a
clap all the city in alarum; shops closed; a world of people in arms run
down to Westminster,' reported the Scot Robert Baillie.[25] There were
shouts of 'Justice!' and 'Execution!' aimed at Strafford. According to
one frightened bishop, some in the crowd threatened to lynch the earl,
or even the king. Names of those MPs who had voted against Attainder
were posted up at the Exchange and at other locations in London and
Westminster. 'Enemies of Justice, and Straffordians'.[26]

To a rapt Commons, Pym revealed the intelligence he had of plots
in the king's army. As usual, he placed the blame on Catholics: 'I am
persuaded that there was some great design in hand by the papist to
subvert and overthrow this kingdom.'[27] The answer was an English
bond of association, or perhaps an English national covenant, like that
of the Scots just over three years previously. The Commons rose: they
would swear an oath – a 'protestation' – to protect the realm and its
king from the papist threat. If this was to be Parliament's last day, then
they would at least have sworn never to relent in the greater struggle.
The 'Protestation Oath' was written and passed. By 7 p.m. everyone –
or nearly everyone – in the Commons had taken it. That night, again,
the Tower was surrounded by Londoners.

The Strafford case was now entering its final act. The Lords were
turning decisively against the earl. Meanwhile Bedford, the linchpin of
a potential moderate compromise, was mortally sick. At some point,
Strafford wrote to the king, releasing him from his promise of protection. 'Sir, to you,' he wrote, 'I can give the life of this world with all the
cheerfulness imaginable', though he still probably hoped to be saved.[28]

---

*Suckling eventually heading to exile where, within a year, he was dead, said to have poisoned
himself.

The Commons, still fearful for their own security, sent up a bill preventing their own dissolution without consent. The Lords, meanwhile, were now debating the Bill of Attainder. They voted to consider the case as one of conscience rather than evidence: 'in the discussing the matter of fact ... the rule shall only be the persuasion of every man's conscience'. All that mattered, in other words, was what the peers *felt* about Strafford's guilt. They debated for three tense days, with no fewer than ten procedural divisions. Many pro-Straffordians, sensing the way things were going, and unwilling to run the gauntlet of the London crowd, simply stayed away. In the end, the Lords voted in favour.

The Bill of Attainder now went to the king. It was presented to Charles at Whitehall by a delegation from Parliament who also brought the bill to prevent a dissolution. More menacing for Charles, they were supported in the streets by a large crowd. It forced an agonising choice. Charles had given his word to Strafford, but Parliament had swung decisively, and the crowd were making their feelings quite clear. Refuse to sign the attainder, Charles worried, and it might unleash a popular fury worse than ever before, this time against him and his family.

On the 8th, Strafford offered his keeper £22,000 to escape the Tower, but the plan went nowhere. The next day, Sunday the 9th, Charles called on his bishops for advice, twice. Outside, the crowd kept a menacing vigil. They had been a constant presence throughout the crisis, and now their threat was pushing the king down a path he would regret for the rest of his life. A mock playbill appeared on Whitehall's Holbein Gate, advertising a 'famous Tragi-Comedy called *A King and No King*'.[29] Eventually, sometime late in the night, Charles signed the two bills.

Earlier the previous morning, the Earl of Bedford had died.

In just two days, any remaining hope for a compromise settlement had finally collapsed. But Charles's assent still didn't give a date for Strafford's death. Perhaps he could save his man by delaying it indefinitely. On the 11th, a delegation of 12 Lords visited the king, impressing on him the knife edge upon which the capital sat. If Strafford didn't die, the safety of the king, of the king's family, could not be guaranteed. If the king didn't order it, perhaps the Lords could issue the warrant themselves. So, on Wednesday the 12th, Charles capitulated. The execution was set for the next day.

8

This is a Remonstrance to the People

Crowds began to assemble at two in the morning. Over the previous days, Tower Hill had pulsed to the sound of sawing, hammering and the shouts of workers, as perhaps as many as seventeen temporary stands rose from the ground. Enough for tens of thousands of spectators. It was welcome employment for the City's carpenters, in a period of downturn; but the hasty job ended in horror when, in a cacophony of cracking wood and screams, one of the stands collapsed. But the performance carried on.

The best views were enjoyed by the nobility, whose seats were close to the scaffold. For the rest, the ritual being enacted on the scaffold was mostly a distant dumbshow, against the expectant hum of the vast crowd. They will have seen the cushion and the block set up; seen Strafford emerge, surrounded by a guard of men. They will have watched the final ministrations, perhaps heard some of the words spoken echo around the makeshift stadium. Then they will have seen the earl bend over and the flash of the blade, before his body slumped and the executioner grabbed his severed head by the hair and raised it.

The ecstatic cheer will have been heard across the City, across the suburbs and out into the neighbouring fields. As people walked home, back into town, they congratulated each other. 'His head is off, his head is off!'[1] Bonfires were raised, and some of those who refused to celebrate found their windows pelted and smashed. This 'great Goliath', wrote the London woodturner Nehemiah Wallington, had been executed 'to the joy of the Church of God'.[2]

Bitter division continued. Lists circulated of who had voted whichever way. 'These are the Straffordians,' one announced, 'the betrayers of their country.' A pro-Strafford list, meanwhile, denounced 'the Anabaptists, Jews and Brownists of the House of Commons'.[3] One MP, a supporter of the earl, was confronted by a constituent who angrily thrust a list of Straffordians in his face. His gutsy reply was that the attainder was nothing but 'murder with the sword of justice', words that were reported to the House, leading to his expulsion.[4] In the coming months, over a hundred publications rolled off the English presses about the dead earl. Some excoriating, others lukewarm, some even positive. Some treated him as a tragic hero, brought down by his own ambition.

The death of Strafford ended the first phase of what would come to be called the 'Long Parliament'. With him out of the way, and a Triennial Act on the books, Charles's rule had been defanged. Now the opposition could move on to a wider project of political reform, removing what they saw as the worst excesses of Personal Rule. But the failure of compromise – of the Bedfordian 'settlement' – would cast a long shadow. With Bedford dead, Pym and St John were now more closely allied to the radicals around Warwick and Essex. The divisive issue of Root and Branch still threatened to pull the reformists apart. And more to the point, the large demonstrations during the trial suggested that the people of London were waking up once more. Meanwhile, Strafford's execution had been a serious defeat for the king, but the chances of him retaliating seemed high. Charles would never forgive himself for allowing Strafford to die, and his minister's death only reinforced his determination, which had been there since November, to not only win back control, but to take revenge.

The king's soldiers and supporters were still rife with plotting and intrigue, so reports said. On 19 May, the tension in the Commons was such that it descended into temporary anarchy when two corpulent MPs broke some wooden lathes causing a loud crack that some thought was gunpowder. But, for all this discord, many now enjoyed a feeling of optimism. 'God send us now a happy end of our troubles and a good peace,' exclaimed Henry Vane, who thanks to his own inglorious role in the trial had more cause than many to be relieved at Strafford's death.[5] The Protestation Oath had now been printed and was being circulated around the country, and people in their thousands were swearing to it. Tonnage and Poundage was soon abolished. So, too, was Star Chamber, the Councils of Wales and North, and the hated court of High Commission. In the summer, Ship Money would be annulled, and knighthood fines declared illegal. Step by step, the apparatus of Charles's Personal Rule was being picked apart.

Pamphlets were streaming off the presses, as an excited and literate capital tried to make sense of what had been happening down the road at Westminster. There are just over 600 surviving titles per year for the 1630s, and this figure had risen slightly, to 848 for 1640. In 1641, there are 2,042. It was an astonishing explosion of print. Henry Burton, who had experienced brutal censorship first-hand, recalled how 'many mouths were stopped, many shut up', but 'Parliament hath opened their mouths ... it has opened the prisons.'[6] Or, in the lavishly biblical allusion of another Puritan author, 'the stone that made the stoppage of the well of Haran is now removed and the flocks of Laban may drink freely'.[7] The works of Prynne, Burton, Leighton were now freely available.

Print helped bring a great flowering of new religious groups, especially in and around London. In July, the Venetian ambassador reported drily that there seemed 'as many religions as there were persons'.[8] Even in the Parliamentary pulpit at St Margaret's, in the small church under Westminster Abbey, radicals told of tearing down Babylon, building up Zion and the planting of a new heaven and a new earth.[9] That summer, Burton declared that the Church of England had become anti-Christian, and advocated the creation of independent congregations, in which people gathered with no direction from above, to worship together as they pleased. Sometimes, so the reports went, groups met on the dark peripheries of the capital: Hackney Marsh and the hills around Hampstead and Highgate. Other congregations gathered in suburban houses, and by the end of the year there was even one led by the radical leather-seller Praisegod Barebone that met in his house on the Strand.

Religious enthusiasts from humble backgrounds, so-called 'mechanic' preachers, were giving sermons in public. One of Henry Burton's followers, Katherine Chidley, scandalised readers by arguing that true ministers could be 'tailors, felt-makers, button-makers, tent-makers, shepherds or ploughmen'.[10] The press made the most of it all, and in the journalists' insatiable desire for sensation, they contributed to a wider sense that old certainties were collapsing. While many stories about weird and worrisome radicals were undoubtedly

written for laughs, more nervous readers still trembled at the lurid
horror. There were reports of naked Adamites, of Anabaptists and
Brownists, even Muslims and 'Bacchanalian' pagans, not to mention
those worshipping the planetary deities of Saturn and Jupiter.[11] One
tract laughed at a mechanic preacher who spoke 'like a Lancashire
bagpipe' so (fortunately) 'the people could scarce understand any
word'.[12] Another delighted and horrified its readers in equal measure
with its cast of concocted female radicals: 'Agnes Anabaptist, Kate
Catabaptist, Frank* Footbaptist, Penelope Punk, Merald Makebate,
Ruth Rakehell, Tabitha Tattle, Pru Prattle, and that poor silly, simple,
senseless, sinless, shameless, naked wretch, Alice the Adamite'.

Much of what happened next revolved around the Scots. Negotiations
continued for the long-promised treaty, finally settling the controversies that went back to 1637. Within hours of Strafford's death, Charles
made the decision to visit the northern kingdom in person. His plan, so
it seems, was to exploit divisions among the Scottish governing class.
Argyll, who was one of Scotland's greatest landowners, was becoming
seen as rather overbearing, using the Covenanter movement to boost his
own wealth and power. Rivals such as the young and impetuous James
Graham, Earl of Montrose, and the courtier Hamilton were looking for
ways to pull Argyll down again. So the king sensed an opportunity to
outflank his opponents in England by winning back Scotland.

Charles was helped by growing tensions in the relations between
the English opposition leadership and the Scots commissioners in
London. English payments to the Scots army were in arrears, and
there had been little progress in the reform – let alone the abolition – of the English episcopacy, which the Scots Covenanters saw as
fundamental to the security of their own, newly Presbyterian, Kirk.
There was therefore a serious threat to men like Pym and his now ally
Warwick that Charles might be able to turn the tables, particularly as
en route to Scotland, Charles would pass straight through his own
dormant army, whose soldiers were still underpaid, still angry and still
largely loyal to their king. It was, after all, Parliament they blamed

*In this case, short for Frances.

for their lack of pay, and if the Scots were encouraged to stand down, there was nothing that stopped the royal army marching on London.

Bold thinking was needed if the opposition were to hold off this new threat. On 23 June, Pym gave another forceful speech: the royal army was full of 'many evil spirits', he argued, 'that might make evil broils'.[13] The answer, adopted unanimously by the Commons the next day, was a set of ten 'propositions', quickly available to the public as a handy pamphlet. These called for the royal army to be disbanded, and the king's departure to be delayed until it was. They asked that the court be plucked of papists; the militia put in the hands of men loyal to Parliament, both of which suggestions would have been offensive to Charles. At the same time, to keep the Scots on side, Parliament turned its attention back to Root and Branch and the everlasting money business, passing a bill for four subsidies and a poll tax.

In the languid heat of the summer, the plague was back, reaching Chancery Lane by the middle of July, ready to skip into Westminster. Then, on 28 July, Charles made the long expected but widely feared announcement: he had a departure date for Scotland, just two weeks away on 9 August. On 2 August, news reached London that the Scottish Parliament had finally accepted the generous peace terms that had been negotiated over the previous months: their episcopacy still abolished, those who had signed the 1638 Covenant protected, and a helpful £300,000 of 'brotherly assistance' from their English friends. The Scots army could at last begin its withdrawal from England. By the end of the month, almost a year to the day since the invasion, it was gone.

It was followed by Charles himself. Despite last-minute attempts to delay his departure, including a Sunday sitting and the appearance of a large London crowd, the king left Whitehall behind and headed for Scotland. With the Covenanters' army gone, the dynamic was changing. The opposition had scored significant victories in disposing of Strafford and Laud (although the latter was still alive in the Tower), by passing the Triennial Act and sweeping away many of Charles's prerogative courts. But reform in the parishes was still barely started, and, now that the Scots army had gone north, Charles suddenly had a freer hand.

Recess was looming. MPs were conscious that they would soon have to return to their counties and towns. Out of the plague-ridden capital, yes, but back to the questioning faces of their constituents. The Parliament was already the longest in English history, having sat for nine months, but what had it achieved? There was still no permanent settlement, in state or in Church. Root and Branch was neither off the table nor had there been any tangible progress, so radicals, moderates and conservatives were all equally unsatisfied. There was still no national plan to eradicate the worst excesses of Laudianism, aside from the arrest of Laud himself and, in August, moves to impeach 13 bishops associated with the controversial Canons of 1640.

With attendances low – perhaps only around 80 MPs were still sitting – and with the king away in Scotland, the time was ripe for a decisive move. Charles's absence provided a window of opportunity, for it allowed Parliament to pass an 'ordinance': an instrument that had temporary force of law, without the need for royal approval. If an ordinance could be passed for the removal of Laudian innovations, then it could be put into effect immediately by ordinary parishioners up and down the country. By the time Charles returned and could veto it, a local reformation of the Church would already have taken place.

By 8 September, the day before recess, the Commons, led by Pym, had put together a mandate for churchwardens to remove 'innovations' in their parish churches, and a declaration that 'the Lord's day should be duly observed and sanctified; that all dancing, wrestling, or other sports either before or after divine service, be foreborne and restrained'.[14] But the Lords were obstructive. On the 9th, they refused to pass the ordinance, albeit by a narrow margin, and instead ordered the printing of an order passed back in January, demanding services observe the Book of Common Prayer. The Commons fought back, ordering the printing of *their* ordinance, together with the names of the 11 peers who'd blocked it in the Upper House. The situation this left was messy, to say the least, but whatever the precise constitutional position, reformists in the parishes finally had at least some of the official backing they needed to tear Laudian innovations down.

Parliament adjourned until 20 October, handing affairs to a committee headed by Pym, and with that its members headed back to their counties. In the weeks they spent at home, the sheer scale of the response to the 8 September ordinance became clear. For there followed a great wave of iconoclasm across the country: altars were pulled down and images smashed. To Puritans and anti-Laudians, these were exhilarating times. '[P]apists tremble,' rejoiced the poet John Bond, 'Arminians tumble.'[15] Robert Harley, MP, returned to Herefordshire from Westminster and smashed the stained-glass windows at Leintwardine parish church, throwing them into the Teme: 'in imitation of King Asa 2 Chron 15:16 who threw images into the brook Kidron'.[16]

But not everyone was as exuberant in their enthusiasm for tearing down Babylon. The 'madness is intolerable,' wrote one conservative.[17] It all added to the fear of that many-headed monster, the English people. 'We must take care,' as one MP put it, 'that the Common people may not carve out a Justice, by their Multitudes. Of this we have too frequent experience, by their breaking down enclosures, and by raising other tumults, to as ill purposes.'[18] Add to this the disquiet felt by many at the tactics of the anti-Straffordians, with their alliance with the unruly London crowd. And the overbearing nature of Pym – who by the end of autumn was starting to be mocked as 'King Pym' – and what people were starting to call his 'Junto'. In all this there was now the potential for the emergence of something new and important in Parliament. A Royalist party.

The man who understood this more than perhaps anyone else was Edward Nicholas. A Wiltshireman approaching his fortieth year, Nicholas was a moderate man, and by the summer of 1641 his politics were drifting far away from those of the opposition leadership.

There were others like him: the cultured Lord Falkland, for example, had been an implacable opponent of Strafford, but his concerns about Root and Branch were burrowing deep into his relatively conservative conscience. Or Edward Hyde, a brilliant, thoughtful barrister, and like Nicholas a Wiltshireman. From September, Nicholas was making concerted efforts to unite such men, and to create a Royalist voting bloc in both Houses, focusing initially on the Lords. First, he persuaded 11 conservative peers to make sure they attended the forthcoming session. Second, he worked to strengthen the voice of the bishops in the House of Lords. Existing bishops were told to be assiduous in their attendance, while Nicholas also – in a particularly smart move – persuaded Charles to fill five vacant bishoprics with solid Calvinists. These were the kind of men who would appeal to moderates, both inside and outside Parliament. Men who disliked Laudianism, but were equally worried about Root and Branch. Charles, whose political nous was improving by the day, saw the logic in switching his allegiance from the Laudians to the Calvinists. 'I have somewhat altered from my former thoughts,' he noted with a wry smile, 'to satisfy the times.'[19] With all 26 bishops sitting, plus a knot of loyal peers, there would be a Royalist choir in the Lords, which could now act as a counterweight to Pym's Junto.

There were also encouraging signals coming from the City. Here, the governing elite were increasingly alarmed by disorder, mechanic preaching and the tide of iconoclasm (which seems to have taken place in around a quarter of London parishes). At the end of September, the mayoral election actually returned an anti-Junto conservative. Meanwhile, a large number of soldiers were appearing in the capital from the royal army in the north, which was now, with the Scots gone, being disbanded. This was in defiance of an order of the Recess Committee on 5 October, demanding they leave London or be imprisoned. Swaggering around the taverns and alehouses of town and suburbs, these 'reformadoes' (as they came to be called) were loyal, leery, volatile and armed: a very obvious threat to the more pro-Parliamentarian London citizens and apprentices. Such was the concern among the Junto that Essex, who had been appointed Lord General in the South, decided to deploy a guard around Parliament, in time for the convening of its second session on 20 October.

Members had gradually drifted back to their lodgings in the capital, ready for the end of recess. Then, the day before Parliament was due to reconvene, a thunderbolt arrived from Scotland.

In Edinburgh, with the king lodged at Holyrood Palace, a plot had been hatched somewhere close to him. Details were not yet clear, but the plan was to arrest several leading figures: Argyll, Hamilton (who was now seeking friendship with Argyll) and Hamilton's brother, and possibly to kill them on the spot. In fact, the intended victims had been forewarned, and had fled to safety. But Edinburgh remained in a state of high tension, not least because it was bristling with the armed retainers of the Scottish nobility. There was talk of a massacre; not idle talk, either, for one of the leading plotters had ordered their tenants to come to Edinburgh on the appointed day each with a musket, a pound of powder and a dozen bullets.

The afternoon after the plot had broken, the king had appeared in the Parliament House (backed by 500 armed retainers) and had tearfully denied all knowledge of this 'incident'. But, as the investigation proceeded over the coming weeks, the central role of one of his most trusted servants, Will Murray, became clear. Charles's complicity seemed obvious. His willingness to countenance violence against opponents, and against one of his capital cities, was worrying indeed.

In Westminster, MPs were now returning to work in earnest, and the sight of a file of militiamen protecting the Palace of Westminster was unlikely to have provided much reassurance against the reformadoes. Worse, five days after the end of recess, the Commons was horrified when a porter delivered a letter to Pym out of which fell 'an abominable rag, full of filthy abominable matter'.[20] It was the dressing of a plague sore, and with it an anonymous letter:

> Mr Pym, Do not think that a guard of men can protect you, if you persist in your traitorous courses, and wicked designs. I have sent a Paper-Messenger to you, and if this does not touch your heart, a dagger shall, so soon as I am recovered of my Plague-Sore: In the mean time you may be forborne, because no better man may be endangered for you. Repent Traitor.[21]

Amid the fear, the Junto's immediate project was to assert Parliament's right for a say in the appointment of Privy Councillors and government ministers. This would be a dramatic step further than the 'Ten Propositions' of the summer, but the Junto knew it was the only way they could ensure their personal safety against the king. With their loss of power in the Lords, though, and with Charles's return from Scotland anticipated soon, the Junto also desperately

needed something to rally their support. So they turned to a project
that had long been in their minds, but had been kept firmly in reserve.
A great 'remonstrance': a declaration of their case against the late mis-
government at the king's command that would unify their supporters,
and present their case to the country. November the 1st was set aside
to open the debate.

On the 1st, MPs filed into the house, expecting to debate this new
remonstrance. But it didn't happen. Instead, at around 10 a.m. the
Commons were interrupted by the sudden appearance of 17 Privy
Councillors at the bar of the house. The day before, an exhausted rider
had arrived at the gates of Leicester House in the West End, asking
for an urgent audience with the Earl of Leicester, Lord Lieutenant of
Ireland. His report was the stuff of nightmares. Ireland was in open
revolt. Dublin had come within an inch of falling to rebels. The biggest
insurgency, though, was in Ulster. Here, the messenger said, the rebel
aims were nothing short of the extermination of the entire Protestant
settler population.

In the Commons, the 17 councillors were given special chairs, from
which they recounted the evidence they had of the new rebellion, to
a horrified audience. Over the coming weeks, England – and especially London – would recoil in shock as sensationalist reports of the
massacre of Protestants filtered through, seized on by an eager press.
The English had little knowledge of Ireland beyond maps, tales and
prejudices. There was little analysis of the causes of the rebellion: few
thought about the gradual bitterness brought by the expropriation
of Catholic Irish land to make way for Protestant settlers, or how
the Scottish example had showed what success rebellion might bring.
Few considered the fear engendered in Ireland by the increasing
strength of a Puritan Junto in England. Or the power of the English
Parliament they dominated, which had established a clear precedent
for jurisdiction over Irish affairs, during the Earl of Strafford's trial.
Few even paused for thought about Strafford's Irish army, disbanded
in the spring, or what the consequences might be of an order of 9
September which prevented former soldiers from enlisting with continental armies, leaving them stuck at home nursing their anger.

With Ireland suddenly aflame, the central question became how a new army might be raised to quell the uprising and protect the Protestants there. How could it be raised with the king absent, still on his way back from Scotland? Who would the commanders be? Would they be men the Junto could trust? On 5 November, Powder Treason Day, and after a thundering oratory from the pulpit of the Temple Church by the Puritan Cornelius Burges, Parliament voted to create a new army, and to demand a Parliamentary veto over the king's ministers.[22] It was a remarkable attempt to win control of the executive, and there was no way the king would willingly assent. The next day, boats carrying refugee women and children from Ireland started landing at the port of Chester.

On the 8th, the great 'Remonstrance' was finally put to the Commons. The document was enormous: history would later call it the *Grand* Remonstrance. It had three parts. First, a long list of grievances going back, pointedly, to the early years of Charles's reign, specifically to 1627, the year of the Forced Loan. Second, it trumpeted the present Parliament's great successes. Third, it set out what was to be done. It was a fierce and angry document, and the debates that followed were intense. If the desire for it was to unify Parliament, the effect was the exact opposite.

To help win moderate support, the Junto gave ground with the religious clauses of the Remonstrance. A critical reference to 'errors and superstitions' in the Prayer Book fell, as did a clause demanding the confiscation of lands held by the bishops. There was also no attempt to defend the controversial 8 September order for pulling down Laudian innovations. It was as if any note of religious radicalism was being sacrificed in the name of the bigger project. But they kept a clause asking for the creation of a 'general synod of the most grave, pious, learned and judicious divines of this island; assisted with some from foreign parts, professing the same religion with us'.[23] The implication was that Scottish, Dutch and (perhaps) French Calvinists would be involved, which made the project a clear threat to the bishops.

On Monday the 22nd, three weeks after it was first moved, the final debate on the Remonstrance took place, starting at noon. Opponents fought hard. Why dig up old grievances, many long since redressed? But most of all, they argued, surely remonstrating *to the people* was dangerous. Democratic, even. 'I did not dream that we should remonstrate downward, tell stories to the people, and talk of the king as of a third person,' said a shocked Edward Dering. 'This is a Remonstrance to the people. Remonstrances ought to be to the king for redress,' declared the moderate John Colepeper. 'We [are] not sent to please the people.' But to Pym, this was the whole point. It was time, he said, 'to speak plain English, lest posterity shall say that England was lost and no man durst speak truth'.[24]

The rancorous debate continued into the early hours of Tuesday when, by the flicker of candlelight, MPs finally voted. The division was astonishingly tight: by just 159 votes to 148, the Remonstrance passed. Exhausted MPs started to file out, but there was one last skirmish. It's not entirely clear from surviving accounts what happened, but the defeated opponents of the Remonstrance seem to have passed a vote – by acclamation – to prevent its 'printing and publishing'. This was a body blow to the whole project, for what good was a grand Remonstrance to the people if the people couldn't read it? So the Junto forced a final vote. In the dead of night, by 124 votes to 101, the thinning House voted to allow *publishing*, but not *printing*. By Wednesday, manuscript copies were already on the newsstands.

The emergence of moderate royalism, driven as it was by a fear of the people, had helped push the Junto towards a more direct appeal to those people. Only time would tell what impact that direct appeal would have. The people had awakened twice already: in May 1640 with the violence against Laud, and nearly a year later with the more peaceful, but nonetheless menacing, crowd action against Strafford. As it would turn out, though, this was just the beginning.

Crucially, too, the split in Parliament was now there for all to see. Charles and Nicholas had been successfully cultivating a Royalist party at Westminster and beyond, while in their way stood supporters of the Junto.

Now, though, the king had almost completed his long journey south, and was near London. By that Wednesday he had reached the grand mansion of Theobalds in Hertfordshire, where his father had died seventeen years ago.

On the 25th, Thursday, Charles was ready to make his grand re-entry to his capital.

9

Dark, Equal Chaos

Despite gloomy weather, the king's entrance to London was a moment of triumph.[1] He was lavished with money and given a banquet at the Guildhall (to which, pointedly, no members of the Commons were invited) and the City's fountains flowed with wine. But there was an unusual military edge to the celebration. Charles had an armed escort of 500 liverymen carrying swords, and the king's bodyguard of the Gentlemen Pensioners carried pistols. 'Drums beat, Trumpets sound, muskets rattle, cannons roar, flags display'd', went one account of the day.[2] Most threatening of all, Charles was accompanied by a band of several hundred swaggering reformadoes, now sometimes known to observers by a new name: 'Cavaliers'.

In fact, Charles had every reason to be optimistic. Since the Edinburgh 'Incident', he had given every concession he needed to placate Argyll and his Covenanters. Even Alexander Leslie, the Covenanter general, had been given an earldom, and Hamilton had been made a duke. Effectively, Charles had conceded defeat in Scotland. But this meant he could turn to England, where the new Royalist caucus in the Lords was actively obstructing the Junto. He also had new support in London, where the City elite were growing seriously disturbed by the explosion in popular religious radicalism.

As the procession left towards Whitehall, the evening flickered with the embers of bonfires and torches. It was a stunning spectacle: the king was showing off his strength. When Essex's commission as Lord General expired, Charles failed to renew it, and he dismissed the guard at Westminster and replaced it with one commanded by the moderate Earl of Dorset. The appointment reduced Parliament's protection from the Cavaliers, but also potentially threatened the crowds of Londoners who were now frequently seen in the Palace Yards, supporting the Junto. To Charles's supporters, they were crowds made up of the unruly rabble. But others took a different view. William Lilly, a well-known astrologer, later remembered the crowds to have been of people of 'a middle quality', neither the rich nor the very poor, 'either such as had public spirits', or those who 'lived a more religious life than the vulgar, and were usually called Puritans'. Very few of them, Lilly recalled, had hair longer than their ears, and so they were know 'by a nickname called Round-heads'.[3]

On 29 November, such a crowd gathered in the yards. They carried swords and staves, chanting 'No bishops! No bishops!' They pushed against the door of the Lords until the peers called upon the Earl of Dorset for help to disperse them. Dorset drew up his men and gave orders to shoot. The order was ignored, but the crowd dispersed anyway. The following day Dorset's men were removed by the Commons.

The Junto needed to tip the balance of power in the Lords back in their favour, so now the bishops became critical. If they (and, ideally also, those Catholics who still sat as peers) could be removed from the Lords, the Junto would be back in control.

On 10 December, a Londoners' petition of around 15,000 signatures against bishops and Catholic peers was due to be presented to Parliament by a huge procession of supporters. The king wanted it stopped so had the Lord Keeper send a guard of 200 halberdiers to Westminster. The Commons, infuriated at this breach of their privilege, dismissed the soldiers, and the petition – 24 yards long – was presented the next day, the anniversary, as it happens, of the original Root and Branch petition.

Again Charles fought back. He issued a proclamation against those who disturbed divine service – a clear sop to conservative opinion.[4] Then, two days later, he ordered absentee MPs and peers to return to Parliament by 12 January at the latest. The order was apparently sent to some 210 members of both Houses, the point being that those who'd stayed away of late were likely to be conservatives. The proclamation itself bore a striking iconography, for – unlike other royal proclamations – it incorporated the image of Hercules slaying the 'many-headed hydra'. The hydra was a symbol of rebellion, but it was also often specifically associated with the 'many-headed monster' of the populace. Not just rebellion, but *popular* rebellion. It was a not-so-subtle message to the socially conservative MPs and peers who'd bolted to their country estates, and who watched with horror as London fell into a whirlpool of mechanic preachers and crowd politics, and as iconoclasts tore up the fabric of parish churches. Come back to Westminster, it said, and slay the demotic beast.

The proclamation set the clock running. When time ran out on 12 January, all the moderate MPs would be back and Charles would have a majority in both Houses. It was now a matter of weeks. But through December, a London smarting under bad trade, fearful of the king's swaggering Cavaliers and shivering in the cold winter became radicalised as never before. The literate population of the capital was mostly pro-Parliamentarian, pro-Junto and increasingly antagonistic towards the bishops, especially as they were seen as blocking the reformist agenda. In order to galvanise popular support, on the 15th, the Junto managed to overturn the ban on printing the Remonstrance and soon the print version was available. Preachers continued to urge the people into action. 'No bishops, no popish lords' was the slogan on the streets.

On the 21st, the annual elections took place for the Common Council, London's governing body, and Puritans swept the board. This was a major problem for Charles, given the Council's role in managing the City's military defences, so he responded by trying to secure control of the Tower. He ordered its lieutenant to resign, and immediately replaced him with Colonel Thomas Lunsford, the swaggering veteran of the Newburn Fight. Even moderates – including the Royalist Lord Mayor – were shocked. The idea of Lunsford, a man who had somehow managed to accrue a reputation for cannibalism, commanding a huge arsenal within cannon's shot of the City was terrifying. The Commons responded with an appeal that he be removed. By the 23rd, there were reports that merchants were withdrawing their bullion from the Tower mint.[5]

At the same time, Charles published a response to the Remonstrance.[*] Drafted by Edward Hyde, the response played on the conservative

---

[*]He still argued the Remonstrance itself was unconstitutional.

fears about 'the irreverence of those many schismatics and separatists, wherewith of late this kingdom and this city abounds'. It was, though, strikingly conciliatory – at least to moderates. At Whitehall, Charles was being pulled in two very different directions at the same time. On the one hand, courtiers like Hyde were advocating moderation; on the other, those around the queen advocated confrontation. The response to the Remonstrance came from Hyde and the moderates, the appointment of Lunsford was driven by the hardliners. In these volatile December days, with order in the capital visibly crumbling, it was unclear which path the king was going to take.

Parliament took two days respite for Christmas. Londoners didn't.

Apprentices announced that they stood ready to match any coup launched by the Cavaliers.[6] The 26th, St Stephen's Day, was a Sunday, and it seems that the pulpits of the capital burned with fiery denunciations of Lunsford, that 'wicked, bloody, Colonel'.[7] Twice an agitated Lord Mayor rushed to Whitehall to warn the king of a rising by apprentices and 'other inferior persons'.[8] At Whitehall, the chants and shouts of the crowd must have been clearly audible to the king – a menacing ostinato against the cold December air. That day, he summoned his Privy Council, and told them he would back down: Lunsford would be removed.

But the news took time to get out. On the 27th, Monday, 'great companies' of Londoners marched down to Westminster to protest against the Bloody Colonel.[9] Told of his dismissal, they still didn't disperse. Instead, they vented their anger against the Lords and the bishops. The chant of 'No bishops! No bishops!' rang out once more across the Palace Yards. Peers were jostled as they tried to pass through the crowds; bishops were threatened with worse.

By happenstance, Lunsford himself was in Westminster Hall with a group of swordsmen, petitioning for pay and the chance to enlist for Ireland. Surrounded by a crowd of protesters, one of the swordsmen, Captain David Hyde, drew his weapon. He said, it was later alleged, 'he would cut the throats of those roundheaded dogs that bawled against bishops' and challenged 'who says no bishops?' 'We say no bishops!' came the reply.[10] At this, Lunsford and the soldiers drew their swords and cut at the protestors, chasing some of them into the Court of Wards (where a startled John Pym was sitting with a committee) and up the stairs into the Court of Requests. As they fled, the protestors – among whose number was the young polemicist John Lilburne and some club-wielding sailors – threw bricks and tiles from the walls back at the swordsmen. Lunsford had to wade into the muddy Thames to escape, finally jumping into a boat and slipping away. The Trained Bands, the local militia, were called out to keep order; the king, meanwhile, demanded military protection, having heard seditious talk under his very windows.

The next day's demonstration was bigger still. This time, the crowd focused on the Abbey, and on chanting against the bishops as they landed from the river. Boys from Westminster School, standing on the Abbey roof, pelted the protesters with stones. Others charged in with pistols and swords drawn. There were reports of shots fired. Lilburne was injured, but the tragic hero of the protesters was Sir Richard Wiseman, who fought sword in hand but took a fatal injury. In the Lords, the Royalist Lord Digby argued that Parliament was under the duress of the crowds, and was thus invalid, but with most of the bishops prevented from attendance his argument floundered for lack of support. Meanwhile, Charles issued a proclamation: the citizens must go home immediately. If not, he gave the Trained Bands the order to shoot to kill. They were, Charles decreed, 'by shooting with bullets or other-wise, to slay and kill such of them as shall persist in the tumultuary and seditious ways and disorders'.[11] The same day, Charles also ordered the construction of a barracks at Whitehall, to house the growing number of soldiers who – like Lunsford – were rallying to him.[12] It looked like a full-blown military confrontation was imminent in the capital.

On Wednesday the 29th, the crowd once more swelled through the morning, chanting at Parliamentarians as they entered the Palace of Westminster. That afternoon the king's soldiers watched as a great gathering of apprentices and Londoners filled King Street from Charing Cross south to Whitehall. They pushed against the royal palace, some demanding to speak to the king himself. Peers still tried to pass in their coaches, but found themselves pressed up with people, faces peering into the windows. The guardsmen were facing off against the crowd. Mud was thrown at them, so they drew swords and attacked. Insults and weapons flew. Swords flashed around, causing grievous wounds. The chant 'No bishops, no popish lords' echoed as the evening sky darkened.

That day, the nerve of 12 bishops snapped. The impetus came from Laud's old enemy John Williams, though behind him lay the hand of Digby. Williams had been promoted to the see of York by Charles that November, thus already earning him the taint of the turncoat from his erstwhile reformist allies. Now his actions were putting him in the camp of the more forward Royalists.

The 12 subscribed to a formal protest, arguing that any action by Parliament since the 27th was null. It was a monumental error, for if Parliament had been under duress during the ongoing London tumults, then had it not also been so during Strafford's trial? What about the early months of this Parliament, when a Scottish army had been camped on English soil? The implication of the bishops' protest, whether intended or not, was that the whole business of Parliament since the defeat against the Scots was unlawful. It was an argument for unravelling the whole of the reformist agenda going back to November 1640.

The Lords were outraged – suddenly swinging behind the Commons. The 12 bishops were impeached immediately, and most of them were hastily decanted to the Tower. The momentum was now firmly with the Junto. It was later said that the Junto considered this reversal to be a result of *digitus Dei* (the finger of God). The real cause, though, was *digitus populi*. The people of London had risen and put the Junto in a commanding position. Suddenly the king's options were much reduced.

On New Year's Eve, a crowd of around two hundred Londoners scrapped with the royal guardsmen outside Whitehall. There was a rumour that the queen herself was about to be impeached. The 12 January deadline for the return of MPs was approaching, and then – perhaps – Charles might be able to claw things back in both Houses. But that was nearly two weeks away, and who knows what the two united Houses might have achieved by then. So, at some point either on the 1st or the 2nd, he decided to strike back.

First, on the 2nd he brought a band of skilled loyalists closer into his government. Hyde preferred to remain as an unofficial adviser, but

Lord Falkland was made a secretary of state, joining Edward Nicholas in the role. These were men who had started the year as reformists but who had been pulled towards Charles by their fears of popular disorder and radicalism in the Church. There were even rather wild rumours that Pym himself was offered the position of Chancellor of the Exchequer in order to keep him quiet, though in the end the position was given to John Colepeper, another moderate.

But Charles made another move that day. He instructed the Attorney General, the Welshman Sir Edward Herbert, that when the Lords reconvened at one o'clock the following afternoon, he was to publicly accuse five MPs, and one peer, of treason.

It was all (mostly) above board. Nothing like the shadowy plot of kidnapping and murder that had been attempted so recently in Edinburgh. At the appointed time, Attorney General Herbert presented the articles of impeachment to the Lords. The men accused were John Pym, Denzil Holles, John Hampden, William Strode and Arthur Haselrig. The peer named was Lord Mandeville, a key ally of Pym, of course, and one of the brains behind the Junto, whose Chelsea mansion had been a regular meeting place for the opposition leadership since 1640. Of the five MPs, Pym's name was self-selecting. Hampden, too, occupied a talismanic position among the Junto. Holles had been at the centre of the disturbances of 1629, and while Strode and Haselrig were smaller fry, they had each proposed pieces of legislation that Charles hated: Strode the Triennial Act, Haselrig the attainder against Strafford.

At this stage, the king's men simply 'required' that the accused hand themselves over. The impeachment articles were printed; indeed, the whole process seemed deliberately designed to take place out in the open and with maximum publicity.

Two slight irregularities caused immediate consternation, though. The first was the fact the impeachment had been presented by the king – until now, impeachments had originated only in the Commons. The other was the seizure, without warning, of the accuseds' papers. And there was something else, too. For the day had seen a confluence of armed men at Whitehall, and one courtier was known to be trying to recruit loyal fighters from the Inns of Court down the road in London.

As things stood on the 3rd, it was doubtful whether the accused would ever be convicted, not least with 12 loyalist bishops now barred from the Lords. But, no matter the outcome, the proceedings were likely to entangle the Junto for some time, certainly until after the 12th. If this was a delaying tactic, it was a smart move by Charles.

For now, the accused were not handed over. Indeed, the Lords ordered their papers – sealed up by the king's agents – to be released again. But that night, something changed. Around 10 p.m., some 30 or 40 cannoneers were added to the garrison in the Tower, which had been under the command of the moderate Royalist John Byron since Lunsford's removal. As news spread, London went into panic. Men ran from door to door, calling people to stand their guard. Chains went across the roads and the gates were manned. But the feared massacre didn't come, and by midnight people were drifting back to bed. The following morning, though, London was taut. Shops stayed shut, and citizens made sure their halberds were ready.

At Westminster, MPs went nervously about their business, condemning the printing of the articles of impeachment as 'scandalous'. Around midday, they received word from the Earl of Essex, who was at Whitehall. It was a warning. He'd evidently seen preparations for something, he wasn't sure what. A group of armed men was milling about in one of the yards.

Then, just before 3 p.m., the king appeared.

Pacing out through the Great Court, he called, 'Follow me, my most loyal liege-men and soldiers', and left by the Palace Gate, onto King Street.[13] He had some 400 men or more in his wake, as well as his nephew Charles Louis, Elector Palatine.

Flagging down a passing coach, Charles gathered his winter cloaks, clambered on board and ordered it to proceed towards the Palace of Westminster.

But the street was muddy, and news travelled faster than the rumbling coach. A lookout posted by the French ambassador rushed to Westminster and told Nathaniel Fiennes, son of Lord Saye. Soon, the accused MPs had left their places in the Commons and fled, hiding in another part of the Westminster warren: the Court of King's Bench.

Now, Charles and around 80 of his men had crowded into the lobby outside St Stephen's Chapel. The soldiers, armed, stood there, allowing their pistols and swords to be seen by MPs through the open door. The rest – several hundred – waited outside in the cold.

Entering the chamber, attended only by his nephew, Charles ascended the Speaker's chair. 'I am sorry,' he announced, 'to have this occasion to come unto you.'[14]

He asked that the five men be handed over, pausing as he spoke, casting his eye around the House. He asked the Speaker where they were. Lenthall, usually such a reticent man, spoke on bended knee. 'May it please your Majesty, I have neither eyes to see, nor tongue to speak in this place, but as the House is pleased to direct me, whose servant I am here.' 'I do not see any of them,' said Charles, 'I think I should know them.' 'All my birds have flown,' he muttered.[15] The anger was showing on Charles's face. He began his withdrawal. As he left into the lobby, he heard cries of 'Privilege! Privilege!' echoing out from the chamber. By now, the accused had slipped out of King's Bench, down the steps to the river and were on a boat heading east, into the arms of London.

The next day, Charles tried again. This time, leaving Whitehall, he headed in the other direction, to the Guildhall to address a special meeting of the Common Council. Here, less than six weeks earlier, Charles had been feted at a grand banquet. Now, after the shock of what looked like a violent coup attempt against Parliament, he came almost as a hostile agent. His reception was a frosty as London's winter streets.

He still had some supporters here: after urging the City not to harbour the Five Members, Charles left the Guildhall to shouts from one side of 'God save the king!' But these were met with cries of 'Parliament! Privileges of Parliament!' Then, as he passed to the outer chamber of the Guildhall, he was confronted with a large crowd, all as one shouting, 'Privileges of Parliament!' His next stop was the house of the sheriff, for dinner. But as his coach passed through the streets, the shops were shuttered, with people standing in their doors, wrapped up against the cold and holding swords and halberds. As Charles ate, the sheriff's house was 'beset, and the streets leading unto it thronged with people, thousands of them', still all chanting 'Privileges of Parliament!'[16] As Charles left dinner, his coach was surrounded. At some point, as it picked its way through the streets back to Whitehall and safety, the ironmonger and pamphleteer Henry Walker managed to push through the crowd and throw a paper towards the king's coach. It contained a biblical text: a radical call to arms: *'To your tents, O Israel!'* When Charles's coach finally pushed down King Street and swung left into Whitehall Palace, his relief was there for all to see.

The following day, the Commons voted to adjourn to the Guildhall, for protection, where they would sit as a committee. That night the City fell once more into panic. There were rumours, possibly set off by a misfiring carbine among the Cavaliers lodging in Covent Garden, of a Royalist attack. There was a great cry in the streets, with banging on people's doors and shouts of 'Arm! Arm!' Thousands came out, armed with halberds, swords and makeshift weapons. Chains were thrown across the streets to stop cavalry attacks and the portcullises were lowered. Women gathered furniture to lob and to build barricades with. Cauldrons of boiling water were prepared to pour down on attackers.

The alarm was false, and the streets cleared quickly, but tension remained. The next day, the Commons put the City's armed forces effectively under the control of their allies in the Common Council. On the 10th, the London Trained Bands were placed under the command of the Puritan soldier Philip Skippon. Apprentices, mariners and the Southwark Trained Bands offered support. Here was a citizen army, ready to defend the privileges of Parliament, against the Cavaliers, even against the king himself.

It was all too much for Charles. The Royalist party he and his allies had been assembling in Parliament was now in pieces. His rash attempt to arrest the Five Members by force, threatening violence against Parliament when the impeachments were already in train, was a terrible blunder. That night, fearing the worst, he left for Hampton Court, abandoning Whitehall and the capital behind him. The next day, the Commons returned to Westminster, processing down the Thames in a vast convoy of decorated barges. As the boats, each carrying a group of MPs, pitched and listed against the flow of the river, musketeers saluted with volleys of gunshot, military bands played and martial music followed the triumphant Parliamentarians back to the House. Meanwhile, the eight companies of Skippon's Trained Bands marched down the Strand and Whitehall, carrying copies of the Protestation. It was the king's city no longer.

This had been a great uprising against an anointed king that had forced him from his capital, and London remained highly fractured. The street fighting had been a 'dismal thing to all men,' recalled one observer; this was the 'saddest and most tumultuous Christmas that in all my life I ever yet knew,' wrote another.[17] Irish refugees were mistaken for Catholic invaders, causing panic. 'I find all here full of fears and void of hopes,' one Kentishman wrote to a cousin back home. Families were at rancour, he said, gentlemen were 'never unanimous'. Nay, 'more I have heard foul language and desperate quarrelings even between old and entire friends'.[18] 'Moderate men are suspected,' wrote one correspondent, while 'violent men are thought saints'.[19]

The dread of armed confrontation grew. The previous four years of tension meant there was much military materiel stockpiled across the country. The biggest prize of all was Hull, where most of the small arms and artillery gathered for the wars against Scotland were being stored: 20,000 arms, 7,000 barrels of gunpowder, 120 pieces of field artillery.[20] On 11 January, Charles, in secret, appointed the loyalist Earl of Newcastle as governor of the town, and sent one of his men to secure it. The next day, Colonel Lunsford, Lord Digby and a band of Cavaliers tried to seize the much smaller magazine at Kingston, a few miles up the Thames, though they were foiled and the disgruntled Lunsford captured.

The queen, now, was crucial. Duly furnished with royal treasure, the plan was for her to seek alliances abroad. Denmark was an obvious potential ally. If the Danes could land troops, perhaps near a Hull that had been secured for the king, this would give Charles an unbeatable hand. But he had to get the queen safely out of the country. He withdrew from Hampton Court to the old royal castle of Windsor, where he called 14 loyalist peers to join him from Westminster. From there, he travelled with the queen to Dover, granting concessions to his opponents as he went, knowing he just had to get her out of England. He dropped the charges against the Five Members, and he finally agreed to exclude the bishops from the Lords. It didn't matter any more. His plan was to fight.

Mid-February, with the queen delayed by bad weather, Charles was sent the most odious bill of all: one that put control of the militia into the hands of men appointed by Parliament. This was a direct attack on the king's ancient prerogative, so he stalled, saying he needed to see the queen safely away before giving it due consideration. On the 21st, the Commons announced that they considered Charles's response as unsatisfactory as a flat denial. Two days later, the queen sailed, with Charles riding along the cliffs to watch as her ship faded out towards the horizon. A few days after that, what had become the Militia Ordinance passed the Lords. As with the previous summer, when Charles was in Scotland, an ordinance could be put into effect immediately, pending later approval from an absent king. But the implications this time were drastic. For Charles wasn't absent. He was still in regular communication with Parliament and had just assented to other bills. Instead, the argument had to be that he was not fit to rule. It was quite the statement.

Through the winter and spring of 1642, a cascade of petitions arrived at Westminster from across the country. They were often put together by county gentry, and passed around for signatures, before being carried to the capital by a suitably grand delegation. The wood-turner Nehemiah Wallington noted seeing one such party coming up Fish Street Hill, having crossed London Bridge, 'many hundreds of them on horseback with their protestations sticking in their hats and girdles'.[21] Most petitions were printed, giving them an even wider audience.[22] They called for accommodation between Parliament and king, but distinctly on the former's terms.

But Charles was far from without support himself. In fact, he was presenting an increasingly assured public face, and whatever his shortcomings might have been as king, he was becoming an adept party leader, helped by a visceral hatred of the upstart Pym among some of the people. One Londoner spoke for many when he announced that 'Pym was King Pym, and that rogue would set all the kingdom by the ears', that the Parliament were all 'fools' and their committees full of 'fishmongers'.[23]

Heading north, Charles's aim was to muster his followers at York, where he arrived on 19 March. But, by the end of the month, only

39 gentlemen had joined him. It seemed to one courtier that he was 'almost abandoned by all his subjects'.[24] Despondent, Charles toyed with leaving the country, perhaps going over to Ireland. In the end, he moved against Hull.

His attempt to take control of the strategically critical North Sea town had started to come unstuck. Parliament had discovered his secret plot to install the Earl of Newcastle as governor and had managed to get their own man, Sir John Hotham, to place a garrison there. On 23 April, Charles appeared outside the town gates, backed by some 300 horsemen and his eight-year-old son, James, Duke of York. But Hotham had directions from Parliament not to yield the magazine until they expressly ordered it. His men pulled up the drawbridges and shut the gates. The king, from outside the town walls, was forced into a humiliating negotiation with Hotham, but in the end – having had him proclaimed a traitor – Charles had no choice but to retreat. It was a great rebuff that was then replayed in a pamphlet debate that lasted well into the year: a public relations as well as a military disaster.

In June, the Junto issued 19 'propositions' which would form the basis of a political settlement. But they had little chance of winning over Charles. In fact, the terms constituted the most radical power grab by Parliament yet. The entire executive and judiciary were to be subject to Parliamentary control, with judges and officers no longer dismissible by the king. Religion was to be thoroughly reformed by the forthcoming Assembly of Divines. The children of Catholics were to be educated by Protestants, while Parliament was to control both the education and the marriages of the royal offspring.

The king's response to the Nineteen Propositions was drafted by Falkland and Colepeper. It was a masterpiece of conservative rhetoric.[25] With the help of his new supporters, Charles was finally becoming adept at managing public opinion, albeit mostly by talking to his natural supporters. Unlike his father, Charles – at least publicly – had come to accept the idea of an ancient English constitution originating in the people and not from the king. It was a balance between monarchy, aristocracy and democracy, represented by the three estates of King, Lords and Commons. But among these, the Commons, while 'an excellent conserver of liberty', was 'never intended for any share in government, or the choosing of them that should govern'.

The *Answer* also played strikingly on fears of the world turned upside down, and the spectres of famous medieval rebels. If the monarch fell, so would the Church, and then 'the common people [would] set themselves up for themselves, call parity and independence liberty', they would 'destroy all rights and properties, all distinctions of families and merit', and so 'this splendid and excellently distinguished form of government [would] end in a dark, equal chaos of confusion, and the long line of our many noble ancestors in a Jack Cade or a Wat Tyler'.

At heart, the Royalists were claiming that they were the defenders of the ancient constitution: the Parliamentarians were the ones trying to make innovations in government. It was a palpable hit: the opposition had moved from trying in 1640 to remove 'illegal' aspects to Charles's rule to making lasting reforms to the government, most particularly by claiming Parliamentary control of the executive and the armed forces. But royalism as it was emerging in 1642 was also strikingly socially conservative, founded on worries about social upheaval, about ordinary people questioning their betters, about mechanic preachers and crowds of chanting Londoners. And such fears were well grounded. Popular petitioning, iconoclasm and mass protests had been a constant feature of English life since 1640. By 1642, not only was the avalanche of pamphlets showing no signs of easing – some 4,038 titles survive from 1642, more than any single year for more than a hundred years – but there were deeper signs of something going seriously amiss. Trade was at a standstill and industry was in severe difficulty. In community, workplace and church, old rules of deference were straining. At Christmas, two men disrupted services at Exeter Cathedral by demanding to hear dance music; when someone threatened to call the Dean, they responded 'Let Mr Dean go shit.'[26] Enclosures were pulled down in Yorkshire, reported the gentlewoman Margaret Eure, by villagers led by a piper and fed with cakes and ale.[27] And some were questioning the king himself. In July, the radical MP Henry Marten argued that 'though the king be king of the people of England, yet he is not master of the people of England'.[28]

The king's *Answer to the Nineteen Propositions* itself provoked a radical riposte. It came from the pen of Henry Parker, son of a rich family from the Sussex downs, whose *Observations upon Some of His Majesty's Late Answers and Expresses* hit London's bookstands at the end of July. Parker understood that the central question was now not about personalities or policies, it was about the origins of power: of sovereignty. Where, he asked, did ultimate authority lie? 'Power,' Parker wrote, 'is originally inherent in the people.' And it was Parliament who properly represented those people. If the Nineteen Propositions only implied Parliamentary sovereignty, Parker's *Observations* announced it out loud. Moreover, Parker reframed the emerging Parliamentarian ideology away from historical justification in the ancient constitution, towards justification by natural law. '[T]he paramount law that shall give law to all human laws whatsoever,' he wrote, 'is *salus populi*.' The same justification, that necessity could override existing human-made laws, had underpinned absolutist theory, allowing kings to act beyond the law. In the absolutists' hands the king was the ultimate arbiter and protector of the people's safety, of the public good. To Parker, the people's safety was best protected by the people's representatives, that is, Parliament. By summer 1642, not only were there two distinctive political ideologies at play, but the Parliamentarian side were starting to argue – grounded in a theory of popular sovereignty – for wresting control of the executive away from the king.[29]

The warm months were spent jockeying for support in the country. Great 'musters' for Parliament took place in a number of counties under the Militia Ordinance, with thousands of men turning out with arms and horses; Charles responded by activating the old medieval device of 'Commissions of Array', which called people out to join him to defend the realm. It was a long-lapsed mechanism, and many considered it of dubious legality. The commissions were also in Latin, which hardly helped. But some musters under the Array did take place. And where both opposing sides were hoping to take control of the same strategic town or arsenal, there were moments of confrontation, even if both sides were reluctant to fire the first shot. In July, in Manchester, a skirmish broke out that resulted in at least one death. The Midlands was said to be 'like a cockpit one spurring against another'.[30] Another scrap took place near Street in Somerset, followed by a confrontation on the Mendips in which the Marquess of Hertford, attempting to recruit for the king, was opposed by a large gathering of 12,000 Somerset men and was forced to retreat.

The navy backed Parliament: both king and Junto tried to get its support, but it was the latter's man, the Earl of Warwick, who got to the Downs first, and it was Warwick the sailors wanted anyway. Most towns, too, were Parliamentarian, although many were split. Oxford and Cambridge universities were Royalist, while the towns themselves supported Parliament. Similarly, in many cathedral cities, the townsmen were Parliamentarian, while the clergy in the close were Royalist. In Canterbury, one Royalist minister worried 'that we can hardly look upon one another in charity'.[31] Some places tried to avoid taking sides: the Isle of Wight, in August, simply declared itself neutral, while Lincolnshire and Staffordshire went so far as to raise men to defend the county borders from all comers. Bulstrode Whitelocke, a lawyer who had been involved in the Strafford trial, was horrified by it all. 'It is strange to note how we have insensibly slid into this beginning of a civil war, by one unexpected accident after another, as waves of the sea.' We 'scarce know how,' he lamented, 'but from paper combats ... we are now come to the question of raising forces, and naming a General and officers of our army.'[32]

The drift to war was shocking and unfathomable. If only Charles had defeated the Scots; if only the Irish rebellion hadn't broken out; if only the king hadn't launched his ham-fisted coup against the Five Members. Charles's own unwillingness to part with his prerogatives without a fight or a plot didn't help, but then isn't it also unfair to expect someone brought up to expect divinely ordained rights to power to give that up freely? More to the point, the coming war had deeper causes. It was born out of fundamental disagreements over faith and government: about religious conformity and about the proper role of Parliament in the constitution, and, of course, also about the monarch: whether they could override human laws and if they did, could the people legitimately resist.

Those disagreements had been played out in a world of rising literacy, particularly among the middle sort of people and the gentry, and particularly in London. The people had been crucial. At key moments, the opposition of a significant segment of the English population – whether their reluctance to mobilise against the Scots, their willingness to elect opposition MPs twice in 1640, the petitions that reached Westminster, the demonstrations against Strafford, the iconoclasm of 1641 and, most of all, the great popular uprising in London in the winter of 1641–2 – had prevented Charles from keeping control. The breakdown wasn't just about mistakes by politicians and the king. It was about the politicisation of the English population.

Now that population was facing the prospect of war. The city militia had, through the spring, been conducting large public musters, sometimes attended by Essex in a sparkling new gilt coach. Then, in July, Parliament voted to create a volunteer army in London, with Essex as its commander. More musters followed the creation of this new force, in the Artillery Grounds and Tothill Fields, with Essex again in attendance in his coach, where he was mobbed by the adoring crowds.

Charles's commander, on the other hand, was to be the Earl of Lindsey. A man with a courtier's good manners, Lindsey had fought together with Essex in the Low Countries, making him a smart choice, for he knew his enemy well. The king also gave command of the cavalry to his own nephew Prince Rupert of the Rhine, younger son of Elizabeth Stuart and the late Prince Frederick. Rupert was a thuggish toff whose youth was spent with the brutal German war raging around him. He was entitled, petulant and had a nasty violent streak, but he had also grown into an effective soldier. Even so, Charles's decision to give Rupert authorisation to act without orders from Lindsey was sure to store up trouble.

In August, Charles issued the fateful summons. On the 22nd of that month he would be at Nottingham, where he would raise his standard, calling his loyal subjects to join him to put down what he was terming the rebellion of the traitorous Earl of Essex. The standard was duly unfurled from a pole, 'like a maypole', in the rain, and it was taken down shortly afterwards. To his cause, a hostile observer wrote, came only 'the scum of the country'.[33] The king moved on, across the Midlands, towards Shrewsbury. Here, in Cheshire, Shropshire, Herefordshire and in Wales, there proved a bounteous seam of loyalists. 'You shall meet with no enemies,' he told his gathering army, 'but traitors', who were 'most of them Brownists, Anabaptists and atheists, such who desire to destroy both Church and state'.[34]

That same month, there was an explosion of popular anger around Colchester and in the nearby countryside aimed especially at Sir John Lucas, a respected scholar of law, philosophy and science, fluent in Latin, Greek and Hebrew, none of which made him a pleasant land-lord. The violence spread, fanning out across the Stour Valley and beyond. Gentry houses were attacked and plundered, Catholics and Royalists sought out. In Oxfordshire, meanwhile, there was talk of countryfolk uttering that 'the gentry have been our masters a long time and now we may chance to master them'.[35] Royalist fears of social revolution were only confirmed.

On 9 September, the Earl of Essex marched out of London at the head of his new army; his own coffin as part of the baggage train. By the 23rd, his army of horse, pike and musket was in Worcestershire. Here, an advance party led by Colonel John Brown ran into a rearguard under Rupert and his brother Prince Maurice at Powick Bridge, over the River Teme. The engagement was small, short and sharp, and the Parliamentarians were routed. Essex still occupied Worcester, though, where his soldiers smashed statues in the cathedral, pulled down the organ and pissed in the font. On 13 October, the king left Shrewsbury, following the Severn to Bridgnorth, swinging south-east towards Warwickshire. On the 19th, Essex left Worcester and pushed east, aiming to put himself between the king and London. The weather was wet, and the thick fields of Warwickshire bogged down with mud. There were two large armies trudging through the Midland country-side, but neither knew where the other was.

By 22 October, the king's army was at Edgecote, on the River Cherwell near Banbury, north of Oxford. That day, foragers of the two armies stumbled across one another at the tiny village of Wormleighton. Royalist scouts were sent out and found Essex's army near Kineton, at the foot of a sharp escarpment called Edgehill. The Royalist army was ordered to deploy on the hill, ready to engage the next day.

On the 23rd, both sides slowly drew up for battle: infantry of pike and musket in the centre, horse on the flanks. By the middle of the afternoon they were ready, though not before Prince Rupert had fallen out with Lindsey, technically his superior officer, over tactics. Charles picked kinship over the chain of command, and Lindsey resigned to join his regiment as a colonel.

The battle started with a loud exchange of cannon fire which did little damage but filled the field with acrid smoke and thunderous noise. The Royalist cavalry on the flanks succeeded in scattering their enemies, and in the centre the king's infantry pressed forward down the hill, firing their muskets before falling on the enemy 'pell mell': that is – using the butts of their weapons as clubs. Then, Essex launched his infantry into a counter-assault, pushing hard with pike and gun against the Royalist centre. In the chaos, Lindsey was killed. But neither army was able to press the advantage. The king's standard was lost, then later recaptured, and as a frosty nightfall came, more than a thousand men lay dead, with no decisive outcome.

It was the king, though, who was able to fulfil his major objective, which was to commence a march on London. Essex's force pulled back to Warwick, but he knew that if the king could get to the capital, the Parliamentarian cause could be decapitated, so he had to move fast. On the 27th, Charles was at Banbury. A few days later both Houses of Parliament had agreed to ask for negotiations. But Charles reached Reading, where he rebuffed any such talk. Then, the king's army marched on to Brentford, a small town just nine miles from London. Rupert was given orders to attack.

By now, Essex had raced back to London, travelling quickly along the old Roman Watling Street. Denzil Holles – who had fought bravely at Edgehill – and Lord Brooke were sent to defend Brentford. On 11 November, Charles wrote to Parliament telling them he was ready to discuss peace, but at the same time he asked Rupert to clear Brentford of its defenders. So, on the 12th, Rupert's soldiers attacked relentlessly through a thick autumn fog. The red-coated Parliamentarian defenders fought hard but were pushed back. Rupert then let his men loose to plunder the town.

London was terrified. Musket fire was audible seven miles away in Chelsea, where Essex had hastily mustered his army. The cannons could be heard at Westminster. News of the defeat at Brentford shocked the City. As Edward Hyde later remembered, the alarm 'came to London, with the same dire yell as if the army were entered into their gates'.[36] Immediately, Essex ordered all remaining troops around London, and any citizens with able bodies and equipment, to rendezvous at the tiny village of Turnham Green. There were cannons on London's gates and in the streets, manned, with fuses lit. Trenches were being dug on the approaches, including Hyde Park Corner and St James's Park. Warships had sailed up to Westminster and sat at anchor outside Parliament.[37]

Essex slept that night at Hammersmith, around a mile from Turnham Green. By eight o'clock on the morning of the 13th, a Sunday, some 20,000 or more had gathered: soldiers, militia, citizens, apprentices, members of both Houses. They were concentrated in the large open common between the village of Chiswick on the river, and the enclosed fields of Acton to the north. It was, wrote the Devonshire diarist Walter Yonge, 'as brave an army as ever was in Christendom', but it wasn't just an army.[38] It was a mass mobilisation of Londoners. Once more, the people of the capital stood ready to resist their king. The professional soldiers rallied the force: Philip Skippon was one, calling out to his men, 'Come my boys, my brave boys! Let us pray heartily and fight heartily.' Another was Essex himself, who rode between the troops, shouting to encourage them. They responded with cries of 'Hey for old Robin!'[39] His popularity hadn't waned one bit since the musters of the summer.

The field of battle was constricted by enclosures in the north and by the walled gardens of Chiswick House to the south. In all, Essex's lines were perhaps just under a mile in breadth. His artillery, protected by earthworks, was trained on the roads that traversed the field.

A few hundred yards away, on slightly higher ground, stood the Royalists, a much smaller army of around 12,000. Their left flank was weak but protected by musketeers lurking in the hedges of Acton. At first, Essex sent four regiments of foot and two of horse towards that northern flank, but any attack would likely have been fraught with danger, so they were pulled back. The Royalists, though, with an army fatigued after fighting the day before, and drowsy after the previous night of celebration and plunder, were even less inclined to strike first.

Shortly before 10 a.m., a Royalist emissary appeared in front of the Parliamentarian lines. He carried a letter from the king. The messenger was ushered to meet Essex, but as the general read the letter, the Royalist artillery opened fire. As a report put it, 'the hope and harmony of peace was lost in the loud voice of a cannon', with one ball 'whizzing by his Excellency's ear'.[40] Royalist horse, meanwhile, were sallying near the Parliamentary infantry, firing carbines while the latter responded with musket fire. In the afternoon, the Parliamentarian artillery finally started up, with two cannons being fired a total of 14 times at the Royalist ranks.

By this point a crowd of spectators had gathered behind the Parliamentarian lines, some bringing food and drink for the soldiers. A hundred carts full of 'good things' streamed out of London and reinforced Essex's men, who were never short of roast beef and hot pies. The contrast with the undersupplied Royalists was marked. Still there was no attack.

As the afternoon slipped away and the long shadows of evening encroached on the Green, the Royalists finally made their decision.

First, half of their horse pulled back, then the artillery train, then the infantry. A thousand musketeers were left to cover the retreat, relieved by the dragoons. Then, last of all, went the remainder of the horse. In the face of the massed ranks of soldiers and Londoners, the king's army had shrunk back from a fight. Once they were gone, Essex's men began their return to London.

The king had failed to get the quick victory he needed.

PART THREE

1642–58
Parchment in the Fire

10

The Sword of His Vengeance

Between three and four in the afternoon on 1 January 1643, the sound of cavalry was heard once more on the battlefield of Edgehill.

With the sun lowering in the sky, three passing countrymen were startled to see a troop of horse thundering towards them at full speed. For a heart-stopping moment, it looked like the horses would charge straight into them. Then, just like that, the troop sunk into the earth, and disappeared. Terrified, and with night approaching, the three men decided they would go no further than the village of Kineton.

The hard-bitten Warwickshire countryfolk didn't believe the men's tall tale of ghostly cavalry, and the next morning the three went on their way. But a few nights later, the doubting villagers were woken by strange noises: the screams of dying men and cries of revenge. Drums rattled and trumpets wailed. Kineton's living cowered in their houses, save for a daring few who peered out of their windows. In the dark they saw horsemen riding through the village.

The next day, at midnight, the drums, horses and men appeared again, in full battle array. They fought out a hideous night battle, until dawn broke when, 'in the twinkling of an eye', they vanished.

Some of the villagers were so terrified that they left. Others consulted 'learned men', who suggested that there might be unburied corpses on the battlefield, whose unquiet souls were haunting it each night. A search was made, bodies were found and buried. Word reached the king at Oxford, who sent six men to investigate. They saw the night battles for themselves, and even recognised a number of the apparitions: comrades lost just weeks earlier.

Meanwhile, the story had reached London, where a pamphlet was produced describing the ghostly night Battle of Edgehill. It prayed of

God, 'with love, fear, and obedience', that he called back his destroying Angel, 'and with the hand of his mercy, sheath up the sword of his vengeance, which his wrath by our multiplying sins caused him to draw against us, unto our fears and terrors'.[1]

But God wasn't listening.

England was divided. Political crisis had escalated and the country's differences would have to be settled on the battlefield. Now that the king's initial plan to take London had floundered in the face of mass opposition at Turnham Green, both sides were digging in for a longer conflict than anyone wanted.

Broadly, the king was strong in the north, the west and in Wales; Parliament in the south and east. But this isn't the whole story: Puritan towns in Royalist regions, like Bolton, Manchester or Dorchester supported Parliament. Even individual families could be torn asunder. When the son of Susan Feilding, Countess of Denbigh, declared for Parliament, she wrote to him trying to persuade him to change his mind. His refusal to support the king, she told him, was more painful to her than childbirth: 'I do more travail with sorrow for the grief I suffer for the ways that you take,' she wrote, 'than I ever did to bring you into this world.'[2] London was split, though control for now lay with Parliament. Hold of the capital was both a blessing and a curse. A grumbling hive of disorder and opinions, it was hard to control, yet it boasted a huge wealth of manpower and money, not to mention the lion's share of the English print trade. It was, though, also a great target: if the Royalists could take London, they might break the Parliamentarian war effort at one blow.

The aristocracy were mostly Royalist, though with some major exceptions like Warwick, Mandeville (now the Earl of Manchester) and Northumberland. In fact, fully a quarter of Charles's old Privy Council ended up as Parliamentarians.[3] Beneath them, the gentry were more evenly divided. In many areas they were instinctively Royalist: it was said because they hated the common people more than they hated tyranny. 'How many of the nobility and gentry were contented to serve arbitrary designs,' asked the radical Parliamentarian Edmund Ludlow, 'if they might have leave to insult over such as were of a lower order?'[4] That said, in parts of the country, notably the south-east, the gentry were largely Parliamentarian.

Beneath the gentry we have less idea, though there were evidently real divides and genuinely heartfelt opinions. Some thought the middling sort were more likely to support Parliament. The Puritan Lucy Hutchinson remembered how most of the Nottinghamshire gentry were Royalist, but 'most of the middle sort, the able substantial freeholders, and the other commons, who had not their dependence upon the malignant nobility and gentry', were Parliamentarian. In Gloucestershire, meanwhile, the king's support was alleged to come from the rich and the 'needy multitude' who depended on them, while 'the yeomen, farmers, clothiers, and the whole middle rank of people' supported Parliament.[5]

There were plenty of members of the middling sort who supported the king, though, and statements such as those just quoted should certainly not be understood as implying the war was neatly divided on a class basis. Rather, they showed that people were taking notice of the apparently newfound political consciousness of the middle sort of people. They were evidently acting independently of their superiors, and this was worthy of comment.

More to the point, the suggestion by some on the Parliamentarian side that those below the middle ranks who followed the king did so simply out of dependence on the rich should be treated very carefully. The reality was that each side's war effort relied on support from across the social spectrum. This wasn't just a mobilisation of the rich followed blindly by the poor. When London, for example, built up its defences against a potential Royalist attack, the work was done by thousands of ordinary women and men from the capital: a vast, collective project. Women, sniffed a Royalist some years later, 'From ladies down to oyster wenches / Laboured like pioneers in trenches.'[6] In the end, perhaps around a quarter of adult males would fight – and they were supported by everyone else, men and women. Women, indeed, would look after soldiers, and would work on civil defences, among so much else. Sometimes they would even fight in battles. Some donned men's clothes and joined the armies, or fought to defend towns, such as the woman at the siege of Gloucester who took potshots at the enemy from the city's defences.[7] The war affected everyone, and everyone took part in one way or another.

The Civil War wasn't a class struggle. It was a clash of ideologies, as often as not *between* members of the same class. The Royalists were anti-Puritan, they stood by the old hierarchies in the Church, notably bishops. They were nostalgic for 'Merry England' before it was ruined by Puritans moping at their books. Parliamentarians claimed they were fighting for God and the constitution; Royalists did, too, but added loyalty to the king and the fact their Parliamentarian enemies were cuckolds. In fact, they delighted in offending their Puritan foes. 'Come out you Cuckold', challenged one of their banners, in particular reference to the Earl of Essex's notorious marital difficulties. Another showed a Cavalier soldier brandishing a sword and an erect penis, with the motto 'Ready to use both'.

But despite such irreverence, the Royalists were also the side of order: to them, the greatest threat to the realm came from upstart Parliamentarians, from the crowd and from mechanic preachers. Royalism was born in response to the social changes that brought crowds onto the streets of London, brought streams of petitions to Parliament, and drew preaching from ordinary men and women. It was a reaction to all these things. It gelled with the old idea that Puritanism was democratical. Royalism stood for tradition, community and the old hierarchies.

Parliamentarians worried less about the crowd or the mechanic preachers. Or, at least, they were less fearful for now, as eventually splits would emerge among the Roundheads – as they were increasingly called by the enemies – over the role to be allowed to the people in religion and government. At the start of the war, they drew strength from popular preaching. They had explicitly appealed to the people with the great Remonstrance of 1641, had benefited from crowd action against Strafford in spring 1641, and against the Cavaliers in the winter of 1641–2, and at Turnham Green.

They were motivated by religious fears, too, not of Puritanism, but of Laudianism and Catholicism, the both of which they considered of a piece. Parliamentarians were also, of course, more likely to be Puritans, or at least sit on the other side of the great cultural divide from those who supported the Book of Sports. Not everyone fitted this pattern: Thomas Challoner was said to be as far from a Puritan as east from west, Henry Marten 'as far from a Puritan as light from darkness', yet both would prove radical adherents to the Parliamentarian cause.[8] However, the correlation between Puritanism and adherence to the Roundheads was strong. Parliament's supporters were those, said the Puritan Richard Baxter, 'that used to talk of God, and heaven, and Scripture, and Holiness', while the Royalists were those who liked to game and drink, and those who were 'for the King's Book, for dancing and recreations on the Lord's days'.[9] To Lady Elizabeth Felton, another Parliamentarian, she chose that side because 'the most religious, and conscientious men amongst the nobility, gentry, and commonality do generally take that way'.[10] The implication that choosing sides was something one did based on personal piety rather than considerations of the social hierarchy was itself very Puritan.

We should not, though, ignore the constitutional side to the Parliamentarian cause. The Roundheads were not democrats – they didn't want to extend the franchise to all men and let alone to all women. But they were anti-absolutist. They tended to have a stronger belief in the Common Law, they wanted regular Parliaments and believed the king could not rule beyond the law. They believed there should not be taxation without consent from the people. By 1642, they had evolved into a movement that was challenging established hierarchies in Church and state, claiming a much greater role for Parliament in the running of the government than had existed before. The Royalists thought their enemies were populist and revolutionary, and, as much as many leading Roundheads tried to protest otherwise, their antagonists had a point.

The horrors of Edgehill had led to a change on the Parliamentarian side. Since the king's attempted arrest of the Five Members in January 1642, the Junto had reigned supreme at Westminster, but now a group started to emerge that wanted to push for peace. It included the Earl of Northumberland and the opposition stalwart Denzil Holles, who had been one of those who held the Speaker down in his chair in 1629, one of the Five Members in 1642, but who had looked on in horror as Prince Rupert wiped out his regiment at Brentford.

Negotiations between king and Parliament began, but as yet neither side was willing to give much ground, so the spring brought new manoeuvres in the field. The Royalists had three major concentrations of force: in Oxford, where the king had established his headquarters; in the west, under the experienced Sir Ralph Hopton; and in the north, led by William Cavendish, Earl of Newcastle. Entering his fifties in 1643, Newcastle was kindly faced, urbane, intelligent, fabulously rich, and with – it was later said – 'the misfortune to be somewhat of a poet'.[11] He was an astonishingly accomplished equestrian, though as yet unproven as a soldier.

The Royalists' aim was to secure territory, for land meant a supply of soldiers and money; and at least to begin with they enjoyed success. In the west, Hopton scored victories over Sir William Waller, a man he still considered his friend. Late that spring, Waller would write to Hopton lamenting this 'war without an enemy', in which 'We are both upon the stage and must act those parts that are assigned us in this tragedy.' 'Let us do it in a way of honour and without personal animosities,' he wrote, for 'Whatsoever the issue be, I shall never willingly relinquish the dear title of your most affectionate friend'.[12]

In the north, meanwhile, the queen had landed in Bridlington on 22 February, almost a year to the day since she'd sailed off from the White Cliffs of Dover. She'd spent the time, depending on which of her enemies you listened to, collecting 'pretty toys to destroy the Protestants', or giving Charles cuckold's horns.[13] In reality, she'd gathered ships, money and troops.

Elsewhere in Yorkshire, the gallant Sir Thomas Fairfax had secured Leeds for Parliament. But in the rest of the county, the position was looking increasingly promising for the king. In the Midlands, the aim was to clear a passage for the queen to march south from Yorkshire. The Royalists were stoutly resisted by Lord Brooke, who stormed Stratford-upon-Avon after an engagement on Welcombe Hill, but then was shot in the eye and killed while besieging the old cathedral city of Lichfield. The advantage in the Midlands then swung back to the Royalists with a sharp and bloody fight at Hopton Heath, near Stafford. Now Rupert could be sent north, although he met brief but tough resistance from the growing manufacturing town of Birmingham, which he burned to ash. In Newark, meanwhile, Royalist forces were gathering, watched carefully by the newly formed Eastern Association army, raised out of the Puritan heartlands of the east and led by the Earl of Manchester.

Soon the Earl of Essex was menacing Oxford, having marched his army up the Thames Valley from London. Despite suffering from sickness and desertions, his army was able to take Reading and then the tiny but strategically useful market town of Thame, not far from Oxford itself. Rupert was recalled from his northern mission, and at this point one of the Parliamentarian officers defected, bringing intelligence that £21,000 was being carried to Essex's army. Rupert was dispatched to intercept the money, but local people rushed a warning to Essex. The earl sent a detachment out, and a sharp cavalry action followed at Chalgrove Field in the plains below the Chilterns at which – although Rupert was unable to take the cash – the Parliamentarians were defeated and John Hampden, the hero opponent of Ship Money, was wounded. Six days later, he died. It was a body blow to the cause.

The queen, meanwhile, managed to reach Newark, then Oxford, but the Royalist forces in the east were shadowed and resisted by the troops of the Eastern Association. Led by the Earl of Manchester (formerly Lord Mandeville), this was a well-oiled Parliamentarian military organisation that drew its resources from the wealthy and Puritan east of England. Manchester's forces took Peterborough and won a minor victory in an engagement at Grantham under Oliver Cromwell, who led an effective body of cavalrymen drawn from the devout yeoman farmers of East Anglia. Nonetheless, this success was small comfort compared to the defeat inflicted on the northern Parliamentarians by Newcastle at Adwalton Moor, which led to the fall of Leeds and Bradford and forced the Fairfaxes, Sir Thomas and his father, Lord Ferdinando, to retreat to Hull. Things could have been even worse had not a plan by Sir John Hotham and his son to betray Hull to the king been discovered at the last minute (they were later beheaded for their treachery). Then, in July, the news got yet more dismal for the Parliamentarians. In the west, the friends Hopton and Waller fought a bloody battle on Lansdowne outside Bath; Waller's forces managed to pull back, but they were then smashed on the windswept Wiltshire hill of Roundway Down. This allowed Rupert to lay siege to the critical port of Bristol, defended by Nathaniel Fiennes. Bowing to the inevitable, Fiennes surrendered. From the comfort of Westminster,

William Prynne accused Fiennes of cowardice, so the young soldier was court-martialled and sentenced to death, though Essex ensured he was pardoned.

The defeats set off a political crisis in Westminster. MPs split, marching Londoners crowded into the Palace Yard. With the emergence of Denzil Holles's peace group, the Junto had evolved into a 'war party', comprised of many of those who had conspired with the Scots in 1640. Essex was a leading figure, plus the earls of Warwick and Manchester and Viscount Saye in the Lords, with Pym, Hampden and Henry Vane the younger, the thoughtful son of the king's former secretary of state. Vane, who had spent his early adulthood in Massachusetts, lay at the more hardline fringe of the war party, where he was joined by men like Arthur Haselrig and the gregarious radical Henry Marten. Born to privilege in a golden-stoned Oxford town house, Marten was certainly no Puritan. A notorious *bon vivant*, he was hated by Charles, who considered him a whoremaster and an 'ugly rascal'.[14] But in the Commons, Marten's flamboyant wit leavened debates and won admiration even from many of his opponents, who may have disapproved of his increasingly republican politics, but still enjoyed his ever-quotable speeches.

Marten was an outlier, though. Most of the war group sat on more moderate ground than he did. They were not republicans, nor did they countenance anything like the abolition of the monarchy. Instead, they wanted total victory over the Royalists in the field, which in turn would allow thorough reform in both Church and state. By late summer, the stand-off between them and Holles's peace group was becoming very difficult. On 7 August – a Monday – the Commons discussed proposals for peace that had been passed to them by the Lords, and which they hoped would form the basis of a settlement with Charles. As MPs debated, the City of London's Common Council, meeting at the Guildhall, organised for a petition to be presented to Parliament against peace, backed by a significant pro-war rally. The Commons rejected the proposal, but only by a slim margin. Then, the next afternoon – Tuesday – Westminster saw an anti-war rally of several hundreds, led by City women wearing white silk ribbons in their hats as a symbol of peace. Some carried babes in arms, 'to soften the hardest hearts'. They swelled around Parliament, haranguing pro-war MPs, although despite at least one guard drawing his sword, it was said that there was 'no hurt done that day'.

On Wednesday, though, things escalated dramatically. The marchers returned, and this time the estimated numbers went well into the thousands. They cried out for peace, they cried out for their slain and imprisoned husbands. They presented a petition to the Commons, via the Earl of Holland, addressing them as 'the physicians that can restore this languishing nation' and 'our bleeding sister kingdom of Ireland'. They asked for a political settlement, for peace, for a restoration of trade. The House offered a reply, assuring the women that they were indeed desirous of peace, and asking them to leave. But it was not enough. Unsatisfied, the petitioners pressed against the door of the House. According to one report, they threw most abuse at those with short hair, the sign of a radical Roundhead, and threatened to hurl the pro-war leaders into the Thames. In the scuffle that ensued, troops waded in, some hitting out at the women with the flats of their swords, some firing blank shots from their muskets. There were casualties, and reports suggested some women were killed, while many others were carted off to prison.

The response from the men who observed the peace march of 9 August 1643 was one of shock. It was monstrous, testament to a world gone mad. According to the Venetian ambassador, one of the leaders was 'a most deformed Medusa, or Hecuba, with an old rusty blade by her side'. The women were 'Oyster wives, and other dirty and tattered sluts,' said one newspaper. '[S]ome say 500 of them were whores,' said another; 'these women,' spluttered a third, 'were for the most part, Whores, Bawdes, Oyster-women, Kitchenstuffe women, Beggar women, and the very scum of the Suburbs, besides abundance of Irish women'.[15] But however the peace marchers might be disparaged by the men, the fact was that with husbands off fighting, trade disrupted and taxes rising rapidly, the war was hurting.

As the winter of 1643 drew closer, Charles was keen to draw Essex into a formal battle before the inevitable bad weather made campaigning impossible. He sallied out of Oxford, and on 20 September the two large armies clashed in the thick hedges south-west of Newbury. Spoils were about even; again the decisive victory had eluded the king. Among his losses was Lord Falkland, the charming, urbane moderate, who – utterly despondent at the war – walked deliberately into a hail of musket fire. Meanwhile, in the east, Oliver Cromwell and Thomas Fairfax, fighting together for the first time, won a resounding victory at Winceby, allowing Hull to be relieved.

In Westminster, Pym's health was starting to fail. He had lost his appetite and was feeling nauseous.[16] At some point, he began to suffer bouts of fainting. His allies feared the worst and wanted to know what would become of him. Late in November, without Pym's knowledge, one of his friends secretly took some of his urine to the astrologer William Lilly for a prognosis. Lilly's calculations were scant comfort. Pym, he thought, was dying.

As the winter nights grew longer and as Pym's life slipped away, he at least could look back on his last great project, which was just about to come to fruition. As peace marches had rocked Westminster, Pym had been working on a new treaty with the Scots. In return for a decisive move towards Presbyterianism in the English Church, the Scots would provide an army to help defeat the king. The Solemn League and Covenant, as it was to be known, was the alliance that would save Pym's cause. But it was to be his epitaph. On 8 December, he died, to be buried with considerable ceremony in Westminster Abbey. What this meant for the cause he'd been so instrumental in guiding, nobody yet knew.

With the Scots gathering their forces for another march into England, the Royalists had made their own deal to bring in reinforcements, in this case from Ireland. These were royal soldiers, released from other duties by a truce Charles agreed with the Irish rebels. They had started arriving in Cheshire in November, and Parliamentarian propaganda eagerly portrayed them as murderous papists.

The two sides were now consolidating. From 1643, they both started using a new tax, the 'excise', on consumption of basic commodities such as salt, meat and beer. The Parliamentarians, meanwhile, were developing a sophisticated – though deeply unpopular – system of local government and taxation, central to which were local governing bodies called 'County Committees'. As the costs of war ballooned, and as volunteers became much harder to attract, territory needed to be squeezed for money, horses and soldiers. It was unattractive work, and the committee men tended to be of lower social status than the traditional local elite: 'all rogues', 'men not born to it', 'men of sordid condition' or 'men of weak fortunes, weaker wits, and yet less merit'.[17]

Charles, by now, had summoned a Royalist 'Parliament' to Oxford, which met at Christ Church College, another attempt to woo constitutional moderates. The old university town itself was transformed by its role as Royalist capital. Charles dined in Christ Church's Great Hall while Henrietta Maria lodged at Merton, hearing mass in the chapel. New College became a magazine and military workshop, and Magdalen Grove was dotted with artillery and housed workshops and forges that spewed fumes across the Cherwell river. The painter William Dobson set up a studio in the High Street, from where he knocked out portraits of the great and good of the king's cause. Bartholomew La Roche, a Walloon, ran a workshop under Magdalen Bridge where he tried to create incendiary devices to aid the king's army. Meanwhile, Royalists crammed into small town houses. Young Ann Harrison (later Fanshawe), daughter of a rich London merchant, recounted the shock: 'from as good houses as any gentleman of England had we came to a baker's house in an obscure street'.[18] The town itself was full and disorderly, and not just because of the soldiers: Charles, for his part, was especially offended by all the pigs that roamed in the streets, and at Christ Church, where he himself lodged, the front quad was given over to a herd of cattle.

The disruption was hard on the dons. Nearing his eightieth year, Ralph Kettell was president of Trinity: a gentleman's son from Hertfordshire who, from his mullioned house that still stands on Broad Street, had worked hard to improve both his college's academic reputation and its buildings. Before the war he had been quite the character, making sure Trinity had the best beer in Oxford (in order – he said – to keep the students away from the disreputable drinking holes of the town), and known for berating the most annoying students as 'rascal-jacks', 'scobber-lotchers' and occasionally 'turds'. He hated luxurious hair and kept a pair of scissors tucked away in his ruff which he would whip out and snip away at any locks he thought too long. But the war brought him indignity and horrors. On one occasion, a soldier came into one of his lectures and, for no apparent reason, smashed the hourglass Kettell used to time himself. And there was the time Ann Harrison and her friend Lady Thynne turned up at chapel 'half dressed, like angels', specifically to tease him. By July 1643, Kettell was dead. Even at his age, it was said the war had taken years off his life.[19]

Women were a striking new presence in the ancient university, for what the dons probably hoped would be the last time, but it was the soldiers who proved the biggest burden. When a terrible fire broke out in 1644, it was rumoured to have been started by a trooper roasting a stolen pig. Such was the military men's propensity for brawling, drinking, duelling and general acts of crime that the authorities had a gibbet set up in the centre of town at the Carfax. Their officers weren't much better: Arthur Aston, who commanded the garrison for much of the war, was remembered as a 'testy, forward, imperious and tyrannical person, hated in Oxon and elsewhere by God and man'.[20] It was some relief to the town when he fell from his horse in 1644, losing his leg and hastening his replacement.

1644 started well for the Parliamentarians, with Fairfax winning a significant victory at Nantwich, Cheshire, in which the king's Irish recruits fought badly. In Yorkshire, the young and thoughtful John Lambert, a minor gentleman from the lonely Dales hamlet of Calton, near Kirkby Malham, was busy recovering the West Riding. The most significant intervention, though, was further north. On 19 January, a Scottish army of around 20,000 began a slow march south through the floods and Northumbrian snowfall, as the local Royalist units fell back, the latter leaving burned bridges behind them as they retreated. On 3 February, the Scots were before the walls of Newcastle, but here they were rebuffed by the town's eponymous (now) marquess.

As spring approached, the icy winds calmed and the next campaign season beckoned. Parliament's new Committee of Both Kingdoms, created to manage the war effort of the Anglo-Scottish allies, was now toying with an attack on Oxford itself, and began to concentrate its forces in nearby Buckinghamshire. But this plan was dropped in favour of another that appeared more promising. With Parliamentarian victories in Yorkshire, York itself looked vulnerable to attack. If the Anglo-Scottish allies could take the old city, it could unlock the whole of the north, landing a devastating blow on the Royalists. So the main Scottish army began another slow march south, and the Earl of Manchester was sent north with his Eastern Association forces.

The response came from Prince Rupert. Leaving the Royalist stronghold of Shrewsbury, and with just 8,000 troops, he swept through Cheshire and Lancashire, gathering soldiers on the way. On 28 April, his army took the Puritan stronghold of Bolton and massacred many of the inhabitants. Charles, meanwhile, took a small force and reached Worcester, whence he wrote to Rupert – telling him in rather ambiguous terms that he should, if he could, relieve York even if that meant giving battle against a much larger force.

Before then, on 23 June, Rupert had left his base at the Lancashire town of Preston and swung east across the Pennines into Yorkshire.

Royalist York was already under siege. Within the walls, soldiers and townspeople alike were reduced to one meal a day while the guns thundered overhead. Outside, the armies of Lord Ferdinando Fairfax, the Earl of Manchester and Leven's Scots had taken up positions. Raids by the defenders burned down suburban houses, outside the walls, that might be used as cover during an assault.

Rupert's march took him up through the Ribble Valley, past the ruined abbeys of Whalley and Sawley, to the old castle town of Skipton, then onwards with the dramatic remains of Bolton Priory to his left, along the River Wharfe past Ilkley to Denton, where his forces occupied Fairfax's birthplace. Then on to Otley, passing north-east across rolling fields, past the recently discovered springs in the tiny hamlet of Harrogate, to the Royalist garrison town of Knaresborough. From here, he swung north and arrayed his forces across the old Forest of Galtres, north of the city of York.

With the sudden appearance of Rupert's force, the Allies pulled back from the siege and prepared to engage. They left behind them their extensive siegeworks (and around 4,000 pairs of shoes) and moved out to the west of the city. On the night of 1 July, they camped out on a vast area of moorland between the hamlets of Hessay and Long Marston.

The next day, they started moving south towards Tadcaster, where they hoped to block Rupert's passage southwards. What they didn't know, but which soon became clear, was that Rupert's army had been up since the early hours, and from 4 a.m. had been ferrying its troops over a captured bridge of boats across the Ouse to the north. By 9 a.m., the size of the Royalist host in the Allied rear was evident.

It was a serious threat, for at this point the Allied infantry was strung out over eight miles of trackways. An urgent order went down the lines, recalling them towards Marston Moor. Over the next few hours, the two armies assembled across the moor, cavalry on the wings, infantry in the centre. Meanwhile, a disagreement between Rupert and one of Newcastle's advisers, Lord Eythin, who bore a grudge against the prince going back to an obscure engagement in Germany, meant that infantry reinforcements expected from York were late to the field. The Allies occupied slightly higher ground in arable fields, with the Royalists ahead of them on the flat moor, behind a ditch lined with musketeers. As the two armies watched each other, just a couple of hundred metres apart, Rupert waited. At around 2 p.m., the cannon on both sides started their intermittent barrages, but the waiting continued, punctuated by the occasional sharp summer rain shower that dampened grass and crops.

Mid-afternoon, Newcastle's infantry finally arrived from York. By 4 p.m., both armies were finally in full battle array. Rupert's horse, led by John Byron, faced off against Cromwell to the west, while those of Charles Goring, one of the king's best generals, stood ready against Thomas Fairfax to the east. By early evening, Rupert was starting to waver, perhaps stung by criticism of his battle plans by Eythin. The sound of chanted psalms from the Allied soldiers drifted across the field. Around 7 p.m., the prince made his decision. The attack would have to wait, so he pulled back, to eat supper. His troops relaxed, Newcastle retired to smoke a pipe.

But it was already too late. At half past seven, the heavens opened: a crack of thunder was followed by a sudden and savage hailstorm, and, just as it cleared, the Royalists looked up to see the Allied ranks advancing steadily down the hill, straight at them.

On the Allied left, Cromwell's horse charged and smashed through Byron's, before fighting (with possibly decisive help from the Scottish cavalry under David Leslie) through a counter-charge by Rupert himself. The prince's horse were scattered. On the Allied right, the story was different: Fairfax found the ground tough, and his troops were trounced by a forceful charge from Goring. In the middle, the Allied infantry crossed the ditch and clashed headlong into the Royalist centre. Meanwhile, Cromwell – now nursing an injury to his neck – managed to pull his disciplined troops back around the Royalist rear. Despite being slowed by Newcastle's lambskin-coated infantry, they wheeled behind Goring. By now, the lanes around the battlefield were streaming with soldiers of both sides trying to flee the infernal chaos. The talk was of a Royalist victory. But two Scots infantry regiments were standing firm, pikemen kneeling with their weapons pointed forwards and upwards, against repeated charges of horse and foot. And Cromwell and Leslie were soon back, charging off the moor at Goring's rear, putting them to flight.

Now the battle had swung decisively, and Allied victory was inevitable. The last resistance came from Newcastle's 'Whitecoats', who fought and died almost to a man, where they stood, even as the evening dusk came in, even as their formation was broken, and even as the battle was long lost. In all, the fighting had lasted just two hours: over 4,000 Royalists were dead; the reports said 300 Allied soldiers died, though this was probably a serious underestimate. Rupert, so the propaganda went, had to escape by hiding in a bean field.

The triumph on Marston Moor should have given the Parliamentarians a path to victory. At Oxford, the mood was dark: tempers were becoming short, arguments too often settled by duel. But there was deliverance for the Royalists, for their enemies now lurched into a catastrophic defeat in the West Country.

As the royal army fell to defeat in Yorkshire, the king's fortunes in the West Country had been rather different. The queen was pregnant, and was sent to Bath where she could take the waters and remove herself from the contested lands around Oxford. Soon she continued on to Exeter, further into Royalist territory.

It was then that Essex tried to exploit her vulnerability. A plan was hatched for Waller to keep the king pinned down in the Midlands while Essex marched into Devon to capture her. Come June, the month before Marston Moor, the Parliamentarian commander was menacing Exeter where the queen, after a very difficult childbirth, decided the danger was too great, left her newborn daughter Henrietta, and fled to Falmouth where she boarded a ship for France.

Then Essex blundered terribly. Leaving Exeter, he moved further south-west into Cornwall, making the unfathomable decision to invade some of the most Royalist territory in the country. By now he was also being pursued by the king, who had defeated Waller at Cropredy in north Oxfordshire, and arrived in late July in Exeter to meet his new daughter for the first time. Soon Charles was on the march again, and by the beginning of August, he had trapped Essex at the small Cornish town of Lostwithiel. Outmanoeuvred, Essex stole away by fishing boat, leaving Philip Skippon and his infantry to surrender. '[W]e desire to know the reason,' crowed a Royalist newspaper, 'why the rebels voted to live and die with the Earl of Essex, since the Earl of Essex hath declared he will not live and die with them.'[21] Women camp followers – the wives and girlfriends of soldiers, and those who supplied more miscellaneous needs of the men – were murdered by the victorious Cavaliers, thrown off Lostwithiel Bridge in cold blood. It was an act of savagery that suggested the war was becoming an increasingly bitter one.

Then, as the various forces manoeuvred through the autumn and as once again it seemed that the king might attempt a march on London, the Earl of Manchester snatched a bloody stalemate from the jaws of victory at a second battle at Newbury, on 27 October. Somehow, despite his losing the great set-piece battle of Marston Moor, Charles's cause was recovering, while Manchester himself was drawing the ire of his subordinates, notably one of his Eastern Association cavalry commanders, the determined Oliver Cromwell.

As war raged in the countryside, in the capital a great synod, known as the Westminster Assembly, was trying to work out the future of the Church. It eventually settled on a fairly careful statement of Calvinist orthodoxy and a new, pared-down liturgy through its 'Directory of Worship' (1644), which was supposed to replace the Book of Common Prayer. Debates in the Assembly were complex, but there were clearly emerging differences of opinion, particularly between the Presbyterians on the one hand, who wanted a strictly regulated Calvinist Church, and the so-called Dissenting Brethren, who were inspired by the experiences of exile in Holland and New England into desiring considerably more flexibility for people to gather in their own congregations without state control over faith. This 'Independent' movement, which had originated half a century ago but had flourished in the years immediately before the war, was to prove a major force.

Then, in 1645, Parliament finally had William Laud executed. His prosecution had been a travesty. Not even William Prynne, who had access to Laud's papers and even his diary, could make the accusations of treason and popish allegiance stick, so once again, as with Strafford, Parliament turned to a bill of attainder. Frail, seventy-one-year-old Laud was killed on Tower Hill on 10 January, his final indignity being to suffer a scolding on the scaffold by the bigoted Anglo-Irish MP Sir John Clotworthy. To Charles, meanwhile, the judicial murder of his leading primate was oddly encouraging. Writing to the now-exiled queen, he suggested that this mockery of justice was sure to incur God's providential wrath. Now, God's 'hand of justice must be heavier upon them and lighter upon us', he thought.[22]

The central political issue at Westminster was now the future of the Parliamentarian armies. The failure, of the old aristocratic generals, particularly Essex and Manchester, were creating serious unease about the leadership of the forces, but the issues ran deeper than this. Aristocrats like Essex were increasingly uncomfortable with the apparently democratic direction of their own side. That December, when the Lords were prevaricating over Laud, the Commons suggested that delay would lead to popular disorder. Essex was appalled, worrying that they were replacing 'the yoke of the king' with that of 'the common people'. 'I am determined,' he announced, 'to devote my life to repressing the audacity of the people.'[23]

Manchester, meanwhile, was in the process of falling out dramatically with his most successful subordinate, Oliver Cromwell. The differences were religious, political and temperamental. The earl was a Presbyterian who valued the existing social order. Cromwell was a fiery radical, an Independent, and had rather less respect for hierarchy. Manchester fought in order to bring the king to a negotiated settlement, Cromwell to bring him to defeat.

More to the point, though, the rich aristocrats weren't getting results in the field, so they were losing the argument at Westminster.

In Parliament, hardliners, linked to the religious Independents and drawn from the war group, were pushing for radical reform of the forces. They were blocked by the more conservative 'Presbyterians', who drew on the peace party and were allied to the Scots. Eventually the debate resulted in an ordinance for 'Self-Denying', decreeing that no member of either House could hold a commission in the forces. The Lords blocked it, so attention then fell on another bill, this time to create a national army – drawn largely from the old Eastern Association – with central funding. It was to be a 'New Model': 22,000 strong: 14,400 infantry all in the same uniform, 'Redcoats all', with two musketeers to every pike; 6,600 cavalry, 1,000 dragoons. Its commander was to be the thirty-two-year-old Thomas Fairfax who though somewhat inexperienced and indeed occasionally unsuccessful on the field, was politically tepid and therefore acceptable to both Presbyterians and Independents. The experienced Philip Skippon, a hero of the European wars and of Turnham Green, was to lead the infantry. The command of the cavalry was left open, for the time being, though many MPs had a particular name in mind.

In April 1645, the Lords finally passed the Self-Denying Ordinance: this version forced everyone to resign their commission but left open the possibility of reappointment. Beneath the veneer of compromise, this was a profoundly important step: the old nobility, traditionally the military leaders of the country, were being sidelined in favour of professional soldiers like Fairfax and Skippon. As the William Lilly put it that year, 'The nobility and gentry who have continued many generations are sinking and an inferior sort of people … are ascending.'[24] The New Model officer corps was made up of soldiers promoted by reason of their skill and zeal, not their birth. If they were gentry, they were from relatively minor families: men like John Lambert, Henry Ireton or Charles Fleetwood. Not poor men, by any means, and they often shared the experience of Oxbridge and the Inns of Court, but neither were they especially wealthy or well connected. And many of the New Model officers, like the firebrand Thomas Harrison and the yeoman's son Thomas Pride, were drawn from outside the gentry entirely.

Then there was Oliver Cromwell. He was the man many MPs expected to take command of the cavalry. Although his position in the new army wasn't yet secure – he was still an MP, of course – for many he was emblematic of that 'inferior sort of people'. Born in 1599, he was in his mid-forties, with an ungainly face, fierce blue eyes and a hot temper. He was known for promoting comrades for talent rather than social position: 'I had rather,' he once wrote, 'have a plain, russet-coated Captain, that knows what he fights for, and loves what he knows, than that which you call a Gentleman and is nothing else.'[25] He himself was, as he put it, 'by birth a gentleman, living neither in any considerable height, nor yet in obscurity', although his wife, Elizabeth Bourchier, came from a wealthy Essex family.[26] After a brief spell at Cambridge, young Cromwell had suffered severe melancholy in his later twenties. Come the 1630s he was a farmer, and his income had fallen to around £100 a year. By that time he'd also experienced a Calvinist 'conversion', bringing a belief that he was one of the elect. His views at this point were probably those of a country Puritan: fiercely anti-Laudian and anti-Catholic. But in the course of a war in which he tramped the country as part of a disciplined force of cavalry 'ironsides', his views moved strongly towards Independency, and he was developing a deep distrust in the idea that state officers should force religious practices on the people.

The New Model Army was well organised and politically committed, but as yet untested in the battlefield. This was soon to change.

In the spring of 1645, as the cold began to recede for another year, the opposing armies took to the roads and tracks again. Desultory manoeuvres in the Midlands and west did little to change the balance of territory. The Scots Covenanters, meanwhile, had become distracted by a brilliant guerrilla campaign in the Highlands by their former ally Montrose, forcing them to pull units out of England and send them north. The Covenanters' army and their commissioners in London were now drawing closer to the peace party and the Presbyterians. Ultimately their aims were for the establishment of a Presbyterian theocracy in England, and they looked in horror at Cromwell, his Independent allies and the new army. '[T]here is some sour Scottish ale a-brewing,' wrote one Somerset radical.[27] He was right.

By late spring, Fairfax was ready to lay formal siege to Oxford. The Royalists responded by taking Leicester, street by street, in an unusually bloody storm. With the king present, soldiers, civilians, women and children were killed. Horrified, London ordered Fairfax to leave off Oxford and give pursuit. On 8 June, he decided to seek battle, and on the 10th he appointed Cromwell as his lieutenant general, commanding the horse. Ratification was sought from Westminster, and the Commons agreed. The Lords refused, but Fairfax decided on balance that he preferred the positive response of the Lower House, so this was the one he accepted. On the night of the 12th, after a rain-sodden day, Fairfax was closing in on the king's army, currently at Borough Hill near the small market town of Daventry, in the gentle Northamptonshire countryside. The king was caught unawares, passing the time hunting in nearby Fawsley Park. But it was late in the long day, so Fairfax's men bedded down in the fields, while he rode around the dark country lanes, scouting the positions, until 4 a.m. Finally, he managed to glimpse the dark mass of Borough Hill, where he saw the embers of fires against the dim morning twilight. More fires than he expected – which could only mean one thing: the Royalists were burning their tents before pulling out.

The following day was critical. At 5 a.m., Fairfax came into some crucial intelligence, an intercepted letter from Goring that revealed that his western army was far away. At 6 a.m., Fairfax conferred with his leading officers, at which point Cromwell finally arrived to join the army – to great cheers from the men. Through the day, the Royalists feinted towards Warwick before swinging north. At every turn they were followed by a detachment from Cromwell's cavalry, led by Henry Ireton and Thomas Harrison. On the moonless night of 13 to 14 June, with the armies nearly touching upon each other in the dark Northamptonshire countryside, the king held a council of war. The next day, they would give battle.

11

Gangrene

The armies started assembling from 2 a.m., and just after sunrise Fairfax's men were ready on the high ground around the village of Naseby. From here, they saw Rupert's cavalry approaching. To many of the soldiers, it looked certain that they would face battle that day. But Fairfax wasn't sure. With his army occupying Naseby ridge, it wasn't clear that Rupert would attack, so he ordered his men forward and downhill. Here, though, the terrain was even worse – marshy and drenched. It was the kind of land, Cromwell was certain, over which Rupert would never attack.

So, Fairfax pulled back again, which meant that when Rupert – on a reconnoitring mission with his life-guard – set eyes on Cromwell's horse, he saw to his surprise they seemed to be withdrawing. The decision was made to pursue, so the Royalists – with their fully armoured king at the head – moved forward in battle formation. They had the wind behind them.

Suddenly they appeared before Fairfax's New Model Army. In response, Fairfax's men tracked westwards, spreading out across the whole field with a hedgerow to their left. Then, Fairfax did something odd. He ordered his men to pull back one hundred paces, behind a gentle elevation, taking them out of the Royalists' line of sight, 'so that the enemy might not perceive in what form our battle* was drawn, nor see any confusion therein'.[1]

Both armies were in the usual formation, infantry in the centre, horse on the flanks. The Royalist foot – mostly veteran Welshmen – were

---

*'Battle' in this case means a battalia.

led by the sixty-six-year-old Lord Astley; their right cavalry flank by Rupert, their left – including many northern veterans of Marston Moor – by Marmaduke Langdale. The New Model's infantry were commanded by the redoubtable Skippon, their left horse by Henry Ireton and their right by Cromwell. On their far-left flank, John Okey lined his dragoons along the hedgerows, ready to pepper Rupert's horse with carbine shot.

Battle began quickly, without much artillery fire. It was the Royalists who attacked first. At 10 a.m. they advanced, quickly but in good order, uphill. At this moment, Fairfax's men moved forward the hundred paces they'd pulled back, and the two armies at last saw each other in full. Now the Royalist cavalry charged. Rupert, riding uphill and facing fire from Okey's dragoons, managed to best Ireton's men. Ireton himself was injured and lost his horse. Meanwhile, the Royalist foot were pushing hard against Skippon's infantry: having exchanged one volley they fell to the push of pike. The Royalists were tired, outnumbered and pressing uphill, but they fought hard and it was Skippon's men who started to concede ground. Gradually, the Parliamentarian infantry began to lose formation: Skippon himself was grievously wounded by a hurtling musket ball.

On the Parliamentarian right, though, the story was different. Cromwell's horse routed Langdale's. Here, ironside discipline paid off. A portion of Cromwell's horse chased Langdale's men off the field, while the rest formed up to charge into the Royalist infantry. Meanwhile, Rupert's victorious horse had galloped off the field in pursuit of the New Model baggage train. This gave Okey's dragoons their opportunity – mounting their horses, they ploughed into the Royalist foot. With the New Model infantry now starting to regroup, the king's infantry found themselves assailed on three sides.

As the Royalists began to surrender, Rupert, rebuffed by the musketeers defending the baggage train, had returned to the field and joined the king at the rear. Here they tried to rally, only for the victorious New Model to reorder themselves into full battle array once more, ready for a final push. The remaining Royalist troops simply melted away.

The last blood shed at Naseby was that of the women followers of the king's army. They were believed to be Irish Catholics, though were probably mostly Welsh – the wives of soldiers. Over a hundred were murdered, the rest slashed in the face and slit in the nose – the mark of the 'whore'.

All the king's artillery fell to Fairfax, but even the loss of these paled behind the capture of his papers, which revealed his evident desire to bring over Catholic Irish soldiers, his willingness to countenance the toleration of English Catholics and – to unsympathetic readers – his unseemly fawning over his wife.

Parliamentarian propagandists in London reacted with ill-concealed glee. By this point, London had emerged as the epicentre of a radically altered landscape of news. Periodical English newsbooks – regular, weekly digests of political and military developments – had emerged in the crisis year of 1641. Unlike the 'corantoes' of the 1620s, which had confined themselves to European news for fear of the censors, the newsbooks of the 1640s were free to cover English affairs. From 1642 these multiplied as the war generated a yearning thirst for information about the latest movements of the armies, not to mention sensationalist tales of strange occurrences, witchcraft and signs from God.

Newsbooks (sometimes called 'diurnals' – i.e. dailies, even though they were usually released weekly – or 'mercuries' after the messenger god) quickly became polemical and argumentative, drawing in information and gossip from multiple sources and fashioning them into invective 'paper bullets'. They were forged on backstreet presses, sold on street corners and read aloud in smoky alehouses. Parliamentarian propagandists depicted Royalists as violent crypto-papists, allied to the savage Irish and wishing to bring in arbitrary government and a return to Laudianism in the Church. The Royalists responded by accusing the Parliamentarians of being anarchic social upstarts who hated their king and whose support came from Puritans and Scots. Both sides produced astrological predictions and accused their enemies of bringing cosmic disorder. Essex was an impotent cuckold, while Rupert's mother was a witch, his father was the devil, and his dog – Boy – was a demon.

Most of London's newsbooks were Parliamentarian, but there was a core of Royalist publications, too.[2] The most important was *Mercurius Aulicus*, written and published by Sir John Birkenhead a man said to have 'great goggly eyes' and be 'not of sweet aspect' but who made up for his unprepossessing physical characteristics by his loyalty to Charles and a mordant wit.[3] *Aulicus* was produced in Oxford from 1643, but copies were widely available in London. A relatively high-quality production, it was characterised by often clever and erudite humour, though as with most Royalist propaganda, it was always happy to play on the idea that Parliamentarians were upstarts who brought social disorder. 'The Parliament', *Aulicus* had scoffed in 1643, 'is ruled by the citizens, and the citizens by their wives'.[4]

In response came *Mercurius Britanicus*, a punchy, funny, more populist offering from the Parliamentary camp. Its leading light was Marchamont Nedham, an impish young journalist with an Oxford education, a riotous sense of humour, but few discernible principles (though it was said, pointedly, that his surname should be pronounced to rhyme with 'freedom').[5] In the run-up to Naseby, *Britanicus* had been inching into particularly dangerous territory, but it was after the battle that Nedham had his first serious brush with trouble. In July, the king's seized correspondence was published, complete with annotations by the propagandist Henry Parker in *The King's Cabinet Opened*.[6] So Nedham used *Britanicus* to print a serialised commentary, culminating in an issue of 4 August in which he went so far as to launch a 'Hue and Cry' against the king, charging him with 'a guilty conscience, bloody hands, a heart full of broken vows and protestations', even mocking the king's stammer. The Lords were furious, so Nedham was briefly thrown in gaol and made to write a public retraction.

With the war now hurtling towards a Parliamentarian victory, and with the simmering tension over how they would deal with a recalcitrant and dangerous king, *Britanicus* had gone way too far.

In the field, the king's cause was collapsing around him. Rupert wrote to Charles suggesting that he might negotiate, but he refused. 'I must tell you that God will not suffer rebels or traitors to prosper,' he retorted. Charles was to spend the rest of the year on the road, bolting from country town to fortress, and the scattered Royalist forces fared no better. Goring, finally, was worsted by a skilful attack by Fairfax at Langport in Somerset at which the Royalists turned and fled through the searing July heat and Thomas Harrison fell into rapture, breaking forth with a loud voice 'into the praises of God'.[7]

By now the war was three years old. It had brought violence, destruction and punishing taxation. By its end, around 62,000 soldiers were dead, and perhaps 100,000 more had died from war-related disease. Some 150 towns had been severely damaged, some set on fire by white-hot cannonballs deliberately designed to enflame timber buildings, and around 10,000 homes had been destroyed. Country houses lay in ruins, and the old medieval castles were 'slighted' – blown up with gunpowder to stop them ever being used again. Today, these have left us with many evocative ruins, such as Corfe Castle in Dorset or Wardour Castle in Wiltshire, but the owners of the time could only lament the tumbling of the old walls.

Some aristocratic estates had seen rents drop to a tenth of their normal levels.[8] Other people lost treasured possessions, like the physician William Harvey, who was distraught by the loss of his scrawled notes on the dissection of frogs and toads, left behind at Whitehall Palace at the outbreak of hostilities. Worst of all was for the former soldiers who now had to live with terrible injuries and post-traumatic stress. Some had seen action and hardship that would live with them for the rest of their lives. William Sumner, a tailor of Leicester, recalled how his house and fruit trees had been pulled down to defend the town. Then, during the king's successful assault his son was killed, 'and most of his goods plundered', and 'with the fright thereof [his] wife has been distracted ever since'.[9]

Both sides plundered. 'I had six oxen the other day, And them the Roundheads stole away', sang a Somerset ballad: 'I had six horses left me whole, And them the Cavaliers have stole.'[10] The New Model Army was, on the whole, different: it had a draconian code against drunkards and blasphemers, and plunderers in the ranks were simply shot. Fairfax also made sure his soldiers had regular pay. Some of the New Model's success in 1645 lay in the fact it was less unpopular with the people whose lands it marched through than the king's men. But all armies, Fairfax's included, brought a heavy tax burden. Indeed, that burden was now much higher than it had been under Charles's Personal Rule in the 1630s, with the excise on basic commodities hitting the poor much harder than the rich. In some counties, the level of tax in the 1640s was ten times that of Ship Money in the 1630s. Meanwhile, many soldiers were quartered on civilian houses, and people complained that they would 'eat the meat out of their children's mouths', and then moan about its quality.[11]

War brought social upheaval. Parents, Edward Hyde later recalled of the wars and their aftermath, 'had no manner of authority over their children, nor children any obedience or submission to their parents'. Young women, meanwhile, 'conversed without any circumspection or modesty, and frequently met at taverns and common eating-houses'.[12] Communities were divided and insults flew as quickly as the cannonballs did. Roundhead dogs, Cavalier rogues.[13] Both Royalists and Roundheads brought cultural destruction. When Thomas Fairfax marched into Oxford at the head of the New Model Army, he moved to protect the treasures of the Bodleian, and it was said that the Cavaliers had done much damage by taking out books and never returning them. But it was the Parliamentarians who committed the most spectacular acts of iconoclasm. They tore down the public cross at Cheapside and would do so to another at Charing Cross in 1647. They pulled up the famous Glastonbury Thorn, said to have grown miraculously from the staff of Joseph of Arimathea when he visited Britain with the Holy Grail. At Canterbury, Parliamentarian troops used a statue of Christ for musket practice, cheering when they hit it in the face.[14] In London, Sir John Clotworthy had personally ripped up a Rubens painting of the crucified Christ, in the Queen's old chapel at Somerset House, with a halberd.[15] In East Anglia, in 1643 and 1644, over 250 churches had been meticulously stripped of anything that looked remotely idolatrous by the eager work of William Dowsing, a wealthy son of a Suffolk yeoman, operating under a commission from the Earl of Manchester.

It was in East Anglia, too, that the most sinister upheaval of all took place. As Civil War gripped, even in areas without significant military action, many seem to have experienced a very powerful sense of crisis: of upheaval and manipulation by demonic forces. East Anglian society, meanwhile, was unusually atomised. The growth of poverty had been especially marked here. There were many old folk who scratched a living on the margins of society, sometimes by begging, and there were many wealthy yeomen and gentry who likely felt some strange, deep-seated pangs of guilt at the fate that had befallen their neighbours. And as often happens in such situations, they projected that guilt onto the victims.

Whether this explains the motivations of Matthew Hopkins, a minor gentleman of Manningtree in Essex and still only in his mid-twenties, is uncertain. Whatever the cause, at some point in the cold months of 1644–5, he started to worry about witches in his neighbourhood, and his investigations led him to an ancient, one-legged widow called Elizabeth Clarke, who was bullied into confessing to keeping 'familiars', a kind of supernatural animal that was believed to be kept by witches to aid their magic. Then Hopkins went on the road, assisted by John Stearne, another small-time gentleman, this time from Suffolk, who dutifully recorded the pair's exploits.

Passing from village to village, Hopkins and Stearne offered to investigate anyone locals suspected of witchcraft. Their approach was unusual. They would subject their suspects to 'watching': keeping them up without food or sleep for several nights, until their familiars appeared. Victims might be searched, often with the help of local midwives, for suspicious marks. Then they would be handed over to the authorities for prosecution. For the first major trial, there were no judges available so the Earl of Warwick, the great Puritan magnate, presided. He had little experience of this kind of thing, and did nothing to stop it. For 20 years virtually no one had been hanged for witchcraft on the Home Circuit. Suddenly, at the Chelmsford Assizes under Warwick, 28 women were sentenced to death. Hopkins and Stearne continued.

Sometimes they used the swimming test, a practice in which victims were thrown in a river, lake or pond and, if the pure water rejected their body and they floated, they were considered to be witches. It had no basis at law, indeed some saw it as a foreign interpolation and therefore rather suspect. But during a civil war, less attention was paid to the normal rules. Watching and swimming – torture, effectively – drew unusual confessions. Not just the standard *malificium* but diabolic pacts and sexual encounters with the devil. One woman, Susan Marchant, confessed that the devil won her over when she was singing psalms, asking her why she was bothering when she was 'a damned creature': the mental scars of Calvinism, no doubt.[16] Another, Ann Usher, described how the devil was able to give her the sensation of 'two things like butterflies in her secret parts'.[17]

The hunt spread across the region. As it did, though, problems emerged. Even after the first trial at Chelmsford, magistrates and clergy questioned the evidence. Warwick's estate steward Arthur Wilson was worried and sceptical of what Hopkins and Stearne were doing. Sleep deprivation was drawing some suspicious confessions. When Joan (or Joyce) Wallis was 'watched', she confessed to having familiars called 'Grissel' and 'Greedigutt'. But after a rest, she said she had no recollection of them; and their names sounded a lot like that of Elizabeth Clarke's imp, called 'Grizzel Greedigutt'.[18] Had Hopkins and Stearne placed the name in her head while torturing her? Had they forced a confession? Or made it up entirely? Wallis was acquitted, it seems.

Some communities, meanwhile, started to baulk at the cost: imprisoning scores of suspected witches was an expensive business. And in 1646, the vicar of Great Staughton, John Gaule, published a stinging attack on Hopkins and Stearne and their methods: 'every old woman,' he warned, 'with a wrinkled face, a furr'd brow, a hairy lip, a gobber tooth, a squint eye, a squeaking voice, or a scolding tongue, having a ragged coat on her back, a skull-cap on her head, a spindle in her hand, and a dog or cat by her side, is not only suspected, but pronounced for a witch'.[19] Gaule went on a campaign of sermons to undermine the witchfinders and this, plus the costs, plus some unwelcome questions from the authorities, seems to have encouraged Hopkins and Stearne to slip back again into the shadows. Hopkins would die in 1647; Stearne, his older companion, retired to his farm and his pen, with which he wrote up a tract, heavily plagiarised, about hunting witches. '[W]hat hath been done,' he wrote, 'hath been for the good of the commonwealth.'[20] In total, their witch hunt had led to over a hundred witches being hanged – nearly nine of every ten were women.

In some areas, war weariness grew into active resistance. In the summer and autumn of 1645, there were risings in several places in the south-west by so-called 'Clubmen', named for the rudimentary weapons they carried. They claimed to be neutrals, but they often had sympathy with one side or the other. In the downlands of Wiltshire and Dorset, a broadly Royalist Clubman association threatened to disrupt Fairfax's siege of Sherborne, but they were surrounded by the New Model Army at the hilltop town of Shaftesbury and their leaders captured. Another group, 2,000-strong and led by two clergymen, gave Cromwell considerable trouble when they assembled on the ancient hill fort on Hambledon Hill. From here, they took potshots at the cavalrymen sent to disperse them, before the troopers attacked, killed around a dozen and captured 300.

But, all told, these were just minor impediments to the relentless progress of the New Model Army. In September, Bristol fell to another skilful assault by Fairfax, this time actually bolstered by sympathetic Clubmen from Somerset and Gloucestershire. Rupert, wisely, accepted terms and surrendered the city. Three days after Bristol, Montrose fell to a catastrophic defeat at Philiphaugh in the Scottish Borders, against a Covenanter army led by the capable David Leslie. Charles then suffered yet another defeat, this time near Chester. He slipped through the country lanes of the north Midlands to Newark, with just a handful of his men as guard. Now Cromwell was working his way through Hampshire, smashing Winchester Castle and capturing the long-standing bastion of Basing House in a fierce and bloody fight. Fairfax, meanwhile, was busy recapturing the West Country. Charles's fortunes continued to slide through the winter. Now back in Oxford, he suggested peace negotiations while still hoping to bring in aid from overseas; but his West Country strongholds were crumbling, and in March 1646, one of the last remnants of his forces was crushed at Stow-on-the-Wold in the Cotswolds. Then Exeter fell, leaving just Newark and Oxford and a handful of minor outposts in Royalist hands.

In April, Fairfax began preparations to besiege Oxford. But at three in the morning on the 27th, Charles managed to slip out of the beleaguered university city – not for the first time in his life passing through hostile territory in disguise. First, he made as if towards London, stopping for three hours at Hillingdon. Was he waiting for something? Someone? Then, he passed on to Harrow, but turned north and slept at Wheathampstead. Carrying on north, he eventually reached Newark, a citadel on the all-important River Trent, where the Scots were laying siege to a Royalist garrison. He found the Scottish army near the old minster town of Southwell a few miles away, and on 5 May, after nearly four years of fighting, he surrendered. Not to Parliament, not to Fairfax, but to the Covenanters.

On 24 June 1646, with colours flying and drums beating, the last Royalist soldiers marched out of Oxford. It was now Fairfax's city. The war, finally, was over.

The question now became what kind of peace might be achieved. The victorious Parliamentarians were splitting more firmly into Presbyterian and Independent factions – 'two juntoes', according to one observer.[21] Since August 1645, meanwhile, 'recruiter' elections had been filling the Commons seats vacated by Royalists – around half of the total. Many of these recruiters were radical and connected to the Army. Despite the Self-Denying Ordinance of 1645, the Commons now had a significant cohort of officers from the New Model: men like Henry Ireton, who married Cromwell's daughter Bridget in June 1646, Charles Fleetwood, Thomas Harrison, or the combative thirty-six-year-old Thomas Rainborough* (Thomas Fairfax, on the other hand, actually failed to get elected for Cirencester early in 1647). But the Presbyterians retained considerable strength. They had suffered when one of their leading figures, the venerable Earl of Essex, had died, from a stroke, in September 1646. Despite his being sidelined by the Self-Denying Ordinance of 1645 he was still something of a hero to his cause and was buried in Westminster Abbey with considerable pomp. New leaders had emerged, though: in particular, the old Commons hand Denzil Holles. They even had an MP, Walter Long, who acted as a kind of Parliamentary whip, making sure allies were present for votes and (at least twice) roughing up opponents.[22]

The king, meanwhile, was currently suffering the hospitality of the Scots at Newcastle. In July, he'd been offered a settlement by Parliament – the so-called Newcastle Propositions. But it was not the kind of thing he could accept, for it was little more than an abject surrender: the complete rescinding of control of the army, of his

---

*Rainborough was elected for Droitwich, where he happened to command the New Model garrison.

government, even of his ability to appoint peers, plus acceptance of full-blown Presbyterianism and the 1643 Covenant, and the prosecution of 58 of his supporters. Instead, Charles thought he had an opportunity: to play one side off against the other. He was right.

The 1646 harvest was bad. In Parliament, the main business was the long-awaited abolition of the episcopacy, in line with the promises made to the Scots in the Solemn League and Covenant. The ordinance was passed in October, but in the country it was the scarceness of the annual crop that caused most trepidation. The Essex clergyman Ralph Josselin noted in his diary that wheat was 'exceedingly smitten and dwindled and rank'. Soon the prices of butter, cheese and meat were rising.[23] On 30 December, peers at Westminster heard a fast-day sermon in the Abbey lament how 'The sword is not yet sheathed, the Pestilence not ceased, and Famine, a plague worse than these, begins to threaten us.'[24] In such circumstances, the continuing costs of maintaining Fairfax's Army cut very deep. Why, it was asked, was such a large army still needed in England. Shouldn't it be dispatched as soon as possible to Ireland, where rebellion raged still?

On the other hand, the New Model itself had good reason to grumble. The soldiers had hazarded their blood for England and its Parliament. So where were their wages? Worse, they worried that once they returned to civilian life they would be prosecuted for acts committed during wartime. Requisitioning might, by a vindictive peacetime magistrate, be interpreted as theft. Horse theft in particular was a capital felony, and in the course of the hostilities, soldiers had requisitioned a lot of horses.

But self-interest was only part of the story. Many of the New Model's soldiers, especially among the cavalry, had volunteered to fight rather than being pressed. They were men – as Oliver Cromwell had once put it – who 'had the fear of God before them, and made some conscience of what they did'.[25] They believed they had fought for religious freedom and political representation, and they listened to voices like those of one of their chaplains, who'd told a congregation of soldiers gathered in Marston church near Oxford, in June 1646, that 'the power is in you, the people: keep it, part not with it'.[26]

To conservatives, including the Presbyterian faction within the victorious Parliamentarian side, the New Model Army was looking highly ideologically suspect. It was not just staffed by social upstarts, but also dominated by Independents, and riddled with lay preaching. In 1646, the fuming Presbyterian Thomas Edwards had produced a comprehensive and bestselling compendium of all the bad opinions he could find abroad in the country. The book was called *Gangraena*, and it detailed tub preachers, atheists, anabaptists and unruly and opinionated women. It came in three parts, and the third, published at Christmas, focused on the New Model Army and the 'desperate sectaries and heretics' it nursed in its ranks.

The success of Edwards's *Gangraena* didn't come out of nowhere. Since the beginning of the war – in fact, since 1640 – the English press had been in overdrive. The mercuries had been one side to this, but naturally there were also many writers who tried to understand the state England was in, and what should come out of her troubles. Ideas that, if not quite unthinkable before, were very much at the radical fringe, were suddenly thrust into the centre of the debate. One such idea – one that caused Edwards particular horror – was religious toleration, and one of the leading voices was a man whose recent experiences in New England had led him drastically to rethink the relationship between Church and state.

Roger Williams was a brilliant minister, famed for both kindliness and Godliness. As a young lad in Jacobean London he had been employed by the lawyer Edward Coke to take notes on sermons and speeches in court. By 1629 he was carving out a career as a private chaplain to the Essex gentry, but his rejection of the Prayer Book led him to leave in late 1630 for Massachusetts. As a Separatist, he gravitated towards the more radical Plymouth Plantation, set up by those who arrived on the *Mayflower*. But here he ran into trouble for insisting the colonists weren't taking Native land rights seriously enough. Back in Massachusetts, in Salem, he was busily causing controversy by claiming the king of England had no right to bestow Native land, and eventually he so irritated the colony's governors that he was sentenced to be sent back to England.

This touched off a formative experience for Williams. Rather than take his family on the next boat home, he fled through the winter snow before – in January 1636 – he settled among the Narragansett people, farming cattle and welcoming his family and some friends from Salem. He learned their language, and – when a war broke out between English settlers and the Pequots – he persuaded his new hosts to join the colonists. Soon, Williams's little community had become the more grandly titled Providence Plantation, a colony based on religious toleration and friendly relations with the Narragansett people. Meanwhile, other dissidents were setting up similar ventures, including one led by the Puritan Anne Hutchinson at Portsmouth. This, though, brought the unwanted attention from the established colonies, so Williams decided to return to England to get official protection, something that had recently become possible because of the collapse of Charles's government, the arrest of Laud and the political rise of the Long Parliament. By spring 1643, with the Civil War in full flow, Williams was back in London.

Within a year, he had gained the patent he needed to found a new colony, one that would later become Rhode Island. But while he was in England, there were religious controversies to be joined, and – ever loving the opportunity for persuasion – Williams leapt in. He became friends with an aspiring poet and controversialist, who introduced him to a publisher. Williams took the opportunity to bring out a remarkable tract, *The Bloody Tenet of Persecution*, based on his own experience in New England, that argued that the state had no right to impose religious forms on citizens.[27] It caused a sensation, provoking a series of ripostes. But it also tapped an increasing desire among some English Independents for something radical and new. Most Puritans – particularly Presbyterians – simply wanted toleration for themselves, and were quite happy, once they had seized the apparatus of state, to use it to restrict the view of their opponents. Williams and his ilk took a different view, extending toleration to include Catholics, Jews, Muslims and even non-Abrahamic religions. It was an idea that could be traced back to the small Baptist communities that had existed in the time of James I. But it was also linked to the older history of Christianity itself. Puritans often saw themselves as the heirs to the Old Testament Israelites, fighting an apostate king and using the sword to cut out bad religion.

Tolerationists, on the other hand, drew inspiration from the New Testament: early Christianity had grown as a counter-culture, in defiance of a powerful Roman state. But for Williams it also grew out of his experience with the governors of Massachusetts and the Narragansett people.

Williams's poet friend had been thinking in similar ways, too. He was a Londoner called John Milton. Highly educated, but unhappily married, Milton had caused a storm back in 1643 by proposing the legalisation of divorce on grounds of incompatibility, his views coloured no doubt by the fact that his own wife was Royalist. The furious reaction to this, and the demands that he be censored for his bad views, then drew from him a brilliant tract, *Areopagitica*, which argued for freedom of speech. Censorship, he argued, took away people's ability to tell truth from lies. 'I cannot,' Milton wrote, 'praise a fugitive and cloistered virtue, unexercised and unbreathed, that never sallies out and sees her adversary.'[28]

Freedom of the press remained a controversial idea, but the reality in which Milton was writing was one in which the old controls such as Star Chamber, the Stationers' Company and the Bishop of London were now either abolished or ineffective. Ideas that would have never seen the light of day in the restrictive world of Charles and Laud were now being printed.

Among the most bracing publications were those beginning to come from a knot of radical polemicists based in London. They were drawn from members of the middling sort and they were asking what kind of England should emerge from the catastrophe of war. Originating in the Independent congregations, their initial concern was for freedom of conscience, but it was shifting to more specifically secular matters, where the breakdown of the old order presented the opportunity to do away with ancient oppressions.

One of these polemicists was John Lilburne, the colourful, charismatic and self-mythologising controversialist who'd fallen foul of Star Chamber in 1638 for smuggling anti-episcopal writings in from the Netherlands. He was self-taught in the law: Prynne sneered that he was an 'upstart monstrous lawyer' whose only legal training was his time in prison. He had clearly made a close reading of the works of Edward Coke, though Prynne snarled at him as an '*Ignoramus*, who understands the law, and Magna Carta, no more than a Jackdaw'.[29] Never someone to shrink from an argument, even his allies acknowledged his belligerence. Henry Marten, the radical MP, once said that 'If there were none living but himself John would be against Lilburne, and Lilburne against John'. His critics, meanwhile, suggested he simply enjoyed opposition: 'a professed enemy to every present government, whatsoever it be'.[30] He'd become a religious Separatist before the war, and since then had an eventful military career that had taken in Edgehill, Turnham Green, a stinking Royalist prison at Oxford and service under the Earl of Manchester. But he had been forced out of the Army in 1645 for refusing to take the Solemn League and Covenant, the 1643 oath that committed supporters of Parliament and the Scots to work towards Presbyterianism.

Lilburne was now residing in Petty France, Bishopsgate, while dabbling unsuccessfully in exports. But he also lived by his pen. 'Oh Englishmen!' he wrote in April 1645, 'Where is your freedoms? and what is become of your Liberties and Privileges that you have been fighting for all this while, to the large expense of your Blood and Estates …?'[31] His ire was particularly aimed at the Lords, for it was the Commons who – Lilburne argued – were 'the supreme power of England, who have residing in them that power that is inherent in the people'. In the summer of 1646, he was hauled before the House of Lords for trial, at which – when the charge was read – he simply put his fingers in his ears and refused to hear it. Eventually, he was debarred from any office, fined £2,000, sentenced to seven years in prison and thrown in the Tower.

Among Lilburne's fellow travellers were Richard Overton, a General Baptist (i.e. one who, unlike the 'Particular' Baptists believed salvation was available to all) with an equally radical wife, Mary. 'For by nature we are the sons of Adam, and from him we have legitimately derived a natural propriety, right and freedom,' he wrote.[32] Toleration should be extended, Overton argued, so that 'Turks, Jews, Pagans, and Infidels' might all live together.[33] Another was William Walwyn, son of a Worcestershire gentleman, grandson of a bishop and a man who said his main recreation was 'a good book, or an honest and discoursing friend'.[34] He made it his habit to walk across London from sermon to sermon, contrasting the views he heard and formulating his

own. He was older than his fellow radicals, being in his forties, and
from a wealthier background. Walwyn was rather more cautious, too,
ending up in prison only once. His writing aimed at gentle persuasion, rather than the verbal grapeshot of the day, and bore disarming
titles like *A Whisper in the Ear of Mr Thomas Edwards* (1646) and
*Some Considerations Tending to the Undeceiving of Those, Whose
Judgements are Misinformed* (1642). But if his prose was gentle, his
ideas were radical, and his enemies thought his pleasant style was
merely a cover for his cunning.[35] Already he had been converted to
a belief in 'free justification': that salvation was open to anyone who
made the effort to open their heart to God. Now he, too, moved into
secular matters.

The London radicals, partly drawing on the networks of the
Independent congregations, had created a web of activism in the capital. Lilburne, Walwyn and Overton were almost certainly working
together by the autumn of 1645. Centred on the district of Coleman
Street, there were meetings and discussions at Salters' Hall and in large
inns like the Windmill at Lothbury and the Saracen's Head in Bread
Street.[36] Sitting over pots of beer and smoking tobacco, they discussed
new ideas and sent manuscripts off to trustworthy printers operating
in alleys. From the printers, their pamphlets were distributed to a
network of street booksellers. Many of those selling these tracts on
the streets were women, who were playing a major role in the radical
movement. Partly this was because radical thought had obvious
attractions to those living under the thumb of patriarchy, and partly it
was because the religious groups it sprung from had always seen more
involvement of women. It also reflected life in London, though, for
it was a city in which male domination had always been less secure.

   As the war drew to a close, the ideology of the radicals became
increasingly sophisticated. They argued that the Commons didn't
just represent the people: it was *answerable* to them: 'We are your
principals, and you our agents.' Their *Remonstrance of Many Thousand
Citizens, and other Free-born people of England to their own House of
Commons* (July 1646) didn't just attack Charles, but monarchy itself.
It was possible, it said, for a 'Nation to be happy without a king'.

It argued for thorough reform: 'Have you shook this nation like an Earth-quake, to produce no more than this for us?' it demanded.[37] The title was indicative: there was a lineage there to Puritan petitions that boasted large subscriptions, such as the Root and Branch of 1640 (or even the 'Millenary' petition of 1603). Ultimately, they were claiming authority from the large numbers of people that put their names to it: a democratic mandate, almost. This was reflected most obviously in the *Remonstrance of Many Thousand Citizens*'s suggestions for Parliamentary elections: they were to be annual, 'upon one certain day in November', and the people would simply turn up, rather than being summoned. Symbolically, they were not serving a higher power, who called them by writs, they were expressing their sovereign rights as citizens.

A central element to the radicals' thought was the idea of English birthrights: not just the idea that the English were 'free-born', something widely accepted, but that this conferred political rights. These were partly expressed in the Common Law, and Lilburne himself saw his rights as being protected by Magna Carta. But the new radicals said something different and more profound, too. They argued that the law as it stood was created by the successors of William the Conqueror. But now, the defeat of Charles, who was the Conqueror's most recent heir, meant the so-called 'Norman Yoke' had been thrown off. Even Magna Carta, to Walwyn at least, was little more than a 'mess of pottage'. Parliament, he complained, had been too enthralled by it: 'when they might have made a newer and better Charter, [they] have fallen to patching the old'.[38] Now, there was a unique opportunity to reform England in line with the laws of God and nature and so to protect the people. It looked forward as much as to an imagined past: '[W]hatever our forefathers were; or whatever they did or suffered, or were enforced to yield unto; we are men of the present age', as the *Remonstrance of Many Thousand Citizens* proclaimed. They would leave the past behind, and forge a 'natural and just liberty, agreeable to *Reason*'.

Not all of the radicals necessarily wanted to abolish the monarchy. The *Remonstrance of Many Thousand Citizens* allowed that kings might remain, were they to 'prove themselves lawful magistrates'. They agreed, though, with the more hardline Parliamentarians that the king shouldn't maintain his veto on legislation. Another fear was that Parliament itself might set itself up as an arbitrary power. The radicals agreed with their fellow Parliamentarians that sovereignty lay with the people. But whereas mainstream Parliamentarian thought claimed that the people had agreed to government by King, Lords and Commons at some distant moment in the past when they consented to enter a governed society, the radicals implied that this consent needed constantly refreshing. Those like Henry Parker, who now represented the mainstream, were settling on a kind of Parliamentary absolutism, whereby MPs represented the people to such a degree that Parliament *was* the nation: 'the Parliament is indeed nothing else, but the very people itself artificially congregated,' Parker wrote.[39] Ironically, this meant Parliament needn't be restricted by appeals to the people, because it already represented those people. But the radicals took a different view. They countered that the power of the legislature was limited by that of the people.

One way to ensure this check on the power of the legislature was to set down some basic fundamental laws that would be unalterable, such as liberty of religious conscience. Another was to ensure that more of the people had a say in choosing their representatives, more regularly: 'the poorest that lives, hath as true a right to give a vote, as well as the richest and greatest,' argued Lilburne from the Tower in December 1646, although in this case with specific relation to London.[40]

It was a critical idea, that was about to have its moment. For 1647 was to be one of the most astonishing, most revolutionary 12 months in the whole of English history. A year in which everything seemed open for debate.

12

To Satisfy All Men

Early in 1647, the burning question remained the settlement of peace, and for the victorious Parliamentarians, this still meant negotiating with the king. There were not yet any other serious options. In exchange for a payment of £200,000 (and £200,000 at a future date), the leading Presbyterian Denzil Holles managed to get the Scots to hand Charles over to Parliament. On 3 February 1647, the Covenanter army marched out of England, having been there for three hard years. Charles was moved to the sumptuous Holdenby House in Northamptonshire. He was lavishly entertained and allowed to pay visits to his new landowner neighbours, including the Spencers at Althorp, with whom the king played bowls.

Seventy-five miles away in Westminster, Holles and his Presbyterian allies now began to move against the New Model Army. By now, though, the soldiers were starting to rise to their own defence. They had fought in the field, now they were beginning to act as a collective political force. For, as yet unknown to Parliament, from around 18 March a petition was being passed around among the cavalry, asking for arrears, indemnity and the guarantees about any future Irish deployment. With the war still raging in Ireland, soldiers knew that some of them would be asked to go over to restore Parliament's control. But they didn't want to go against their will, and if they did go, they wanted their old commanders. They weren't the only ones circulating petitions, either. In London, the civilian radicals were stirring, launching a great appeal, known to posterity as the *Large Petition*. It asked for legal and social reforms and was presented to the Commons, addressed as the 'supreme authority of this nation'.[1]

Near the end of the month, a delegation from the Presbyterian-controlled Derby House Committee, currently operating as the Parliamentary executive from its building at Whitehall, was sent to Saffron Walden. Here, in the timber-framed Essex market town, Fairfax had made his headquarters. Here, the delegates saw the full nature of the Army's solidarity.

The soldiers' grievances had now been distilled into a single petition. It was addressed to Fairfax, but somehow the Derby House men got hold of a copy. On 27 March, Clotworthy revealed the document to the Commons. Two days later, Holles was tasked with drafting the Commons's response. He left the House at around 9 p.m., returning shortly afterwards with a hasty declaration expressing 'high dislike' for the petition, fuming that the officers who encouraged it would be considered 'enemies of the state and disturbers of the public peace'. Holles's so-called 'Declaration of Dislike' passed the Commons that night, and the Lords the next day.[2] It was ordered to be read out to each regiment – an act of gross provocation against Fairfax's army.

By early April, tempers were flaring in the Commons, with things so hot that Denzil Holles nearly came to a duel with the officer–MP Henry Ireton. Meanwhile, the Presbyterians' plan to reduce the Army's size began to come into force. In response, Fairfax summoned nearly 200 of his officers to meet in Saffron Walden's great medieval church – everyone down to the captains and lieutenants. Here, John Lambert spoke up. Where was Parliament's response to the Army's concerns of March, he asked? The officers declared they would go to Ireland, but only under Fairfax and Cromwell: 'Fairfax and Cromwell and we all go!' they cheered through the church. Soon, some 151 officers would sign a document: the *Vindication of the Officers of the Army*. It preached solidarity between officers and men, not just for the good of the soldiery, but for England. 'We hope …' it said, 'that in purchasing the freedoms of our brethren that we have not lost our own.'[3]

Still Parliament pushed on.

By this point, though, something had happened in eight of the eleven New Model cavalry regiments. Since the middle of April, they had elected representatives, known as 'Agents' or 'Agitators', two from each regiment. At the end of the month, three Agitators, William Allen, Thomas Shepard and Edward Sexby, presented a paper on behalf of all 16 to Fairfax before putting it to the Commons. It accused MPs of trying to break the Army and set themselves up as tyrants. The Commons ordered an emergency sitting, at which its officer–MPs, Cromwell, Ireton, Skippon and Fleetwood, were told to ride hard up to Saffron Walden and to settle this smouldering discord. Arriving, they found the town on edge. Soldiers were standing ready to fight, some posted on street corners with drawn swords.

In the shadows, the Agitators were creating their own administrative network and were starting to think about propaganda, looking to employ 'able pen men' and printers 'to satisfy and undeceive the people'.[4] They were cavalrymen, so likely to be literate members of the middling sort, and their horses meant they could communicate quickly with each other by racing across the byways of Essex and Hertfordshire and down to London. Soon, contact was being made between them and the London radicals – Edward Sexby seems to have acted as a go-between. He, William Allen and others travelled to the Tower, where they visited John Lilburne.

On 20 May, the Lords voted to invite the king to Oatlands, just 19 miles from Westminster. Here, they hoped he could be persuaded to strike a deal with the Presbyterians. Even with the crescendo of the previous weeks, this was a major escalation, for a royal treaty would have drastically weakened the position of the Army and their Independent allies. The person of the king remained critical, for even now few dared imagine a constitution without him.

Holles thought he might be able to raise a force of his own, to counter the New Model, made up of the London Trained Bands, the northern Parliamentarian army – which wasn't under Fairfax's command – and the growing band of 'reformadoes'* who were gathering in London. Then, on the 25th, Parliament finalised the plan for disbanding Fairfax's army: it was to take place over the first two

---

*Unlike the reformadoes of 1641–2, these were mostly men who had fought for Parliament.

weeks of June, at separate rendezvous locations. Divided, they hoped, the New Model Army could finally be conquered.

Now, though, the Agitators were acting fast. 'Pray, Gentlemen, ride night and day,' wrote one of them from London to his fellows.[5] In Hampshire, Thomas Rainborough's regiment of foot, without orders, suddenly started moving north towards Oxford.

On the 29th, Fairfax called a council of war at Bury St Edmunds, where the Agitators had established a headquarters. It was to be a critical moment. The Agitators presented a petition asking Fairfax to call a general rendezvous, in direct defiance of Parliament. It would bring together the whole of the New Model in solidarity. Fairfax, who was staunchly loyal to the interests of his comrades, then asked nearly a hundred of his officers two questions: first, whether they were happy with the terms already offered (they voted 'no'), and second, whether the Army should hold a general rendezvous. On the second question, they voted overwhelmingly yes. Fairfax agreed. The whole New Model would gather, at Newmarket, the following week.[6]

By this point, though, a gambit was in motion that would escalate things dramatically. It came not from the high command. It came from the Agitators.

On the evening of 31 May, Cromwell received a visitor at his lodgings in Drury Lane in the West End of London. His name was George Joyce, a cornet – the lowest rank of commissioned officer – in Fairfax's lifeguard. In a previous life, Joyce had been a tailor. He was here to tell Cromwell of a plan that would change everything.

Over the last couple of days, probably under the direction of the Agitators, Joyce had gathered a force of 500 cavalry troopers. His original purpose seems to have been to seize the Army artillery train at Oxford, to make sure it stayed loyal to the New Model. This was to be in coordination with Rainborough's men, the ones who'd suddenly gone off the grid somewhere in Hampshire. It was a smart move, for on the 31st the Derby House Committee ordered the artillery to pack up and move to London. Supposedly this was part of the disbandment, but surely also hinted that the Presbyterians were making active moves to fortify the capital against Fairfax.

At some point, though, Joyce also heard that Parliament had decided to move the king from Holdenby, perhaps even bringing him to London. This was an immediate danger to the Army's cause, so he left new orders to his men at Oxford, telling them to ride hard the next day to Holdenby, where Joyce would later rendezvous with them. Then he set off for London for his meeting with Cromwell.

On the day of the Drury Lane meeting, the 31st, the Oxford artillery were seized in a brief skirmish on the dusty High Street. The next day, 1 June, Cornet Joyce's troopers had been sighted within 30 miles of Holdenby.

Joyce, riding up from London, arrived before them, on 2 June. The troop of soldiers guarding the king (who was at Althorp playing bowls) immediately welcomed Joyce. They were ordinary men, so perhaps sympathised with the cornet and the Agitators he represented. But, that night, their commander Graves slipped away. If Graves, who was fiercely loyal to Parliament, returned at the head of a larger force, who knew what might happen.

In the morning, Joyce wrote urgently to Cromwell for further instructions.[7] Then, later that day, he consulted his fellow soldiers, and they were agreed: they would have to move the king. So, at 10 p.m., the cornet entered the royal bedchamber and informed the startled Charles that he would be moved in the morning, promising that he would be unharmed.

The next morning, in the early hours, Charles was roused from bed. Joyce's troopers were gathered outside the great Elizabethan mansion, horse hooves scuffing at the gravel of the yard, ready to join the road, destination as yet undetermined.

At this point, Charles attempted a brief moment of defiance.[8] He asked Joyce what commission he had: whom did it come from? It came from the soldiery of the Army, Joyce replied. Have you no document, Charles pressed. Joyce gestured to the men behind him: 'Here is my commission.'

'Where?'

'Behind me', pointing at the men.

Charles wryly conceded the point. 'It is a fair commission and as well written as I have seen a commission written in my life.'

Did Joyce mean that his commission was simply one of force? Perhaps that's what Charles thought. More likely, Joyce meant that his warrant came from the ranks. It came from the wills of the men, not the steel of their swords.

But where should they go?

Joyce suggested Oxford or Cambridge. Charles had a different idea. He had fond memories of Newmarket, where – he remembered – the air was clear. Joyce agreed. Can Charles have known that Newmarket was the chosen location for Fairfax's general rendezvous of the Army? It was an astonishing coincidence.

'Certainly God hath appeared in a mighty manner,' wrote Joyce that evening. 'Let the Agitators know,' he told his messenger, 'we have done nothing in our own name, but what we have done hath been in the name of the whole army.'[9]

That same day, Oliver Cromwell would leave Westminster, and ride north. He, too, made for Newmarket.

As Fairfax's army was gathering on Kentford Heath outside Newmarket, 75 miles from Westminster, Parliament began to appreciate the hornet's nest they'd stirred. Sitting all through the night of 3 June, they agreed to retract March's notorious Declaration of Dislike. But it was too late.

On the 5th, a new document was being read and acclaimed by the Army on the heath. The Agitators had been consulted for this one, too, but it was largely written by Henry Ireton. It would come to be known as the *Solemn Engagement of the Army*.[10] A respected officer, and now Cromwell's son-in-law, Ireton was to be a central figure, perhaps even *the* central figure, of the next two years. His outlook was complex, as it would turn out. He would become infamous for his defence of the voting rights of property holders against those who would argue for wider democracy, but he was nonetheless prepared to take his own constitutional thinking to its own, potentially radical conclusions. In particular, he believed in the sovereignty of Parliament as a representative of the people, though with one major caveat, which was that ultimately all human law was subject to the overriding principle that the safety of the people was the ultimate law: *salus populi suprema lex*.[11]

The full flowering of Ireton's ideas lay in the future. For now, his *Solemn Engagement* was focused on the task in hand. It was read to all the present regiments and assented to by the officers and men. It vowed only to disband once their grievances had been met, and once the 'freeborn people of England' were safe from the tyranny of Holles and his allies, and once 'common and equal right, freedom and safety to the whole' had been established. Critically, it also called into being a new army governing body to monitor exactly when these demands had been met: to be comprised not only of the high command, but also of two representatives of the soldiers of each regiment. It would be a general council of the whole army: officers and ordinary soldiers alike.

The Army packed up its tents, ready to march south. On the 10th, Fairfax sent a letter to the City, assuring them that despite his army's march, he wished for no coup against the government. Parliament responded by ordering his army to stay at least 40 miles away. In the early hours of the 12th, MPs created a Committee of Safety for defence. From London, though, the signs weren't encouraging. Drummers raising men for the militia that would fight the Army were roundly jeered by local lads. The Trained Bands were refusing to rally against the New Model.[12]

That day, the Army reached St Albans, 25 miles from Westminster. Now a group of officers were preparing impeachment charges – to be lodged by their allies at Westminster – against 11 leading Presbyterian Members of Parliament, including Holles. A declaration was issued, in which the Army claimed to speak for the nation. '[W]e were not a mere mercenary army,' it avowed, 'hired to serve any arbitrary power of a state, but called forth and conjured by several declarations of Parliament to the defence of our own and the people's just rights and liberties.'[13] It called for liberty of conscience, a purge of the present Parliament, a statutory limitation to the length of Parliaments and to the reapportionment of seats so that they better matched each constituency's tax burden. Royalists, save an egregious few, were to be pardoned: renewal was to be the order of the day, not retribution. But the current Presbyterian leadership had to go.

On the 23rd, the Army issued an ultimatum to Parliament, giving them until the next night to suspend the accused 11 members. The deadline passed, so the next day Fairfax moved the Army to Uxbridge, just 15 miles from Westminster, spreading his infantry out from Watford to Staines. On the 26th, the worried 11 members asked for permission from their fellow MPs to leave the House. It was granted.[14]

With the 11 gone, thanks to the threat of Fairfax's advancing force, the Presbyterians in Parliament were broken. The Army now – on terms – agreed to withdraw its headquarters to Reading, 40 miles away from Westminster. Charles, meanwhile, asked to come to Windsor and – after careful thought – Fairfax allowed him to move to Caversham, helpfully adjacent to the new Army HQ. His confinement under Fairfax was fairly genial: he was allowed to communicate with the queen, to worship with the Prayer Book and to see his children. To Charles this all suggested how desperate the Army was to please him. It was a dangerous miscalculation on his part.

The key players in the three camps – king, Parliament and Army – were now converging on a small patch of Berkshire and Buckinghamshire, in the wooded foothills of the Chilterns, just north of the winding River Thames. The king arrived at Caversham on 3 July, while the day before emissaries from Parliament had begun negotiations with the Army at a High Wycombe inn. Charles spent several days pressing representatives of the Army to make him an offer. Henrietta Maria, meanwhile, who was in exile in Paris, had sent her own representative to Reading to negotiate a settlement. His name was Sir John Berkeley, a former diplomat and once a rather tempestuous Cavalier, whose years of military experience had now left him with a genuinely pragmatic bent. He was a smart choice, for he was respected by the officers of the New Model as an honourable and capable opponent from the war. Ireton and Lambert were sent off to prepare a document setting out the Army's expectations of a future settlement.

On 16 July, the first General Council of the Army met in Reading. It included the Agitators, who called for an immediate march to London. Cromwell and Ireton argued against: this would be a wholly illegitimate use of force, and in any case they hadn't even decided what they would do once they took power. At some point, Ireton slipped away.

That night, he sat up late. With him, deep in discussion, was the queen's agent Berkeley.

In the morning, as the General Council sat down for another meeting, Ireton entered the room, bringing with him the first draft of a remarkable document. It was a set of proposals for the final settling of the kingdom, to be offered to Charles as a basis for peace.

The *Heads of the Proposals*, as Ireton's document came to be called, was the most promising set of terms produced yet – considerably more generous to Charles than the Newcastle Propositions of the previous year. It proposed a new, balanced, monarchical constitution. Parliaments were to be time-limited, constituencies reformed; the armed forces controlled by Parliament for ten years (Newcastle said 20). In constitutional terms this was about achieving balance between king, Parliament and people, not about taking power for themselves. Only a small handful of Royalists were to be prosecuted, and most were to get off much more lightly than under the Newcastle terms. Crucially, the Book of Common Prayer was to be allowed, though not mandated; bishops could return, and there was to be no coercion in the Church. Unlike the Newcastle Propositions, this would have allowed Charles to maintain the rudiments of his old Church, but it would also allow for the protection of the Independent congregations.

The new proposals, reported a newsletter, could ensure that 'Monarchy may be so settled, but not to be so hurtful as formerly.'[15] Ireton acknowledged, though, that the *Heads* were still a work in progress. The Agitator William Allen asked for more time to consider them for 'I suppose it is not unknown to you that we are most of us but young Statesmen.'[16] So the document was sent to a committee of 24: half officers, including Ireton and Lambert, and half Agitators. At some point, quite possibly as a result of discussions in committee, a series of additional 'common grievances of this people' were added.

These suggest significant dialogue with the London radicals: an end to the excise as well as fairer taxation, free trade and simplification of the law.

The king wasn't yet willing to treat. He distrusted the officers, he said, largely because they hadn't asked for personal preferment and favours.[17] What on earth could their motives be if it wasn't for advancement and wealth? But Parliament was at last starting to move in the right direction. On the 20th, it heard the *Heads*. The Army began to withdraw into Bedfordshire, away from Westminster.

The king was relocated to Woburn Abbey, the grand country estate – as it happens – of the Russell family, Earls of Bedford. Perhaps, in the house of the great moderate of 1641, the wounds of war might finally start to heal.

But in London and Westminster, the reaction was already under way. On 20 July, demonstrations by conservative crowds around Parliament became so rowdy that a halberdier guard had been placed outside. On the 21st, there was a gathering at Skinners' Hall in the City, where a crowd of conservatives, including watermen, disbanded reformadoes, and apprentices, met to sign a 'Solemn Engagement' calling for the return of the king to London and his restoration on generous terms. It was passed around the City by men calling themselves 'agitators'. The following evening, thousands of reformadoes gathered in St James's.

Then, on the 26th, came anarchy.

It began with a procession by the City leaders to Parliament, to present petitions about control of the City militia. Gathered with them was an angry crowd of apprentices and reformadoes – making fearsome noise and egged on by Presbyterian ministers, they knocked, bustled and hooted outside the Palace.[18] First they invaded the Lords, then the Commons, where they threw street ordure in the faces of MPs. The House was forced to vote to invite the king to London – the invaders even joined in the division themselves.

Denzil Holles made his way back to the Commons, ready to lead the Presbyterians once more. Parliament briefly adjourned, and the City prepared for battle. Drums beat through the town and a letter was sent to Fairfax telling him to stay away. With a counter-revolution now in full swing, Independents were making themselves scarce. The Speakers of both Lords and Commons, plus eight peers and some 57 MPs fled Westminster and made their way to the Army. 'Let the rogues tug it out by the ears' was Charles's gleeful reaction, according to gossip in London.[19]

On the 28th, Fairfax announced the inevitable. His army, after all the debates, would march on London, at the request of the two Speakers. Its hand had been forced, finally, by events.

At Woburn, Charles was mulling over the *Heads*, still believing he held all the cards. Berkeley was exasperated: under the offered terms, he thought, 'never was a Crown (that had been so near lost) so cheaply recovered'.[20] Then, perhaps believing developments in the capital would encourage a better offer from the Army, Charles sent word he was ready to negotiate. Fairfax and Cromwell dispatched a delegation of four officers, including Ireton and Rainborough. They rode out to the king at Woburn and were ushered into the royal presence. Charles eyed the four men suspiciously, but negotiations began. They lasted for three intense summer hours. If, in this fleeting moment, an agreement could be reached, then the Army could march to London with the king at its head and settlement would be ensured.

What if Parliament didn't accept the settlement? pressed Berkeley. They would, said the soldiers. But what if they didn't? 'If they will not agree, we will make them,' declared Rainborough.

But Charles was implacable, despite Berkeley's efforts: 'You cannot be without me. You will fall to ruin if I do not sustain you,' he insisted.[21] The Army commissioners genuinely believed the *Heads* would be an acceptable solution, protecting the religious Independents and a balanced political settlement. Charles saw it as just more evidence of the divisions among his enemies, just one more chance to play them off against each other. Rainborough was so disgusted that he left the negotiations and returned to camp, fuming. The moment slipped away.

Now London had to be secured.

By Sunday 1 August, the army was near Windsor, 24 miles from Westminster. On the 3rd, a Tuesday, the 15,000-strong army marched out onto Hounslow Heath, just 12 miles from Westminster. That evening, joined by their MP supporters, the Army was marching towards London, strung out over a mile and a half. By owl-light, forward units under Rainborough took Southwark; as the sun rose, the City's western defences yielded without a shot fired.[22] Then, on Thursday, the returning MPs were paraded through Westminster, as the church bells sang out, escorted by Fairfax's soldiers, who wore laurel leaves in their hats like conquering Romans. The next day, Parliament was sitting again, and the day after that Fairfax's army paraded in triumph through London. Their discipline impressed everyone: they took not so much as an apple, it was said.[23] Denzil Holles fled the country.*

In August, as poor farmers cast forlorn eyes over a second bad harvest in a row, the Army's headquarters had been moved to Kingston, and the king to the rather comfortable Hampton Court nearby. Then, in early September, Fairfax moved his headquarters again, this time to the small Thameside village of Putney.

Six miles from Westminster, Putney was a quiet community – notable for its large houses with spacious gardens, its breezy open spaces and its rough heath, now dotted with fluttering Army tents. By the Thames sat the compact medieval parish church, its handsome ragstone tower rising into view as boats from London rounded a wide bend in the river. In this church, the General Council of the Army now sat, meeting every Thursday. With the New Model in control, after the failed counter-revolution of the summer, Putney church became the driving saddle of the nation.

---

*He fled to Normandy, to which he'd prudently already dispatched his mother, heir and £2,000. Like many a political exile, he started writing his memoirs, complaining of how England had become a place where 'servants should ride on horses', and 'the meanest of men, the basest and vilest of the nation' had 'got the power into their hands; trampled upon the crown; baffled and misused the Parliament; violated the Laws; destroyed, or suppressed the nobility and gentry'. Underdown, *Pride's Purge*, p. 59.

Initially the Council's focus was on the *Heads*, about which Charles was starting to make positive noises. Leading Independents were using their control of a Parliamentary committee, that for revenue, to lavish him with horses, clothing and luxuries.[24] Parliament, still not fully sold on the *Heads*, had tried sending a new version of the Newcastle Propositions, but these had once more been rebuffed by Charles, to the surprise of absolutely no one. At the same time, an attempt by the radical MPs Henry Marten and Thomas Rainborough to pass a vote in the Commons against any further 'addresses' to Charles had been defeated, with Cromwell and Ireton among those joining the 'noes'. As the Army quartered around the capital, though, and with its arrears still seriously delayed, the civilian radicals, milling around the camps sharing pamphlets and slogans, were gradually creating stronger bonds with the soldiery.

Central to the radicals' efforts was Lilburne. Currently stuck in the Tower, he was visited by a cordial Cromwell, who tried without success to buy him off. Asking Lilburne why he had fallen from those who were his friends, Lilburne replied that it was his friends who had fallen from him. Instead, Lilburne penned an open letter to the soldiers warning them against the leadership. They shouldn't trust the Army 'grandees', he wrote, 'further than you can throw an ox'. The letter was enthusiastically seized upon and published in a new and ardently Royalist mercury that was just hitting the stands. Entitled *Mercurius Pragmaticus*, it was the brainchild of none other than Marchamont Nedham.[25] The previous year, his *Britanicus* had once again attacked the king far more than was prudent to his Parliamentary masters, so they fired him and closed the newspaper. He'd made ends meet for a while as a physician but now the former radical war-party Parliamentarian had re-emerged as an apparently equally convinced monarchist. No doubt the pay was good.

The most startling development, though, was the appearance around the end of September of new agitators, 16 in all, across five cavalry regiments. On 18 October, two of their number got an audience with Fairfax, where they presented him with a forceful, if rather convoluted, manifesto. Called *The Case of the Army Truly Stated*, it was probably written – at least in part – by a twenty-five-year-old ex-soldier named John Wildman.[26] Fiercely bright and iron-cast in his convictions, he had the knowing sneer of exactly the kind one would expect of a man with the motto *Nil Admirari* – 'Let nothing surprise you'. He was someone perpetually convinced that those in power would turn out to be hypocrites. And to be fair they frequently did.

The *Case* had been signed by the New Agitators at Guildford a few days earlier. It castigated the grandees and the General Council for their political failures. Power, it claimed, was originally vested in the people and their representatives. The current Parliament should be dissolved within ten months, followed by a general election in which all Englishmen aged twenty-one and over – except Royalists – should have the vote. It also demanded liberty of conscience and drastic reform of the law.

Soon, *The Case of the Army* was available to buy on London's streets. This was dangerous stuff, but Fairfax – perhaps against his better judgement – agreed to discuss it at the next General Council, due to sit on the 21st. At that Council, the *Case* was referred to a committee, expected to produce a stern rebuttal. Instead, it wrote to the New Agitators and asked them 'in a friendly way' to attend the next General Council, scheduled for Thursday 28 October.[27] It was to be a monumental decision.

The day before this meeting was due to take place, one of Cromwell's soldiers, Robert Everard, was at the Army headquarters at Putney. Here he presented yet another document. The leadership were expecting to discuss the *Case*, but what Everard brought was something completely different. It was a short pamphlet – just a few pages – approved the same day at a meeting between the New Agitators, Wildman and some other civilian radicals.

Its pages contained a strident statement of first principles. Parliament was sovereign – there was no mention of the king or the Lords – but it could not override certain basic rights: freedom of religion, freedom from conscription and equality before the law. These could never be given away by the people: they were inalienable. There should, meanwhile, be biennial Parliaments, inferior in authority only to the electorate itself. Crucially, it suggested that the franchise should be reformed so that constituencies reflected not tax contribution – as in the *Heads* – but the number of people. It was a document of quite fundamental radicalism: based on the premise that the defeat of the king – and the 'Norman Yoke' he represented – had left the people a blank slate on which to scrawl their own, new, rational and equitable laws. Even the document's name conveyed its democratic character: it was an *Agreement of the People*, and its approval by the whole population, the authors hoped, would form the basis of a new English democracy.[28]

The next morning, the 28th, the General Council met, as usual, in Putney church. Over the next three days, one of the most remarkable meetings in the whole of English history took place, in which soldiers and civilians argued about the future of the constitution, the nature of sovereignty and the right to vote. It was a pivotal moment in the revolution, one of those times in history when events stood on the edge of a knife.

Fairfax was unwell, reposing at nearby Turnham Green, so Cromwell took the chair. It was a sign of things to come, as the gentlemanly Fairfax, very much someone on whom greatness had been thrust, began a long withdrawal from political activism. He had stood by his men as they challenged Denzil Holles, but he was hardly a firebrand. In fact, he was something of a political ingénue. Few doubted his courage, but, as the Royalist Countess of Derby put it, 'there are various opinions about his intellect'.[29]

He was leaving the stage to more committed revolutionaries – of many stripes. Henry Ireton, one such revolutionary, was there at Putney, a man whose undoubted intelligence was outrun only by his own belief in it. Also there was the very different Thomas Rainborough, someone whose presence probably raised some eyebrows. He had been at headquarters for over a month, where he had been in a heated and occasionally table-thumping feud with the generals. Cromwell had opposed Rainborough's recent commission as a vice-admiral in the navy, leading to a disagreement in which the two men had to be physically separated. Fairfax – perhaps not unreasonably – then made the assumption that Rainborough's new navy commission would make his regimental duties in the army more difficult, and had given them to someone else. The whole debacle had left the ever-irascible Rainborough furious with his commanding officers and – one suspects – rather spoiling for a fight.

Also in Putney church was Edward Sexby, along with two civilian radicals: John Wildman and Maximilian Petty, and two New Agitators. Such was their obscurity that the secretary William Clarke, taking detailed notes, identified one, Robert Everard, by his clothing ('Buffe-coat') and the other (still unidentified today) only by his Bedfordshire accent ('Bedfordshire Man').

Sexby began. 'The cause of our misery is upon two things,' he said. 'We sought to satisfy all men, and it was well; but in going to do it we have dissatisfied all men.' They had laboured to please a king who would only be happy if they cut their own throats, and they had supported Parliament that was just a 'Company of rotten members'.[30] He told Cromwell and Ireton bluntly that their reputations had been 'much blasted' by their attempts to please the king and the Presbyterians.

The *Agreement* was then read. Cromwell, responding, tried imme-diately to pour cold water. The *Agreement* promised 'very great alter-ations of the very Government of the Kingdom', he agreed, but he wondered if 'the spirits and temper of the people of this Nation are prepared to receive and go along with it'. Perhaps it was 'good in the end', but how would it be implemented?[31] Critically, he and Ireton argued both that adopting the *Agreement* – however desirable – would in practice be very difficult; and they argued that the Army was bound by its previous promises since June, namely to obey Parliament and promote settlement with the king. The new path forged by the radicals would force them to go back on these.

Rainborough responded, speaking with fluent eloquence and no little sarcasm. He scoffed at the suggestion that this would all be too *difficult*: when Parliament embarked on the wars, surely they had considered there might have been some *difficulties*? And he turned to history: 'If writings be true,' he averred, 'there hath been many scufflings between the honest men of England and those that have tyrannised over them.'[32] Wildman and Ireton then faced off, often in very abstract terms, over the question of the prior 'engagements' (i.e. commitments) that would necessarily be broken if the Army pursued a radical constitutional path. In the end, Cromwell acknowledged he was not 'wedded and glued to forms of government', indeed he was prepared to acknowledge that 'the foundation and supremacy is in the people, radically in them'. But all that came out of the first day's debate was the appointment of a committee, which would look through previous Army declarations and see where the *Agreement* might be compatible.

The following day's meeting of this committee took place not in Putney church, but in the lodgings of the quartermaster-general.* In the morning, a prayer meeting was held. Then, after refreshment, the civilians joined with Everard, first gathering by the door – engaging no doubt in hushed conversation – before Cromwell, again in the chair with Fairfax still indisposed, called them to come closer.[33] At some point, Rainborough entered. He was late, he said, because he'd been forced to visit London the previous night. Whom could he have been meeting?

Cromwell tried to get the committee to consider previous 'engagements' – pulling out a handy 164-page compendium of the Army's declarations. Rainborough, though, wanted to discuss the *Agreement* as a matter of urgency: 'to see whether it were a paper that did hold forth justice and righteousness'. Rainborough held the room. So the *Agreement* was read, then the first clause read again. It was the one that stated that Parliamentary constituencies 'ought to be more indifferently proportioned, according to the number of inhabitants'.

This, Ireton thought, would be an easy win. Surely, he argued, this implied giving every male inhabitant the vote. It implied universal male suffrage. Whether this was the actual intention isn't clear: it had been one of the demands stated in the *Case of the Army*, though the text of the *Agreement* was much less specific, merely saying that distribution of constituencies should be based on population size not tax contribution. But what happened in the heat of the debate was that Rainborough – not, himself, one of the authors – decided to press the point that it was. '[F]or really I think,' he said, 'that the poorest he that is in England hath a life to live as the greatest he; and therefore truly, Sir, I think it's clear, that every man that is to live under a government ought first by his own consent to put himself under that Government.'

Ireton countered: 'For my part I think it is no right at all. I think that no person hath a right to an interest or share in the disposing or determining of the affairs of the Kingdom, and in choosing those

---

*He just so happened to be Henry Ireton's brother.

that shall determine what laws we shall be ruled by here, no person hath a right to this, that hath not a permanent fixed interest in this Kingdom.' Rainborough was advocating universal male suffrage; Ireton, on the other hand, believed voting rights should be vested in those who owned property: those with what he termed 'a permanent fixed interest' in the nation.

Ireton was forensic and clever; Rainborough eloquent, logical and passionate. 'I do not find any thing in the law of God,' Rainborough said, 'that a Lord shall choose 20 burgesses, and a gentleman but two, or a poor man shall choose none.' Ireton argued that manhood suffrage was a threat to property. Rainborough questioned 'what we have fought for', is it a law 'which enslaves the people of England that they should be bound by laws in which they have no voice at all'?

The debate was hot, and Rainborough in particular argued with considerable force, but it never quite boiled over into full-blown acrimony. Ireton specifically disavowed *ad hominems*: 'We speak to the paper, and to that matter of the paper, not to persons.'

As the debate opened up, Ireton was gradually losing the room – save for his father-in-law Cromwell – and even Cromwell was ready to compromise. Sexby and Wildman both made heartfelt pleas for democracy: to Sexby, if the soldiers had been fighting for anything other than 'a right to the Kingdom', then 'we *were* mere mercenary soldiers'. Now, it seems, 'except a man hath a fixed estate in this Kingdom, he hath no right in this Kingdom. I wonder we were so much deceived!' Winning the vote, Sexby argued, 'was the ground that we took up arms, and it is the ground which we shall maintain'. To Wildman it was 'the undeniable maxim of Government: that all government is in the free consent of the people'.

Other officers tried to foster a compromise: could foreigners be excluded? Maximilian Petty, the civilian radical, thought that perhaps they could. Maybe servants, apprentices and the very poor shouldn't have the vote, either? Debate continued, though Clarke's shorthand notes eventually tailed off. By the end of the day, it seems, an agreement had been made that the vote should go to all men save servants and almstakers. After all this, the very poorest he (let alone the poorest she) was to be excluded. But it would be a radical redistribution of power nonetheless.

On Sunday, a break allowed Rainborough to visit Lilburne in the Tower. Then, Monday's debates brought some startling statements against Charles: he was, said one Captain Bishop, a tyrant and a 'man of blood'. The radicals were arguing that there could be no safety with Charles still enjoying any power. Cromwell, though, still thought that the Army couldn't legitimately overthrow him. In any case, simply sweeping away the constitution in favour of a new one wasn't going to solve everything: even the best regime, Cromwell pointed out, was but 'dross and dung in comparison of Christ'. There then followed a lengthy argument over the king's right to veto bills from the Commons, in which Wildman was provocative, Ireton once again enjoyed himself rather too much, and nothing was agreed.

By now, though, the momentum was elsewhere. Wildman had written a pungent denunciation of Cromwell, Ireton and the 'grandees', entitled *Putney Projects*, and it was already circulating among the regiments, even while Rainborough and Ireton were arguing over the franchise.[34] New agitators were appearing across the whole Army, and the men of Robert Lilburne's regiment* were already in open defiance. In fact – on that momentous second day of debate, officers had been repeatedly called out of the room to discuss how to deal with them after they had refused orders to march to Newcastle and remained in the Dunstable area. Agents were trying to get the soldiers to subscribe to the *Agreement*. Perhaps the radical takeover of the Army could be completed not by persuasion at Putney, but by infiltrating the ranks in the field.

At Putney, progress was gradually being made towards a statement of the Army's desired settlement, but the radicals were pushing for a general rendezvous and arguing against further dealings with the king. On 8 November, there was another battle over the franchise in which Cromwell suggested that manhood suffrage 'did tend very much to Anarchy'. By this point, though, Fairfax and Cromwell had decided that the debates had gone far enough. The radicals were winning the

---

*Robert was John's less radical brother; there was also a third brother, Henry, who eventually became a Royalist.

argument; they couldn't under any circumstances be allowed to win
control. Under a motion by Cromwell, the officers and Agitators
were sent back to their regiments. Clarke's notes were finally brought
to a close.*

On the 9th, Fairfax ordered the rendezvous, but – in order to prevent the New Agitators turning it into a mass uprising against the
grandees – it was to be spread over three places and four days starting
the following week. Events were now moving very fast. If no settlement could be found, wrote a Royalist mercury, 'a general insurrection against the wealthier sort' was surely inevitable.[35] That day, John
Lilburne happened to have been granted bail from the Tower. Who
knew where he might turn up next?

Nor was he the only one at large. On the evening of the 11th,
Charles escaped from Hampton Court. He had received warning, he
said, that the Agitators were plotting to kill him. On hearing the news,
Fairfax thought Charles was going north. He wrote an urgent letter
to Lambert at York, telling him to post guards on the main roads.
But Charles turned the other way, and by the morning of the 14th he
had reached the Isle of Wight, where he placed himself in the hands
of the moderate Colonel Robert Hammond (who also happened to
be Cromwell's cousin). He was soon installed at Carisbrooke Castle,
which while not especially comfortable, did at least have an excellent
bowling green.

By now the radicals had gained a new name – one that recalled the
anti-enclosure riots of 1607 – the Levellers. And they were ready to
make their play. If they could take control of the New Model Army,
they could usher in a true revolution. In print, they urged the Army
to disobey orders and commit to a single general rendezvous. On the
15th, the first official rendezvous began at Corkbush Field near Ware in
Hertfordshire. As the troops gathered, civilian radicals passed around
them distributing copies of the *Agreement*. John Lilburne had travelled up from London, and was waiting at Ware for the opportunity

---

*They were eventually squirrelled away in an Oxford college until rediscovered – the lost words
of Rainborough with them – by an understandably excited Victorian archivist.

to give a stirring oration. Fairfax arrived, trying to soothe the ranks. Then – some considerable time later – another regiment appeared on the field, that of Thomas Harrison, but without its officers. Many carried copies of the *Agreement*, stuck in their hatbands, with the words 'England's freedom and soldier's rights' scrawled over it. It seemed that a wholescale radical mutiny was taking place.

But Fairfax met them with determination. A group of his officers, probably including Cromwell, rode into the men, plucking some of the papers out of their hats before the rest, duly chastened, voluntarily took them out. Then, Robert Lilburne's regiment also arrived, again without most of its officers. It had been in open revolt for three weeks already, and Fairfax already knew they were coming. By the time they arrived they had already marched 20 miles, and Fairfax was able to address his other regiments – to noisy cheering – while Lilburne's waited nearby. When Lilburne's men refused to back down and remove the copies of the *Agreement* that they, too, kept in their hats, a group of officers charged them with swords drawn. The officers, again almost certainly including Cromwell, then plucked the papers from the mutineers' hats, and they submitted. Eight or nine of the mutineers from Corkbush Field were subjected to instant court martial and sentenced to death, all were pardoned bar three, who were left to draw lots. The loser was shot.

The Levellers' attempt to win control of the New Model Army had failed. John Lilburne, 'sick of the sullens', returned to London.[36]

13

Blood Defileth the Land

The radicalisation of the New Model Army in 1647 had utterly changed the direction of the revolution. Even with the defeat of the Levellers, the rise to prominence of men like Oliver Cromwell and Henry Ireton had drastically transformed the scene. Just as important, Charles's sudden escape from Hampton Court had thrown the Army's plans for a negotiated settlement into complete chaos. Now, the Army closed ranks to deal with this new threat, which of course bore a striking resemblance to the old one: royalism.

At Christmas, decorations appeared across London, in defiance of a Parliamentary ban on celebrations. In Kent, there were demonstrations in favour of the king and the old Church: 'For God, King Charles, and Kent'.[1] Charles finally made a treaty with someone. Not Parliament, or the Army, but the Scots. Their secret 'Engagement' committed England to three years of Presbyterianism, before settling the Church for good through an augmented version of the Westminster Assembly. It was signed, sealed and buried in lead in the garden at Carisbrooke, so no one would know about it until it was too late. It was a terrible deal for both king and Scots, and there seemed little doubt that Charles would go back on it if he ever got the chance. But it meant the Scots were likely to march into England again, this time as soldiers for the king.

On 3 January 1648, the Commons responded to the King's escape by passing a Vote of No Addresses, ruling out further negotiations with Charles. It was followed shortly afterwards by an angry Army declaration,

quite possibly drafted by Ireton, calling for the 'settling and securing of the Parliament and the Kingdom without the King and against him'. If the king went against the safety of the people, it was him that would have to go.[2]

Economic conditions got worse. In Cheshire, 'many doleful and hideous lamentations' poured forth from the poor.[3] A Leveller petition, exclaiming the 'warning tears of the oppressed', told its audience to 'hark, hark at our doors, how our children cry Bread, Bread, Bread'. '[N]ecessity,' it threatened, 'dissolves all laws and government and hunger will break through stone walls.'[4]

Through spring, hundreds of reformadoes and former Royalists flooded north to join the Scots. On the king's accession day, 27 March, there were disorderly celebrations and bonfires in London, aimed at goading Parliament and the Puritans, followed by a serious riot in early April. Royalists were drawing support from those who hankered after the old world of Christmas and merriment, which was now very visibly under attack. The Parliamentarian authorities hardly helped: their prohibition of stage plays was renewed in February, together with an order to pull down theatres, fine audiences and have actors whipped. In May, Parliament ordered capital punishment for those who committed 'Blasphemy'.[5] In Norwich, arguments over bonfires and feasts for Charles's accession day led to a petition, a riot and the accidental detonation of the county magazine at the cost of some hundred lives. Royalists also continued to draw support from people shocked at the social levelling that had been linked to Puritanism before the war, that had exploded in the heady days of 1641 and 1642, and that had only become more pronounced after the war had ended. A rhyme that circulated in 1648 encapsulated this perfectly, when it mocked the Parliamentarians as upstart democrats whose support came from unruly women and the poor:

> Come clowns, and come boys.
> Come hober-de-hoys.
>> Come females of each degree;
> Stretch your throats, bring in your votes.
>> And make good the anarchy.[6]

That spring there were a series of conservative petitions from the counties. When Essex petitioners came to London in May, they were cheered through the streets. Surrey freeholders gathered at Dorking with a conservative petition on the 8th, agreeing to reconvene on Putney Heath on the 16th. From there, they marched downriver and crowded into Westminster Hall. Troops had to clear them and a few were killed in the fracas. By now, a major Royalist rebellion had broken out in South Wales, and Royalists had seized Berwick and Carlisle in the north. Military confrontation was now inevitable.

Cromwell was dispatched with a force to South Wales. Before he left, he took time to attend a special prayer meeting at Windsor Castle. It was urgent, passionate and angry. Charles was reviled in biblical terms. 'It was our duty,' it was recalled, 'to call Charles Stuart, that man of blood, to account for the blood that he has shed.'[7]

In a wet May, the counties of the south-east slid into rebellion against Parliament, followed by much of the navy, stationed in the Downs. At the beginning, Kent was the epicentre. Fairfax was sent in, gathering his troops on Blackheath and pushing the enemy back towards Maidstone. The Royalists were disorganised and badly led, so within a few weeks, the seasoned general had retaken the county, but a body of Royalist soldiers had made it across the Thames into Essex. There was now a threat that East Anglia might rise up; and with Fairfax's army already scattered across England and Wales stamping out local Royalist uprisings, defeat in Essex would have been very dangerous. It was a crucial moment.

In June, the Royalists made their stand at Colchester, led by the veteran Sir Charles Lucas – himself a native of the city and brother to unpopular landlord Sir John. Thomas Rainborough – who was an expert in siege warfare – was dispatched to the town. In London, the Royalists were recruiting openly. Even Thomas Lunsford, the arch-Cavalier former Lieutenant of the Tower was abroad again in the City, drumming up support for the king.[8] That month, Pontefract Castle in Yorkshire, a huge medieval fortress overlooking the Great North Road and thus one of the keys to the north, had been surprised by Royalists.

Then, in July, came the main act. On the 8th, the Scottish army that
had been gathering finally crossed the border, led by Charles's old
Scottish friend the Duke of Hamilton. Through streaming rain and
driving wind, they slogged and plundered southwards, not down the
east coast, but through Cumberland, Westmorland and south into
Lancashire, via the wilds of Shap Summit with the howling scarp of
the Pennines to their left. By now it had been joined by 3,000 seasoned
Royalists under the Yorkshireman Marmaduke Langdale. But though
Hamilton's force had grown to over 20,000-strong, many of his
recruits were very poorly trained. Some could barely fire a musket,
even had their powder been dry.

Fairfax was still laying siege to Colchester in Essex, so Cromwell
raced north from Wales to deal with the threat. Lambert, now a major-
general at just twenty-eight, was already in the north, shadowing
Hamilton. The Scots continued on their ponderous march. They
stopped for seven days at the grey old cloth town of Kendal, and
five at the tiny castle-village of Hornby on the Lune. Everywhere
they went they exacted a heavy price on the local peasantry, already
straining under an awful harvest.

Immediately south of Hornby was the mass of Bowland Forest,
wild moorland, impassable to an army even without the bad weather.
So Hamilton would either have to march south-east into Yorkshire,
and strike towards the besieged Royalist-held castle at Pontefract. Or
turn south-west, follow the River Lune towards Lancaster, then march
south through Lancashire, where he might recruit more from the old
Royalist strongholds of that county and Cheshire, and beyond. The
decision was a fraught one, but eventually Hamilton picked the latter.

Meanwhile, between Leeds and Knaresborough, Cromwell had
finally joined up with Lambert. Now they turned west, across the
Pennines, searching out Hamilton for battle.

By the time Cromwell caught up with the Scots, Hamilton was near
Preston. Or at least, his infantry was. The cavalry had pushed forward
and was now somewhere near Wigan. Battle began on 17 August as
Cromwell attacked hard through muddy fields: 'There was nothing
but fire and smoke', while '[t]he bullets flew freely', wrote one of his

officers.[9] It was a complex day of skirmishes and fierce fighting. But the outcome was decisive. Hamilton's Scots were put to total rout. The next day, the Scots cavalry – their powder soaked by the rain – were chased away. Finally, the sorry and sodden remnants of Hamilton's army were crushed near Winwick. Ten thousand Scots were captured, and Hamilton himself was hurried to London for trial, his days now very much numbered.*

The Royalists effort had collapsed once more. What would come to be known as the Second Civil War was over. On the 28th, Colchester finally surrendered.

Fairfax, furious at the unnecessary loss of life caused by the Royalist insurgency, sentenced four commanders to death by firing squad. One escaped, another was spared on discovery that he was a foreigner. Two, Sir George Lisle and Sir Charles Lucas, were shot. Pontefract was now the only major stronghold to remain.

Still, though, Parliament continued to offer negotiation to the stricken king. In fact, the popular violence of the year had only served to convince MPs that a settlement was all the more urgent. As the New Model Army fought the Royalist resurgence, Parliament – terrified by where this all might lead – had moved back towards a more moderate posture. The 11 members, including Denzil Holles, had been readmitted, and now Parliament had sent emissaries to the Isle of Wight to begin negotiations on what would hopefully develop into the Treaty of Newport. It looked like after everything – after all the blood spent – Parliament would betray the cause and come to a weak peace.

The torrential summer rains brought yet another terrible harvest, now the third in succession. In Cheshire, market officers wailed that 'the poor were very harsh with us and thought it to be our fault'.[10] The Levellers were resurgent and now had a regular newspaper, called *The Moderate* (the jokes were predictable). In the summer, the radical MP Henry Marten had ridden home to Berkshire and raised a regiment committed to fighting 'all tyrants whatsoever'. He

---

*He was tried in the new year and beheaded on 9 March 1649.

also – probably – penned an urgent pamphlet in the name of the 'plain men of England against the rich and mighty'. It promised a continued fight against the rich: 'we shall make bold with our servants and families to visit your rich houses, barns, butteries, cupboards and tables', and to take what they wanted.[11] A huge petition, claiming to represent thousands of 'well-affected persons', was presented on 11 September, calling for the abolition of tithes, monopolies and the excise, an end to enclosures, the relief of beggars and for justice against the 'capital authors' of the wars. Parliament ignored it, and two days later a crowd pressed against the Commons door with another. Demonstrators were heard saying that there was 'no use of a King or Lords any longer'.[12]

In was in the Army, though, that the real revolutionary spirit was stirring. The soldiers seethed with anger. How dare Charles go against God's providence that had brought victory to Parliament; how dare he force them to risk shedding their blood once more. Charles was 'guilty of all the bloodshed in these intestine wars', said a petition from Ireton's regiment.[13] He had 'polluted the land with blood', said another.[14]

Parliament was desperate for a treaty, so they threw concessions at the king. As Charles chafed over the followers he was supposed to abandon to punishment, Parliament agreed to revise the number down. When he rejected the abolition of his bishops, which had been passed in October 1646, Nathaniel Fiennes took to the floor to argue that moderate episcopacy was, in fact, acceptable. Charles, though, was just waiting for a chance to escape again. MPs were so desperate for a deal that would bring Charles back to Westminster that they couldn't see the obvious: the king was simply stalling, looking for an opportunity to evade his captors and slip away to the Continent.

He had been helped by Jane Whorwood, a tall, red-haired loyalist with a pockmarked face, whose court connections went back to her Surrey childhood. Earlier in the year, she had consulted the Parliament-supporting astrologer William Lilly, who had put her in touch with a locksmith who provided a file and some acid to aid the king's escape from Carisbrooke. The plan had come to naught, and by September,

Cartmel Priory, photographed in the mid-twentieth century. In 1604, it was the scene of a raucous invasion by cross-dressing youngsters.

London in 1647, from an engraving by Wenceslaus Hollar. The old medieval city was growing fast and spilling out from the old walls. One of the fastest growing areas was Southwark, south of the river.

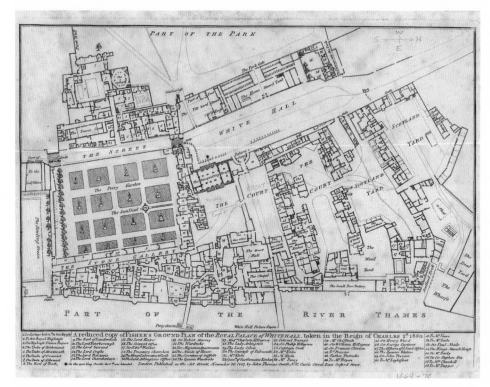

Plan of Whitehall Palace in the reign of Charles II. The long street (now called Whitehall, then bifurcated by the Holbein Gate) that ran from Parliament and the Abbey to Charing Cross would be the scene of mass demonstrations in the 1640s that changed the course of English history.

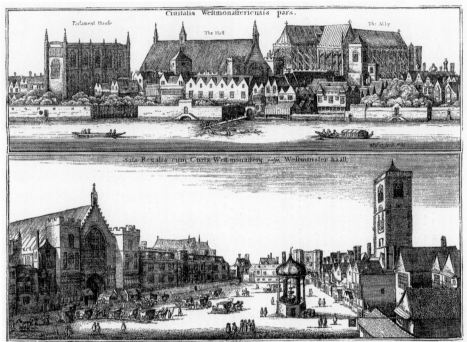

TWO VIEWS OF WESTMINSTER. *(From Original Etchings by Hollar, 1647.)*

Westminster, 1647, after an engraving by Wenceslaus Hollar. While London was by far the largest city in England, its neighbour Westminster housed Whitehall Palace, the great medieval abbey, the main law courts, and Parliament itself.

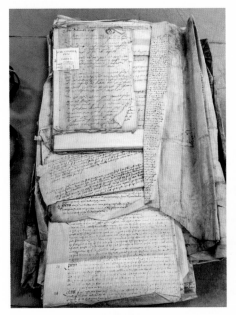

The records of the Star Chamber suit from 1604, relating to the nefarious activities of James Anderton, a Lancashire Justice of Peace. The case file includes a vivid description of the Cartmel wedding of 1604.

James I of England (VI of Scotland), painted in later life. He was an enigmatic, elusive figure, whose attempts to maintain peace fell to ruin in the 1620s.

Hoghton Tower, Lancashire. It was here that in 1617 James I witnessed a 'rushbearing', prompting him to issue a proclamation in support of Sunday sports and traditional pastimes.

COTSWOLD GAMES.

'The Cotswold Games', from *Annalia Dubrensia* (1636). Created by the lawyer Robert Dover, part of the fun of the games was the annoyance they would cause to local Puritans. Like the traditional society they were supposed to reinforce, the games were clearly hierarchical.

George Villiers, Duke of Buckingham, painted by Peter Paul Rubens. He was staggeringly good looking.

Archbishop William Laud. Hailing from a relatively humble background in Reading, Berkshire, Laud was pompous, authoritarian and donnish. But it was his belief in ceremony, hierarchy and beautification – and the exaltation of the clergy – that won him most enemies.

King Charles I, painted on horseback under a triumphal arch. Like his kingship, this was supposed to be a vision of order and good government.

The *Sovereign of the Seas* was launched in 1637. It was the pride of Charles's 'ship money fleet', which hoped to bolster England's naval strength. But the levy was constitutionally dubious and caused considerable opposition.

The Earl of Strafford's trial in the House of Lords, 1641. Spectators were encouraged to come and witness, except the king himself, who was forced to watch from a box, incognito, though – it was said – 'conspicuous enough'.

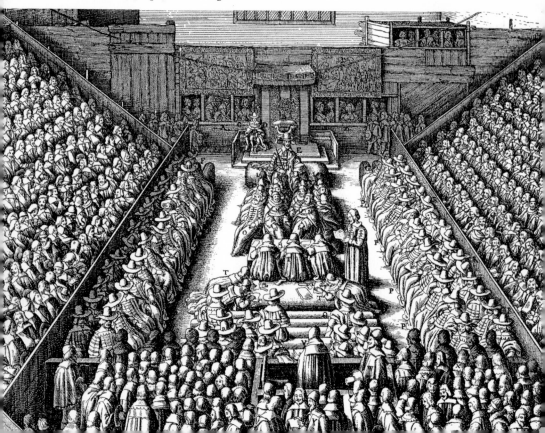

The Arch-Prelate of St Andrewes in Scotland reading the new Service-booke in his pontificalibus assaulted by men & women, with Crickets stooles Stickes and Stones.

The rising of Prentises and Sea-men on South-wark side to assault the Arch-bishops of Canter-burys House at Lambeth.

Charles's rule unravels. The riot at St Giles's Cathedral, Edinburgh, 1637, and the March on Lambeth Palace, 1640.

a Letter sent to Mr Pym

Mr Pym, doe not think that a guard of men can protect you, if you persist in your traiterous Courses and wiked designes, I haue sent a Paper-messenger to you, and if this does not touch your heart, a dag—ger shall soe soon as I am recouered of my plague=—sore: In the meane time you may be forborn, because no better man may be endan-gered for you. Repent, Traitor

Colonell Lunsford assaulting the Londoners at Westminster Hall, with a great rout of ruffinly Cavaleiros

Tension mounts in 1641. John Pym receives a letter containing a plague sore, and Thomas Lunsford fights with crowds at Westminster.

Oliver Cromwell leading cavalry at Marston Moor, in a nineteenth-century painting. The battle was as much a Scottish victory as one for the English Parliamentarians, but it also marked a key moment in the rise of the East Anglian farmer who would become head of state in the 1650s.

The Battle of Naseby, 1645, from a contemporary print.

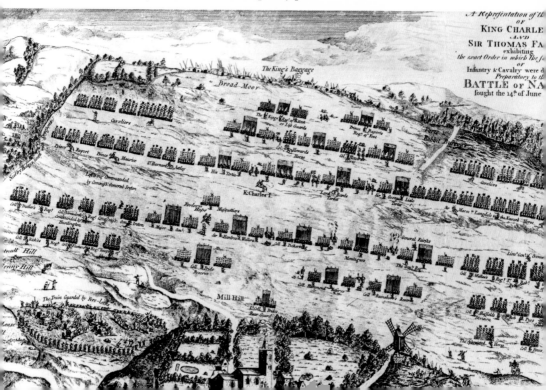

THE
Parliament of Women:

With the merry Laws by them newly
Enacted, To live in more Ease, Pomp, Pride,
and Wantonness : But especially that they
might have Superiority, and domineer over their
Husbands. With a new way found out by them
to cure any old, or new Cuckolds, and how
both parties may recover their credit
and honesty again.

LONDON, Printed for *W.W.* and are to be sold by *Fra.Grove*, at
his shop on Snow-hill, near the Sarazens-head. 1656.

The Parliament of
Women: a contemporary
satire mocking the way
the wars and political
conflict had turned the
world upside down.

Matthew Hopkins, the
notorious Witchfinder
General, interrogating
two of his victims. The
image references the imp
Grizzell Greedigutt, who
in a roundabout way
helped one of the accused
women to be acquitted.

Thomas Rainborough, from a contemporary engraving. His stirring arguments at Putney saw him emerge as a major leader of the 'Leveller' movement.

Henry Ireton, Cromwell's son-in-law. Ireton was a sophisticated political thinker, and although he acted as a conservative opponent to Rainborough at Putney, it was his revolutionary drive which led to the trial and execution of the king.

The execution of Charles Stuart, 'that man of blood', from a cheap woodcut. The late king's trial and execution took place in the public eye. Those who couldn't attend could follow through cheap print.

The English Improver Improved, by Captain Walter Blith. A classic text on farming by a member of the 'Hartlib Circle', it encapsulated the spirit of 'improvement' that took hold during the Republic and the later seventeenth century.

A Quaker meeting with a female preacher, by Egbert van Heemskerk the Elder.

A London coffeehouse. From the later seventeenth century the consumption of coffee took off in urban society. Coffeehouses were a place where people (mostly men) could get together, read newspapers and discuss the latest political gossip.

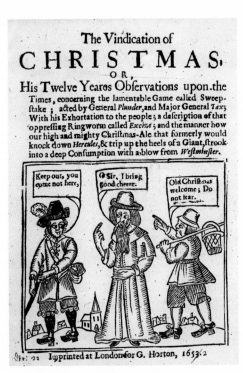

The Vindication of Christmas (1652) by the impish Royalist poet John Taylor. During the Republic, dissident monarchists liked to hark back to an old age of warm hospitality and bawdy fun, in contrast to what they saw as the cultural austerity of the Puritan regime.

Margaret Cavendish's weird, wonderful, and prescient *Description of a New World Called the Blazing-World*. Such a rich and strange text invites multiple readings. In many ways it anticipates modern science fiction, but it's also a meditation on power, science and imperialism, told from a proto-feminist perspective.

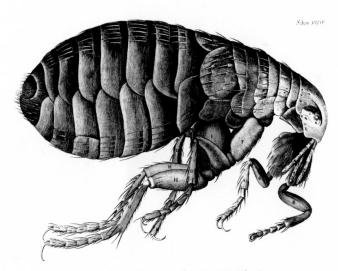

The famous flea from Robert Hooke's *Micrographia* (1665). The images were part of a revolutionary new vision of the world – and the universe – allowed by new technologies such as microscopes and telescopes.

King James II of England (VII of Scotland). He is often blamed for losing his Crown from a position of strength in 1685, but the seeds of his downfall were longer.

Mary of Modena, James II's second wife. When, to general surprise at the age of twenty-nine, she gave birth to a healthy son, it pushed England into yet another political crisis, leading to yet another revolution.

in what would prove her last correspondence with Lilly, he simply advised that her master accept the proposed Treaty of Newport.[15]

Fairfax, too, still favoured a negotiated peace. Cromwell, meanwhile, was out of London. In October, Thomas Rainborough had been sent from Colchester to Pontefract. But on the 29th, a group of Royalists had invaded his quarters and tried to kidnap him. The garrulous radical put up a stout fight, ended only by the cold blade of a Cavalier sword. His death, sudden and shocking as it was, became a martyrdom thanks to the capable publicity machine of the London Levellers. His coffin, trailed by mourners wearing ribbons of green (Rainborough's colour), was processed through London to its resting place at Wapping, while *The Moderate* exhorted its readers against the Royalists: 'The Lord stir up your hearts to be avenged of these bloody enemies.'[16]

Rainborough's death left his task of leading the siege of Pontefract empty, so it was filled by Cromwell. It was something that allowed him the luxury, at least for a time, of avoiding involvement in politics, and immersing himself in the considerably less dangerous business of war.

So it fell to Henry Ireton to take on the monarchy.

His fundamental position hadn't changed. The key underpinning to everything was the safety of the people: *salus populi*. Constitutions and human laws were all very well, but in extreme circumstances they could be broken. These, now, were extreme circumstances.

Late in September he'd attempted to persuade Fairfax to use the Army against Parliament. Fairfax had refused and Ireton had tendered his resignation, though Fairfax also refused that. Instead, Ireton rode down to Windsor, to turn his fierce intelligence to a new manifesto eventually to be called the *Remonstrance of the Army*. It was a complex, sometimes abstruse document. But its main aims were clear enough: justice against the king, and for revolution.

By mid-November, it was ready, so Ireton presented it to a General Council of the Officers, which had just convened in the great nave of St Albans Abbey.* They debated it from the 10th. Persuading the officers was no easy task: even with the bloodshed of the Second Civil War laying heavy on their minds, the senior soldiers were unwilling to let go of the idea of a treaty with Charles. Then, on 15 November, everything changed. That day, the Commons, still hoping for that elusive deal, voted that the king should be restored to 'a condition of honour, freedom and safety', and that he should be allowed to return to London, once the treaty was completed.[17]

This was too much. The next day, the Army's General Council approved Ireton's *Remonstrance*.[18] On the 18th, it was put before the Commons. It took four hours to read, for it was long and very badly written.[19] Supporters watched their fellow MPs like hawks to gauge their reaction. The *Remonstrance* implied that the people were sovereign; that rule should be contractual; and that the Army had the moral backing of God's providence. Its recurrent motif was *Salus Populi, Suprema Lex*: the Safety of the People is the Supreme Law. It was the *Safety of the People* that the proposed Treaty of Newport threatened, for the king had shown no remorse, no likelihood of holding to his promises. It was the *Safety of the People* that demanded thorough constitutional reform, too: more representative government; an agreement of the people, modelled on that of the Levellers, to protect the constitutional fundamentals, assent to which would be a requirement for all office holders including any future kings. And, ultimately, the *Safety of the People* demanded something more. It demanded 'capital punishment upon the principal author and some prime instruments of our late wars'; that 'the Person of the King may and shall be proceeded against in a way of justice for the blood spilt'; that the king and his worst associates be 'speedily brought to justice, for the treason, blood and mischief he is therein guilty of'.[20]

Moderates were horrified and the House put off discussion of the *Remonstrance* for a week, instead turning to discuss the latest offer from Charles. Nedham's *Pragmaticus* reported that, as anti-Army MPs slipped back to their lodgings at the end of the day, they were followed by pairs of soldiers, muttering threats.[21]

---

*This body was a version of the old General Council of the Army, but it had no Agitators.

Around this time, Cromwell changed his mind. It was now, he believed, inevitable that the Army would need to stop Parliament's treaty with Charles. On the 25th, Cromwell wrote to Hammond on the Isle of Wight. There had been, Cromwell wrote, 'some remarkable providences, and appearances of the Lord'. Now was Hammond's time to do the work of the Lord. He had sought out retirement on the island: 'Did not God find him out there?' Cromwell asked. '[T]hen tell me, whether there be not some glorious and high meaning in all this.' Was not the Army 'a lawful power, called by God to oppose and fight against the King'? 'My dear friend, let us look into providences; surely they mean somewhat.'[22] Cromwell needed Hammond not to waver: to hold fast to God's plan rather than his sympathy with a stricken king.

But Hammond was no longer in charge. On 21 November, he'd been relieved. Next day, the Army had moved from St Albans to Windsor.

Ireton's plan was to dissolve Parliament. He needed friendly MPs to declare against the Parliament and come to the Army. This he could use to declare that Parliament had lost legitimacy, as a pretext for sending it away. But others argued for a purge: to keep the current Parliament sitting, while removing the most troublesome moderates. The General Council was meeting in Windsor Castle. On the 26th, officers prayed from nine in the morning until five in the afternoon, asking that they be made instruments of justice, and 'that righteousness and judgement may flow in the land'.[23] On the 28th, the order was given that so many at Westminster and London feared. The Army, once more, would march on the capital.

As news passed along the Thames, Royalists began to flee the City. Some buried their money. A letter was rushed north to Pontefract, summoning Cromwell to ride immediately to London. He set off, slowly.

On the 30th, the Army issued a declaration, impugning Parliament and calling 'upright', i.e. supportive, members to withdraw. Meanwhile, they would draw up in London, 'there to follow Providence as God shall clear our way'.[24]

The same night on the south coast, a detachment of soldiers crossed the Solent, passing from the mainland to the Isle of Wight in a ferocious rainstorm. The king, at Carisbrooke, was writing a letter to his queen when his trusted servant Henry Firebrace rushed in with news that Newport was teeming with soldiers from the New Model. By the middle of the night, the rain still lashing the grounds of the old stone castle, the new guard at Carisbrooke was in place. First thing, as the dawn broke, the king was woken by two soldiers and hustled into a coach. As the party prepared to leave, one of the soldiers, Major Rolfe, tried to board the coach, hat still on his head, but the king rose and pushed him back out again: 'It is not come to that yet,' Charles snapped, 'Get you out.'[25] The party rumbled west along rutted roads to the coast at Yarmouth, where, after an hour's wait, they boarded a boat and made the three-hour crossing on the churning waters of the Solent, to Hurst Castle. It was a grim fortress on a jutting spit, surrounded by weedy salt marshes and 'noxious' air. The ground was stony, uneasy and 'offensive to his feet', though the king did at least enjoy taking in the view and watching passing ships, among them the tall white sails of his old Ship Money fleet.[26] Once they had been the pride of his kingship. Now they were guarding him against escape.

The same day, the Commons rejected the *Remonstrance* by 125 to 58. William Prynne tried to have the Army denounced as 'rebels and traitors'.[27] But it was already too late.

That afternoon, the Army was at Kensington and Fairfax had 7,000 men in Hyde Park. All weekend Westminster was crawling with red-coated soldiers. Horses of the New Model were tethered to the doors of the great mansions of the rich in Covent Garden. Soldiers commandeered people's beds and, where these weren't available, slept on their floors. All eyes turned to the Commons. On Monday, they reconvened after the Sunday break. They debated whether they should continue negotiations with the king. A resolution was passed by a tight margin to bring in candles. Sitting through the night, as the winter wind rattled the Palace windows, the debate continued. Prynne gave a three-hour speech laced with *ad hominem* attacks on those foolish enough to disagree with him. Slowly, MPs drifted out: 340 became 214 by the early hours. Then, as the twin cities of London and Westminster woke up, the House passed the resolution. Negotiations with the king would continue. With the Army literally at their gates, they had chosen defiance.

The House risen, Ireton, Ludlow, Harrison and others gathered in Whitehall, where they met with sympathic MPs. The debate was 'full and free', Ludlow would recall, by which he probably meant that it was thoroughly acrimonious.[28] Ireton still wanted to dissolve Parliament and start afresh: a Parliament that had merely been purged of recalcitrant members, he said, would be a 'mock-power, and a mock-Parliament'. But he couldn't hold the room. Instead, it was decided to purge.

Preparations began through the night.

As the day broke over the capital, soldiers filtered through the streets, giving shouts and cries as they went. They took up position outside the Palace of Westminster. When the normal guard provided by the City Trained Band came to assume their usual stations around 8 a.m., there was a stand-off. The professional soldiers of the New Model told them to go back to their workplaces and their wives. It was lucky that Skippon was on hand, to make sure the militiamen could take the joke.

At the Palace, at the top of the stairs leading to the lobby, stood Colonel Thomas Pride. He had a list of Members he was supposed to arrest. From 8 a.m., the MPs started to arrive.

Pride the soldier, former drayman, had little idea who many of the MPs were. At first he was aided by a doorman, but he was soon also joined by the elderly and diminutive Lord Grey of Groby: 'This is the person,' Lord Grey would announce as an unwitting arrestee approached the stairs. The colonel treated each with punctilious courtesy, his hat in his hand. But he was assiduous in his work.

Throughout the day, as soldiers huddled under driving sleet in the Palace Yard, more than 40 MPs were arrested. They were herded through into the nearby Queen's Court and their guards were informed that it was these men who'd withheld their wages for so long. In the evening, they were told that coaches had arrived to take them to more comfortable lodgings at nearby Wallingford House.

Instead, they were shunted just around the corner into a victualling house called 'Hell'. Here they spent the night stuffed into just two rooms, their sleep interrupted by the constant sneezing of one of their number – Sir Robert Harley – who had a terrible cold. In the morning, they weren't even given breakfast.

Cromwell had arrived late on the day of the Purge. He knew nothing of it, he is reported as saying, but since it had happened, he was content. Two days later, the Army entered the City. In the biting winter cold, the seats of St Paul's were pulled up and burned as firewood. Churches were used as stables. On the international exchanges, the value of the pound began to sink.[29]

At Whitehall, Ireton and a committee of officers had sat down once more with the Levellers. Their aim had been to hammer out a new constitutional settlement, underpinned by a new *Agreement of the People*. The arguments were forceful once more: Wildman, Lilburne and the Levellers pushed for complete religious toleration, but Ireton held fast.

Everyone at Whitehall accepted that the state shouldn't have power to force people into conformity, but the grandees differed from the Levellers in their insistence that secular power should be able to restrain people from disorderly or blasphemous religion – a subtle, but important difference. Despite the differences, by the 11th the meeting had been able to draft a new *Agreement*. Was this meant to be final? The Levellers seem to have thought so. But instead, to their fury, it was presented to the Army's General Council of Officers, and it was debated again. Discussions were heated and evidently in earnest: some 160 officers and civilians are known to have attended. At one point, the conservative young Surrey gentleman John Evelyn managed to listen in to a debate chaired by Ireton, and was shocked at the 'horrid villainies' he heard from the earnest soldiers.[30] The upshot was a new Officers' *Agreement* that was to be readied by January.

But the Council of Officers had other things on their mind.

On the 15th, it appointed a committee. Its job was to decide what to do with Charles, 'to the bringing of him speedily to justice'.[31] On the 27th, an abridgement of the *Remonstrance* hit the stands, helpfully summarising the convoluted original into just 13 pages complete with fiery marginal glosses from Scripture. The call for punishment against the king was explicit: he would be 'brought to Justice for the Treason, blood, and mischief he is therein guilty of'. Among the stream of scriptural references to gloss this statement was the fearsome words of Numbers 35:33: 'So ye shall not pollute the land wherein ye are: for blood it defileth the land: and the land cannot be cleansed of the blood that is shed therein, but by the blood of him that shed it.'[32] On the 28th, an ordinance was introduced in the Commons. It would establish a High Court of Justice and put the king on trial.

At this point the House was a fraction of its former membership. Around a hundred MPs had now been arrested or excluded. Many more had stayed away after the Purge, partly in protest, partly in fear. The Lords chamber was nearly empty. Wags started to refer to this as the 'Rump' Parliament. Out of the public gaze, though, Cromwell was trying to bring moderates onside. Politicians were seen attending meetings in rooms deep in Whitehall, where men puffed tobacco and talked in hushed tones about what needed to be done. The lawyer Bulstrode Whitelocke recalled Cromwell receiving him at Whitehall, lying in the king's sumptuous beds, persuading him to join the cause and inviting him to discuss a future constitutional settlement. The Army's intentions, wrote a French agent, 'are so concealed that it is difficult to get to the bottom of them'.[33] In a climate of uncertainty, rumours of backroom deals and secret negotiations abounded in the press. Nedham's *Pragmaticus* mocked the 'frighted Junto', claiming they needed the king, and wrote hopefully of a mission of peers led by the Earl of Denbigh to the army headquarters that would finally offer the king a way out. More and more politicians left London. Whitelocke slipped away on the 26th, and was soon relieved to be enjoying the fresh air, woods and partridges at his country estate in Berkshire. Lord Saye disappeared, probably bolting to his island retreat on Lundy. For once, even the man known to contemporaries as 'Old Subtlety' for his political wiles wanted to be as far from the action as he possibly could be.

The Ordinance passed on 1 January 1649: 'Whereas it is notorious', its preamble thundered, that Charles 'hath had a wicked design totally to subvert the ancient and fundamental laws and liberties of this nation. And in their place to introduce an arbitrary and tyrannical government.' This design, the Ordinance claimed, had been pursued 'with fire and the sword'.[34] A resolution was passed claiming that the act of levying war against Parliament and the kingdom constituted treason.

The Lords immediately blocked the ordinance, without even needing to vote. Three days later, the Commons passed it anyway, declaring that 'the people are, under God, the original of all just power'. It became the first Act of Parliament passed solely by the Commons, without the need for the House of Lords or the monarch.

The Commons were engaged in strange business. On the 9th, the House resolved that the 'Name of any one Single Person' should be removed from all legal proceedings. The same day, it approved a new design of the Great Seal, which made no mention of king or Crown, but instead carried an icon of the House of Commons, inscribed 'In the First Year of Freedom, by God's Blessing Restored, 1648'.[35] Whatever rumours were passing around about continuing negotiations to save the king's life, his monarchy, or *any* monarchy, the 'Rump' was already preparing for a kingless government.

On the 20th, the Officers' *Agreement of the People* was finally presented to the House. It was a forward-looking constitution, offering franchise reform and separation of powers: workable and intelligent. The Commons thanked the officers, ordered it printed and promised to return to the new draft constitution 'as the necessity of affairs will permit'.[36]

The necessity of affairs, though, had moved on, for that day in Westminster Hall, the trial of Charles Stuart began.

The trial was so controversial that many of the leading lights of the legal establishment refused to be a part of it. In the end, the presidency was given to a fairly obscure, though evidently talented and committed, Cheshire judge called John Bradshaw. The prosecution, meanwhile, was led by the firebrand John Cooke, a man of fierce conviction for whom the trial was 'not only against one tyrant, but against tyranny itself'. Fairfax never attended – though his increasingly Royalist wife Lady Anne did, haranguing the court from the gallery during its initial roll call. But despite being approached by envoys of the young Prince Charles, asking him to intervene, he did nothing.

The charge stated that, having been 'trusted with a limited power to govern by, and according to the laws of the land, and not otherwise', Charles had engaged in 'a wicked design to erect and uphold in himself an unlimited and tyrannical power to rule according to his Will, and to overthrow the Rights and Liberties of the People'. He had levied war against Parliament and the people it represented, had solicited foreign invasions and renewed the war, all to uphold his own interests and those of his family, against the 'public interest, common right, liberty, justice and peace of the people of this nation'. Thus Charles was a 'Tyrant, Traitor and Murderer, and a public and implacable Enemy to the Commonwealth of England'.[37] Such a charge, which hinged on the simple point that Charles had levied war against Parliament, was tactically astute. *If* you accepted that waging war against the people was treason, and *if* you accepted that the Long Parliament represented the people, then there was a strong case.

The trial was public. Any temptation simply to murder Charles in a backroom, a fate that had befallen more than one of his medieval predecessors, was stoutly resisted. This was to be a revolution for the people, if not exactly by them. As the Royalist Edward Hyde noted with some sadness, this was a court that swept away the 'distinction of quality', making 'the greatest lord and the meanest peasant undergo the same judicatory and form of trial' as each other.[38] Its guiding principle was a crucial one, that rulers are – ultimately – accountable to their people.

On the 20th, Charles had been conveyed, surrounded by soldiers, from St James's to Whitehall in a closed sedan chair which had been lent by the Earl of Pembroke. In an earlier life, the earl had shared a passion for art with the king, though he had always been a reformist, even a Puritan. Now he was about to witness the unthinkable.

Once at Whitehall, Charles was transferred onto a barge and carried down the river, with spectators lining the banks of the Thames. At Westminster, he was lodged in the old house of Sir Robert Cotton, a man who had been imprisoned and ruined by Charles in the 1630s. During the trial, spectators crowded into the galleries that overlooked the Hall.

Those who couldn't attend listened to gossip and rumours, and read and heard accounts of the trial published in the mercuries.[39] They heard of how the king laughed at the charge that he was a 'traitor', how he refused many times to plead, denying the validity of the court. They heard that he challenged Cooke's assertion that he was 'elected' king: 'England was never an elective Kingdom, but a hereditary kingdom for near these thousand years.' They heard that an irritated Bradshaw had to have the king removed, to shouts of 'Justice! Justice!' from the soldiers in the Hall. They heard that Charles had pointed out that the Commons wasn't, and never had been, a court of judicature (the Lords was, but he didn't see any peers in the room). They also heard various stories about how a masked lady – Anne Fairfax – had scoffed at the idea that the trial was being carried out in the name of the people, by shouting that 'Not half! Not a quarter of the people of England. Oliver Cromwell is a traitor!'

Perhaps, some may have speculated, Charles might have saved his neck by entering a plea, thus acknowledging the validity of the court and the 'Act' of the Commons that created it. This would have confirmed the supremacy of the Commons and, by extension, the sovereignty of the people, and their right to bring the king to justice. Or maybe he was always done for: a man of blood, whose own blood needed to be shed, to cleanse the kingdom and bring some kind of resolution. The fact is that nobody really knew, though there were plenty in the Army who wanted Charles dead.

In any case, Charles's refusal to plead was a problem – technically, a defendant in a treason trial who refused to plead could simply be taken as guilty, but this robbed the court of its ability to bring forth

witnesses in public, proving to the wider world of the prisoner's guilt.
So, on the 25th, they held a public session, in the Painted Chamber,
where the prepared witness statements were read out: everyone
from a farmer who saw Charles encourage violence at the sacking
of Leicester, to a Nottingham man who had painted the pole that
bore the royal standard in August 1642. The witnesses were giving
testimony, said the prosecutor Cooke, 'on the people of England's
behalf'.[40] It was the people *versus* Charles Stuart. They emphasised
the blood shed on both sides of the war, showing Charles's guilt for
it. When Charles himself listened to his people testify against him,
he was sarcastic and scornful, pulling faces and scoffing. The Puritan
Lucy Hutchinson, whose husband was sitting in judgement on the
king, thought it suggested Charles thoroughly lacked remorse. He
was little more than a bloody tyrant.

Royalists hoped for deliverance – perhaps from Rupert, perhaps
from the queen of Sweden. Dutch envoys, persuaded by the eighteen-
year-old Prince Charles, arrived urging arbitration. But it was to no
avail. On the afternoon of the 27th, after a tense session with multiple interruptions, sentence was passed. Bradshaw gave a 40-minute
oration, castigating Charles for breaking his oath to the people. Then
the clerk rose and read out the sentence, prepared in advance by the
Commissioners: 'that the said Charles Stuart, as a Tyrant, Traitor,
Murderer and a public enemy, shall be put to death, by the severing of
his head from his body'.[41]

There then followed days of silence. Rumours passed around. Would
Charles Stuart be saved? Perhaps by an insurrection, or perhaps by
Fairfax. At St James's, the radical army chaplain Hugh Peter preached
brimstone to the soldiers. At Whitehall, Charles was ministered to by
William Juxon, the loyal former Bishop of London. On the 29th, he
was allowed to see those two of his children still in England: Princess
Elizabeth, the elder of the two, just thirteen years old, and Henry,
Duke of Gloucester, five years younger.[42] 'Sweetheart you will forget
this,' he reassured the inconsolable Elizabeth. 'I shall never forget it
whilst I live,' she replied. To little Henry, Charles warned: 'they will
cut off my head, and perhaps make thee a king: but mark what I say

you must not be a king so long as your brothers Charles and James do live: for they will cut off your brothers' heads (when they catch them) and cut off thy head too, at last; and therefore I charge you, do not be made a king by them.' 'I will be torn in pieces first,' the eight-year-old replied.

From morning the next day, a huddled crowd gathered outside the grand Banqueting House at Whitehall, where a scaffold had been hastily thrown up, draped in black and surrounded by troops and their horses.

But there was a delay. Why? Nobody in the crowd knew.

At last, at around two in the afternoon, there was movement. As the crowd watched, Charles Stuart appeared, accompanied by Juxon. After a short speech, and a few formalities, he lay his head down on the low block in front of him, gave a signal and the executioner cut off his head. As the axe fell, a terrible groan came forth from the assembled crowd.

Within half an hour, the troops had cleared them all away.

A week later, the Commons abolished the monarchy. The 'office of a king,' they declared, 'is unnecessary, burdensome, and dangerous to the liberty, safety, and public interest of the people of this nation; and therefore ought to be abolished'. The reason it took a week to abolish the monarchy was that the Rump was busy with another matter – what to do with the House of Lords. In the end, they plumped for abolition of this, too: declaring it 'useless and dangerous', although not before a debate in which Henry Marten quipped that it was 'useless, but not dangerous'.[43]

News of the king's execution filtered out to a stunned nation. The first Sunday after the execution, the ultra-Royalist former Bishop of Rochester gave a sermon likening the execution of King Charles to the killing of Jesus. He later published it, with its anti-Semitism blazoned in the title, as *The Devilish Conspiracy, Hellish Treason, Heathenish Condemnation, and Damnable Murder, Committed, and Executed*

by the Jews against the Anointed of their Lords, Christ their King.
When Oliver Cromwell's sister, Catherine Whitstone, found out, she
was utterly shocked. 'I was very troubled at that stroke which took
the head of this poor kingdom from us,' she wrote to a cousin, 'and
truly had I been able to have purchased his life, I am confident I could
with all willingness have laid down mine.'[44] Some Royalists simply
preferred not to talk about it: the regicide was, said the Countess of
Derby, a 'fatal stroke which I cannot name without horror'.[45]

Was this what the wars had been fought for? Virtually no one,
in 1642, let alone 1640, had envisaged the execution of the king and
the abolition of the kingly office. To get this far, events had taken on
a life of their own, driven by political accidents and unfathomable
decisions. Charles himself must carry much of the blame: he had been
a stuffy authoritarian, but never ruthless enough to be a successful
tyrant. He had emerged as a competent – even charismatic – leader,
though we must take care to separate the charisma of the man from
that of his office. But he was only ever successful at inspiring those
who already agreed with him, and his pathological inability to understand his opponents' position would cost him dear. His great opportunity had been in 1647, when he could have accepted Ireton's *Heads*,
and marched into London, garlanded by a grateful New Model
Army. Parliament would surely have fallen in line, and a new, tolerant
Church could have been created, with room for both Independent
prayer meetings and the old Book of Common Prayer. It would have
left a balanced constitution with regular parliaments. But instead
Charles tried to hold out for a better deal, costing him his own head
and – much more importantly – the blood of countless thousands of
innocent people.

In the beginning, many had fought for religion – to protect a Church
in danger from either papists, sectaries, Laudians or Puritans. Others
had fought for the 'ancient constitution': they believed it had become
unbalanced by the tyranny of the king or the pretentions of Parliament
or populace. Thomas Fairfax, shown a copy of Magna Carta in 1647,
had announced that this was what the Army had shed so much of its
blood for. Cromwell, later, would say, 'Religion was not the thing

at first contested for' – rather, it was matters of secular government, although no lesser figure than Thomas Hobbes would disagree: 'the cause of the civil war,' he wrote, was 'nothing other than the quarrelling about theological issues'.[46]

But even if religion was always a major issue, the question had also evolved into one of lawful government: where did it come from? What can the people do if their leaders break the law? By the end of the 1640s, many on the more radical wing of the old Parliamentarian cause had come to the conclusion that laws and government originated in the people, and that kings were only useful if they protected the people. The first part had been implicit much earlier, notably in Henry Parker's famous polemic against the king's response to the Nineteen Propositions and in anti-absolutist writers well before even that. The second part, which implied that a wronged people might actually depose a tyrant king, was the more fundamental breach. The king, the Rump declared in March, had been set up as a 'public officer for the common good', by 'Agreement of the People', yet this system had evidently failed in its fundamental purpose of protecting that common good. All government, wrote the republican John Parker the following year, 'is in the people, from the people, and for the people'.[47] What had happened, so the theory went, was that the chief officer of the state had become a danger to the people, so they had exercised their right to depose him.

The obvious trouble with all this was that the role of the people remained rather hypothetical. The regicide was carried out in the name of the people, but – as Lady Fairfax famously shouted – most of them wanted nothing to do with it. The new regime had toppled the monarchy and established the power of the Commons, but they had done so without rooting the new government in actual popular consent. They spoke of popular sovereignty, without allowing new elections or – as the Levellers desired – a new Agreement of the People. Very soon the old radicals were just as disillusioned as everyone else, and at the end of February, John Lilburne exploded back into print. His latest intervention was to launch a broadside against the new regime, *England's New Chains Discovered*, which attacked the newly created

Council of State, the Army grandees and Westminster oligarchy, and the way they were clamping down on the press and petitioning – the key tools of the Leveller movement.[48]

Spring brought further Leveller activity and publication. In March, the Levellers printed *The Hunting of the Foxes*, claiming that the Rump was 'a more absolute arbitrary monarchy than before. We have not the change of a Kingdom to a Common wealth; we are only under the old cheat, the transmutation of Names, but with the addition of New Tyrannies to the old.'[49] This in turn led to a violent overreaction by the new government. The Leveller leadership was voted guilty of treason in the House, and Lilburne was arrested by soldiers in a dramatic dawn raid. Walwyn, Overton and Thomas Prince were also detained. According to Lilburne, while he was being interrogated in Whitehall, Cromwell could be overheard in an adjacent room thumping a table and announcing to the Council of State that 'you have no other way to deal with these men but to break them in pieces'.[50]

By the end of April, demonstrations against the imprisonment of the Leveller leaders were becoming a regular occurrence at Westminster. Women were still at the forefront: 'Bonny Besses, in the sea-green dresses', as a sympathetic mercury put it, were striking fear into 'Nol [Cromwell] and his asses'. The sea-green colour had become a Leveller symbol, originating at the funeral of Thomas Rainborough late the previous year.[51]

The reaction to the petitions from those in Parliament was dismissive. On one occasion, protesting women were told by an MP to go home and wash their dishes. Another MP made the mistake of commenting on how strange it was to see women petitioning: 'It was strange that you cut off the King's head, yet I suppose you will justify it', came the stinging retort. In the end, the serjeant-at-arms confronted the women, told them the matter was too complex for them to understand, that an answer had already been given to their husbands and 'therefore that you are desired to go home and meddle with your housewifery'.[52] It was not the most helpful intervention.

At the same time, Levellers in the Army were close to open defiance. Things began in London, where a young trooper named Robert Lockyer – just twenty-three years old yet a veteran of Naseby – staged a minor act of insubordination. He was arrested and publicly shot in St Paul's churchyard, on the insistence of Fairfax. His funeral was another occasion for grand Leveller public propaganda, attended by thousands.

But if the Army command hoped this act of swift brutality would quell the discontent, they were quite wrong, for by the early days of May, an uprising was already under way in the west. For the second time, the Levellers were attempting to win control of the New Model Army.

The mutiny began in Salisbury, and within weeks there was an unauthorised Leveller rendezvous at Abingdon in Berkshire. News reached Cromwell, so he gathered his forces in London and addressed them in Hyde Park. Some Leveller sympathisers had turned up with sea-green ribbons in their hats. But Cromwell talked them down. Any who wished not to fight could be discharged with their arrears paid; the rest would have to head out to the west, to face down the rebels. In all, he and Fairfax left London with five regiments: two cavalry and three foot.

It was a formidable force, and the Levellers had little choice but to retreat, especially as their numbers dwindled and as supporters melted away into the countryside. First, the Levellers were trapped near Newbridge, on the Thames, so they pulled back along the quiet River Windrush, through the Oxfordshire countryside, towards the small market town of Burford in the low dip slope of the Cotswolds.

It was here that Cromwell caught up. A midnight attack through the town did what it needed to do, and, despite a brief show of resistance, the Levellers were corralled into the great medieval parish church. In all, around 300 were kept there overnight, one of them scratching his name into the wall: 'Anthony Sedley. 1649. Prisner.' In the morning, the mutineers were pardoned, save three – a corporal, a cornet and a private soldier, who were taken out of the church, into the open air, and shot.

The Levellers had been defeated. The revolution was not to be theirs. As Cromwell's soldiers packed up to leave Burford, the town could get back to the rhythms of springtime. While the lambs cried in the nearby pastures and the wood pigeons called out from the resplendent trees, Private Church, Cornet Thompson and Corporal Perkins were buried in the soil of Burford churchyard. Another quiet corner of England, manured with the blood of its people.

In the course of some 19 months, the New Model Army – increasingly Oliver Cromwell's New Model Army as Fairfax shrank back from politics – had defeated the Levellers, the social radicals within its own ranks, the Royalists, the Scots and its enemies in the Long Parliament. In just four years, a force led not by aristocrats but by members of the lower gentry and middling sort had crushed all before it, overthrown an ancient monarchy and carried out a revolution in the name of the English people. Military conquests in Ireland and Scotland lay ahead, of course. But now, with the Army's allies in what remained of Parliament, the main challenge was going to be to govern, to bring peace and stability to a country torn apart by seven years of war, while protecting the religious congregations that had flourished but which were still viewed with great suspicion by most of the country. It was a daunting task.

14

To Translate the Nation from Oppression to Liberty

In March 1649, two months before the Leveller rising that ended at Burford, Francis Thorpe, serjeant-at-law, stood up to address the York Assizes. This was the main local criminal court, which dealt with the most serious offences, the felonies that – in theory at least – carried the death penalty. But the assizes were more than this: they were an occasion of great pomp, in which judges rode into the county town, on circuit from London, and conveyed the power of the central government. They were traditionally accompanied by sermons and speeches, and increasingly by lively social gatherings as the local gentry came out to see the awesome power of justice begin. It was, quite simply, one of the great moments in which the seventeenth-century monarchy projected its power.

But this was no ordinary assizes, for England was no longer a monarchy. The stakes, this time, were much higher. This was an opportunity for a shaky new regime, with little popular support, to make its case. And this was what Francis Thorpe offered. Thorpe was a local: born to a gentry family in Birdsall, on the northern edge of the gentle Yorkshire Wolds. His father had been a lawyer, too, and a courtier under James I. In the 1630s, Thorpe the younger had clashed with Thomas Wentworth, later Earl of Strafford, and during the war he had provided legal support to the House of Lords. Then he was elected, as a 'recruiter' to the House of Commons in 1646, from which he supported the Independents and the New Model Army. During the Second Civil War of 1648, he stayed in Yorkshire, helping organise the Parliamentarian army, and he was able to survive Pride's Purge that December.

For all his alliance with the Army and the more radical wing of the Commons though, Thorpe stayed away from the king's trial. Named as one of the trial Commissioners, he didn't show. But once the regicide was done, he found himself trusted by the Rump – now in charge of the government – to ride out on the northern assize circuit, which he did that February.

He cleared his throat. 'Gentlemen, Friends, and Countrymen,' he began. He admitted, immediately, and disarmingly, that the change in authority by which the court was sitting 'works divers effects upon the tempers and spirits of men'. But he was there to justify the Republic, which he did with a series of historical and constitutional reflections. Ultimately, he argued, it was the 'People (under God)' who were the 'Original of all just Power'. They could 'let the Government run out into what form it will, Monarchy, Aristocracy, or Democracy, yet still the Original Fountain thereof is from the consent and agreement of the people'.[1] As it was, the people's consent had been given to the Rump Parliament for it to govern.

Shortly after Thorpe's assize speech, on 1 April, a small group of peasants, wearing the rough-hewn clothes of agricultural labourers and carrying spades on their back, went out onto the heather-carpeted common at St George's Hill, Surrey. Here, they began digging. They would work the land in common, sharing the spoils of God's earth. Known as 'Diggers', or 'True Levellers', their leader was Gerrard Winstanley.

He was a true visionary. Quite literally, in fact, for Winstanley experienced trances. But he also took inspiration from the most radical tendency among the Levellers, which argued that the earth should not be exploited as private property, but was a common treasury for all – *true* levelling. In December 1648, an anonymous tract called *Light Shining in Buckinghamshire* had made the case, calling for 'common right and equity', and for 'a just portion for each man to live, that so none need to beg or steal for want'.[2] Over the next two years, Digger communities sprang up Northamptonshire, Kent, Buckinghamshire, Hertfordshire, Middlesex, Bedfordshire and Leicestershire. The

Diggers at St George's Hill were dispersed by Fairfax's soldiers (after on one occasion being chased away by angry club-carrying local men of whom some – presumably to mock the way the Diggers were turning the world upside down – were dressed in women's clothes). But Winstanley persisted with a sustained pamphlet campaign, culminating in 1652 with *The Law of Freedom*, which set out the basis for his Christian communist utopia. In this, people would '[w]ork together, eat bread together'.[3] He didn't just want to overturn the oppressions of the Norman Yoke, but – as he had told Fairfax – to restore 'the pure law of righteousness before the Fall'. The earth, he argued, was a common treasury to all. There would be free, universal education for boys and girls, but it would all be backed by a savage penal code, with the death penalty not just for murder and rape, but also buying and selling, or even being a lawyer or parson.[4]

The revolution brought an extraordinary moment of ideological creativity. The monarchy had been the keystone to the entire social order, from politics to the family, but the regicide had the potential to bring all this crashing down. 'The old world,' wrote Winstanley, 'is running up like parchment in the fire.'[5] Monarchy itself would fall across the Continent: 'first in England, then in France, then in Spain, and after all in Christendom', 'then Christ would rule', thundered a Winchester minister, recounting a vision he claimed to have had in September 1647.[6] Perhaps the fall of monarchy would bring private property tumbling down soon afterwards, and England and then the world would become an egalitarian utopia: the country 'hath lain under the power of that Beast, kingly property,' Winstanley enthused. 'But now England is the first of nations that is upon the point of reforming.'[7]

Winstanley was at the radical fringe, but some of those closer to the government were dedicated to far-reaching reform, too. A circle of intellectuals centred on the remarkable Polish-born polymath Samuel Hartlib committed itself to rethinking society's problems, with an emphasis on providing practical solutions. 'Improvement' was their buzzword, so as to make sure people could 'enjoy that liberty which we have so dearly purchased'.[8] It could be applied to everything from poor relief to the textile industry. Walter Blith, a former Army captain and 'lover of ingenuity', sought to improve farming, publishing *The English Improver* (1649), arguing for the use of new crops like sainfoin and clover. 'This very nation may be made the paradise of the world,' he argued, 'if we can but bring ingenuity into fashion.'⁹ Such was the book's success that it, too, came to be improved, as *The English Improver Improved* (1653).¹⁰ Enclosure had its advocates, too. Increasingly, it was being seen as beneficial to society, for it allowed marginal land to be improved and made profitable. The English, enthused one writer, were 'an ingenious and industrious people', who would wring 'desolate wastes into fruitful fields' and 'howling wildernesses into comfortable habitations'. This would at least bring 'some benefit by all our revolutions, transplantings, and overturnings in authorities'.¹¹

One of the rising champions of improvement was a young Hampshire twenty-something called William Petty. From a middling background, Petty's childhood had been spent in the small market town of Romsey, which was one of those places, like Cartmel, where an old monastic building had been saved and used as a parish church. It was, you might say, a monument to a practical approach to religion, and William grew up to be anything but a fanatic. He was a tall, handsome man, noted both for his prodigious gift with numbers and for his sense of humour. He was also able, to much mirth of anyone lucky enough to be present, to give mock sermons in the manner of any of the religious groups of the day: Episcopalians, Presbyterians, Jesuits. The last of these he had particular experience of. As a youth he had left Hampshire to work as a cabin boy on a merchant vessel. Shipwrecked in France, and recovering from a broken leg, he had tried to make the best of the situation by joining a Jesuit college at Caen. At one point he fell into deep poverty in Paris – an experience that brought a lifelong appreciation of the need to improve the economy. And it was his beloved numbers that he saw as key to doing this. 'Little small threads of mathematics', he thought, could be put to 'vast uses'.¹² He'd even, in 1649, suggested that difficult political questions should be settled by referendums, thus – he hoped – leaving 'no room for any factions'.¹³

Back in England after the war, Petty became friends with Hartlib, for whom he penned a fascinating tract of 'advice', which was published and printed. In it, he extolled the transformative virtues of education, to ensure that there was no one 'now holding the plough which might have been made fit to steer the state'.[14] Petty's largely secular outlook was remarkable, but he was unusual in this, for the religious radicals were also at the forefront of drives for social reform. One religious enthusiast, the mysterious millenarian George Foster, reported a vision in which a man on a white horse cut down anyone higher than the middle sort, raising up anyone lower, chanting 'Equality, Equality, Equality'.[15] Both the New Model Army chaplain Hugh Peter and the Baptist preacher Elizabeth Attaway argued for the legalisation of divorce (following John Milton, of course). Samuel Herring, a radical from the freethinking hotbed of Coleman Street, London, prepared a document that suggested everything from free access to lawyers and something akin to a national health service, to go hand in hand with religious renewal.[16]

Naturally, given the upheavals, some turned to theorising power and politics. Thomas Hobbes, who was tutor to the late king's eldest son, Charles, in exile, composed a tract on the origins of the state, publishing it in England in April 1651. He called it *Leviathan* after a biblical monster. His argument was that states came into being to protect people who would otherwise exist in a 'state of nature'.[17] It suggested that the people should give obedience to the state in return for protection: in other words that government was reciprocal – indeed, it argued that since the 'king' (the pretender Charles Stuart) could no longer provide protection, Royalists should submit to those that could, namely Parliament, a suggestion that caused horror among his former sponsors and led to him being banned from the exiled court.

The fiercest debates, though, were over faith. About a quarter of the parish ministry had been ousted as Royalists, the universities purged and the bishops abolished. But the remaining clergy were still a diverse bunch, from Puritans to old-school Calvinists to secret Episcopalians, not to mention some serious oddballs. The Independents carried a new confidence, borne of political success and Godly zeal. 'Beware Nol Cromwell's army,' a 1650 pamphlet warned the Pope, 'lest Hugh Peter come to preach in Peter's chair.'[18] Presbyterianism, on the other hand, had struggled to take hold, and the Directory of Worship of 1644 had steadfastly failed to stir people's souls. The bishops were gone, but no formal Presbyterian apparatus – as there was in Scotland, for example – had been put in their place. England would never evolve a fully fledged Presbyterian system of local classes, synods and elders. Milton, famously, summed up some of the reason for this failure, for – he said – was not 'New Presbyter just old priest writ large': similar tyranny, different name.[19] In reality, longing for the old ways was as powerful as the wish to avoid the oppression of new dogmas. But, either way, Presbyterian roots failed to find fertile soil.

The Rump, in September 1650, repealed the Elizabethan law enforcing attendance at church. The hope was that people would voluntarily attend another congregation, but of course many simply found other distractions of a Sunday. And the new diversity, together with the sheer (and probably deliberate) weakness of government oversight, meant that English theology started moving in some quite unexpected directions. Orthodox Calvinism remained strong, but some Puritans even began to embrace Arminian ideas about justification by good works. At Cambridge, scholars turned away from a belief in harsh predestination and towards a spirituality based on the goodness of God and the dignity of man. In fact, there developed in English parish life a genuine nostalgia for the rhythms of the older church, its calendar and the Book of Common Prayer. Lots of people still happily used the old Prayer Book on the quiet, such as the ousted minister Thomas Preston, who used it for illicit sermons in an abandoned church in a Winchester suburb.[20] Ironically, the Puritan victory of the 1640s, was paving the way for the emergence of something genuinely recognisable as the beginnings of 'Anglicanism' even if, for now, it was technically illegal.

The most remarkable development, though, was in the sheer diversity of ideas. Publications ranged from full-blooded defences of Arminianism to the first English translation of the Quran (1649). Some continued to argue for complete separation of religion and the state: 'heathens, Jews, Turks, or pagans' should all be left in peace to worship without being bothered by the authorities, one tract argued, following the American Roger Williams's lead.[21] There were the Socinians who followed the anti-Trinitarian Italian Lelio Sozzini, 'Muggletonians' who followed the London tailor Lodowick Muggleton. There were 'Seekers' who believed the truth was effectively unobtainable and only the second coming of Christ would reveal the true Church. Some even said that there was no god but nature, and others were said to be worshipping the stars.[22] The Royalist Countess of Derby, writing to her French Protestant sister-in-law, lamented how the radical sects increased 'daily', and 'it makes one's hair stand on end to think of it. The Quran is printed with permission. It is common to deny both God and Jesus Christ, and to believe only in the spirit of the universe.' Everyone was now permitted to preach, she bewailed, 'even women'.[23]

The Baptists were thriving – though they were split, like the wider Protestant Church, on whether salvation could be gained through good works. Smaller in number, meanwhile, though perhaps greater in influence, were the so-called Fifth Monarchists. Their intellectual world was complicated, but their crucial desire was to prepare England as a Godly commonwealth for the Second Coming, which they saw as imminent. Their following was strong in London, and among clothworkers and craftsmen, but also in the Army; and it now included the charismatic senior officer Thomas Harrison, a man whose political importance was growing.

Others completely rethought the meaning of the Fall of Humankind in the Garden of Eden. What if it was reversible?[24] What if a state of grace could be attained in this life? It was not an entirely new idea, but now it chimed with the radical desire for social equality. To the conservative viewpoint, the social hierarchy was an apparatus of control necessitated by man's innate wickedness. But if humans could achieve grace on earth, then inequality was no longer necessary. Some suggested that hell didn't exist, and in a society where the fear of eternal damnation was used as a tool of control, such ideas could be truly liberating.

Some claimed that those who had achieved grace had no need to obey man's laws. The most notorious proponents were those called 'Ranters'. Never much of a movement, and without doubt amplified by journalists who enjoyed being shocked, the Ranters were nonetheless real. At their most extreme, they believed that if all acts came from

God, then all acts must be good. 'Consider any act, though it be the act of swearing, drinking, adultery and theft; yet these acts simply, yea nakedly be as acts nothing distinct from Prayer and Praises,' wrote one of their most prominent authors, the Lancashire-born Laurence Clarkson.[25]

Ranters revelled in upturning the morals and mores of the age, not least about sex. One claimed to have conceived a child by the Holy Ghost.[26] Another, Thomas Webbe, was a flamboyant country rector with powdered and frizzled hair, and was supposed to have announced in 1650 that 'there's no heaven but women, nor no hell save marriage'.[27] Among his followers was one John Organ from the nearby village of Castle Combe. In their theological discussions, the two men became intimate, so much so that Webbe took Organ as his 'man-wife', and for a time they enjoyed a public relationship, though it ended when this became too much for the local community and Organ was forced to flee the county. And there was Abiezer Coppe, whose *A Fiery Flying Roll (Parts 1 and 2)* (1650) was condemned as containing 'many horrid blasphemies'. 'Have ALL THINGS common,' he wrote fierily, 'or else the plague of God will rot and consume all that you have.'[28] In 1650, Coppe shocked Londoners by ascending the pulpit in St Helen's Bishopsgate and issuing a stream of profanities that lasted an hour.

The biggest new religious movement was to be neither the Ranters, nor even the Fifth Monarchists or Baptists, although eventually all of these groups – not to mention the Levellers – would feed into it.

During the war, a restless Leicestershire man became dissatisfied with the Church. His name was George Fox, and he tramped the local countryside, making shoes and talking to whomever would listen about his faith. Then, in 1647, still in his early twenties, after hearing a voice in his head, he started preaching that even the Bible held less authority than people's conscience, their inner guide, or inner light. Gradually, as he passed through Derbyshire and Nottinghamshire and back into Leicestershire, where it was said 'the mighty power of the Lord was manifest', he gathered more followers.[29] In 1650, having gained some unwanted attention from the authorities, Fox found himself in Derby gaol. Here, a magistrate noticed how his followers would physically tremble as they channelled their inner light. The magistrate called them 'Quakers'.

Fox's followers preferred a different name – 'Children of the Light', or 'Friends'. He languished in gaol for some time, at one point refusing to join the army as a condition for parole. Late in 1651 he was released, and immediately celebrated by stomping barefoot into Lichfield, shouting, 'Woe to the bloody city of Lichfield!' Then, the next year, he ventured north. First, he wandered through Yorkshire, where his ideas found a ready audience. One of his most important converts was James Nayler, a small farmer from near Wakefield who, unlike Fox, had seen active service. He'd risen to become quarter-master to his fellow Yorkshireman John Lambert. And Nayler was also intensely charismatic, indeed mesmerising to the eye. With long, dark hair to his shoulders, some even said that he resembled Jesus.

Quakers had strange ways. One striking characteristic of Fox's movement was their refusal to doff their hats to their social superiors, and their use of the familiar 'thou' to address people who were used to the more formal 'you'. Another was the prominent role of women. For all the radical thought of the post-war period, and for all the role played by women in the Leveller movement, male domination remained sturdily immovable. Indeed, one argument against monarchy used by the regicide John Cooke had been that it was 'against the Law of God and nature to make millions of men subject to the commands of a woman'.[30] Quakerism was different, for unlike virtually any other form of religion at this point, it allowed equal participation by women and men. As a result, women provided much of the movement's early dynamism: something that drew inevitable criticism from conservatives and helped ensure the Quakers were widely associated with witchcraft. Yet for the women involved, it was exhilarating and liberating. Among them, for example, was a Selby maidservant called Mary Fisher. Her devotion to the cause was astonishing. It would see her travel to Cambridge, where she would be whipped for claiming to be the bride of Christ and for denouncing Sidney Sussex College as a synagogue of Satan. The next few years would take her twice to the West Indies and then deep into the Ottoman Empire, where she and her companion Beatrice Beckley even gained an audience with Sultan Mahomet IV in a military encampment at Adrianople.

June 1652 was the turning point for the movement. From Yorkshire, Fox had turned west and into the Pennines. Here he was driven to climb the looming mass of Pendle Hill, and, looking across the surrounding country, Fox later recalled, God 'let me see, in what Places he had a Great People to be gathered'.[31] From Pendle, Fox headed north-west, passing farmhouses and streams and fields of cattle and sheep, bedding down for nights on the bracken. On the 13th, he was at Firbank Fell, hemmed in under the Howgills, where he preached to a crowd of several hundreds, drawn from the local peasantry. Then he turned south-west again, via Kendal along the gravel paths of low, rolling hills, through tiny stone hamlets set among limestone walls.

Eventually, passing through the tiny town of Ulverston, on the sandy coast of Morecambe Bay, he arrived at a stocky grey manor house, with mullioned windows set seemingly at random. Swarthmoor Hall was owned by Thomas Fell, a judge and an MP. He was away on duty. At home was his wife, Margaret. She was a local woman from a wealthy family. She'd married Thomas in 1632, aged just seventeen, and they'd had nine children, of whom one son and seven daughters were still alive in 1653. She was to become one of the leading lights in Fox's new movement. She and her husband had supported local Independents, helping to get a New Model Army chaplain installed as curate at Ulverston. But Fox was different: 'listening to him opened me so, that it cut me to the heart; and then I saw clearly that we were all wrong'. Converted, she allowed Fox to preach at Ulverston parish church. From now on, Margaret Fell would provide financial and operational support to the Children of the Light, writing letters to Friends across the country and becoming to them 'a nursing mother'. Later widowed, she and Fox would eventually marry, but for now they had secured the future of a major new religious movement.

All the while, England's constitution remained resolutely unsettled. Seldom can an English regime have begun its rule with less political capital. As early as June 1649, a day of thanksgiving for the defeat of the Levellers, saw preaching against the regime and prayers for the young pretender Charles Stuart from London's disillusioned

Presbyterian clergy.[32] Indeed, much to the embarrassment of the new government, the late king's spiritual autobiography, *Eikon Basilike*, was proving a runaway bestseller, justifying all he did and setting him up as a Christian martyr.[33] The battle for loyalty, or at least tacit acquiescence, needed winning as a matter of some urgency.

A carefully worded 'Engagement' was introduced, initially for members of the new Council of State, and then extended in October 1649 to all MPs, clergymen, soldiers, court and local government officials. It ordered them to 'declare and promise' (not swear) to live quietly under the new regime. Then, in January 1650 it was expanded to all adult males, and most took it though many naturally did so in entirely bad faith. Meanwhile, a declaration of September 1649 announced proudly that God had blessed the commonwealth, and it had already made great strides in 'procuring the blessings of pure religion and just liberty into this nation'. That same September, a new Licensing Act prohibited many publications the regime deemed problematic. John Milton, meanwhile, prepared an erudite riposte to *Eikon Basilike* which, though it only gained a fraction of the latter's sales, did at least make a sophisticated case that monarchy itself was inherently tyrannical, while skewering Royalist supporters as an 'inconstant, irrational, and image-doting rabble'.[34]

The bigger coup at the time, if not to posterity, was the employment of Marchamont Nedham, now sporting a fashionable wig which enemies said made him look like a 'portable pillory'. A salary of £100 a year from the government was enough to divest him of his current Royalist allegiance, retire *Pragmaticus* and create a new republican mouthpiece, *Mercurius Politicus*. He also produced an effectively argued pamphlet, *The Case of the Commonwealth of England Stated*, in defence of the Republic. 'How sweet the air of a commonwealth is beyond that of a monarchy!' he enthused in an early issue of *Politicus*, rather against the inclinations of his former self.[35] The Republic would be a bastion of liberty, against the former tyranny of the monarchy, though Nedham was keen to ensure the people didn't pursue the wrong *sort* of liberty. After all, he wrote, 'the multitude is so brutish'. This was to be a Republic founded on popular sovereignty, i.e. the theoretical idea that power ultimately lay with the people, and on Parliamentary government. But it was not a democracy. After all, Nedham thought, true democracy would only lead inevitably back to tyranny.

The propaganda war was important, but there were also real battles to fight. Shortly after the regicide, in Scotland the young Charles Stuart had been proclaimed king of Great Britain, though he would be expected to accept the Covenant of 1643, committing him to Presbyterianism. European powers, meanwhile, mostly reacted with horror to the killing of one of God's anointed; the only exception – for now – was Switzerland, which welcomed England to the Continent's tiny family of European republics.[36] Now that the German 'Thirty Years War' (1618–48) had finally ended, there were a number of potential adversaries suddenly free to avenge their fellow monarch.

The immediate concern, however, was Ireland. In the spring, after selecting regiments by getting a London child to draw papers out of a hat, the Army was deployed, led by Cromwell. The situation remained fluid and complex. Many soldiers had changed sides over the inter-vening nearly eight years of bloodshed: two highly capable ex-Royalists, George Monck and Roger Boyle, Lord Broghill, had now come over to the regime, in the former case after a spell in the Tower. Then, in August, another ex-Royalist, Michael Jones, had scored a crucial victory at Rathmines, which prepared the ground for Cromwell's Irish landfall.

Cromwell's strategy was to take the key eastern and southern towns. The decisive engagements took place in the autumn. In September 1649, Drogheda was taken by storm; it was a fierce fight, and, with victory ensured, Cromwell ordered every one of the defenders who'd borne arms to be killed. Some 3,000 died – including some civilians and a number of priests. '[T]his is a righteous judgement of God upon these barbarous wretches, who have imbrued their hands in so much innocent blood,' Cromwell wrote to the Speaker of the Rump.[37] Many of the dead were English Royalists, led by the hapless Arthur Aston (beaten to death with his own wooden leg, according to the stories, because the soldiers thought it was filled with gold). But Cromwell's language was designed to appeal to English bigotry against the Irish specifically. He claimed the massacre would pre-vent future bloodshed, though it didn't. There was another slaughter at Wexford, the next month, with another 2,000 corpses added to Cromwell's name.

By May 1650, Cromwell was ready to return to England. Ireton was left in command, though he died, exhausted by the campaign, before the year was out. Ireland was now well on the way to being conquered. It had suffered plenty already: brutal and complex civil war since 1641, and now an effective and violent conquest. In 1652 William Petty estimated that the pre-war (i.e. 1641) population of 1.5 million had fallen as low as 850,000 (a loss of over 40 per cent). Petty's calculations were fairly dubious, and the real figure was undoubtedly lower, probably less than half that. The 1640s, before Cromwell ever set foot in Ireland, had already seen much death, and famine was at least partially caused by bad weather. Population loss isn't all caused by mortality either: emigration and a drop in the birth rate will have contributed. But even taking all these into consideration, and giving a fairly conservative figure of losses resulting from the actual conquest, Cromwell's campaign remains a moment of brutal savagery.

More pain was to come. The 'Cromwellian' land settlement was planned by the Westminster Parliament from 1642, legislated by them in 1652 and would be kept in place long after Cromwell died. But without Oliver's army, it couldn't have happened. He and his soldiers won the military victories that made it possible. The 1652 act put into place the long-planned confiscation of 2.5 million acres, and – in theory – rendered some 80,000 Irish people liable to capital punishment (the relatively poor were exempted). A court was created to oversee the process, and hundreds of people were executed (though the court had virtually ceased activity by the time Cromwell actually came to power in 1653). Former insurgents who surrendered were allowed to leave to serve foreign armies, and perhaps 34,000 did. Some Irish prisoners of war were shipped to the West Indies as indentured servants. Then, in 1653, the English government put into place the mechanisms for planting the many 'adventurers' and former Parliamentarian soldiers who'd been promised Irish lands. This meant forcibly removing those who already lived there, mostly to the barren county of Connaught. There was a debate as to whether every Irish Catholic should be cleared from the settlements, but in 1655 – with the Irish government under the hand of young Henry Cromwell, Oliver's son – the decision was made only to remove landlords. Gradually, a new Protestant landlord class emerged in Ireland. But this was a slow process – incomplete by the end of the decade. And it brought resistance: Irish cattle raiders known as *tories* (meaning 'bandits') caused continual trouble for the settlers; and by the time William Petty completed his vast 'Down Survey' of the island, several of his surveyors had been assassinated.[38]

By the spring of 1650, Charles Stuart was finally ready to make good his alliance with the Scots and launch a war to claim the throne of England. Everyone knew what was coming, so the question became whether to launch a pre-emptive strike. Fairfax believed it was against the 1643 Solemn League and Covenant to do so, resigned his post and finally retired to Yorkshire, leaving Cromwell as commander-in-chief. It was the end of a long process of withdrawal from the revolution by the old commander of the New Model.

In the summer, Cromwell invaded Scotland. He faced his former comrade David Leslie, with whom he had fought side by side at Marston Moor. Leslie knew Cromwell's strength, so pulled back, burning the Scottish countryside as he went. Eventually the two faced off at Dunbar. Cromwell was outnumbered, but his second-in-command Lambert managed to find a weakness in the Scots' position. The attack came before dawn, and in a fierce fight the Scots were utterly defeated. It was a stunning victory, which Cromwell put down to God's providence. He wrote to the Speaker the next day describing his men as the 'chariots and horsemen of Israel', calling for Parliament to grab the opportunity they had for social reform, for, 'if there be anyone that makes many poor to make a few rich, that suits not a commonwealth'.[39]

But the war wasn't over. On New Year's Day 1651, Charles Stuart – now in Scotland – had been crowned at Scone. Through the first part of the year, Cromwell and Lambert continued to make progress in conquering Scotland, which pushed Charles into a last, desperate gamble. In the high summer, he marched his army into England. His force was large, but it was so poorly equipped that, in an age of firearms, it had to resort to the use of a few dozen archers. Its only hope was that it would touch off a major Royalist uprising as it passed south down the west of England. But nothing significant came, and now – leaving Monck in charge of Scotland – Cromwell had returned to England to face down Charles. Eventually, the forces met at Worcester where, after a complex and bloody battle – exactly a year to the day after Dunbar (3 September), Charles was routed. It was, Cromwell wrote, a 'crowning mercy'.[40] All Charles could do was quietly slip out of the country (via a famous night spent in a conveniently symbolic Shropshire oak tree) and head to the Continent, a forlorn figure: a king without a country.

By now, the Rump's position was secure. The London Presbyterians were quieted somewhat, thanks to Cromwell's glory at Worcester and to a major recent show trial, in which a Welsh Puritan called Christopher Love had been executed for intriguing with Charles Stuart. Even the problems presented by Prince Rupert, who had taken to piracy after the regicide, were on the wane thanks to a major investment in the Commonwealth's navy. With the *Charles* renamed the *Liberty* and the *Henrietta Maria* rather acidly rechristened as the *Paragon*, the Republic's navy had doubled in size. Led by Robert Blake, English ships bested Rupert in a cat-and-mouse game of sail and gunpowder from the Tagus to the Mediterranean. Eventually, Rupert sailed out to the Atlantic where he filled his time bothering English merchant ships and trading in enslaved Africans.

Meanwhile, relations with the Dutch – brothers in republicanism but enemies in trade – were collapsing. Initially, the friendship had been warm, helped by the death in 1650 of William of Orange, the late king's son-in-law. In 1651, the lawyer Oliver St John was even sent to The Hague to propose a political union between the two nations. His delegation met serious hostility, though, for The Hague remained the residence of Charles I's daughter Mary. The biggest provocation by the English, however, was the Navigation Act of 1651, which decreed that all goods imported into England, Ireland or the colonies should be carried in English or colonial ships. It was, therefore, a direct attack on the Dutch, whose ships tended to be the other option available to importers. Tensions rose gradually, and in late May, the English and Dutch fleets were eyeing each other off Dover. As these were English territorial waters, it was accepted that the Dutch should dip their flags, but they were slow in doing so, so the English admiral Blake opened fire.

It was to be a naval war, and England was well equipped to fight it, but as battle raged on the seas, there was a growing sense of political malaise at home. Especially among the Army command, it was coming to be believed that the providential opportunity presented to England by abolition of monarchy was being squandered. The most pressing problem was what to do about Parliament, for this was technically still the same one that first sat in November 1640. It was time for a change; but what should that change be? In 1652, having run into Bulstrode Whitelocke in St James's Park one sunny November afternoon and fallen in to conversation, Cromwell suddenly asked, 'What if a man should take it upon him to be king?' Whitelocke thought it was a bad idea.[41]

The crisis came in the winter and spring of 1653. With little else to put their minds to, an increasing number of Army officers were in London, meeting regularly. Firstly, the Rump had angered the religious tempers of the Army by dropping their one really important reform programme. In 1650 they'd set up new bodies to propagate the gospel in Wales and the north, the 'dark corners of the land' (as those in London would have it). This was a cause close to many Puritans' hearts, including Cromwell's, and these commissions had been generally effective, but that in Wales in particular was dominated by radicals, notably the charismatic millenarian Vavasor Powell. They had support in the Army, especially from Thomas Harrison – now himself a convinced Fifth Monarchist. But on 1 April 1653, the Rump conspicuously failed to renew the Welsh commission, meaning the end of one of the government's most important religious projects.

A tepid religious policy was one thing, but there was more. Cromwell was keen to leave the divisions of war as far behind as possible, and was infuriated that the Rump was acting too harshly towards former Royalists. In early 1652, Parliament had finally passed an 'Act of Oblivion' protecting those Cavaliers who had put down their arms. Cromwell had been a strong promoter, hoping to win generous terms for his former enemies. He had support from both Army officers like Lambert and some radicals within the House, including Henry Marten. But there was still considerable anti-Royalist feeling in the Rump, and Arthur Haselrig in particular had fought back and managed to get the act wrapped up in various exceptions, 'clogged with so many provisos', that rendered it only dubiously effective.[42] Meanwhile, the Rump undermined the whole project by selling estates confiscated from the losers of the wars. Seventy-three the previous summer, then 29 more in July 1652. Then, in December 1652, a new act specifically went for the property of some 678 smaller Royalist landowners. In Cromwell's view the Rump's leaders were doing so simply for their own enrichment.[43]

Most controversial of all, though, was the increasingly rancorous debate over new elections. Nearly everyone agreed that they had to come at some point, but when? And what form should they take? The debates didn't seem to be going anywhere, and by mid-April 1653 Cromwell had lost patience. On the 19th, he summoned a group of officers and sympathetic MPs to his apartment at Whitehall. His proposal was for the Rump to dissolve, leaving in its place an interim government of around 40 men – MPs and officers. These would then govern until the country was ready for elections. The next day, 20 April, Cromwell dressed in casual clothes and chaired another meeting, discussing the same.

The meeting, though, was disturbed. A first messenger brought news that Parliament was discussing their own bill, and were hoping to pass it the same day, thus dramatically outmanoeuvring Cromwell and the Army. He didn't believe the report; but a second messenger came, then a third. Gathering up his cloak and putting on a broad-brimmed black hat, he summoned a small detachment of soldiers and rushed down the street to Parliament. It was a relatively full session – perhaps a hundred members as against 50 the previous day. Cromwell took his seat – his usual seat – and listened to the debate. Then, the Speaker prepared to put the final question. At this moment, Cromwell rose, taking off his hat. He praised the Parliament for its past work but denounced its recent failings. His voice rising with anger, he told them they were corrupt and oppressive – in bed with the lawyers and Presbyterians. His hat back on his head, he marched up and down the floor of the house, bearding individual members as drunkards, whoremongers and more. Then, he turned to Thomas Harrison: 'Call them in! Call them in!' and around 40 soldiers filed in, and swept the reluctant and bewildered MPs out. The Long Parliament, which had sat since called by a reluctant Charles I in November 1640, had finally been dissolved, not by a king, but by a man who grew up on a Cambridgeshire farm.

Why Cromwell acted thus is shrouded in mystery – not least because he never published the proposed bill that he took from the clerk. Presumably its contents were embarrassing for him and his Army colleagues, so its fate was to be incinerated in some Whitehall fire. But neither did his enemies rush to explain themselves: in fact, both sides were tellingly quiet about what the bill contained. The most plausible explanation is that its provisions were for the Rump to reconvene and manage the new elections, which was both an affront to the Army, albeit one they couldn't really admit to, but also left MPs open to accusations that they were seeking ways to perpetuate their own sitting. In any case, with Parliament gone, the question now was what to do next.

There was no doubt that Cromwell was the leading political figure in the nation, although for now he shared power with the Council of State. It was the Council of Army Officers, though, in which decisions about the political future were being made. Here, John Lambert suggested giving power to a small group of men, but the Fifth Monarchist Thomas Harrison argued for a more biblical solution: an experiment based on the Jewish Sanhedrin. It was Harrison whose views won out, and plans were made for a Nominated Assembly to be called up. It would comprise 140 trusted representatives ('Saints', in the eyes of some of them), mostly from England but with six from Wales, six from Ireland and five from Scotland, making it the first representative body for the whole archipelago. They were picked by the Army, though letters survive from some Independent congregations enthusiastically suggesting suitable candidates.

It convened on 4 July, amid much heartfelt enthusiasm from Harrison and the Fifth Monarchists. Radical saints in Herefordshire, meanwhile, told Cromwell he was God's instrument 'to translate the nation from oppression to liberty, from the hands of corrupt persons to the Saints'.[44] William Lilly held the new assembly to be 'the first of our redemption from Norman Conquest in England'. And Cromwell himself reached transcendent heights of enthusiasm in his opening speech. 'I confess I never looked to see such a Day as this,' he gushed, 'when Jesus Christ should be so owned as He is, this day, in this Work ... Jesus Christ is owned this day, by the Call of You; and you own Him, by your willingness to appear for Him. And you manifest this, as far as poor creatures may do, to be a Day of the Power of Christ.'[45]

The Nominated Assembly soon voted itself to, in fact, be a Parliament. Enemies griped that it was full of 'inferior persons', though most of the members were gentry, albeit lesser. Even Praisegod Barebone, whose surname was mockingly attached to the assembly (even today, it is usually called 'Barebone's Parliament'), was a rich London leather-seller as well as the tub-preacher of legend. There were religious radicals and of course the Independents still dominated, but many members were comparatively moderate – they were members of the landed gentry who hankered most of all after some return to stability. Still it was on shaky ground, and even its sponsors in the Army generally considered it only to be a temporary expedient: to set a good example with saintly rule, in advance of future elections.

As Barebone's Parliament began its work, the war against the Dutch was going satisfactorily well. The enemy was losing ships, and struggling to feed her people as their British adversaries harried their supply lines. In the spring and summer, the plain-speaking former Royalist George Monck had won two major engagements in the North Sea, costing the Dutch dozens of ships and the life of their admiral, Maarten Tromp. But at home, things were far from happy. The government, for one, had been deeply embarrassed when the Leveller John Lilburne returned from exile. He'd been tried by the Rump in 1651, for having alleged in print that Sir Arthur Haselrig had tried to murder him and cheat him out of a fortune. The Rumpers pleased themselves to take on the old judicial powers of the House of Lords, and decided somewhat creatively that Lilburne's attack on Sir Arthur constituted treason. So, as well as a fine and swingeing damages, they imposed exile on Lilburne, compounded with a death sentence should he ever return. Thus, when he did appear again in England in 1653, he technically required a trial only to confirm that he was, in fact, John Lilburne. However, a sympathetic jury decided he was 'not guilty of any crime worthy of death' (a thoroughly irregular verdict, it must be said), so the case was referred to Parliament, who sent him, once more, to the Tower.[46]

Meanwhile, attempts at domestic reform achieved virtually nothing. Efforts were made to reform tithes – the system by which parish churches were still funded by a local tax on agricultural goods – and the rights still held by laymen to appoint members of the clergy to parishes. But these angered the Assembly's many moderates. When the Assembly came to discuss reform of the law, its efforts were scuttled both by members' own incompetence and by the sheer deviousness of the moderates. First, the Assembly voted to abolish the Court of Chancery – infamous even then for its backlog of cases – without deciding what would replace it, a move that would have caused complete chaos. Then, a motion was passed by reformists to create a committee to 'consider a new model of the law' (i.e. to reshape it), but the Speaker misheard this as a new 'body' of the law (i.e. a radical overhaul). The reformists tried to get this changed, but – counter-intuitively – conservatives insisted the word 'body' remain, knowing that such a radical remit would never win favour and would effectively kill the bill.[47]

In the end, Barebone's Parliament fell victim to an alliance of convenience between its moderates and the Army. On Monday 12 December, moderates took their seats early and simply voted to dissolve themselves, before the rest of their colleagues had even arrived. The next day, John Lambert was ready with a new plan, called the 'Instrument of Government'. He had spent the last few weeks at his home, the old royal mansion of Wimbledon House, writing his draft for a wholly new constitution. It instigated a government with something monarchical in it, in which a single person would hold the executive. This single person was to be Oliver Cromwell, who was then installed as 'Lord Protector'. Shortly afterwards, Cromwell formally moved into Whitehall Palace, and in the spring of 1654 his family – including his eighty-nine-year-old mother – joined him. It was a new court, for a new head of state, one whose position was based on something entirely new for these islands: a written constitution.

It took the shock of Civil War, the politicisation of the New Model Army and the regicide to bring things to this point. Lambert had been a protégé of Henry Ireton, though he himself was present at neither the Putney Debates nor at the regicide itself. He was no Puritan, indeed some suspected he may have even been a secret Catholic. He enjoyed a happy marriage, to Frances, the daughter of a family friend. Some even thought he was rather too domesticated – spending time not only in his garden, which he loved, but according to Lucy Hutchinson, 'working at the needle with his wife and his maids'.[48] He was an eloquent speaker and writer. It was on the battlefield that he first made his mark, and he was as good a soldier as any. But it was as a constitutional genius that he was most accomplished, and here he was surpassed by few of his contemporaries, and certainly not by Cromwell. Lambert's Instrument of Government was born out of revolutionary circumstances, even if it tried to balance these with a certain texture of conservatism. Its setting down of unalterable fundamentals showed it owed something to the Levellers. And in its willingness to reform based on *reason* rather than custom, it is a remarkably modern document. Whether it would work in the turbulent 1650s, though, was another matter entirely.

15

A Good Constable to Keep the
Peace of the Parish

The Instrument of Government provided for government by a single person, Lord Protector Cromwell, who was to be assisted by a Council of State and regular Parliaments.[1] The fuller republicanism of the Rump and Barebone's Parliaments was replaced by something different: a semblance at least of the old monarchical constitution from before the regicide. Yet there was no House of Lords, and both the franchise and the old constituency map were drastically reformed. Now, any man with property worth £200 or more (save active Royalists or Catholics) could vote, while growing towns like Manchester and Leeds were given representation, at the expense of rotten boroughs.* MPs would sit in Westminster from Ireland and Scotland, as had been the case with Barebone's Parliament. England and Wales remained over-represented, though, with 400 MPs. Scotland and Ireland had 30 each, even though in population terms they should probably have had twice that number each.

It was a constitution based on checks and balances. Cromwell, said the lawyer Bulstrode Whitelocke when asked about it on a diplomatic mission to Sweden, would only have the 'limited power of a chief magistrate'. Parliaments, meanwhile, were to be summoned at least once every three years, and last at least five months, but the very existence of the Instrument as a written constitution limited their power, as well as that of the Protector. The Protector had a temporary veto over legislation (though this could be overturned by a second vote).

---

*This was neater than the older franchise, but it wasn't wider: £200 was the equivalent of £10 a year, five times higher than the old 40-shilling freehold.

Critically, the Instrument enshrined religious toleration. There were to be no penalties to compel people to any particular faith (Clause 36); instead, 'endeavours be used to win them by sound doctrine and the example of a good conversation'. Meanwhile, all 'such as profess faith in God by Jesus Christ' were to be protected in their worship (Clause 37), so long as they eschewed 'papacy and prelacy', i.e. Catholicism and bishops, and so long as they didn't disturb others. It was an imperfect toleration, no doubt, but it was still remarkably broad by the standard of the day.

Whatever its merits, though, the Instrument always had its enemies. To republicans, it was a transfer of power to a single person, Cromwell, and offensive to the ideals of the kingless commonwealth. They looked in horror at the Protector's partial veto over the will of Parliament. To conservatives, on the other hand, it was an attack on the 'ancient constitution', and too liberal in its provision for religious tolerance. Most fundamental of all, to civilians, it was a constitution that had come directly from the Army rather than from Parliament. Its origins lay in the politicisation of the New Model Army in 1647, not in the ancient constitution or consent from the representatives of the people. John Lambert, though undoubtedly one of the greatest political intellects of the day, remained to many civilians just a plain old Yorkshire gentleman, and not a very prominent one at that. Worse, he remained a soldier.

Cromwell and Lambert's hope was that, once Parliament sat again, it would endorse the Instrument, giving the new constitution the official support of the people. For now, though, as the turbulence of 1653 passed and as winter became spring, government proceeded without a new meeting of the legislature. Cromwell's Council of State made itself busy, passing 82 ordinances in the next eight months, and bringing the Dutch War to a broadly successful conclusion. Both sides agreed not to harbour rebels against the other – bad news for those Royalists who had set up in the Dutch Republic. And the English got to keep their Navigation Act, which had been a major *casus belli*. Finally, on top of this, the Dutch agreed to Cromwell's demand for the Princes of Orange to be excluded from the office of Stadtholder. The previous Stadtholder, William, had married Princess Mary of England, daughter of Charles I, so the Orange family and the Stuarts were closely linked, hence the exclusion. But that William had died young, in 1650, leaving his son as the sole hope of his line. As the Anglo-Dutch treaty was being concluded, that William of Orange was just three years old, and had – as it turned out – a long future ahead of him.

At home, a simmering uprising in Scotland, led by the Earl of Glencairn, was now under control, thanks to the efforts of George Monck, who was back on dry land and enjoying a return to soldiery. In England, the Protectorate was evidently more palatable to some moderates, conservatives, and even former Royalists than the regimes of the Rump and Barebone's Parliament, something helped by the reduction to just 11,000 in the number of troops stationed in England. In March 1654, Presbyterian exiles were offered an amnesty and freedom to return home: Denzil Holles was one who gratefully accepted, heading to retirement in the Dorset countryside.

Even Catholics found the Protectorate more sympathetic. Still subject to the old recusancy laws, they had an unlikely guardian in the Protector himself. Cromwell had begun his career imbued with the usual anti-Catholic bigotry of the English Puritan gentleman. But his experiences in the 1640s had given him a healthy distrust of the state's role in forcing people's religious consciences, something that he now extended to Catholics. He allowed the Venetian ambassador to administer mass to Londoners and restored the Irish and colonial estates of the Catholic Lord Baltimore of Maryland. When a Jesuit, John Southworth, was hanged, drawn and quartered in 1654, Cromwell was furious, and arranged for the poor man's remains to be put to rest in Douai in northern France, home of the English Catholic seminary.

Within a couple of years, even the ex-Royalist poet Edmund Waller was happy to laud Cromwell as a European colossus, like Edward III, Henry V or (rather more fancifully) the Emperor Augustus. Marchamont Nedham was, of course, on hand to write a defence of the new regime, as a bastion against the anarchy of Barebone's Parliament and the previous corruption and tyranny of the Rump. 'Parliaments always sitting,' the one-time doctor Nedham wrote, 'are no more agreeable to the temper of the people, than it is to a natural Body to take always Physic instead of food.'[2] But all this came at the cost of alienating some radicals, not least the Fifth Monarchists like Thomas Harrison, who had pinned their hopes on Barebone's

Parliament only to have it flushed out by Cromwell's soldiers and Lambert's Instrument. John Rogers, a Fifth Monarchist preacher, had seen Cromwell as a new Moses when he dissolved the Rump, but now decided he was the Antichrist.

The constitutional problems of a fledgling political entity remained real and potentially very tricky. The biggest early setback came with the Protectorate's first Parliament, which – it had been hoped – was supposed to have given the Instrument the endorsement of the people. After the first general election in 14 years, Parliament had convened on 3 September 1654, the happy anniversary of Cromwell's great triumphs of Dunbar and Worcester. Cromwell's opening speech called for 'healing and settling' and praised the traditional social order: 'a nobleman, a gentleman, a yeoman; the distinction of these: that is a good interest of the nation, and a great one!' It was time to reinforce 'the ranks and orders of men – whereby England hath been known for hundreds of years', which had been challenged by 'men of Levelling principles' who had tried 'reducing all to an equality'.[3]

But if this conservative rhetoric was supposed to prevent criticism of the new regime, it failed, for MPs immediately began challenging the Instrument. Parliament had only sat for a few days before Cromwell came in, gave a rather more angry speech and insisted MPs sign a 'recognition' promising not to try to alter the government. Around a hundred MPs couldn't square this with their consciences, and so absented themselves. The case of the Protectorate was not helped by inelegant contributions like that of the gruff soldier John Desborough, who on 10 November told Parliament they should be grateful the Protector had given them half the power, since he previously had all of it, and 'might have kept it without any competitor'.[4] It was embarrassingly close to a truth Cromwell would have preferred unspoken, that his Protectorate's authority, ultimately, rested on the Army. And it was all the worse given that Desborough, who was a much better soldier than politician, was Cromwell's brother-in-law.

Even with Parliament effectively purged after November's 'Recognition', MPs persisted with a new Constitutional Bill, aimed at rewriting and replacing the Instrument, to Cromwell's considerable annoyance. There was also fresh discontent in the Army in the form of a petition, accusing the Protectorate of being a military tyranny and calling for Parliamentary government as set out by the old Officers' *Agreement of the People*. It was written by the Leveller John Wildman and signed by three colonels (including the hero of the Naseby dragoons, John Okey). The three colonels were promptly arrested and dismissed. Eventually, Cromwell lost patience with everybody and – taking a very creative interpretation of the Instrument's stipulation that he could dissolve Parliaments after five months – waited until 22 January, five *lunar* months since they convened, and sent the MPs home.

As Parliament was bickering, a merchant named George Cony had refused to pay Cromwell's taxes on the grounds that they had not been granted by Parliament. It was a palpable hit, not least because illegal taxation was one of the reasons Cromwell had taken arms against Charles Stuart in the first place. The authorities had Cony fined and imprisoned, and the government tried to bully his lawyers, interrogating them and sending them to the Tower for 'using words tending to sedition, and the subversion of the present government'.[5]

There was worse news from the West Country. Since 1653, Charles Stuart had actively engaged a small group of mostly aristocratic Royalists and charged them with plotting the overthrow of the Republic. Known as the 'Sealed Knot', they had achieved nothing. By late 1654, a rival syndicate had emerged and were actively planning an actual uprising. Cromwell's hawklike spymaster John Thurloe knew about it, and that winter the regime recalled 3,000 men from Ireland and placed cannons to defend Whitehall and St James's Park.

Thankfully for Cromwell, the uprising was a catastrophe. On 8 March 1655, the drunkard Earl of Rochester succeeded only in mustering 150 men on Marston Moor, who were promptly scattered by Robert Lilburne. Other assemblies did little better, save for one in Wiltshire, led by John Penruddock. However, even this was a fiasco: shrinking from their plan to take Winchester, they instead entered Salisbury, before Penruddock's forces fled west to their inevitable defeat, mocked as 'Tories' after the Irish Catholic bandits.[6]

Penruddock's rising necessitated a trial, but here the regime found itself on shaky constitutional ground once more.[7] In 1654, the Council of State had passed a Treason Ordinance, but this hadn't been approved during the fractious recent Parliament. The defendants thus argued that this ordinance didn't hold force of law, in which case they would have to be prosecuted under the medieval treason laws for levying war against the king. Yet, as they pointed out with no little irony, the Rump had, in 1649, abolished all kingly government. Penruddock's men had a point, and even the judges saw this, but as a result their arguments had already been anticipated, so instead the judges argued that levying war against the Lord Protector was treason by the 'fundamental laws of the land'. Effectively, killing the supreme magistrate was a common-law offence, whether that supreme magistrate was a king (as it had always been) or a Lord Protector (as it now was). In any case, the defendants' arguments didn't get them off, for after trial, some 39 were sentenced to death, and around half – including the hapless Penruddock – were executed.

The Marston Moor rebels fared better. They were prosecuted by Francis Thorpe, the judge who had given the stirring speech at York when the Republic was young. The problem was the rising had been a flop, which meant the only people who had witnessed it were those actually involved. Thorpe's misgivings led him to be replaced by a Walter Strickland, sent up from Whitehall to sort things out, but when the trial eventually did take place, it was scuppered by the old issue of a lack of evidence. The rebels, much to their relief no doubt, could only be convicted of rioting, and got off with mere fines.

Still, with the Royalist rebellions defeated, Cromwell could turn his attention to a wider initiative, to projecting the power of his new regime on the high seas. He had a large, well-furnished navy, fresh from a successful war against the Dutch, ready to use. But should he point his cannons at France, or against England's traditional enemy, Spain? Suffering a bout of Elizabethan nostalgia, he decided to attack Spain. Their weak spot, he thought, was Hispaniola in the Caribbean, but it turned out to be nothing of the sort. The 'Western Design' to capture it was forcefully rebuffed, though the Republic did – somewhat by accident – conquer Jamaica, which had yet to be extensively cultivated, and was then seen as a rather poor substitute. As news reached the Protector, he went into a bout of miserable introspection, and decided that God had finally deserted His new Israel. It was Cromwell's first substantial military defeat, and even though it had taken place on the other side of the Atlantic while he was in England, he took it hard.

The only answer, surely, was moral reform. This would be driven by a radical new experiment. England would be divided into military cantons, each overseen by a major-general. These would combine security with the reformation of people's manners. Of the two, security was the bigger priority, but the second was an old Puritan desire, and now they had the tools to make it work.

Cromwell's rule was wading into deeply unpopular territory. Military government like this was offensive enough to English sensibilities, but, worst of all, the major-generals would be supported by a cavalry militia to be paid for by a 'Decimation' tax on former Royalists, which was not only extra-Parliamentary (for now at least), it also directly contravened the 1652 Act of Oblivion. Cromwell's Protectorate had been edging towards reconciliation with former Royalists; now it threw that progress away.

Cromwell's major-generals were of widely varying impact, but pretty much everywhere they were wildly unpopular. William Prynne, the old Puritan scourge of Charles I who had been excluded at Pride's Purge, thought they were tyrants, opening people's 'houses, studies, trunks, chests, both by day and by night', and closing inns, taverns and alehouses 'without any legal authority'.[8] Those, like Edward Whalley in Leicestershire and Warwickshire, who worked with the traditional local elites, were more successful than the uncompromising swordsmen like Charles Worsley in Lancashire, Cheshire and Staffordshire, or John Desborough in the south-west. But none of them were loved, and when a fresh general election was called in the summer of 1656, their continued presence was likely to be hugely contentious. The major-generals assured Cromwell that they would be able to manage the elections and secure a pro-regime Parliament, which, of course, would then give legal backing to the Decimation Tax. But they were wrong.

The overt threat posed by militant royalism, at least, was now receding rather quickly. Penruddock's failure showed up the weakness of organised resistance, and the military successes of the regime meant that Charles Stuart found his reputation among Europe's political elites relegated from useful pawn to minor irritant. Royalists were reduced to mockery, although some of them were quite good at it. The old tropes about their enemies were still there: they were Puritan killjoys who hated their neighbours, and brought anarchy, levelling and weird sects. The war and regicide had overturned the old order: London was now 'Nodnol' (itself a convenient reference to 'Nol' Cromwell), and the people were now in charge. One scurrilous 1652 pamphlet, *Mercurius Democritus*, pretended it was avoiding politics, but in reality mocked the new order by presenting a topsy-turvy world. It pointedly used the subtitle *A Perfect Nocturnal*, making it an upturned version of the respectable *Perfect Diurnall* and offered up jokes about hypocritical Puritans and rebellious women, including an invented sect called the 'Sisterhood of the Tumblers' who liked to 'exercise on their backs in many obscure alleys'.[9]

Now Royalists also had the figure of Cromwell to mock, for his devilish ambition, his obscure origins and, not least of all, his oversized nose. He was 'Beelzebub's Ale-brewer', 'Nose Almighty' or 'His Noseship'.[10] His supporters were 'Lord Plebs'. Meanwhile, Royalist humour also revelled in its rejection of Puritan morality more generally, celebrating hard drinking, bawdy comedy and the merits of good company. Royalist tales included those of an Irishman who buggered an eel and Puritans so strict that they tried to impose fines on people for farting. The aim was to show themselves as fun-loving Cavaliers, an antidote to the dowdy Puritans in power. It was, and is, an enduring stereotype, though it owes nothing to the famously civilised late king Charles. Indeed, to the moderate gentry, it may have made the new Cavalier cause considerably less attractive, for even swordsmen might be preferable to degenerates.

Part of the reason the Royalists found so much to poke fun at was that Cromwell's regime did throw its energies into thoroughly Puritan projects of moral reform. Now, after decades on the sidelines engaging in local projects for 'reformation of manners', Puritans controlled the state, and they were not about to miss the opportunity to make society more Godly. 'You must be a terror to drunkards, swearers, Sabbath-profaners, whoremasters, seducers, blasphemers, and all the rabble of Hell', magistrates were told at one point.[11]

In most cases, ambition naturally outpaced achievement. In the case of sexual regulation, for example, the Protectorate carried on the work of the Rump, whose Adultery Act of 1650 had ordered the death penalty for adulterous women and their partners, and imprisonment for fornicators. But convictions were vanishingly rare, and the law was considered a 'mere scarecrow'. It was so savage that few considered it just to make use of it. Ironically, indeed, since the old church courts had been abolished, you were actually much less likely to be prosecuted for illicit sex under Cromwell than you had been under the previous monarchs, albeit the penalties were now rather more severe.

There was legislation against swearing, too, especially by London's porters, watermen and dockworkers. Some local authorities fined people for bad language and gave the proceeds to the poor. The whole thing proved a thankless task, though. When the Puritan Henry Newcome asked a woman why she swore on the sabbath, she replied that she swore on every other day, so why should Sunday be any different.[12]

Sabbath observance was enforced, and it did become much harder to find an alcoholic drink, or even a barge across the Thames, on a Sunday. Alehouses were regulated with new vigour (they were 'hell-houses' and 'the seminaries of devils incarnate', said a sermon in Lancaster, presumably not just referring to the local ones).[13] Rowdy sports, too, were regulated, though bear-baiting, bull-baiting, dog-tossing and cock-fighting all managed to survive. Music became controversial, though it had many defenders: 'Music is a lawful science, and I love it,' said one MP, and Cromwell himself was something of an aficionado.[14] He had the great organ at Magdalen College, Oxford, packed up and carted down to Hampton Court for his aural enjoyment, and the corridors of his Whitehall echoed to the sounds of an eight-part orchestra and polyphonic Latin motets sung by choirboys.

The biggest problem was the wrong sort of music in the wrong sort of place, especially if it had the wrong sort of audience, and particularly, of course, if it was on the Sabbath. One Leicester man, for example, committed the error of playing the bagpipes in an alehouse within earshot of Major-General Whalley's lodgings. The soldier's sensibilities were offended, and the piper was sent to the local House of Correction. Eventually the issue of music would come to be debated in Parliament, at times at a rather comical level of specificity. Were harps immoral, it was asked? What about bagpipes, fiddles and singing? In the end, Parliament only prohibited fiddlers and minstrels from playing in alehouses for money. Hardly a great change, all told.

Theatre was seriously hit, however, and nearly all of the London playhouses closed. One that survived was the Red Bull in Clerkenwell, which carved out a role as home for populist 'drolls'. These were lively and slapstick performances comprising acrobatics, rope-dancing and suchlike, which would remain as one of the most ironic legacies of Cromwell's England. Another such legacy was a new form of art entirely, at least in England. In the autumn of 1656, after testing the waters earlier in the year, William Davenant, a flamboyant playwright who had written masques for the late king and his queen, put on a show that focused on music rather than acting, in a style that had developed in Italy. By doing so it avoided the official frowning upon dramatic performances. Davenant wisely gained official permission from Bulstrode Whitelocke and from John Thurloe, arguing that such entertainment would cheer people up and discourage them from sedition. The performances even featured a female actress – reported to be the first that ever appeared on the professional stage. Davenant called the new art form by its Italian name: 'opera'.

Dancing, meanwhile, survived in elite circles, but was disapproved of in it rowdiest forms. Some dances, indeed, were wilfully bawdy – no doubt an enjoyable way of irritating Puritan killjoys. A popular collection of dance music and steps, sold at John Playford's shop in the Inner Temple, by the church door no less, included mixed-sex dances entitled 'Up Tails All', 'Punks Delight', 'Rufty Tufty' and 'Bobbing Joe' no doubt to considerable horror in some quarters.[15] Morris dancing, meanwhile, seems to have taken on an additional political significance – not only anti-Puritan but actively Royalist. It largely disappeared in London (for now), though it remained strong in the West Country.

And fashion was irrepressible. The old Puritan taste for short hair had fallen out: flowing locks were in. Nor did everyone dress as plainly as the ageing Lord Protector. John Lambert and his wife Frances were notoriously fashionable. Ladies' dress in London continued to form the object of derisory comments (from men), although the reason for such scorn depended on the beholder. Puritans fumed at 'whorish attire' such as 'naked breasts, bare shoulders, powdering' and 'spotting the face'. Royalists, meanwhile, laughed at the sartorial pretensions of jumped-up tradesmen. 'O bedlam world!' scoffed one. 'When every trade, and every greasy kitchen maid / with gold and silver lace is overlaid.'[16]

As might be expected, the regime put considerable energy into religious reform. Here, much more was achieved – in theory at least. Cromwell's first Parliament established a dual system of 'triers' and 'ejectors', who would ensure the ministry was ideologically sound by vetting new appointees and ousting existing ones considered problematic. But attempts to create a new confession of faith remained stubbornly on the drafting table. Locally, meanwhile, Puritan ministers often faced open resistance from parishioners, whose mockery ran from hooting, hollering, sleeping and making monkey faces during sermons, or even hitting cricket balls at the church. One Puritan minister at Kirklington, Yorkshire, was 'hissed out' of the pulpit by an elderly woman who called him 'old hackle back' and threatened to lob her chair stool at him.[17] Others were called names like 'devilish roundheaded priest' and 'Sirrah Jack Priest'. Puritan ministers were, one complained, 'exposed to the dirt, drivel, foam and rage of the very scum of vain, deluded and profane wretches'. But they hardly helped themselves. 'It is a sure sign commonly that a minister is good,' wrote one Puritan's son, 'when all the parish is against him.'[18]

Most infamously, Christmas remained under official disapproval (dating back to 1644). Essentially, Puritans here had three goals: they wanted churches closed, they wanted celebrations ended and they wanted people to work as normal. They largely succeeded in the first of these, but not the other two. People still, it was said, spent Christmas Day 'carding, and dicing, drinking, bellowing, roaring'.[19] And celebrations continued in private houses: crackling winter fires, mince pies, drinking and gambling would be encountered in the houses of many members of the rural gentry, including many Cromwellian loyalists.

Interestingly, the English republic did not go after witches. The major-generals were never asked to seek them out, nor is there any evidence that Cromwell had much interest in the topic. The contrast with Scotland was remarkable: here, the Puritan revolution brought added impetus to witch-hunting, and in 1649–50, during a particularly vicious 'hunt', some 150 witches were killed there. But in England, once the Hopkins trials had petered out in 1647, only a handful of witches were prosecuted, let alone convicted or executed.[20] The evidence we have suggests around two-thirds of those put on trial at this point were found not guilty, though some were still hanged, including victims like Anne Bodenham of Salisbury, who happened to be a former servant to John Lambe, the Duke of Buckingham's sorcerer, and who had told a maid suffering convulsive fits that she should pray to Jupiter. The biggest burst of prosecutions took place in Kent in 1652, and resulted in nine convictions, though interestingly this drew a stinging response in print from the local gentleman Sir Robert Filmer. Dripping with sarcasm, Filmer pointed out that witchcraft was a crime of dubious legal basis, for it depended on people acting as accessories to the devil. In English law, Filmer acidly remarked, one could not be tried as an accessory until the conviction or at least indictment of the principal, something singularly unlikely when the principal was Satan.[21]

Nor was Filmer the only sceptic. The Hopkins trials had been attacked in print as early as 1646 by a local vicar, John Gaule. Then, in 1651, the classic attack on the notion of witchcraft by Reginald Scot, written in the 1580s, was republished for the first time since, by a printer who specialised in radical texts. And another writer, the Essex Puritan Thomas Ady, published a tract that ridiculed popular beliefs about witches. Why, he asked, would Satan use women, the weaker vessel, for his terrifying schemes? Why, he wondered, did Scripture not come with a warning that witches were more likely to be women? Folkloric beliefs like those of the familiar, Ady thought, were idolatrous: he likened them to indigenous belief systems of the

New World, and poured scorn. Who indeed didn't themselves have marks on their body that could be taken as witches' teats? Some, Ady noted, had been condemned simply for suffering from piles. More to the point, since Christ had said, 'A Spirit hath not flesh and bones' (Luke 24:39), how could the devil as portrayed in traditional culture be real: 'that he is some ugly terrible creature to look upon, some black man with a pair of horns on his head, and a cloven foot, and a long tail or some monstrous beast that inhabiteth in woods, and walketh about in the night to scare people'.[22] Like Scot before him, Ady didn't just think witchcraft was difficult to prove, he thought the very notion as it existed in English popular culture was utterly ridiculous.

By 1656, many of the most radical groups that had sprung up in response to war and revolution were in retreat. The Levellers and Diggers had lost their lustre and the Ranters were no longer quite the bogeymen they had once been. Laurence Clarkson, the Ranter, seems to have lived as a cunning man and astrologer during the mid-1650s, before converting to follow Lodowick Muggleton, the London tailor whose small sect was still attracting supporters. But the Quakers were different. They had flourished. They were frequently disrupting services in the 'Steeplehouses' of the old faith – as they called parish churches – and welcoming new adherents to the Inner Light. Many claimed healing powers, including no lesser figure than George Fox himself, whose cures would run to well over a hundred.

In London, though, the otherworldly Fox had been slightly overshadowed by the charismatic former soldier James Nayler, who had made a name for himself as a witty orator and a pithy pamphleteer. Lurking around town with his long hair and a group of female disciples, he propounded a theology based on the idea that those who accepted the Inner Light literally had Christ in them, meaning they were without sin.

That summer, the Quakers suffered an unexpected crisis. Members of Nayler's group, particularly the effervescent Martha Simmonds, had started disrupting other Quaker meetings. Some decided that Simmonds was having a malign influence on Nayler, and asked him to leave her behind and come to the West Country, where Fox was in prison. But when Nayler left London, Simmonds followed him, and anyway, Nayler was arrested under a law against vagrants and thrown in Exeter gaol. On Fox's own release from confinement, he visited the still-imprisoned Nayler, but the latter man refused to offer subservience, and when Fox asked the lank-haired Yorkshireman to kiss his hand as a gesture of reconciliation, instead Nayler kissed his foot, which Fox took as an insult.

Nayler remained in Exeter gaol as summer turned to autumn, until help came from Martha Simmonds. She had taken work as a nurse in the household of Major-General Desborough, the rather despotic military governor of the region. Specifically, she was looking after Desborough's wife, who had a rather influential brother: Oliver Cromwell himself. In return for her work, Simmonds got Desborough to allow the release of all the Quakers in Exeter gaol, with the order signed by the Protector.

Nayler's release took place on 20 October. Within a couple of days, though, he was stirring up trouble once more when he and his followers staged an unusual, and largely unnoticed, procession into the tiny hillside town of Glastonbury. Then, on the 24th they repeated the performance at Bristol, a much more populous town, through driving rain, with Nayler's followers throwing garments in front of him, singing 'Holy, holy, holy, Lord God of Sabaoth'.

Bristol's Quakers, who were trying to live in peace with their neighbours, were mortified. Nayler's biggest problem, though, was that he was promptly arrested and interrogated by the local authorities. Any doubts about the performance were quickly dispelled by his followers. Dorcas Erbury, one of Nayler's fellow prisoners at Exeter, announced that Nayler was 'the only begotten son of God'; in fact, she had literally died in the gaol before the Yorkshireman resurrected her. It didn't take a particularly unsympathetic observer to consider that this may have crossed the line into blasphemy.

All the while, elections for a new Parliament had taken place. Supporters of the major-generals had suffered bruising defeats as election-day crowds chanted, 'No swordsmen! No decimators!' Some, like the Dorset landowner Anthony Ashley Cooper, were able to get elected by co-opting the language of the 'Country' against the military. In the end, the Protector's Council decided to exclude around a hundred newly elected MPs, out of 460, on the basis that, under the terms of the Instrument, they were not 'persons of known integrity, fearing God, and of good conversation'. It was only when Parliament met, after a military-dominated opening ceremony in which Lambert shared the Protector's coach, that members learned of the exclusions. Some stayed away in protest, and a letter of remonstrance on behalf of the excluded was quickly presented to the Speaker by the moderate Cheshire MP George Booth.

Then, at the end of October, Parliament was made aware of Nayler's entrance into Bristol. Horrified, they appointed a committee of 55 MPs to investigate. After five weeks they were back in the House, reporting that Nayler, as well as having sexual relations with his followers, was guilty of assuming 'the gesture, words, names, and attributes of our Saviour Christ'.[23] The report was met with astonished silence.

Finally, Philip Skippon, the wounded hero of Turnham Green and Naseby, rose. 'I do not marvel at this silence,' he said. 'Every man is astonished to hear this report.' The problem was toleration. Too much of it.

Others piled on. 'My ears did tingle, and my heart tremble, to hear the report,' said Major-General Boteler. 'I am satisfied that there is too much of the report true. I have heard many of the blasphemies of this sort of people; but the like of this I never heard of.' He thought that the punishment should fit the horror of the offence. 'By the Mosaic law, blasphemers were to be stoned to death.'

Parliament then exploded into ten days of fierce debate about what to do. The language veered from the measured to the positively Old Testament. 'To supplant your God, oh, horrid!' cried George Downing, the rather unpleasant Anglo-Irish MP after whom Downing Street would eventually be named. 'These vipers are crept into the bowels of your Commonwealth,' warned Colonel Milton (not in any way to be confused with the poet), 'and the government too. They grow numerous, and swarm all the nation over; every county, every parish.' 'The eyes of the whole nation', the House was reminded, 'are upon you in this business, and say, Is this the issue of your government and reformation?'

Eventually, Nayler himself was summoned to the bar.

'King of Israel: assumed you thus?', he was asked.

'As I have dominion over the enemies of Christ, I am King of Israel spiritually' was the careful reply. 'I was set up as a sign of Christ's coming. The fullness of Christ's coming is not yet, but he is come now,' he declared. In fact, he confessed everything except the allegation of sexual relations with one Mrs Roper. 'It might be she kissed me. It was our manner; but when I found their extravagancies I left them. All that knew me, in the army and elsewhere, will say I was never guilty of lewdness; or so reputed. I abhor filthiness.'

Even this left Parliament with a big problem. At worst, Nayler had contravened the Blasphemy Act of 1650, and – as the reliably pedantic Bulstrode Whitelocke argued – he should therefore be tried in the ordinary courts. But conviction for a first offence, which is what this was, would only bring six months imprisonment. Scarcely enough to satisfy the furious House.

So they explored other options. One was to proceed by legislation: use the same method that had dealt with Strafford. But this, just as in that case, would have required assent from the executive, and Cromwell was not necessarily a willing persecutor. The other was to use the judicial powers that had been vested in the old House of Lords, act as a court of law and convict Nayler of something else. Yet even here there were problems. It was not quite clear what had happened to those old judicial powers. Had they been abolished with the Lords, or had they passed to the new, single-chambered Parliament? Not only this, but surely the Instrument of Government, with its famous toleration clause, gave constitutional protections to those who professed a belief in Christ, which Nayler, for all his idiosyncrasies, evidently did.

It was a problem quite clear to Skippon. The Instrument of Government, specifically its 'toleration clauses', numbers 37 and 38, was protecting blasphemers. 'These Quakers, Ranters, Levellers, Socinians, and all sorts,' he grunted, 'bolster themselves under thirty-seven and thirty-eight of Government, which, at one breath, repeals all the acts and ordinances against them … If this be liberty, God deliver me from such liberty.'

Downing, meanwhile, brought yet more brimstone: 'As to the Instrument of Government, I hope it shall never be made use of as an argument to let this wretch escape.' 'I am as much for tender consciences as any man,' he lied, 'but I deny that this has any share in such liberty.' 'God,' intoned Downing, 'could have made him a pillar of salt immediately, if he had pleased; have struck him dead, but he has left it to you to vindicate his honour and glory.' Parliament needed to act.

A very few MPs stood up for Nayler, though even most of the so-called 'merciful men' agreed that he'd gone too far. They argued, though, that Parliament was about to set a dangerous precedent, setting itself up as the ultimate arbiter of blasphemy, while making blasphemy a potentially capital crime. Not everyone, indeed, agreed that Nayler had really committed that particular offence. And even if he had, the idea that Christ was in every person was widespread and theologically defensible. A telling speech by Lord President Henry Lawrence, whose thoughts were particularly important because he was a key ally of Cromwell, warned the House: 'If you hang every man that says, Christ is in you the hope of glory, you will hang a good many.' The execution of religious radicals was no way to secure the regime. Lambert, meanwhile, defended his former quartermaster. 'He was a man of a very unblameable life and conversation, a member of a very sweet society of an independent church.' He'd lost his way – become 'puffed up' – Lambert admitted, but still he must be proceeded against within the law.

Ultimately, though, such voices were in a minority. In the end, on 8 December, Nayler was voted guilty – not of blasphemy, but of *horrid* blasphemy. It was a new crime altogether, created retrospectively to fit Nayler's particular offence, and it was based on the old jurisdiction of the Lords.

Eight days later, 82 MPs voted that Nayler should be killed. But this was too much for many, and 96 votes were cast against. Nayler would live. But he would still be punished. The diary of Thomas Burton, a backbench MP from Westmorland, records MPs words as they stood up to smite Nayler down.

Colonel White proposed that his tongue might be bored through.

Colonel Barclay, that his hair might be cut off.

Major-General Haines, that his tongue might be slit or bored through, and that he might be stigmatized with the letter B.

Colonel Coker, that his hair might be cut off.

Sir Thomas Wroth. *Slit his tongue, or bore it, and brand him with the letter B.*

One of the few to suggest restraint was Major-General Whalley, though his argument was scarcely of much comfort: 'Do not cut off his hair,' he pleaded, for 'that will make the people believe that the Parliament of England are of opinion that our Saviour Christ wore his hair so, and this will make all people in love with the fashion.'

In the end it was ordered that Nayler was to be whipped through London, be branded with the letter B, have his tongue bored; then to be carried to Bristol backwards on a bareback horse, there to be whipped through the town, then back to London where he was to be imprisoned until Parliament ordered his release (not, one will note, until the Protector did). He was to be kept to hard labour, with no writing materials. Not only this, he was to be kept from the company of both men and women.

Nayler wasn't allowed to speak. As he was being led out of Parliament, he did say he hoped his body would endure the punishment, and telling MPs, 'The Lord lay not these things to your charge.'

Over the next few days, he suffered the ordeal of pillorying, branding, boring and whipping. According to Burton, 'He put out his tongue very willingly, but shrinked a little when the iron came upon his forehead. He was pale when he came out of the pillory, but high-coloured after tongue-boring ... Nayler embraced his executioner, and behaved himself very handsomely and patiently.'

His companions were allowed to accompany him, and Martha Simmonds, Hannah Stranger and Dorcas Erbury adopted positions around the pillory that apparently mimicked those of the women at the Cross at Golgotha. One Quaker, the merchant Robert Rich, licked

Nayler's wounds, and put up a sign: 'This is the King of the Jews.' It was exactly the kind of scene MPs didn't want.

Cromwell himself was less than impressed by the whole debacle. He had enjoyed fairly cordial relations with Quakers, and as much as he disagreed with them, he had no desire to see them persecuted. But his conscience didn't stretch to doing anything, save for sending a message to the House, on 25 December, noting that he detested blasphemers, but asking to know the 'grounds and reasons' on which Parliament had punished Nayler specifically. Behind this, though, lay Cromwell's realisation that Nayler's persecution had exposed some of the constitutional fragility of his regime.

The case had seen a genuine revulsion among Parliamentarians against the new sect, but it also provided a handy way of attacking the Instrument of Government – not just its loose religious toleration, but also its failure to sort out the issue of the judicial function of the former House of Lords. It exposed the Instrument as unsatisfactory to all sides. To conservatives, it offered too much protection to the sects through its toleration clauses; yet because it apparently allowed the Commons to act as a law court and to use this power to tyrannise over the Quakers, it also provided insufficient checks and balances, and therefore protection, for the religious radicals.

Civilian enemies of the Instrument and its military sponsors also now scored a significant victory over the major-generals. The Decimation Tax, the levy on Royalists that funded the new militia, was due for renewal, so Major-General Desborough introduced a bill to the House on Christmas Day, when he knew many moderates would be away, still marking the old festival. Somehow, though, this 'Militia Bill' disappeared, only to return on 7 January 1657, after Twelfth Night. But it wasn't quite the same: someone had attached an 'indemnity clause', forgiving the major-generals for any unlawful acts. Desborough was furious at the implication, namely that the major-generals might have broken the law. He sarcastically thanked the proposers. 'It is our swords must Indemnify us!' he then thundered, unhelpfully (and once again rather openly admitting the origins of their power).[24] Lambert supported the bill, but it was opposed by 'civilian' Cromwellians like Lord Broghill as well – tellingly – as Cromwell's son-in-law John Claypole. Decision was delayed, partly because of the discovery of an assassination plot by the old Levellers Edward Sexby and Miles Sindercombe (supported by John Wildman), which would have involved blowing up Whitehall with gunpowder. Eventually, at the end of the month, the Militia Bill was defeated.

By now, it was clear that the 'civilian' faction around Broghill were about to make a major play. On 23 February, their gambit began in earnest. That day, the backbencher Sir Christopher Packe rose and presented a new paper. It was a new constitution. It would bring back a bicameral Parliament. Religious toleration would be carefully scaled back, explicitly excluding those 'who publish horrible blasphemies'.[25] Crimes like Nayler's would be placed decisively outside the law. And, most startling of all, Oliver Cromwell would become king.

The debate was fierce, both in the House and outside. Lord Broghill supported the new constitution, now known as the 'Humble Petition and Advice'. Lambert, Fleetwood and Desborough – the Army high command – were 'violently against it'.[26] They knew it would represent a wresting of power away from them and towards the civilian faction. More than this – the new constitution would change the rules about succession, a major consideration as the Protector aged. As things stood, under Lambert's Instrument of Government, the next Protector would be decided by the Council of State, on which the army were well represented. Some thought Lambert himself was eyeing up the role. But under the Petition and Advice, the decision would fall to Cromwell alone.

Punters made bets on the future of the regime, much to Puritans' irritation. For many observers, the offer confirmed Cromwell's own insatiable ambition for power. But the reality was that a King Oliver would have a much more restricted power than Lord Protector Cromwell. As Protector, his authority was based on the sword, and on the Instrument of Government that had come from the soldier Lambert, and which had never been agreed by Parliament. It was a constitutional novelty and the fundamental limits to executive power were still decidedly uncertain. Kingship, on the other hand, was 'known by law', bounded by years of custom and practice.

Moreover, because the crown was explicitly being offered by Parliament, Cromwell's reign would be expressly grounded in the sovereignty of the people. William Lenthall, the old Speaker of the Long Parliament, suggested the offer was the voice of the people itself: 'for it is the voice of the three nations in one Parliament'.[27] A Cromwellian monarchy would, then, have been the final repudiation of the old absolutist argument that kings were made by God.

But what if God had already spoken against the title of 'King'? On 27 February, a delegation of a hundred army officers met with Cromwell to persuade him against accepting the new constitution. He was furious with them for everything that had gone wrong with his Protectorate, and with their presumption to tell him what he should do. Sure, the royal title was nothing to him – just a 'feather in a man's hat', he said, but what made the officers think he should listen to them?[28] He'd followed them, but where had it taken him and the country? Perhaps the most stunning moment, though, was when Cromwell revealed that he had been offered the crown already, in December 1653, with the Instrument. Did all of the hundred officers already know? The heads of those who didn't will have turned accusingly towards Lambert.

Yet for all Cromwell's anger, he remained unconvinced. Had not God's providence 'laid this title aside?' he wondered. Many of the religious groups who had flowered under kingless government wrote to him to ask him to refuse. Would not his acceptance of the crown 'rejoice the hearts of the profane party?', asked a Gloucestershire congregation. Would it not 'greatly sadden' the hearts of the Saints? These were men whom Cromwell had fought and prayed with, and God had rewarded their sufferings with an end to the tyranny of monarchy. 'We beseech you in the Bowels of Christ,' London Baptists implored him, 'remember what God did for you and us, at Marston Moor, Naseby, Pembroke, Tredah [Drogheda], Dunbar and Worcester, and upon what grounds.' 'Those that are for a Crown,' an old comrade-in-arms wrote, 'I fear you have little experience of them: the other, most of them, have attended your greatest hazards.'[29] Even George Fox visited Cromwell, telling him that taking the kingship would 'bring a shame and ruin on himself and his posterity', advice that Cromwell seemed to take well, and thanked the Quaker for.[30]

In the end, he could only refuse. He drew on the language of a
parish officer: 'I am ready to serve not as a King, but as a Constable …
a good Constable set to keep the peace of the Parish.' And he spoke
as a Puritan: 'I would not seek to set up that which Providence hath
destroyed and laid in the dust, and I would not build Jericho again.'
Ultimately he convinced himself that God's Providence had cast down
monarchy, that the institution itself was an 'accursed thing'. That if he
picked up the crown, then the Lord would rain punishment down on
His new Israel.

But the 'kinglings' weren't ready to give up just yet. Over the
course of April, the offer was repeated, again, and again. Gradually,
they became convinced he would accept. On 6 May, a small group of
Army officers drafted a petition against him doing so. The same day,
Desborough met Cromwell in St James's Park, telling him he'd resign
if the crown was accepted. Fleetwood and Lambert made it clear they
would do the same. Two days later, Cromwell gave a speech to MPs,
at James I's Banqueting House. 'I cannot undertake this government
with that title of king,' he told his dumbfounded audience.[31] Finally,
the kingship issue was dead. There would be no King Oliver I.

It was a supremely ironic twist: the Parliamentarians in the Civil War had
fought for the notion that kingly authority came from the people, against
a king who thought his title came from God. Now, the ultimate beneficiary of their victory was refusing that same title, offered to him by the
representatives of the people, on the grounds that God found it offensive.

It was a matter of conscience: God's providence, Cromwell
thought, had cast down the monarchy – who was he to pick up the
accursed thing again? It didn't help that the army – his old comrades –
were against, but this wasn't the primary reason. For the rest of the
Humble Petition was accepted. The Instrument of Government was
gone, and there was now an 'Other House' as a balance against the
Commons. The Council was rebranded as a 'Privy Council', and the
Protector himself took on more elaborate rituals and trappings. The
change in constitution, even without the kingship, was a civilian coup
against the army and against the Instrument of Government. Lambert
was forced into retirement at his mansion at Wimbledon, though his

erstwhile allies Desborough and Fleetwood – both, unlike Lambert, married into the Cromwell clan – were able to make their peace with the new government.

The Protectorate fell back into relative peace, though not without threats to its stability. The Other House was packed with Cromwellian supporters, which meant they weren't where they were needed: in the Commons. There were still plots, and harvests took a turn for the worse towards the end of the 1650s. By this point, though, England was returning to some kind of stability and the economy was strong, meaning that the system of poor relief could cope. Whereas during the crisis at the end of the 1640s, magistrates had been forced to scramble to reactivate formal poor relief in the face of a crushing burden, now parishes simply increased the amount they spent.

There were other reasons to be positive about England's future, too. Despite the setback of Hispaniola, England only got stronger. Scotland and Ireland were quiet, and there was an increasingly successful alliance with France against Spain. Local government was back, by and large, to normal. Royalists, radicals, Quakers and republicans were still present, but all told they posed little real threat.

The process of healing and settling was well under way. Cromwell had created two new hereditary peers and around a dozen baronetcies. The old order was on its way back. London was as vibrant as ever. Most of its theatres remained shut, but despite the Puritans, it was still full of 'alehouses, pie-houses, and tobacco-shops'. So full of vice was the town in 1657 that at least one author was prophesying that God's wrath would come, in the form of fire.[32] Former enemies were even socialising. One rather unexpected lubricant was gardening. In May 1657, Henry Lawrence, Lord President of the Protectorate's Council of State, had paid a visit to the arch-Royalist John Evelyn to admire the latter's gardens. John Lambert, whose horticultural hobby had led him to fill his gardens at Wimbledon House with botanical wonders from places as far away as Algiers and Constantinople, corresponded with a Royalist in Paris about flowers.

Tulips, anemones and irises were not the only exotic commodities taking hold in Cromwell's England, either. In 1657, a London jury prosecuted James Farr, a barber, 'for making and selling a drink called coffee whereby in making the same he annoyeth his neighbours by evil smells'.[33] Coffeeshops had appeared in Oxford in 1650, where it had been drunk in the university in the 1640s, and in London in 1652 (opened by an Armenian).

Far from being the international pariah it had been in 1649, England was now opening itself up to the world, with London the centre of a growing empire of trade and power. Cromwell's most remarkable project, though, was to make England welcoming to the world's Jews. In 1655, the chief rabbi of Amsterdam, Manasseh Ben Israel, had arrived in London. Lodging on the Strand, he was entertained by Cromwell, who agreed to try and facilitate the readmission of Jews to England, largely because he hoped to convert them and thus usher in the Second Coming. In the end, Cromwell was blocked by a combination of the self-interests of English merchants and the anti-Semitism of his political class. However, because the expulsion in 1290 had been by royal decree, Cromwell could use his Protectoral power to reassure Jewish representatives that they wouldn't be prosecuted. The rabbi himself was given a state salary of £100 a year, a burial ground for Jews was purchased and a synagogue on Creechurch Lane became established from 1657, where it remains today, in the heart of the City.

The courting of Manasseh Ben Israel is a reminder that, even as Cromwell grew old and his Protectorate inched back towards something close to the traditional constitution, kingless England still had some radical goals, even at the top. Among the English people, Cromwell's rule was never especially popular except for the stability it brought. The English did, however, retain a radical streak, though the experience of the 1650s had seen the baton passed from the Levellers and Diggers towards religious groups, especially the Quakers. Religious radicalism, not secular, would be the immediate legacy of the Republic. Reform of the commonwealth had been supplanted by the radicalism of the soul.

Cromwell's rule must be accounted a success, at least in terms of realpolitik. The atrocities in Ireland cannot be excused, though it speaks volumes of his English contemporaries that they saw his part in the regicide as the worse crime. His defenders point to his religious toleration, and they are right to do so, but even here he often failed to stand up to those who would persecute the sects. He abandoned Nayler to his fate, and, when the Humble Petition and Advice was accepted, he allowed the constitutional protections for religious dissent contained in the Instrument of Government to be quietly dropped.

On the other side, the more excitable bouts of Puritanism under his rule were rather less about him than the people who came to power with the Revolution. He is remembered for cancelling Christmas, even banning mince pies. He is the man who closed the theatres and stopped music and dance. But the Christmas ban originated in 1644, the theatres were closed by the Long Parliament and any legislation about pies exists only as a figment of the popular imagination. The notorious Adultery Act was passed by the Rump, and even the slightly bizarre act of 1657 which proscribed such offences as 'profane walking' was a Parliamentary initiative not a Cromwellian one.[34] Clearly he was in favour of moral reform, but the fact that the Republic ended up so Puritan was not just about the obsessions of one particular man. The truth is, the revolution brought to power a group of people who had grown up in a world of rising population, social stress and a crime wave. No wonder they wanted to reform society. Many of them could quite happily have worked with Charles I – who himself was a committed reformist – and many of them did end up working with his son.

Either way, the country was settled and now becoming respected on the international stage. How much this can be attributed to Cromwell himself is moot. In reality, stability owed much to the fact that people were sick of the chaos of war, and to the existence of a sizeable force of arms. Modern commentators sometimes suggest the Republic was a military dictatorship, backed only by the threat of violence. There's a degree of truth here: certainly Cromwell's army was stronger than that of the late king, though monarchies themselves are not averse to using violence to quell dissent – just ask the Scots Covenanters or Prynne, Burton and Bastwick. Cromwell always tried to rule with a veneer of constitutionalism based on checks and balances. He claimed that constitutions were 'but dross and dung' compared to Godliness, but this didn't stop him ruling through Parliament. It's sometimes pointed out with glee that Cromwell ended up dissolving more parliaments than Charles I ever did. Given that Parliaments were always dissolved by the executive, it's not the telling point many think it is. In the five years of his Protectorate, Parliament was an almost constant presence, and regular elections were written into the constitution. That can't be said for the reign of Charles I. Cromwell's dissolution of the Rump in 1653, by military force, needs to be seen in the context of a Parliament that had sat for nearly thirteen years. Even the Levellers might have admitted that he had a point.

But one of the great tragedies of Cromwell was that he prevented the Republic being so much more. He was, at heart, a conservative East Anglian landowner. In the laudable goal of healing and settling, he took the path of least resistance, cosying up to the traditional rulers: 'a nobleman, a gentleman, a yeoman'. Had Providence put another figure as Fairfax's deputy, one of the many great constitutional brains of the New Model Army, someone who thought forms of government were more than just 'dross and dung', then who knows what could have been achieved. Had John Lambert occupied Cromwell's position, England could have gone down the path of a balanced, written constitution. Lambert was if anything the finer general and certainly the greater intellect. Instead, Lambert's fate was to have his constitution harried and hassled by republicans and conservatives alike, picked apart and undermined because it dared give protection to Quakers and because he happened to be a soldier. Then, in 1657, Cromwell betrayed him, looking for new counsels among the old social elite, the kinglings, even as he had rejected the kingship itself.

Or what if Thomas Rainborough had risen in Cromwell's place? He was of similar background, similar charisma and similar military potential. But he was murdered by Royalists. If this had been Rainborough's revolution, could it have been a democratic one? In the end, the fact it was Cromwell who took the reins was one of the crucial factors that ensured England would turn back to its monarchy. He not only prepared the ground for the coming Royalist coup, but his own unattractive Puritanism, his apparently vaunting ambition and of course his brutal conquest of Ireland, helped taint republicanism for centuries and still does, to a point. Perhaps Cromwell's statue today should stand not outside the Houses of Parliament, for whom he is a rather ambiguous hero, but beside Buckingham Palace.

PART FOUR

1658–89
The Original of Power

16

Providence and Power

The Republic was doomed from the afternoon of 3 September 1658. Cromwell's health had been in freefall for weeks, partly thanks to the death of his beloved daughter Elizabeth on 6 August, just a few weeks after her twenty-ninth birthday. On 17 August, he had improved enough to ride out in Hampton Court Park and meet the Quaker George Fox. Later Fox remembered feeling a 'waft (or apparition) of death' about Cromwell, who already, he thought, looked 'like a dead man'.[1] The ageing Protector clung onto life for a couple more weeks, wondering whether it was possible for the saved to fall from grace. But on the afternoon of the 3rd, the anniversary of his triumphs at Dunbar and Worcester, the man whom so many wished to assassinate, execute for treason or simply kill in the rush of a cavalry charge, passed away peacefully in his bed. 'Cromwell died, people not much minding it,' wrote an Essex clergyman.[2]

It's not quite clear whether he named a successor, but it quickly became accepted that he had: his eldest surviving son, Richard. The Republic was to be a hereditary one, for now. Richard immediately got the assent of his father's Privy Council, and the senior army officers under Charles Fleetwood, another Naseby veteran who was also Richard's brother-in-law (having married Henry Ireton's widow Bridget). Richard's rule was proclaimed across the capital to hearty, possibly even heartfelt, applause. Congratulations came in over the following months from the fleet, and no fewer than 24 towns and 28 counties. Only Oxford struck a sour note, as the sheriff tasked with proclaiming Protector Richard was bombarded with carrots and turnips by boisterous students.

In Dublin, Henry Cromwell, Oliver's intelligent younger son, ensured the new regime arrived without trouble. In Scotland, things were kept under control by General George Monck. The son of a relatively poor Devon gentleman (the fourth child of ten, no less), Monck was a bluff, coarse infantryman who had risen through talent and hard work. He was fifty-seven years old and had been a soldier for forty-seven. He'd fought against Spain for England, France and the Dutch Republic, before fighting for Charles I against Parliament and then – after a moderate spell in the Tower – for Cromwell in Ireland, Scotland and the High Seas. He loved tobacco and pots of ale, and found it resoundingly funny when people referred to his wife Anne, who had once done the laundry for him when he was in the Tower, as 'dirty Bessie'.[3] Appropriately, he traced his ancestry to a bastard son of the warlike Yorkist king Edward IV. Those who knew him thought him honest and quite lacking in guile. Oliver Cromwell, who fancied himself as a good judge of character, liked to think of Monck as 'plain hearted George'.[4]

But they were wrong. Monck was to prove quite capable of keeping his cards close to his chest. 'Monck is so dark a man,' a Royalist in the exiled court of the Pretender would remark, that 'no perspective can look through him, and it will be like the last scene of some excellent play, which the most judicious cannot positively say how it will end'.[5] Perhaps life at the Stuart court left one better equipped to get the measure of such man than did service in the New Model Army.

Richard for his part was likeable, popular and got on well with Royalist and Parliamentarian alike: even the former admitted he wasn't a 'traitorous hypocrite' like his father.[6] He was morally upstanding, but no zealot. He had spent most of the previous decade living in obscurity in the quiet Hampshire village of Hursley where he would hunt deer in the park with local Royalists. Neither especially Puritan nor a military man, he was thus shorn of the two most unpopular characteristics of his father: a 'very good neighbourly man' as one who had lived near him at Hursley recalled, which may have been a roundabout way of saying he was definitively non-Puritan.[7]

Yet Richard also had nothing of Oliver's political drive or intellectual heft. Most of the men who surrounded him were mediocre, and he never gained the respect of the military. His father had been their comrade-in-arms, Richard was just 'the young gentleman'. Ultimately, he was way too likeable to succeed as a politician, never something that could have been said about his father.

Still, at the start of 1659, the astrologer William Lilly offered the prediction that May would be the month when Richard Cromwell showed the world 'that he hath the abilities to govern'. But when May came, Richard was in protracted dispute with the army high command, including his brother-in-law Charles Fleetwood, over attempts to cut the regime's debt by reducing the size of the army, and after an unsuccessful Parliament and a springtime stand-off at Westminster, the military simply deposed him and shuffled him off to retirement. Lilly put this down to the hand of God, which he said no one could be expected to predict.[8] But the truth is the army had never had much loyalty to Richard Cromwell, or to the Petition and Advice of 1657 on which his succession and rule was based.

In order to bring down Richard, Fleetwood and the army had allied themselves with the old republican enemies of the Protectorate, and so, with Richard gone, the old Rump Parliament was recalled. The 'Commonwealthsmen' Arthur Haselrig and the younger Henry Vane were among the leading lights, taking the moment to reignite what they called the 'Good Old Cause' of republicanism before the Cromwells had imposed themselves. But the Rump had about as much chance of balancing the interests of the army and the country as Richard did. It had just 78 recognised members, and a number of these never sat. None of them represented Scotland or Ireland. Some of the MPs excluded by Pride tried to take up seats, but they were barred by the army. One of them, William Prynne himself – now sporting long hair to cover his mutilated ears – even managed to sneak in and rail against those sitting, before the army was called on to keep him away. The new version of the Republic was unpopular and ineffective – not least in its policy of releasing Quakers where possible, much to the horror of conservatives. In August 1659, discontent blew up when Sir George Booth, a moderate ex-Parliamentarian, tried to raise rebellion in Cheshire. He was joined by some old Cromwellians and Presbyterians, and even one of the regicides: Richard Ingoldsby. But most Royalists stayed at home, and although Booth was able to hold much of Cheshire and Lancashire for three weeks, calling for a 'free Parliament' (though not yet a restoration of the monarchy), his force was eventually scattered by John Lambert. Booth tried to escape disguised in women's clothes, as 'Lady Dorothy', but his cover was blown in a Newport Pagnell hostelry, when his attendants tried to buy him a razor.

The call for a 'free Parliament', one based on traditional elections, not the purged husk that the Rump represented, nor one hobbled by Cromwellian expulsions and restrictions, was emerging as a common slogan. It combined the old Presbyterian interest – that which had been defeated at the end of 1648, with a resurgent royalism, which looked at the political churnings since Oliver Cromwell's death and wondered whether, just maybe, these offered a chance for the late king's son, the pretender Charles Stuart.

The Pretender and what was left of his court-in-exile were now holed up in Bruges. It was one of the many territories of the Spanish crown, and Charles had made it his base when the French, despite their monarchy's family ties to the Stuarts, joined in alliance with Cromwell's Protectorate against Spain. In 1658, a Spanish army, sponsored by Charles and featuring his brother James as one of its commanders, was routed by an Anglo-French force at the Battle of the Dunes, near Dunkirk. All this left Charles rather despondent, but as he played and drank and danced away the hours in Bruges over 1659, he began to sense that his fortunes might just change.

In England, as the year progressed, the prospects of stability remained distant. There seemed no immediate way that the respective demands of military and civilians could be settled, now their shared goal in the spring of toppling the Protectorate had been achieved. In autumn, the Rump picked a fight with the army, voting on 12 October to dismiss Lambert and Desborough, and to demote Fleetwood. It was an unnecessary provocation and it led to another stand-off at Westminster, with troops gathering ominously around the Old Palace Yard. Amazingly, the government sat in limbo for two whole weeks, but effectively the Rump was dead, Lambert and Desborough still very much active, and the constitution up for question. The army created its own executive, called a Committee of Safety, but it was finding it increasingly difficult to keep control. Many of the law courts stopped sitting and a new deluge of political pamphlets came from the presses. Maybe the rule of saints could be tried again as it was in 1653? Or perhaps a new *Agreement of the People* would work? A club called the Rota was founded by James Harrington, a genial intellectual who had been a confidant of Charles I but who had now become a convinced republican, and indeed had penned *Oceana*, a remarkable tract outlining a case for a rational, kingless constitution. The Rota met at a coffeehouse in the New Palace Yard, to discuss constitutional and republican ideas. It was jammed every evening, and its debates – attended by some of the brightest (male) minds of the day – were settled using a ballot box. In the City of London there was agitation for a free Parliament. People were resisting the Committee's demands for taxation after the Rump, in one of its last acts before the latest Army coup, had passed a bill making it treason to pay taxes raised without Parliamentary consent.

In Scotland, General Monck watched. In October, he wrote to the army leaders, deploring their course of action and demanding that Parliament be recalled. Despite a life spent almost entirely in arms, he thought soldiers should stick to fighting. Politics should be left to civilians. His aim was to 'reduce the military power in obedience to the civil'.⁹ Preparing for a showdown, he purged his army of officers he thought likely to be disloyal: to him, not to the commonwealth. Then he began moving his men to the Anglo-Scottish border, setting up his headquarters at Coldstream on the Tweed on 8 December.

The Committee of Safety knew what was at stake, and mobilised a large force under Lambert, while planning new elections under yet another new constitution (favourable to the army grandees, of course). On 3 December, a group of republicans led by Arthur Haselrig managed to take control of the garrison at Portsmouth, supported by its governor. In a wintery London, things were especially tense. On 5 December, a squadron of horse loyal to the Committee was pelted with ice and tiles at the Royal Exchange. Apprentices were trying to petition the City's Common Council for a return of Parliament and free elections, but soldiers opened fire and at least two rioters were killed. A coroner's inquest found the deaths to be wilful murder, and the officer in charge was indicted. There were rumours that a massacre was about to be committed by religious radicals; apprentices took potshots at soldiers from the rooftops; the shops were shut. Only by the skin of his teeth was Desborough able to take command of the Tower on the 12th, from a lieutenant who was about to declare in support of the republicans at Portsmouth. Then the fleet intervened. Vice-Admiral Lawson, a Baptist republican from Scarborough, wrote to the City setting out his support for the Rump and backing political reform. The City ignored him, so Lawson left the Downs with 22 ships, sailed around the North Foreland and entered the Thames.

The Committee was quickly losing control of all three realms. In Ireland on 13 December, a coup led by the old New Model officer and Cromwellian loyalist Sir Hardress Waller took Dublin Castle and declared for Parliament. Monck then secured Scotland, in negotiation with the ex-rebel Glencairn. Monck's army was smaller than Lambert's, but Lambert's men were demoralised and underpaid; moreover the Yorkshireman's position at the head of his force meant he was out of the capital, where the Army interest was represented by the much less capable – and much less steadfast – Charles Fleetwood.

In London, Common Council elections on the 21st brought in new representatives, many of whom wanted the return of a king. At this point the lawyer Bulstrode Whitelocke visited Charles Fleetwood. There were two choices about how to oppose Monck, Whitelocke suggested. Either Fleetwood could gather his forces, see if enough rallied to him, and, if they didn't, then call for a free Parliament; or he could try to pre-empt whatever Monck's plan was by joining with the Presbyterian faction and sending an emissary to Charles Stuart. Fleetwood knew the military option was unpromising, so he asked Whitelocke if he would go to the king in exile. Whitelocke agreed, but as he was leaving, another delegation, including Henry Vane and John Desborough, arrived. They argued that Fleetwood had promised Lambert that no such moves would be taken without his assent. Fifteen minutes later, Fleetwood emerged from his room and confronted Whitelocke again. 'I cannot do it! I cannot do it!' he cried. Instead, the next day he surrendered the keys to the Commons, and with support from the army, the Rump returned for a third time. God, admitted Fleetwood, 'had spat in our faces'.[10]

At the end of December, a small rising took place in Yorkshire. Made up of local gentry and dissident soldiers, it assembled on the old battle site of Marston Moor before moving against York itself. The rising was large enough to be a potentially significant problem for Lambert. But what was more worrying was not so much the numbers, but the man leading it. Old, gout-ridden and moving across the icy roads of Yorkshire in a coach, it was someone who knew Marston Moor well; a talismanic figure for so many, not least because he'd stood aloof from pretty much every political experiment going back to the regicide – Thomas Fairfax.

On 2 January 1660, York submitted to Fairfax. The same day, Monck moved. By the 7th, the Rump could see where things were going, so wrote to Monck and rather tamely invited him south. Lambert's army was recalled by the Rump, and simply crumbled. There were calls to readmit those MPs 'secluded' by Pride's Purge, 11 years earlier in 1648. Discontent spread through the country: apprentices in Exeter rioted, while there were calls there, in Gloucester, Kent and Northamptonshire for a free Parliament. Monck entered York on the 11th. As he moved south through the snow, the church bells rang. A desperate Haselrig tried to get MPs to take an oath not to restore the monarchy, but hardly anyone did. By the 23rd, Monck was at Leicester, where he wrote a letter apparently disavowing monarchy. By the end of the month, he was in striking distance of the capital. On 2 February, his army reached Whitehall, where some soldiers laid violent hands on the Quakers who'd been meeting in the Palace Yard. The next day, Monck entered the City.

The Rump was deeply unpopular. Harsh economic conditions over the winter, stemming ultimately from a poor harvest, were blamed on the government. Printed declarations for a free Parliament had been produced as Monck moved south. In Bristol, William Prynne helped the apprentices draft a declaration that bore an impressive level of attention to the medieval history of Parliament for something supposedly produced by angry youths. Demonstrations in towns called for bread and a free Parliament, while young lads kicked footballs at government soldiers to try and provoke them. In Bristol, 'Kiss my Parliament!' became a popular expression of contempt.[11] On 8

February, London's Common Council debated whether it should continue to pay taxes collected for the Rump. This touched off the crisis: Monck was ordered by the Rump's Council of State to occupy the City, dissolve the Common Council and take down the great gates that protected it. As the sun rose the next day, his men marched in, watched by hushed crowds.

But then the Rump overstepped: it began proceedings to take control of Monck's army. On the 11th, a Saturday, the general fought back by demanding that the Rump proceed with elections, and on the same day he met with the Corporation of London at the Guildhall. Suddenly it appeared that he was about to come out against the Rump and in favour of a free Parliament. The celebrations that night were recorded in the diary of a twenty-six-year-old teller in the Exchequer. 'In Cheapside,' he wrote, there were 'a great many bonfires, and Bow bells and all the bells in all the churches as we went home were a-ringing.' The diarist's name was Samuel Pepys, and as he returned home that night, the winter air crackling with heat as at least 31 bonfires burned, he saw rumps of meat tied on sticks and paraded down King Street, and he saw butchers in the Strand clattering their heavy knives 'when they were going to sacrifice their rump'. On Ludgate Hill, there was a rump on a spit. To Pepys, it felt like the whole street was ablaze. Beef, mutton and poultry were cooked and gorged upon. The windows of old Praisegod Barebone in Fleet Street were smashed as Londoners vented their anger against radicals. Beacons and bonfires were lit across the countryside on hills and other prominent places. In Oxford, the republican warden of All Souls had his windows pelted with fresh-roasted rump.[12]

The Rump offered elections, but the conditions they planned to impose were too much for Monck. This would be no free Parliament while Arthur Haselrig kept control, for the old republican knew exactly what one would bring: it would spell the end of the Republic he had devoted himself to, the final death of the Good Old Cause. But Sir Arthur was so unpopular now that, so it was said, he refused to have a candle lit in front of him for fear of showing his face. Monck, under suitable pressure from loyal officers and his wife, decided that the old secluded MPs – the victims of Pride's Purge – would be returned. On the 21st, the general met with 73 excluded members, then escorted them to the House to the evident surprise of the MPs already sitting. Again the City rang to bells and smouldered with bonfires, for everyone knew what this new political coup meant. Again, Praisegod Barebone's windows were smashed.[13]

Parliament, a body now much less dominated by republicans, quickly set new elections in motion, selecting a new Council and installing a raft of new militia commissioners in the counties, including none other than Sir George Booth who by that time had been released from the Tower (and, it was to be hoped, had found a razor). Baptists, Fifth Monarchists and Quakers were attacked and plundered in Wales, Bristol and Gloucester. On the 27th, while Pepys was visiting Audley End in Saffron Walden, he was ushered into a cellar where the house-keeper offered him 'a most admirable drink, a health to the King'.[14] Everywhere the talk was of government by a single person: George Monck, perhaps, or Richard Cromwell, or Charles Stuart.

The last piece of the jigsaw was the army: Monck faced down much of the opposition in a tense meeting on 7 March; some of the key hardliners were cashiered and John Lambert was sent off to the Tower. By this time, Charles Stuart was being openly toasted across town. There was another bonfire and people cried out, 'God Bless King Charles the Second'.[15] Parliament, meanwhile, on the 16th, finally agreed to dissolve itself.

The stage was set.

The final drama was played out in three acts. The first, in April, came in the form of elections to the new Parliament (technically, because not summoned by royal writ it would be known as a 'Convention'). In theory, active Royalists were excluded, but no one really cared. There was an avalanche of pamphlets: many pro-Royalist, but some arguing against the restoration of the Stuarts, like Marchamont Nedham's *News from Brussels*, which alleged Charles was plotting brutal reprisals on all who'd opposed his father.[16] Then there were the rhymes, scurrilous as ever. They attacked the Rump, bearing titles like *Arsy Versy*, and they attacked religious 'fanatics'.[17] More than one known song accused Quakers of bestiality: *The Four Legg'd Quaker* was one, the work of Sir John Birkenhead, eventually published in

1664; or, for those for whom that title was a little subtle, there was *A Relation of a Quaker that, to the shame of his profession, attempted to Bugger a Mare near Colchester*, attributed to the Royalist poet John Denham.[18] The elections, meanwhile, saw the highest number of prospective candidates so far in English history. Even Lambert managed to stand while still in prison (he lost). The question had become not whether there would be a restoration, but what kind of restoration it would be: at the hustings, the critical issue was whether candidates were in favour of imposing conditions on Charles. The harder line Royalists, i.e. those generally against conditions, tended to win.

By now, Monck and the king were finally in communication. Charles moved his court to the town of Breda near the Dutch coast. The English fleet stood ready off the coast of Kent, the old Cromwellian Edward Montagu in command as General at Sea, Pepys on board as his employee, spending pleasant evenings supping, drinking wine, conversing, playing music and singing songs. Rather embarrassingly, Lambert escaped from the Tower (dressed in woman's clothes, having swapped places with Joan, the lady who made his bed), and drew some support from disgruntled soldiers and old radicals. It looked as if there could be a general uprising in the army: 'the agitators and Lambert's agents are all over England,' warned one of Monck's captains, 'privately creeping amongst us & tempting our men from us'.[19] It was rumoured that 7,000 Quakers and Anabaptists would join. But in the end, humiliation fell on the old army man, who declared for Richard Cromwell, staged a desultory muster on the old battle site of Edgehill and was promptly arrested by the turncoat Richard Ingoldsby. After that there was little trouble from the old republicans. Haselrig submitted to Monck, who offered him his life and his estate if he paid him tuppence. On 30 April, Haselrig wrote to Monck to plead innocence of any conspiracy with Lambert. His letter included two pennies, for which Monck fulfilled his promise.

The new Parliament, complete with a House of Lords, met on 25 April. It was an overwhelmingly Royalist body in what was still, technically, a republic. And so Parliament ushered in the second act: the return of the king. On 1 May, a declaration from Charles was read in Parliament. It had been penned at Breda on 4 April. It offered a pardon for everyone who gave allegiance to the king within 40 days (although Parliament, it allowed, could make exceptions). It promised 'liberty to tender consciences', and that Parliament would be allowed to sort out disputes over property created during the revolution. It promised, naturally, that Monck's army would get their arrears and be retained under the new regime.

That afternoon, Parliament voted that 'the government is, and ought to be, by King, Lords, and Commons'.[20] They voted, in other words, for the restoration of the Stuarts.

London rejoiced, as did the rest of the country. At last, people thought, the return of the king might bring stability, an end to upheaval. In Boston, Lincolnshire, young men took down the arms of the Republic, had the town beadle whip them, then – taking turns – 'pissed and shitted on them'. Even in Dorchester, long a Puritan stronghold, the town clerk celebrated the deliverance from a 'world of confusions' and 'unheard of governments'.[21] On 9 May, almost as an afterthought, Richard Cromwell, who was still somehow Chancellor of Oxford University, hung up his robes and disappeared into obscurity.[22]

On the 14th, Monck's ships were in sight of The Hague, where, in a moment that looked both back to the past and forward to the future, they made rendezvous with Elizabeth, James I's daughter, once queen of Bohemia, and paid due respects to the nine-year-old William, the late king's grandson, son of Princess Mary, now Prince of Orange.

The month of May 1660 would be remembered as one of the most joyous in English history. '[A]ll the world,' wrote Pepys, was 'in a merry mood because of the King's coming.'[23] The return of Charles, brought back by Monck's fleet, was celebrated with maypoles, church bells and bonfires. From his landing at Dover on the 25th to his entrance to London on the 29th, the restored king was met by cheering crowds. Some 120,000 were said to have greeted him at Blackheath. In London, his entourage took seven hours to pass through. The streets became a kaleidoscope of tapestries and flowers; there were fountains flowing with wine. Oliver Cromwell, and his widow Elizabeth, were burned in effigy on a Westminster bonfire.[24] After the austerity of the Puritan republic, it was a time for riotous celebration. According to

Marchamont Nedham, seething at what he saw as the credulousness of the people, the return of the king was widely expected to bring 'peace and no taxes'.[25]

The rejoicing, though, was stained with reprisals. Within a day, the king was forced to issue a proclamation against 'debauched and profane persons, who, on pretence of regard to the King, revile and threaten others' (or simply sat in taverns and tippling houses drinking endless healths).[26] Independent congregations suffered abuse, as did those ministers who'd taken the place of clergy ejected by the Republic. Quakers were attacked in at least 15 counties.

In many ways the new government was fairly conciliatory. The Privy Council had four Cromwellians and eight former Parliamentarians (including old Denzil Holles) to balance the 16 Royalists. The old Wiltshire moderates Edward Hyde and Edward Nicholas were to be Lord Chancellor and Secretary of State, respectively – roles they'd occupied in titular form in exile. The navy went to the king's brother James, Duke of York. But there were places in the administration for former Parliamentarians such as the superannuated earls of Manchester and Northumberland. There was, however, a new Commission of the Peace, which meant the Royalist gentry were brought back into local government, and inevitably this meant some servants of the Republic were squeezed out. And at Oxford and Cambridge there were Royalist insertions, sometimes leading to quite nasty conflicts among the dons.

The immediate priority was a Bill of Indemnity and Oblivion, which sought to draw a line under the previous troubles. But there were debates about how far forgiveness should go. William Prynne, for example, thirsty for revenge, specifically argued that Francis Thorpe, the lawyer whose speech at York had set out the case for the Republic back in 1649, should be executed. Thorpe had already petitioned the king for a pardon on the grounds that he had opposed the regicide, had not bought any Crown lands and had been gentle on the Royalist rebels of 1655. He had allies in the Commons, too, and Prynne's vindictiveness found little support. In the end, though, some of the more egregious republicans were exempted from pardon, with some

33 men specifically singled out for punishment. The 33 were mostly regicides who had sought to evade capture, particularly those who were not lucky enough to have powerful friends. Eleven were already in custody.

Thus, finally, things were set for the third and final act. After the April elections and the return of the king came the revenge.

In October, during Parliamentary recess, all 11 were tried. Only one witness was considered necessary for each act of supposed treason, but then, with the evidence there in plain sight, maybe such niceties didn't matter. Six signatories to the death warrant, together with the lawyer John Cooke and the preacher Hugh Peter, suffered hanging, drawing and quartering at Charing Cross (two of Charles's guards, Daniel Axtell and Francis Hacker, were executed at Tyburn). The butchered men were defiant to the end: one of them even managed to land a punch on his executioner. Thomas Harrison, when the crowd taunted him asking, 'where is your Good Old Cause now?' replied it was 'Here, in my bosom, and I shall seal it with my blood.'[27] But the jeering crowd had its way, and their remains were duly displayed on the City gates. Such was the smell at Charing Cross that local inhabitants petitioned the king to stop the executions, 'for the stench of their burnt bowels had so putrefied the air'.[28] When Parliament returned, their fugitive colleagues were subject to Attainder, which meant they lost their property. Then, in January 1661 – on the anniversary of the regicide – the bodies of Cromwell, Ireton and John Bradshaw (the king's trial judge) were dug up and hanged. John Evelyn thought this was one of the 'stupendous and inscrutable judgements of God'.[29] Those other republicans who'd been buried at Westminster Abbey were also disinterred on orders of the Dean, and their bodies cast into a nearby pit.

Not everyone welcomed the Restoration. 'What!' cried Margaret Dixon of Newcastle on 13 May, so it was alleged, 'Can they find no other man to bring in than a Scotsman?' 'Cromwell ruled better than ever the King will,' said Richard Abbott, according to an indictment against him.[30] These were minority views, though. Overall, as the wild celebrations attest, the return of the king was popular. Had it not been, it might never have happened.

Certainly the leading politicians made sure to acclaim Charles. 'Almighty God', thundered an Act of Parliament in August, had 'by his all-swaying providence and power' occasioned the King's 'most wonderful, glorious, peaceable and joyful restoration'.[31] And so to mark this, it declared 29 May, Charles's birthday, to be an annual celebration, known as Oak Apple Day after the wasp galls people plucked from oak trees and wore in celebration. For his part, Charles appreciated the need to show off his own majesty. 'Nothing keeps up a King more than ceremony and order', he had been advised by the old Marquess of Newcastle. Charles should appear godlike, so the people prayed to him 'with trembling fear, and love, as they did to Queen Elizabeth'.[32] The coronation took place, to much general rejoicing, with new crown jewels, on St George's Day 1661 at Westminster. One of Charles's first acts was to commence touching for the 'king's evil', the traditional ritual in which the royal touch was held to cure sufferers of scrofula. By the end of the decade, he was 'healing' around 1,800 people a year in an elaborate ritual overseen by members of the Anglican clergy. The Quakers were not the only ones who thought their God-given powers stretched to magical cures.

Indemnity protected many, notably those former republicans who'd supported the Restoration. Many, indeed, were promoted. Monck, unsurprisingly, was on the way up, and became the Duke of Albemarle. Richard Ingoldsby lied that Oliver Cromwell had forced his signature onto the late king's death warrant, and not only escaped reprisal but was made a Knight of the Bath. For the most part, aside from the 33, the old guard of the Republic were able to find their place within the new regime, though they often found it sensible to retreat as far as practical into obscurity. Henry Cromwell and Charles Fleetwood retired, although the ever-irascible John Desborough spent the next few years in and out of trouble. In fact, some old Royalists smarted at the alleged favour shown by Charles to erstwhile enemies. To be fair to Charles, though, he also ensured peers created since 1642 could sit in the Lords, gave substantial rewards to some former Royalist soldiers and their families and repaid from his own purse 54 men who'd lent money to his father. There were also awkward conversations to be had with those former Royalists who had worked for the Cromwellian regime. The poet Edmund Waller was on hand to provide a congratulatory address to Charles II, but the new king, so legend would have it, pointed out that it was rather inferior to the one Waller had written for Cromwell in 1652. 'Poets, Sire,' Waller quipped, 'succeed better in fiction than in truth.'[33] The king was satisfied, and the poet made sure the Cromwellian ode didn't appear in later editions of his works.

The Army was mostly all pensioned off: a poll tax and a new assessment ordered in the summer saw to that. The king was provided with apparently bounteous revenue of £1.2 million a year from customs and excise, allowing him to retain Monck's regiment of foot, now named the Coldstream Guards after his base while he waited on the Border the previous year, and still wearing the old red coats of the New Model. The old lands of Crown and Church were clawed back, though often with due compensation given. Meanwhile, Royalists who'd seen their lands confiscated during the last regime had them restored, although the decision to ratify all legal proceedings during the Republic meant that any lands they'd had to sell – for example, to pay the decimation tax – were now probably gone for good. It was a point that generated much bitterness among the old Cavaliers.

Meanwhile, the old episcopal church was reinstated. In the immediate months following the Restoration, many parishes went back to the old liturgy, buying copies of the Book of Common Prayer even though there was widespread expectation that a new version would soon be produced. Returning bishops were cheered and copies of the Solemn League and Covenant, which had been a key reason for their abolition, were enthusiastically burned. The cathedrals were in a parlous state: Durham had seen use as a prison, St Paul's as a stable and a marketplace. Bishops' palaces at Chester, Salisbury and Exeter had been converted into (respectively) a gaol, a tavern and a sugar factory. But funds were found, and within a couple of years, the old cathedrals were resplendent once more.

Initially there were moves towards a compromise with Presbyterians, potentially 'comprehending' them within the Church of England, i.e. granting enough latitude within official Church practice to allow them to worship within it. But Parliament voted comprehension down. In fact, England was about to take a dramatic swing towards a more restrictive Church. Perhaps this was always going to happen. But partly, too, it was a reaction to the events of January 1661, when, the same month in which the bodies of Cromwell, Ireton and

Bradshaw were dug up, a quixotic rising by Fifth Monarchists broke out in London, with shouts for 'King Jesus, and the Heads upon the Gates!' It was led by one Thomas Venner, and ended in a brief occupation of St Paul's, a clampdown by the Coldstream Guards and 14 executions.[34] A new round-up of Quakers and other undesirables followed, prompting – incidentally – George Fox to write a stirring tract declaring that his Quakers would utterly renounce war and violence. Given they had made up many of the ranks of the Republic's army, this was some about-turn, though the principle has since become one that defines the movement.

Through March and April 1661, new elections took place. With Venner's rising fresh in the minds of the country gentry, the elections were a resounding victory for royalism. Yet, although the new Parliament would come to be known as the 'Cavalier', it was actually rather careful in what *kind* of monarchy it endorsed. In religion, Laud's notorious Canons of 1640 were explicitly disavowed, while at law the courts of High Commission, Star Chamber and Requests all remained duly abolished. Taxation was now almost entirely controlled by Parliament. During the Revolution, Parliamentary taxation had grown vastly, not least with the creation of the excise (a tax on domestic consumption), while older prerogative revenues had been transferred from Crown to Parliament, most notably the customs (a tax on imports), including Tonnage and Poundage. The upshot was that while only a quarter of state revenue came from Parliament before 1640, after 1660 some 90 per cent did. There had been a revolution in public finance, and the Restoration of the monarchy did nothing to reverse it. Frankly, the king liked having the money, wherever it came from.

Parliament thus remained a crucial part of the constitution. The Triennial Act, which enforced regular sittings of Parliament, stayed on the books, for now. Indeed, despite usefully confirming Charles as supreme commander of the small remaining military (itself one of the trickiest issues of 1641–2), and instigating a handy new tax on hearths, whereby English householders would be assessed based on the number of chimneys their house had (as a rough proxy for their value), this was to be anything but a pliant legislature. 'We have our King again, and our Laws again,' Edward Hyde, now Earl of Clarendon, would

tell the Lords, before adding, pertinently: 'and *Parliaments* again'.[35]
This was not absolutism.

Charles presented himself, outwardly at least, and for now, as a
king who would rule through law and precedent, not military force or
arbitrary power. Unlike his father, Charles II accepted that he would
have to work with Parliament. He did, though, try to control as much
as possible who got elected. To this end local government was purged,
with suspect magistrates and town officers forced out. Control of the
towns was especially important: with the old franchise and constituencies restored for good, the cities and boroughs once more controlled
four-fifths of the MPs elected to Westminster.

The most dramatic work of the Cavalier Parliament was a sustained
assault on the Presbyterians and the Independents. In the summer
of 1661, its Corporation Act allowed Parliament to purge city
governments of anyone vaguely disloyal. Town governors were forced
to take the Oaths of Allegiance and Supremacy, to declare a belief that
taking arms against the king, in any circumstances, was wrong, and to
renounce the Solemn League and Covenant of 1643. The last two of
these were very difficult for anyone who had supported Parliament in
the previous wars. Quakers, meanwhile, suffered imprisonment under
an act against those who refused the Oath of Allegiance (Quakers
refused *all* oaths); other nonconformists were prosecuted under older
laws against recusants. Then, an Act of Uniformity forced all clergy
to abjure the Covenant and accept a new Prayer Book – which bore
Laud's influence and indeed borrowed from the Scottish Prayer Book
of 1637. If they hadn't done so by St Bartholomew's Day (24 August),
they would be removed. Eventually no less than 10 per cent of the
clergy were deprived. In some counties it was as much as a fifth; in
London, a third.

It was much more than Charles had wished for: so much so that
in December 1662, he issued a Declaration of Indulgence, aimed at
suspending penalties against nonconformists and Catholics alike. But
the agenda was being pushed by a revitalised Episcopalianism in the
Church, and a radically Royalist Parliament, so when Charles asked
Parliament in February for a 'dispensing power' allowing him to protect individuals from the penal religious laws, it caused a major controversy, and he was forced to back down.

Parliament also went after those republicans it felt to have escaped too leniently the previous year. Those who had sat in judgement on Charles I without actually signing the death warrant were dispossessed and (if they were still alive) thrown in prison. Henry Vane was executed on Tower Hill on the anniversary of the Battle of Naseby, 14 June 1662, an unrepentant martyr for his cause. Charles himself had insisted the old republican must die, for he was 'too dangerous' for any other fate, and the jury were pressured to return a guilty verdict.[36] The government even arranged for musicians to play and drown out his scaffold speech. This time, many Londoners thought Charles had gone too far. Lambert was also tried, and sentenced to death, but Charles allowed the old Yorkshire soldier a reprieve, and he was shuttled back to Guernsey where the regime periodically threatened to shoot him if anyone attempted a rescue. The governor of the island did, at least, share Lambert's interest in gardens, and his wife Frances was allowed to move there, too, with some of their children. In 1670, he was transferred to Drake Island, off Plymouth. Frances died in 1676, her husband following in 1684. It was a sad end to one of the geniuses of the revolution, and to one of its most attractive characters.

The people remained quite stubbornly opinionated about politics, and there was now a new fashion for drinking in coffeehouses and discussing the news over a hot drink and tobacco. To the Restoration regime, this was all very dangerous, for they had seen where rampant political discussion had got the country in the previous 20 years. It was thanks to coffeehouses, grumbled the conservative Roger L'Estrange, that 'every carman and porter is now a statesman'. In some places, coffeehouses were regulated: in Cambridge the vice chancellor only licensed them if they agreed to 'suffer no scholars of this University, under the degree of Masters of Arts, to drink coffee, chocolate, sherbet, or tea . . . except their tutors be with them'.[37] But the regime also made careful efforts to reduce freedom of political activity and the press. Petitions of 20 or more 'for alteration of matters established by law in Church or State' were banned without approval from the local authorities. In 1662, a new Licensing Act helped dramatically reduce the outpouring of print, banning anything contrary to Christianity and/ or Anglicanism; 'the exorbitant liberty of the press', after all, had 'been a great Occasion of the late rebellion in the kingdom, and the schism in the church'.[38] The clampdown brought a number of victims, none more pitiful than a printer named John Twyn, who in 1663 was raided by Roger L'Estrange, the new surveyor of the press, at 4 a.m. while printing a seditious tract. Twyn tried to throw the printed pages out of a window, but to no avail; he was tried for treason and executed.

Within a few years, the goodwill towards Charles II's regime was waning fast. Part of the problem was the obvious moral decay at the court – something of a shock after the stern propriety of both Oliver Cromwell and Charles I. The scandals started as early as October 1660, when Edward Hyde's daughter Anne was revealed to be pregnant. She named the king's brother James, Duke of York, as the father, claiming they'd secretly married. She had credible witnesses, so the duke was forced to recognise her as his duchess. The raucous behaviour of other courtiers didn't help either. By 1663, one of their favourite haunts, the spa at Tunbridge Wells, was becoming known as a den of erotic misadventure. Then, in June that year, one courtier, Sir Charles Sedley, was thrown in gaol for a bizarre performance, with two other rakish companions, from the balcony of a Bow Street tavern in London. According to Pepys, Sedley 'showed his nakedness', gave a mock sermon and announced, 'there he had to sell such a powder as should make all the cunts in town run after him'. Apparently a thousand onlookers then watched as he 'took a glass of wine and washed his prick in it and then drank it off, and then took another and drank the King's health'. And the story somehow gained more nudity with each telling: in Oxford, the party was now thought to have been entirely naked, and by Flintshire there were also six naked serving girls.[39]

Charles himself was fun-loving, curious, personable and thoroughly lecherous. Even before the Restoration, he had one son, by his mistress Lucy Walter. In 1660, he'd started an affair with the Catholic Barbara Palmer (née Villiers), who in five years would bear him five children. Then, in 1663, while he was still sleeping with her, Charles tried desperately to seduce another Catholic, Frances Stuart, who was fifteen.* Meanwhile, he had married. His wedding to Catherine of Braganza had cemented an alliance with the Portuguese crown, Charles having let it be known that he hated princesses from cold countries and especially Germans. The marriage brought with it a dowry which included the towns of Algiers and Bombay, but there were no children. Predictably, Queen Catherine – who understandably shared little love for Lady Castlemaine (as Barbara Palmer now was) – quickly quarrelled with Charles over the role he was allowing to his mistress. Charles chose sex over marriage, and Catherine was cold-shouldered until she conceded defeat.

Perhaps the fact that unease about Charles centred on his sexual misadventures, rather than anything more serious, can be taken as evidence that the regime's foundations had grown much sturdier. The king may have been a lecher, but at least he was no tyrant. There was still opposition, though. In the autumn of 1663, a plot by republicans and Quakers had led to some minor disorders in the north, of which Charles's press made the most. This, in turn, meant that Parliament returned from recess in March 1664 with both king and Cavaliers in a bellicose mood. Charles demanded the repeal of the Triennial Act, and it took less than a week for Parliament to oblige. New legislation did recommend that Parliaments *should* sit at least once every three years, but they left off any mechanism for enforcement, so it was politically meaningless.

Then hardliners within the Cavalier Parliament went after the nonconformists once more, passing the Conventicle Act, which laid down tough penalties for those who attended unofficial religious gatherings. Repression was severe, at least where local magistrates wanted it to be, particularly of Quakers – who made no effort to evade the act and instead actually made a point of accepting punishment. Some local bigots made it their business to harass Dissenters in general and Quakers in particular. On the Isle of Wight, the deputy-governor Colonel Walter Slingsby, a veteran of the Royalist army, took particular delight in persecution, even boasting of how he had

---

*Frances, 'La Belle Stuart', was a famous beauty, not short of suitors despite some disparaging comments being passed around about the sharpness of her intellect. She ended up being the model for 'Britannia', and so her likeness – of sorts – could be found on coins until the twenty-first century.

sent two Quakers a translation of the Quran, hoping to goad them into converting to Islam and discrediting the whole movement.

At Whitehall, the Privy Council was now explicitly pushing for greater persecution. Even the Elizabethan recusancy laws were used. In 1664, 12 Buckinghamshire Baptists (ten men and two women) were sentenced to death under them, though this time Charles had them reprieved. Worse was to come in 1665. That year, the notorious Five Mile Act banned ejected ministers from living within five miles of their former parish, or any corporate town. Whatever will for tolerance had existed in 1660, England was quickly becoming an Anglican tyranny.

By late 1662, the mock-poem *Hudibras*, by Samuel Butler, was available to buy.[40] Butler had been of a modest Worcestershire background. Even as young boy, 'he would make observations and reflections on everything one said, or did, and censure it either well or ill'. *Hudibras* was his censure of Presbyterians, Puritans, the Parliamentarian cause and the times in which 'The Oyster-women lock'd their Fish up / and Trudg'd away to cry No Bishop', and where 'The Rabble are the Supream Powers'.[41] The lead character, Sir Hudibras, fitted the Puritan stereotype of a pompous hypocrite. The poem lampooned the world turned upside down of the Civil War and Republic. At one point in the poem, the eponymous Puritan anti-hero encounters a skimmington, which featured a man carrying a truncheon, droning bagpipes and an 'amazon' sat 'face to tayl, bum to bum' accompanied by a man carrying a spindle and a distaff. Hudibras was suitably appalled at 'so profane a show' and such 'Paganish invention'. But the joke was that for twenty years it had been men like Hudibras who had been the ones turning things topsy-turvy.

Naturally *Hudibras* became a runaway bestseller. Such was the book's success with former Royalists that Lord Clarendon had Butler's picture placed on the chimney in his great library, though Samuel Pepys was less impressed when he read it that Christmas.[42] 'It is,' he wrote in his diary, 'so silly an abuse of the Presbyter Knight going to the wars, that I am ashamed of it.'[43] Presumably it was less funny to those who had sympathised to at least some degree with the Parliamentarian cause, as Pepys evidently still did. People kept informing him of the book's wit, though, so he gave it another go, then another, but still he couldn't see the appeal.

The success of *Hudibras* reminds us that Restoration culture, in its fun-loving hedonism, was also about the defeat of Puritanism. As much as Charles talked about forgetting the past, there were plenty who were quite willing to rake up the radicalism of the Republic and remind people of the days when Christmas was banned and the theatres were shut, and soldiers stomped up and down the country closing horse races and fining people for their loyalty to the king. *Hudibras* was a way of crowing about this. The culture war, that we saw at the start of the century in events like the Cartmel wedding, had been won. Puritanism had been cast out. Momus's day had come and gone. Merry England was back.

But Pepys is a reminder that there was more to it than this. We think of Charles as a 'Merry Monarch', given over to celebration and parties, to theatre and pleasures of the flesh. It's not a false view as such, but it obscures a lot. For Dissenters, especially Quakers, his reign was one of brutal oppression, harder than anything experienced by the Puritans under his father. In its controls on the press, his government tried to stop the mouths of the English people once more.

The legacy of the Republic remained. Puritanism may have been defeated politically, but it lived on in the dissenting tradition which became such an important element to English religion – and indeed eventually political – culture. Meanwhile, the degree to which the constitutional issues of the earlier seventeenth century had been resolved was quite unclear. Technically, now, the vast majority of revenue came from Parliament, though the king might try and circumvent this by seeking other sources. Taxes on trade, for example, specifically the customs and excise, were increasingly lucrative, and yet were subject to less Parliamentary control than direct taxes because they tended to be granted for the life of the monarch.

The idea of a standing army was now, thanks to the Civil Wars and to Cromwell and his Protectorate, even more anathema to English sensibilities. Yet the realities of European geopolitics, in which armies were generally becoming much bigger and more professional, meant that it would be hard to maintain the country's clout without one. The press and public opinion were not going away. The world of pamphlets and coffeehouse politics was here to stay. Finally, the country's religion remained unsettled. The apparent supremacy of Anglicanism masked the resilience of Dissent. More to the point, while in exile both Charles and his brother James had been surrounded by Catholic influences. The nightmare scenario, perhaps, was a king trying to use his prerogative powers to promote Catholicism and to build a standing army that he could use to cow opposition, all funded by indirect taxes – or even a pension from a foreign monarch – while Parliament lay sidelined.

As people danced away on Oak Apple Day, as they laughed at *Hudibras* and as they settled into the covered seats of the newly vibrant London theatres, they had little sense of how soon this situation would come about, how the old wounds of the century would come to be reopened. In any case, the 1660s would bring plenty of other delights to distract them, as well as some quite unexpected horrors.

17

The Blazing World

A single plague death was nothing to worry about.

It appeared in London's Bills of Mortality, weekly published lists of deaths within the City and its suburbs. Instigated in the 1520s as a count of those dying from plague, the Bills had evolved into weekly and annual printed totals of burials and baptisms in London parishes. In 1629, the Bills started to record the cause of death. They were read closely by the wealthy, it was said, in order to see when it might be necessary to leave town.[1]

But a single death from plague was nothing to worry about.

It happened in St Giles-in-the-Fields, the ramshackle Westminster suburb running north from Covent Garden, home to a smattering of the rich, but a much greater concentration of the poor, some living in tiny rented rooms and cellars.

It was also theatreland. Restoration London was vibrant, colourful, noisy and malodourous, and plays were back, now performed in sophisticated covered theatres rather than the older, rain-sodden pits. King Charles was a keen aficionado, not least because of the new fashion for giving female parts to pretty young actresses rather than boys.

London was also a capital city at war: 1664 had brought a new conflict with the Dutch, touched off by trading and colonial rivalries. For London, this meant some hardship: hostile waters meant slower trade, and coal – which still came down from Newcastle by sea – was harder to transport. But even so the capital remained prosperous. Great building projects continued. Bloomsbury Square, a majestic piazza, was under construction. In Piccadilly, grand residences were planned for the great Royalist politicians Clarendon, Sir John Berkeley (who'd negotiated the Heads of the Proposals with Henry Ireton) and the poet Sir John Denham, he who had once caused chaos in London by drunkenly blotting out the street signs. Westminster Hall, outside which still stood the impaled skulls of Cromwell, Ireton and Bradshaw, was busy with traders and shoppers. It was a city of curiosities, where you could drink English beer, French wine, Arabic coffee, Asian tea and South American chocolate. In St James's Park, newly planted with trees and astride an elegant watercourse, you could see pelicans gifted by the Russian ambassador.

One especially delectable focus for the discerning man about town was the new Royal Society of London for Improving Natural Knowledge. Founded late in 1660, 'to shake off the shadows and to scatter the mists which fill the minds of men', the Society's first meeting had been at Gresham College.[2] It began with an address from the polymath Sir Christopher Wren.

Members tended to see themselves as the heirs of Francis Bacon, the one-time Lord Chancellor who – once his political career had collapsed – published a series of books in the 1620s extolling the importance of experience and observation, and the free sharing of knowledge.* And the Society tapped into the great European thirst for knowledge of the natural world. Of the first 550 fellows of the Society, 72 were foreigners. It was, said one founding fellow proudly, 'a ferment of the inventive heads of the world'.[3] Although the Polish Samuel Hartlib was pushed aside because of his connections to the Republic (he died in 1662), his network of correspondents was taken up by the German Henry Oldenburg, who became one of the Society's two secretaries.

Across Europe old uncertainties were under pressure from new ideas and new technologies. Things like thermometers, barometers, air-pumps and microscopes were all making unthinkable new discoveries possible. 'There be daily many things found out,' Sir Robert Filmer had written, 'and daily more may be which our fore-fathers

---

*The reality was that Bacon wasn't the first great English experimental philosopher, nor, indeed, does he seem to have actually done any experiments (unless you count the story of his dying from a cold after trying to freeze a chicken). In England, Londoners had engaged in observation and experimentation in Elizabeth's reign – though these men tended to be of middling status, so did not gain the lasting fame of the aristocratic Bacon. Most important, William Gilbert had, in 1600, published a path-breaking report of experiments on magnets.

never knew to be possible.'[4] Nowhere was this more so than in the heavens. A remarkable pair of bright supernovae in 1572 and 1604 had shown the heavens beyond the moon to be changeable, contradicting one of the central beliefs of the time. This was confirmed when comets, which also came and went, were proven to be superlunary. Then the Italian Galileo had used a telescope to show that Jupiter had moons, that the earth's own moon had a pockmarked surface and that Venus had phases. The last of these proved that at least some of the planets didn't revolve around the earth.

There was also, though, a context specific to the English Restoration, for natural philosophy, observation and experimentation proved attractive to those wishing to leave the traumas of the previous decades behind. They were a counterblast to the 1640s and 1650s, and the 'passions, and madness of that dismal age'.[5] The society saw itself, in the words of one member, as a 'famous academy of our philosophical sceptics that believe nothing not tried'.[6] Ideas were developed not from dogma, or suspiciously Puritan things like personal revelation. They were based on precise observation, experiment and recording. They were based on facts: 'numerous observations of sense', as Robert Boyle put it, would be 'diligently sought after and procured' before conclusions were drawn.[7]

Even so, Restoration science also built on a culture of enquiry and philosophical diversity already well entrenched under Cromwell and the Republic. John Aubrey, a member from 1663, was happy to admit that 'the searching into natural knowledge began but since or about the death of King Charles the First'.[8] The Society men also picked up on the desire for 'improvement' that had flourished in the 1650s, looking for science that was 'new, true, and useful'.[9] Perhaps most important, new ideas electrified an already highly sophisticated world of urban leisure, which had been taking hold in the capital for decades. In London, discoveries were discussed in coffeeshops and in the town houses of the rich.[10] So-called 'cabinets of curiosity', collections of wonderous knick-knacks from across the Continent and beyond, became centrepieces to the fashionable town house. Even the king had one at Whitehall.

Charles also had a laboratory, and the palace hosted lectures by William Petty and others. The braying Cavalier courtiers often found the intellectual content rather baffling, though; on one occasion, the exasperated Irish-born astronomer Thomas Streete upbraided Prince Rupert, the king's cousin, for his poor maths, setting off a flutter of gossip and earning him the epithet of 'the man who huffed Prince Rupert'.[11] In reality, the court at Whitehall was less important to the sharing of science than the publishing industry, centred on London. The way science was shared in print meant that people could cross-reference, double-check and correct in a way that simply wasn't possible – at least to the same degree – with cumbersome manuscripts.[12] Print helped foster a culture of corroboration, allowing an experiment to be repeated and validated, or a theorem or prediction to be tested by others. *Nullius in verba* ran the motto of the Royal Society: Take no one's word for it.

One of the biggest publishing sensations was a 1665 book by Robert Hooke, a striking-looking minister's son from the Isle of Wight. Grey-eyed, pale-faced and with a shock of curly brown hair, Hooke had experienced tragedy as a young lad when his father committed suicide. Now he was the darling of the Royal Society. His *Micrographia*, with its astonishingly lifelike drawings, of such fine-grained detail, showed the wonders of the world to be seen beyond the confines of unaided human vision.[13] It featured the fearsome eyes of a grey drone fly, the intricate wings of a gnat, even a breathtaking pull-out drawing of a flea with the very hairs on its back and legs visible. And the same year the Society started publishing an academic journal, the *Philosophical Transactions*, in which the latest ideas and experiments could be recorded. Aimed, wrote Henry Oldenburg, at 'such Englishmen as are drawn to curious things, yet perhaps do not know Latin', it was, in many ways, the heir to the Civil War mercuries, albeit infinitely more refined.[14]

One thing the Royal Society shared with the old mercuries was an interest in celestial prodigies, though theirs was scientific rather than providential. So it was that, in December 1664, Society members found themselves pondering a new 'blazing light' in the sky. It was, noted Pepys, the talk of the coffeeshops; and it also set off a rather intemperate academic dispute, adjudicated by the Society, between two astronomers, the Frenchman Adrien Auzout and the Danzig-born Johannes Hevelius.

The new blazing star was reported in New England, too, where a Puritan minister named Samuel Danforth noted its small parallax, which.– he understood – showed that it lay beyond the moon. It was, he would write, 'not a new fixed star, but a planetic or erratic body, wandering up & down in the etherial firmament under the fixed stars'. His understanding was an advanced one, accepting the modern belief that the superlunary cosmos could change. But he also worried about what the comet portended. 'The Histories of former Ages,' he wrote, 'do abundantly testify that Comets have been many times Heralds of wrath to a secure and impenitent world.' Had not one appeared in 1618, and 'the same year brake forth the Bloody Wars in Germany'?[15] Like a good Puritan, Danforth urged repentance.

Back in England, the winter had brought some suspicious deaths in the busy port town of Yarmouth. The previous year, reports of pestilence in Amsterdam and Hamburg had led to plans for quarantine. The plague was poorly understood: 'It is a mysterious disease,' Henry Oldenburg would write that September, 'and I am afraid will remain so, for all the observations and discourses made of it.'[16] There were two main theories as to its origin. One held it to be caused by *miasma* – bad air rising up from unsanitary places – the other blamed it on contagion – disease spreading from place to place. Either way, it was evidence of God's displeasure. This didn't, though, mean that humans couldn't take action. Miasma could be tackled by cleansing and by perfuming the air; contagion by quarantine and by locking down infected households. God's anger, meanwhile, could be sated by the reformation of public morals – though this was currently rather out of fashion.

Such thoughts, as the comet receded from visibility and into memory and observational record, will have crossed the minds of those who read the Bills of Mortality, and learned of the plague death in St Giles.

But a single death from the plague was not necessarily something to worry about.

In February 1665, there was another death in the same parish. The Bills showed an unusual growth in all deaths. Rumours began to spread, and Londoners made dire predictions, terrifying each other with tales of past outbreaks.[17] But the theatres and coffeehouses and the shops stayed open. The Duke's Playhouse, run by William Davenant, was one. Located in St Giles parish itself, its visitors that April included the twenty-four-year-old Lady Castlemaine and her conspicuous escort, the king.

On 24 April, the Bills revealed another two plague deaths in St Giles. There was a suspicion that the disease had taken hold elsewhere, too, but wasn't yet showing in the official statistics. The order was made to set up pesthouses on the outskirts of the City; affected households were subject to quarantine. Then, in May, there was a death within the walls of the City, on Bearbinder Lane. The Lord Mayor, fearing miasma, ordered bonfires and a deep cleanse of the streets. Still the theatres stayed open.

In June, temperatures rose. So did the numbers of deaths. Forty-three one week, then 112; 168 the next week, then 267. Now people started to evacuate. In July, perhaps 30,000 inhabitants left London, including members of the Royal College of Physicians. The king and court decamped to Salisbury. The roads out of town were choked with coaches.

London fell quiet. Now the death toll was 470 in a week; then it was over a 1,000. By the end of a hot, dusty, silent July, nearly 2,000 people were dying every week. In August, this rose to over 6,000. Streets were deserted, doors painted over with the red cross. Infected families were shut up inside and supplied only by food packages brought by the local community. '[E]verybody's looks, and discourse in the streets,' wrote Pepys, 'is of death.'[18] Those in the know thought the official figure of deaths was an understatement – the real toll was perhaps 25 per cent higher.[19] Quack doctors preyed on the fearful. Trade ground to a halt; most coffeeshops were shut. Rumours spread that the plague had been brought over from France, carried in bottles of infected air.[20]

By September, all but four of the 130 London parishes had outbreaks. Some argued that shutting people up in their houses was a mistake – it only ensured that every member of the household would be infected. Across England, towns tried to protect themselves. In Bath, you could not enter if you'd been to an infected place within 20 days. In Cheshire, the inns were closed. At Salisbury, now home to the court, entry was conditional on a valid certificate of health, though of course the rules didn't apply to the king. Meanwhile, when plague caught hold in the Peak District village of Eyam, the inhabitants closed themselves off to protect their neighbours. Three-quarters of them died. The Dutch press were delighted about the whole thing. 'The English nation,' one newspaper chirped, 'is now brought down so low with Plague that a man may run them down with his finger.'[21]

In September, the court moved to Oxford, where they won no friends. The courtiers were 'rough, rude, whoremongers'. 'Though they were neat and gay in their apparel,' complained the academic Anthony Wood, 'yet they were very nasty and beastly, leaving at their departure their excrements in every corner, in chimneys, studies, coalhouses, cellars.' Nor was it just the rowdiness of courtiers shit-ting in people's chimneys. There was also the king's open affair with Lady Castlemaine. 'The reason she is not duck'd', went a rhyme, was 'Because by Caesar she is fuck'd'.[22]

By autumn, the epidemic in London was peaking. Winter brought abatement. By Christmas, deaths were dropping to under a hundred a week. At the end of January 1666, the court was starting its move back, initially to Hampton Court. Gradually, life in London started to grind back to some form of normality.

As the new year progressed, plague was spreading around the country, hitting small towns one by one. Norwich, the second largest city, was recording 200 burials a week by the late summer.[23] Londoners looked anxiously at the Bills for signs of the expected summer second wave. Meanwhile, the war raged on. In June, the English and Dutch navies fought an infernal four-day battle in the North Sea, resulting in thousands of casualties on both sides, and an English retreat. Then, on St James's Day, in the midst of one of the hottest, driest Julys in recent years, another fierce North Sea engagement brought English revenge, with Prince Rupert and George Monck commanding an English fleet that killed 1,200 Dutch sailors and took two of their ships. Shortly afterwards, the slave-trading Rear-Admiral Robert Holmes sailed up the Vlie estuary and burned 150 merchant ships plus the town of West-Terschelling.[24] The outraged Dutch hoped for divine vengeance on the perfidious English. The resurgence of the plague didn't come; but August was hot, and so very, very dry.

In September, retribution came.

Shortly after midnight on Sunday 2 September, the baker Thomas Farriner woke to find smoke filling his house on Pudding Lane. It was a tangled, timbered part of the City; near the river front and full of 'old paper buildings and the most combustible matter of Tar, Pitch, Hemp, Rosen, and Flax'.[25] The alarm was raised with cries and drums. The Lord Mayor was summoned from his bed in Maiden Lane. A true Cavalier, known for drinking and dancing, he was an overpromoted man whose political success owed more to the strength of his royalism than the wisdom of his judgement. He underestimated the threat from Farriner's fire, refusing to pull any surrounding buildings down to break the path. 'A woman might piss it out,' he said.[26]

By 3 a.m., Samuel Pepys was woken at his house in Seething Lane, and told of the fire: he looked out of his window and saw the glow, a few streets away to the west, and returned to bed. By the time he woke again, at 7 a.m., the blaze was furiously out of control. He went down to the river and took a boat towards Whitehall. Passing under London Bridge, he looked to his right to see the whole river front aflame, with people clambering to throw their possessions into boats. At Whitehall, Pepys rushed to an audience with the king and the Duke of York. They told him to hasten back into the City, and to tell the Mayor to start pulling down houses to stop the spread. Pepys took a coach and travelled back east. He got off at St Paul's and walked east down Watling Street, into the face of a crush of people, horses and carts. On Canning Street, he found the Mayor, sweating, sleep-deprived. 'Lord what can I do? I am spent: people will not obey me.'[27] In the afternoon, the king and duke arrived by boat near St Paul's. The fire, swept westwards by the breeze, was now making the timbered old city rattle, a deathly sound accompanied by the 'thunder of the impetuous flames, the shrieking of women and children, the hurry of people, the fall of towers, houses, and churches'.[28]

The fire continued through the night and into the next day. People scrambled to save their possessions, tossing everything from furniture to virginals onto boats. As some of the goods caught fire, the river itself began to appear as if it was burning. Militia from surrounding counties were called up. The wealthy scrambled to save their riches: heavy merchants' goods were hard to move, but paper money and gold was easier. Alderman Sir Richard Browne managed to get £10,000 away in a chest, giving a miserly tip of £4 to those who helped him carry it.[29] Rumours spread that the fire was the work of Catholics, the French, of Puritans, or part of a Dutch attack. Women were said to be assaulting those who couldn't speak good English; at Moorfields, a Frenchman was attacked because he was carrying tennis balls, which were believed to be grenades. Another man was arrested because he had 'the appearance of a Frenchman'.[30] The Spanish ambassador had to turn his residence into a bolthole for terrified foreigners. As night fell on the 3rd, the searing flames had reached just 300 yards from the Tower; the order went out to bring all the fire engines kept at Woolwich and Deptford, together with 'all persons, capable either by hand or judgement'.[31]

By Tuesday, the fire had crossed the River Fleet, and spread outside the western walls. Bridewell Palace was destroyed, taking with it £40,000 worth of grain. So was Bulstrode Whitelocke's house on Fleet Street. Livery halls, churches, mansions and private dwellings were burned to the ground. White-hot cinders drifted through the city streets as the water in the city fountains boiled. The Guildhall was gutted, the medieval fortress of Baynard's Castle destroyed, the glorious Royal Exchange, with its shops and its clock tower, was left smouldering in ruins, little remaining but the stone statue of its Elizabethan founder, Thomas Gresham. Old St Paul's Cathedral, already earmarked for a radical rebuild, caught fire that evening. The scaffolding acted as kindling; so did the stacks of personal possessions that people had brought to what they thought was the safety of the old stone cathedral. Inhabitants fled anywhere they could – Moorfields was transformed into a canvas suburb of fluttering tents, each full of refugees. Hatton Gardens, Lincoln's Inn Fields and the piazza at Covent Garden all filled, so people moved out towards the villages of Islington and Highgate. Ash fell as far away as Eton.

As the wind dropped on Wednesday, and the authorities began to put out the fire, it became clear what damage had been done. London had become a hellish landscape of charred timber, ash and molten metal. The fire had raged for four days, but it seemed like a week: Pepys – for one – had lost track of what day it was. All told, some 52 livery halls, 87 churches and 13,000 houses were destroyed. The landscape was flattened so much that you could see the river from Cheapside. Trade goods were incinerated. One merchant lost £20,000 worth of tobacco, and the burning of Blackwell Hall took with it huge quantities of woollen cloth. Overall, the cost of the fire was somewhere in excess of £8 million. The old City, to all intents and purposes, was gone.

That winter was particularly cold; a cruel twist after such a hot summer. Many were still homeless, and coal was still in short supply. One Justice, Sir Edmund Berry Godfrey, who had earned his knighthood as a hero of the fire, fell from public favour when he was accused of hiking up the price of coal to extort money from the poor. Gradually, though, the rebuilding began.

It had been, said some, a judgement of God 'upon us for our sins'. Parliament even placed the blame on atheistical books, notably Thomas Hobbes's *Leviathan*, which had incurred God's wrath. Others suggested conspiracy: perhaps the Dutch, perhaps the French, perhaps religious fanatics. An unfortunate Frenchman even confessed, and was promptly hanged, though few in high places really believed him guilty. In government, the accepted view was that of Joseph Williamson, that the fire was caused by 'the hand of God, a great wind, and a very dry season'.[32] Perhaps, some wondered, it might not be such a terrible thing for the king: London's role in the Civil War was forgotten by no one. The Keeper of the Privy Purse even suggested that, after the Restoration, this was 'the greatest blessing that God had ever conferred' on the king; because it destroyed the walls and gates of the City.[33] No more could London defy the monarchy, as it had in 1642.

After the fire, at the instigation of the king the buildings of Gresham College on Bishopsgate were commandeered by the City government. The Royal Society was forced to move, first to the lodgings of the astronomer Walter Pope, where Robert Hooke presented a scale model for what he thought the rebuilt city should look like, then to Arundel House, one of the great aristocratic mansions on the riverbank south of the Strand: a rambling collection of buildings set around a spacious courtyard.

It was this world that Margaret Cavendish, née Lucas, wife to William Cavendish, Duke of Newcastle, dramatically entered in 1667.

Margaret was from Colchester. Raised by her mother, Elizabeth, but under the influence of her brother, Sir John, Margaret wrote with honeyed nostalgia about her country childhood. Her mother never beat the children, she said, but 'reason was used to persuade us'.[34] She never went to school, instead being taught to read and write by 'an ancient decayed woman' at home. She was drawn to intellectual pursuits from a young age, later remembering her ignorance at dancing, needlework, spinning, preserve-making, cooking and baking, 'as making cakes, pies, puddings, and the like'.[35] 'I was never very active,' she wrote, 'by reason I was given so much to contemplation.'[36] She claimed to have spent her youth in love with three men: 'the one was Caesar, for his valour, the second Ovid, for his wit, and the third was our countryman Shakespeare'.[37]

Unlike many she had no aptitude for languages, something which proved rather a burden when, during the wars, she followed Queen Henrietta Maria in to exile on the Continent. Here, though, she met her husband, William Cavendish, then Marquess of Newcastle, fresh from his humiliation at Marston Moor. In Paris, Margaret and William read, discussed and peered through telescopes and microscopes. He was already a keen poet and playwright, as well as an extremely accomplished equestrian; she was a budding writer and wit. Together they entertained Thomas Hobbes and his assistant William Petty, and a galaxy of French intellectuals including René Descartes. After 1648, their exile moved them to Antwerp, where they rented the old house of Peter Paul Reubens from his widow. William took to writing political philosophy, in which he argued that the common people had become too educated, and proposing a state in which they had regular entertainment but no access to newspapers. Margaret, meanwhile, found her mind buzzing 'like a swarm of bees'; and so, she too started to write.

She wrote poetry ('not excellent, nor rare, but plain,' she declared) and she gathered a reputation for flamboyant dress. Not everyone was impressed. 'I have seen it,' wrote the gentlewoman Dorothy Osborne of Margaret's first collection, 'and am satisfied that there are many soberer people in Bedlam. I'll swear her friends are much to blame to let her go abroad.'[38] But Margaret claimed not to be disheartened by dislike or neglect of her work: 'my mind's too big,' she noted.[39] In 1655, she published her pithy and caustic *World's Olio*, a collection of observations named after a kind of Spanish stew. Many readers were convinced her books must have been plagiarised. To William's mind, the problem was simple. 'Here's the crime: a lady writes them, and to entrench so much upon the male prerogative is not to be forgiven.' It was all a product, Margaret thought, of 'the overweening conceit men have of themselves and through a despisement of us'.[40]

After the Restoration, Margaret and William returned to England. Most of their time was spent on their country estate in Nottinghamshire, where they studied astronomy. William agreed to forgo money owed by the king (originally lent to Charles I during the First Bishops' War) in return for a dukedom, so Margaret became Duchess of Newcastle. The duke and duchess had paid a brief visit to London, in some considerable style, in spring 1665 – just as plague was tightening its grip. By that winter, now back in Nottinghamshire, Margaret was becoming engrossed in the writings of the Royal Society. The more she read, though, the more perturbed she became.

Particularly bothersome was Hooke's *Micrographia*. To Margaret, microscopes and other scientific instruments gave only 'fallacies' and distortion. For her, observation must be tempered with reason. Her response came in print late in 1666, when she published her *Observations upon Experimental Philosophy*. It castigated men like Hooke as thieves and rebels: 'like those unconscionable men in civil wars, which endeavour to pull down the hereditary mansions of noblemen and gentlemen, to build a cottage of their own'.[41]

In its first edition, the *Observations* was also appended with a short piece of fiction, a 'work of fancy', as she termed it: *The Description of a New World, Called The Blazing-World*.[42] It tells the story of a young lady, abducted and taken on a ship to the North Pole where she found a whole new planet attached to the earth. Here, having learned the language at remarkable speed, she became empress.

The Blazing World was a place of immeasurable wealth and luminous colour, peopled by strange, technicoloured beings and with cities of amber, coral, marble and sparkling diamonds. It was a world with just one religion and a monarchical government, for 'as it was natural for one body to have but one head, so it was also natural for a Politick body to have but one Governor', indeed 'a Commonwealth, which had many Governors', was like 'a Monster of many heads'. It was also a place grappling with new ways of seeing. Telescopes had brought discordance about scientific questions, the movement of the earth and sun, and about how many stars there were. Microscopes, meanwhile, were able to inspect fleas, but not do anything useful like stop the damn things from biting.

Soon the empress decided she needed a 'Spiritual Scribe' so she called for Margaret Cavendish herself, 'which although she is not one of the most learned, eloquent, witty and ingenious', yet she is 'a plain and rational Writer, for the principle of her Writings, is Sense and Reason'. So Margaret's soul was sent for, and the two protagonists proceeded to discuss philosophy and theology, and embark on 'such an intimate friendship between them that they became platonic lovers, although they were both females'. Together they travelled to England, but the empress was called back to the Blazing World, where disorder was taking hold. Having settled things down, the empress then learned that her old country, 'ESFI', was beset by war and foreign enemies. So she travelled there in dazzling imperial robes, with a navy and an air force of mythical creatures carrying fire-stones, and – vanquishing hostile armadas and setting fire to cities – she made ESFI 'the absolute Monarchy of all that World'.

'ESFI', her readers will have known, was England, Scotland, France and Ireland – the dominions of Charles II (he still, rather incongruously, maintained the old Plantagenet claim to France). Margaret had created her own world: 'Though I cannot be Henry the Fifth, or Charles the Second,' she wrote, 'yet I endeavour to be Margaret the First; and although I have neither power, time nor occasion to conquer the world as Alexander and Caesar did; yet, rather than not be mistress of one ... I have made a world of my own.' But like all great writers of what we would call science fiction, she clearly had another society in mind. And it was an ambivalent picture, for though the Blazing World was rich and powerful, it was beset by disorder, its attempts to settle on one religion and an absolutist monarchy hampered by discussion and discord. Eventually the Blazing World harnessed technology to dominate others: to become a great empire based on violence. Was this what the new science should be used for?

In April 1667, the Newcastles arrived back in London. Margaret had written a biography of her husband, and it was about to come out, while the duke himself had a new play to promote – a throwaway comedy called *The Humorous Lovers* which Pepys saw and, thinking Margaret had written it, thought 'the most silly thing that ever come upon a stage'.[43]

They stayed at their grand Palladian town house in Clerkenwell, where Margaret held court – discoursing freely with favoured guests. She was now several years past forty, by her own reckoning shy and awkward, but still a striking and glamorous presence on the outskirts of the scarred, smouldering City. John Evelyn was suitably taken, and visited four times, recording how he was 'much pleased with the extraordinary fanciful habit, garb, and discourse of the Duchess'.[44] John's wife, Mary, though, was rather horrified. 'Women are not born to read authors and censor the learned,' she wrote: they should content themselves with raising children (Margaret had none), assisting the sick, relieving the poor and obeying their husbands. 'I hope, as she is an original, she may never have a copy.'[45]

As was befitting, of course, Margaret attended the theatre, to see her husband's play, on which occasion she dressed in a dramatic 'antique' style with 'her breasts all laid out to view'.[46] She visited the king at Whitehall, travelling in a cavalcade of three coaches. Pepys was desperate to catch a sight of her: 'The whole story of this lady is a romance, and all she doth is romantic.'[47] He finally did within a few weeks of her arrival, as she passed from Whitehall towards the City in her elaborate coach.

At some point, Margaret let it be known that she wished to do something no woman had done so far. She wanted to attend the Royal Society. Revolution, Republic and Restoration had done nothing to change the deep granite of patriarchy that underlay English society. Rather, the horrors of women preaching, petitioning and stripping to their smocks in the name of Quakerism and whatnot had probably hardened male attitudes. The world had been turned upside down, but now under Charles II the proper order was back. Women's education was no priority. The few who pushed back against this knew how difficult their position was. As the teacher Bathsua Makin, said to be the best educated woman in England, drily noted, '[a] learned woman is thought to be a comet, that bodes mischief, whenever it appears'.[48]

Nonetheless, aristocrats – even controversial ones like Margaret Cavendish – tended to have allies, and she was duly proposed, seconded and the visit confirmed by a vote. It was Thursday afternoon, 30 May: the meeting place in Arundel House was crowded in expectation of her visit. As ordinary society business continued, word arrived that the duchess had appeared at the gate, in a gilded coach, with tassled horses, a gown with an eight-foot train and a broad-brimmed hat. To describe the outfit as striking would have been an understatement: and it combined both men's and women's fashion. John Evelyn thought she looked like a beardless Cavalier.[49]

The Society pulled out all the stops. Margaret was treated to a demonstration of their pride and joy – Boyle's air-pump, as well as a display of magnetism, to the generation of hot liquid from the chemical reaction of two cold liquids, and given the chance to inspect a louse under Hooke's microscope. She also watched as a piece of roasted mutton was dissolved in acid – a demonstration that Pepys, also in the audience, particularly enjoyed.

But it was all rather overwhelming. It put her, she recalled, 'extremely out of countenance'. She had no idea how to respond, a situation undoubtedly made worse by the presence of Boyle and Hooke, whom she'd criticised in print. In the end, asked for her thoughts, all she could muster was to say that she was 'full of admiration, all admiration'.

Pepys was now distinctly unimpressed. Margaret had been a 'good comely woman,' he wrote in his diary, but 'her dress so antic and her deportment so unordinary, that I do not like her at all, nor did I hear her say anything that was worth hearing.' She was, he later wrote, a 'mad, conceited, ridiculous woman.'⁵⁰

But there is more to life than impressing Samuel Pepys. As Margaret Cavendish travelled back north, she no doubt reflected on her appearance at Arundel House, lamenting the wit that just wasn't quite ready on the tip of her tongue. Yet she had transcended the limitations placed on her by the dead hand of patriarchy. And her cynical vision of her own Blazing World, where scientific endeavour is used for domination, and where the state worries about dissent from a free-thinking population, was a lot more perceptive than it might at first appear. To the naked eye, you might say.

18

All the Blessings of Heaven and Earth

In late June 1667, the restored monarchy was humiliated. A Dutch squadron, sailing up the Medway, was able to overrun the English defences at Chatham, wreak havoc on their fleet and tow away the flagship, the *Royal Charles*. That the ship had cleared the dock under Cromwell, known then as the *Naseby*, only highlighted the depths to which the nation had sunk since the victories of the Republic. Soon, Dutch ships were buzzing all around England's coast: 'By God,' cried one infuriated naval administrator at the dinner table, 'I think the Devil shits Dutchmen.'[1]

An unsatisfactory peace beckoned. The Dutch kept lucrative Surinam, Pulo Run and Tobago, and the English retained the backwater of New Amsterdam, now renamed as New York after the king's brother. But the nation's confidence was shattered.

Whatever the country's failings in warfare, though, it was prospering. Two years after the Medway humiliation, Edward Chamberlayne, Fellow of the Royal Society, published a handbook entitled *Angliae notitiae, or, The Present State of England* (1669).[2] It covered religion, history, politics, but also social statistics, providing data on trade, resources and social structure. It was avowedly optimistic about Charles II's realms:

O happy and blessed Britannie, above all other Countries in the World, Nature hath enriched thee with all the blessings of Heaven and Earth. Nothing in thee is hurtful to Mankind, nothing wanting in thee that is desirable.

And it was a huge success, running to three editions, with a French translation, within a year.[3]

Restoration England was going through a rebirth, a cultural and economic flowering that, though much less well known than that under the Tudors, was much wider reaching. The new natural philosophy – science, as we would call it – continued to flourish, not just in the Royal Society but in institutions and networks across the country. In 1668, Robert Boyle set up his own laboratory at his house on Pall Mall. Gresham's College and the Royal College of Physicians vied for prominence in the capital, joined in 1673 by the Royal Mathematical School, and in 1675 by the Royal Observatory at Greenwich. The latter's purpose was to put astronomy to practical use, particularly finding a way to reckon longitude while at sea.[4]

There were still the universities, too. Here, scientific experimentation was easing out the conjuring of spirits as the academic fashion of the day. Meanwhile, local scientific groups sprang up in country houses. In Lancashire, far from the calm banks of the Isis or the Cam, a group met to discuss Galilean physics, astronomy and meteorology – taking barometer readings on the wild reaches of Pendle Hill. Over 1679–83, Oxford's Ashmolean Museum was founded by Elias Ashmole, with a laboratory. 'Though London be the seat of the wits,' wrote the astronomer John Flamsteed, 'yet the country is the seminary.'[5] Communication between capital and provinces was improving, and science reaped the benefits. In 1668, a new London publication, *Mercurius Librarius*, helped spread the word about new books.

The new world that was springing up in the later seventeenth century was growing amid the remains of the old. Everywhere, in the economy, in society, in ideas, change was gradual, incremental and contested. The new always had to compete with the old.

Belief in the occult, the supernatural and in astrology and the like remained, for example, intertwined with the new experimental science. Between 1650 and 1680, more books were published on alchemy than any time before or since, and both Isaac Newton and Robert Boyle were serious practitioners.[6] Oxfordshire's Robert Plot, meanwhile, hoped to get an endowment for a college to search for the elixir of life, and Joseph Glanville, one of the leading advocates for the new science, spent much of his time trying to prove the existence of witches. Members of the Royal Society corresponded about astrology, witchcraft, magic and unicorns.[7] John Aubrey recorded phenomena such as the apparition seen near Cirencester in 1670, that – when challenged on its intentions – returned no answer 'but disappeared with a curious Perfume and most melodious Twang'.[8] William Lilly, the old astrologer, was consulted, and he thought it was a fairy.

Many remained very suspicious of the metaphysical implications of the new philosophy. If, in particular, one accepted René Descartes's idea that matter in motion explained all natural phenomena, then God might no longer be necessary. Perhaps, therefore, the universe spontaneously generated itself? It was a troubling thought. 'This way of philosophising all from natural causes, I fear, will make the whole world turn scoffers,' wrote the Bishop of Hereford.[9] To the pious, indeed, it was all rather dismal: 'I never yet read of any anthems composed for the contemplation of atoms,' wrote Oxford's Thomas Manningham in 1681.

But the scientists were mostly devout Christians themselves. Few careers epitomised the bonding of religion and science as did that of Seth Ward. Born in Hertfordshire in 1617, he studied at Cambridge where, in fulfilling the rather bizarre role as official university jester, he so offended the vice chancellor that he was temporarily suspended. After the war, he was forced out of the old university, but for royalism rather than jollity. He found himself instead at Oxford, where he fell in with the scientists around John Wilkins at Wadham College. He devoted himself to the study of mathematics and astronomy and became the first Oxford professor of the latter to teach the works of Copernicus. Following the Restoration, though, this brilliant scientist became a favoured son of the Church: Bishop of Exeter in 1662, then Salisbury in 1667. Dividing his time between Wiltshire and Knightsbridge, he was politically and socially well connected, and eventually very rich. He managed his diocese with careful attention, annotating the historical records, rebuilding the bishop's palace and guildhall at Salisbury. Always a bachelor, his wealth allowed him to found the beautiful almshouses next to the great cathedral that still bear his name.

Ward's enquiring mind didn't stretch to religious toleration. Such was the force of his attempts to harass Dissenters in the diocese that it was said he was singlehandedly causing depression in the cloth trade in which many of them worked. Nor was he the only one who combined a scientific mind with devotion to religious causes. Robert Boyle helped fund projects to translate the Bible and religious texts into Arabic, Turkish, Irish and Lithuanian, as well as working to evangelise Native Americans.[10] If anyone suggested that the scientists were diminishing God's work, they would point out that, rather, their discoveries showed the great wonder of Creation. As John Ray wrote, in a publication of the 1690s but based on lectures given in the 1650s: 'There is no greater, at least no more palpable and convincing argument of the existence of a deity than the admirable art and wisdom that discovers itself in the make and constitution, the order and disposition, the ends and uses of all the parts and members of this stately fabric of Heaven and Earth.'[11]

Eventually, indeed, a crucial piece of the divine puzzle was provided by Isaac Newton. A rival to Hooke, Newton had already revolutionised the understanding of light in his experiments on refraction, reported to the Royal Society in 1672 (and eventually published as his *Opticks* in 1704). These were able to demonstrate that white light was made up of the colours of the rainbow, allowing him to pen a 'theory of colours'. Around the same time, Newton was formulating a new set of theorems that would dramatically change humans' understanding of celestial mechanics and would eventually be published in his revolutionary *Philosophiae Naturalis Principia Mathematica* (1687).[12] They depended on a well-established idea, that there was a powerful force pulling bodies together, for which Newton used a Latin term, *gravitas*, meaning 'weight'. It was a stunning step forward: 'the greatest discovery in nature that ever was since the world's creation,' thought John Aubrey, though to him it properly belonged to Hooke rather than Newton.[13] Indeed, Hooke would go to his grave claiming that he had done the groundwork and Newton had merely plagiarised him.

Whoever was the real pioneer, gravity not only gave a satisfying mathematical model for the universe in motion, showing that – against the ancients – the same laws applied on earth as they did in the heavens; it also put God back in the picture. René Descartes's mechanics was not enough, without the mysterious – perhaps even occult – force holding it all together. In Newton's universe, God could now be seen as some kind of divine watchmaker, setting up Creation to work like clockwork. Few people as yet read Newton's mathematical modelling, not least because it wasn't published in English for nearly 40 years, and even fewer understood the complex mathematics. But it had the potential to create a radical new metaphysics: the whole of Creation was governed by mathematical laws, yet the whole thing still depended on a mysterious force; and where did *that* come from?

As famous as Newton was (and is), a more characteristic figure of the age was John Aubrey. If Newton was the genius of the age, Aubrey was its soul.

Born in Wiltshire in 1626, Aubrey had a whole sweep of interests, running from science to historical and antiquarian matters, to topography, geology, botany, the weather, fossils and even folklore. He was fascinated by mathematics, and considered it central to understanding the world, even admitting at one point to doing geometry and algebra while on the toilet.[14] About the only thing he really didn't care for was politics.

A member of the Royal Society, Aubrey engaged in wide correspondence with his fellow gentlemen, including many luminaries of science and philosophy. His views could be reformist, lamenting, for example, the 'tyrannical beating' that was often used in old-fashioned English schools. But he had no truck with the social levelling that had characterised radical thought during the Revolution: '[a] cobbler's son,' he thought, 'may have a good wit, and may perchance be a good man, but would not be proper for a friend to a person of honour'.[15] Like many at the time, he saw England as uniquely blessed by natural resources: 'there is no nation abounds with greater variety of soils, plants, and minerals'.[16] He was fascinated by curious medical remedies, like the information he received from a Dutch scientist that deafness could be cured by putting the dripping of a roasted eel in one's ear. He had a deep interest in astrology, and he personified an age when the supernatural was under attack, yet retained a significant hold. He knew of a witch in the parish of Chalke on the Wiltshire downs in the 1670s who had fits and vomited crooked pins, and he accepted the tale of a Jesuit the same decade who said he had seen a ghost. But he also saw that some of the old stories were dying out. Remembering his childhood ('and so before the Civil Wars'), he recounted how 'the fashion was for old women and maids to tell fabulous stories', about 'sprites, and walking of ghosts, etc'. They had been passed down from mother to daughter since before the Reformation, but were now on the way out. 'When the wars came and with them liberty of conscience and liberty of inquisition – the phantoms vanished.'[17]

He surveyed Stonehenge and Avebury, and collected a vast array of information about ancient monuments in the West Country. He formulated theories about the distribution of place names, and thought about the geological arguments for an ancient globe, feeling that strati-graphic evidence supported a much older Creation than many allowed. Meanwhile, the soil and the landscape could explain much, he thought, about the mysteries of human geography. People, he suggested, had different accents because of variations in soil and air. Aubrey even considered this to explain the various qualities of church singing: richer soils meant better singing. Not only this, but on sandy soils like those of Gloucestershire, people had droning voices and were spiteful, as well as inhospitable, envious, malicious, and more likely to be 'bigots and witches'.[18] Most remarkably, he suggested a theory of how top-ography influenced culture and religion. In Wiltshire, he thought, the people of the 'chalk' country, the downlands, were different from those of the 'cheese', the dairy farming areas. He believed the hard work of the chalk downs brought religious conformity: 'being weary after hard labour, they have no leisure to read and contemplate religion'. In the cheese, by contrast, people had little hard work to do, spent their time reading and so were 'apt to be fanatics'.[19]

His was a mind in which observations of the natural world were being used to explain the human: it was a mind conditioned by the new science, but also by the incredible complexities of a society that had recently fallen into revolution. Aubrey has sometimes borne the reputation as something of a dilettante, but he was a celebrated scholar in his day. Such was his renown that when Charles II was told in 1663 of the glories of Avebury, the Wiltshireman was immediately sent for and was able to provide a plan of the stones from memory. Nearly a decade later, Aubrey was commissioned by the Scottish-born cartog-rapher John Ogilby to undertake a survey of the county of Surrey.

Aubrey then spent much of 1673 perambulating, noting antiquities, churches, graves and topographical features, drawing houses and gardens. He enjoyed himself a lot.

There is a fascinating passage in the *Natural History and Antiquities of the County of Surrey*, which was published posthumously in 1718, in which Aubrey – evidently visiting the ancestral estate of his friend John Evelyn at Wotton in the thickly wooded valley of the Tillingbourne River – climbs to the top of nearby Leith Hill.[20] From the summit, the highest in the area, Aubrey is able to identify the country that swept away far below him to the distant horizon: 'the whole county of Sussex, as far as the South Downs, and even beyond them to the sea', while to the north and west the vista rolled away over parts of Hampshire, Berkshire, Oxfordshire, Buckinghamshire, Hertfordshire, Middlesex, Kent and Essex, as well as the City of London. Aubrey also knew – perhaps by observation or maybe by discussion with a willing guide – that with a telescope one could see his native Wiltshire. The view, he felt, far exceeded that from Windsor Castle, Leith Hill being 'much the highest eminence in this county (which has many other Alps)'.

Aubrey is not exactly 'romantic' in his appreciation of the view from Leith Hill and the 'Surrey Alps': his discussion is almost dispassionate, to a large extent merely listing the visible counties. But rather than anticipate the poets of a later period, he was characteristic of his own age. For in the later seventeenth century, climbing up and taking in the view was becoming something one did, as travel became more common and as some of England's wilder spots like woodlands and hills were enclosed, cultivated, explored, mapped and ultimately lost some of their danger. Aubrey's England was a land of improvement and prosperity, and one of the emerging pleasures of the later seventeenth century was looking at it.

The country was becoming visible. If not, for everyone, from the summit of a hill, then at least on the paper of a map. Long before the Civil Wars, great county maps made by Christopher Saxton (1579)

and John Speed (1611) had already laid out England to view. Since then, these maps had only become easier to come by, as print runs expanded and cheap versions appeared. And now they were joined, too, by the incredible prospects of Wenceslaus Hollar – most famously of London – and the road maps of John Ogilby. No wonder Aubrey, who himself drew a remarkable map of the ancient sites of Wessex, could identify all those counties from the top of Leith Hill.

The new visibility of England wasn't just confined to the landscape either. It could also now be seen through statistics and data. One of the most lasting developments was the appearance of the new academic discipline of 'political arithmetic': what one practitioner would later define as 'the art of reasoning by figures, upon things relating to government'.[21] The origins went back well before the Civil War. Even at the start of the century, estate surveys, parish records, documents relating to poor relief, and local population and tax listings existed as raw quantitative data. As the century progressed, these became more common. Thanks to the Poor Law, for example, each parish wrote a list, every year, of everyone receiving relief (and sometimes also of everyone who paid the poor tax).

In London, the leading light in the new 'Political Arithmetic' was William Petty, whose service to the Republic had done nothing to stop his career under the restored monarchy. Now he was a handsome court favourite and raconteur, with a natural daughter who had grown up to be a famous actress and who happened to look just like him. This he somehow combined with being the realm's most celebrated statistician. The first major publication in his field, though, was by the similarly affable John Graunt. In 1662, Graunt produced an analysis of the London Bills of Mortality in which he tabulated baptisms and burials, calculated mortality and fertility, and generated life tables – a remarkable exercise in what would become statistical demography. He calculated the population of London to be 460,000, a huge number but much lower than the 'millions of people' commonly spoken of at the time. He used data from Petty's home parish of Romsey to show that population growth was coming from the countryside. He even had an inventive stab at working out the total national population, reaching the not disgraceful figure of 6.4 million.[22]

The consequences of all this were impressive. In 1600, no one had much idea what the population of England was; now, it was being calculated. In 1688, another political arithmetician, Gregory King, would get the number nearly right at 5.5 million, and he had a go at predicting how it would grow in the future. It would, he thought, reach 6.42 million in 1800, 7.35 million in 1900. The maximum, was 11 million, which would be reached around the year 3500.

Even the physical size of the country was unknown until the 1680s, when Edmond Halley found an ingenious way to work it out. Taking the best recent map, he carefully cut out the shape of England and weighed it on a scale. He then took out a circle from the centre of the map, knowing that it wouldn't be hard to find the acreage this represented. Once he had this figure, he could calculate the total acreage.[23] A fundamental question of economic statistics had been answered using cartography, geometry and mathematics, all performed by someone most famous as an astronomer.

By 1701, it would be possible to produce a compendious description of the country boasting up-to-date maps, county acreages, population sizes, tax contributions, numbers of houses, natural history, mineral resources, soils and products, as well as the inevitable list of eminent families.[24] Thanks to these 'men of numbers' (as Pepys called them),[25] England was coming into view: not just as a landmass, or as a monarchy, but as a territory full of people and resources. And knowledge was power, of course: 'the more we know of the Islands,' the great advocate of improvement John Houghton wrote, 'the better, I presume, may they be managed'.[26]

By now, England's population had stopped growing – and was even starting to decline: around 5.3 million in the 1650s had dropped below 4.9 million by the 1680s. Some of this was caused by emigration, especially to the growing colonies on the North American mainland. But the primary reason was that people were marrying later, and more women were not marrying at all: of those born in 1666, for example, something like one in ten didn't marry. At first, this was a result of wage pressures: high population had caused wages to fall, meaning that people married later or didn't marry at all, so they had fewer children. But this pressure on earnings started to abate as the population stopped growing and started to decline. So there must have been other reasons the population stayed low. One suggestion is that the death rate was very high, partly thanks to the virulence of smallpox at the time. Another was that the growth of towns was attracting young women, who worked in the domestic trades. This meant that towns had more young women than men, while the countryside had the opposite. Intriguingly, a third theory suggests it might also have been a result of changing expectations. With more consumer goods available to buy, there were more attractions to enjoy in one's youth. Perhaps, so this theory goes, young women especially wanted to hold off on marriage because they were enjoying life without children too much. It's a fascinating possibility.

What is not in doubt is the sheer importance of population stagnation. It was as if a great tide was ebbing away, easing the pressure on English society. Thus, whereas before the Civil War, any gains in gross domestic product were immediately eaten up by the growing number of people, now those gains translated into higher individual living standards. Rents and food prices were stagnant, even falling. So great were the falls in wheat prices that the government in 1672 began to encourage exports, an unthinkable development in the hard 1590s or 1620s in which scarcity had been a constant companion.

This price shift not only meant ordinary people could afford more goods like meat and clothing: 'We are the greatest flesh-pots that ever lived', it was said in 1713.[27] But it also forced farmers to innovate and improve efficiency. Writers looked back on the spirit of improvement that had taken hold amongst English agriculture. To John Houghton, writing in 1682, the decades since the Civil Wars had seen 'such an improvement as England never knew before'.[28] Every acre of land must be 'improved that is capable of improvement,' wrote one commentator in 1670.[29]

Improvements included everything from better weeding, marling and drainage to the wider use of horses rather than oxen. One major innovation was the water meadow: a technical feat in which valley lands were artificially flooded in winter to produce a better crop of grass. New and relatively new fodder crops were making a difference, too, notably clover, sainfoin and the humble turnip, all gradually becoming more common as the century went on.[30] Cheaper food, helped by the introduction of the potato, even meant labourers were better fed: in a world where human effort was needed at every turn, more nourishment meant a physically stronger and healthier work-force (and thus more weeding).

The crucial thing, though, was that the whole rural economy was fitting together much more effectively. Everything was becoming more market-oriented and efficient. Regions were becoming more specialised: arable in the south, pasture in the north. Enclosure was continuing apace, despite occasional riots like those in Worcestershire in 1670, when a band of 'Levellers' under the leadership of 'Robin Hood' and 'Little John' threw down fences.[31] But thanks to generally higher wages, this opposition seems to have been much weaker now. And those who lost out could increasingly find relief in the Poor Law, which was expanding rapidly. By the 1690s, the money funnelled into Poor Law spending through the parishes was able to feed around 5 per cent of the whole population (and, as this was a local tax, it didn't cost the central government a penny). Paupers were increasingly seeing it as a right and, most important of all, it was one reason – along with better agricultural productivity and higher wages – that England remained free from famine.

Such was the success of this nascent welfare system that some were starting to grumble that it cost too much, and was making people shun work. 'There is no nation I ever read of,' wrote one disgruntled commentator, 'who by a compulsory law, raiseth so much money for the poor as England.' It was making them lazy, he thought: 'our charity is become a nuisance'. Indeed, the Poor Law, he claimed, had been the greatest mistake of Elizabeth I's reign, for it was 'the idle and improvident man's charter'.[32] But a revolutionary change had taken place: in the early part of the century, the poverty problem had seemed unmanageable, and there were still occasional famines in which pitiful souls starved to death. In the latter part, the country was regularly redistributing large sums to its neediest residents, and famine in England was gone for good.

The commercial beating heart of the kingdom was still London, now being rebuilt at remarkable speed in stone and brick. It remained unhealthy, though. In fact, the number of burials in London was about 5,000 per year higher than baptisms. Yet it grew. The capital must have had around 7,500 migrants per year to grow as it did. The vast majority of them came from the English provinces, but more than ever were now coming from further afield. By the end of the century, London had thousands of Huguenots, around 1,000 Jews and the lion's share of the roughly 10,000 people of colour who lived in England (a proportion of whom, likely a majority, were enslaved[33]).

By now, the urban areas of the City and of Westminster were beginning to intertwine, though there was an increasingly stark distinction between the East and West Ends. The tight lanes of the east were dominated by the port of London with its associated trades: a working city of dockyards and poverty. The west was now given over to the brick and tile mansions of the wealthy and the middling sort, set in spacious and ordered streets. Together, London and Westminster formed a great city of pleasure, of theatre, music and art. Between 1660 and 1700, some 440 new plays were performed, plus 120 revivals. By the end of the century, Shakespeare was coming back into fashion: nobody, wrote Mary Astell, 'has given us nobler, or juster pictures of nature than Mr Shakespeare'.[34] More populist than the plays, though, were the 'drolls': albeit there was a Shakespeare connection here, too, for one of the most successful collections of drolls had been published in 1662 by Francis Kirkman as *The Wits, or Sport upon Sport*, and whose comic sketches included the gravediggers' scene from *Hamlet*.[35]

Such a vibrant city was a lucrative market for the rest of the country. By 1700, London was consuming 200,000 tons of grain a year, drawn from a hinterland that extended to Sussex, Norfolk, and even Yorkshire. Internal shipping grew by two-thirds over the century, as English traders increasingly took advantage of the country's lengthy and accessible coastline. One set of beneficiaries were Cheshire dairy farmers: from virtually none in 1650, the amount of cheese shipped to London rose to 2,000 tons by 1680.[36] Inland trade was even more important, and here – again – there were significant improvements. Roads were getting better, and publications like Ogilby's *Britanniae* (1676), which mapped out the major trunk roads in remarkable detail, meant people had access to better information about them.[37] There were more coaches, and the postal service was improving. In 1680, a new penny-post was created, described by Evelyn as 'useful, cheap, certain, and expeditious', a 'mighty encouragement to trade and commerce' and was soon handling up to 700,000 letters a year.[38] Even more spectacular were river navigations, in which established waterways were dug out in order to make them passable to commercial vessels, and which required a not insignificant application of capital and technical expertise. One of the earliest had been of the River Wey, connecting the Thames with Guildford in Surrey, constructed between 1651 and 1653, after an act was passed by the Rump Parliament. Then, between the Restoration and the end of the century, some 200 miles were added to England's navigable rivers (from 700 miles to 900 miles; another 200 would be added by the 1720s).

All this buoyant trade was reflected in the vitality of England's towns, each hosting an increasingly diverse cornucopia of amenities, from shops to sports events and coffeeshops to theatres and concert halls. There was much rebuilding of homes, particularly in brick and tile, and with sash windows. And towns became centres of a new, urbane culture that promoted 'politeness' and consumption. Coffeehouses, said Houghton, were places where 'an inquisitive man' could learn about 'arts, merchandize, and all other knowledge'.[39] The great spa towns were booming: Bath took off after a physician, Thomas Guidot, published a bestselling description of the hot springs, and their medicinal properties, in 1676. By the end of the century it had its own season: 'five months in the year 'tis as populous as London, the other seven as desolate as a wilderness'.[40] Tunbridge Wells drew patronage from the royal court and became immensely fashionable. Soon it had 'shops full of all sorts of toys, silver, china, milliners, and all sorts of curious ware', as well as two large coffeehouses which also served tea and hot chocolate.[41]

As these products suggest, part of the new prosperity was driven by the remarkable growth of international trade. Between the 1620s and 1700, the merchant marine tripled in size.[42] Meanwhile, after enduring a period of failure and financial vulnerability in which the Dutch managed to push them out of their bases in South-east Asia, the East India Company was thriving again. Shifting its focus from spices to textiles, it was doing a booming trade centred on the Bay of Bengal. By the 1690s, about 13 per cent of England's imports were arriving from Asia.

Atlantic commerce was escalating rapidly, too, and this included the slave trade. On the American mainland, a string of colonies had been established in New England in the north, based on small family farms. In the south, meanwhile, were plantation economies based on the farming of tobacco, together with cattle ranching, rice, cotton and indigo cultivation, deer hunting, and pitch and tar production. The colonial population everywhere was growing. By 1700, the mainland colonies had a white settler population of about 234,000, while Caribbean colonies had 32,000. All the while, between 1651 and 1700, English ships, mostly those of the new Royal African Company (founded in 1660), transported some 350,000 Africans into slavery, of whom around a quarter died en route. The growth of Atlantic slavery was most marked in the Caribbean, where there had already been 15,000 enslaved people in 1650, but where the number had risen to 115,000 in 1700, or around four times the white population.

The slave plantations brought incredible wealth to those who owned them, supplying a growing demand at home for sugar in particular, but also tobacco. But the Caribbean colonies also created a significant demand for food, clothes, and much more that was largely supplied by the mainland. In this way, the whole of English North America was tied into the slave economy. Indeed, the mainland colonies sometimes actually supplied slaves. In the 1670s, an aged Roger Williams, founder of Rhode Island, aided the New England colonies in fighting a war against local Native Americans, including the Narragansett who had welcomed him as a young exile. When the war, known to the English as 'King Philip's War', was over, Williams helped the colonial militia round up Native prisoners for sale in to slavery in the Caribbean.

The monarchy profited from all of this. At home, the growth of internal trade led to a sharp increase in revenue from the excise, while the East Indies and Atlantic trade, including the slave trade, brought growing customs revenue. Charles II personally benefited from slavery, as did his brother James, Duke of York, who was governor of the Royal African Company, and its largest shareholder.

Increased consumption by the people provoked debate – not so much because of the miseries inflicted on enslaved Africans, though some questioned those – but because of an older concern about covetousness. Here, though, some startling new ideas were developing. By the 1670s, writers like John Houghton and Nicholas Barbon (son of the Puritan

Praisegod Barebone) argued that luxury, for want of a better word, was good. High living, wrote Houghton in 1677, made 'everyone strive to emulate his fellow'. He defended wine, linen and brandy as necessities.[43] Barbon, meanwhile, went about 'as fine and as richly dressed as a lord of the bedchamber on a birthday',[44] placed emphasis on emulation – something he felt was particularly strong in the towns. Urbanisation not only increased the number of shops (which were gradually overtaking markets as the main places people bought goods), but it also brought you into contact with people who'd recently been shopping: 'the cobbler is always endeavouring to live as well as a shoemaker, and the shoemaker as well as any in the parish ... and thus the people grow rich'.[45]

Even rural households were buying better furniture, household linen and cooking utensils, and across the whole country, chimneys and glass windows spread to more areas. Houses had more rooms, including parlours and bedchambers.[46] Labourers were better clothed and better fed, and bought better shirts, smocks and underclothes and smoked tobacco. Consumption fuelled growth in the country manu-facturing areas: metalworking in Birmingham and the Black Country, steel around Sheffield, wool in the West Riding and cotton around Manchester and Bolton. In Newcastle, the coal industry continued to thrive, something which had the potential to be transformative, for it was unlocking energy like never before. By 1700, over half of English fuel requirements came from burning coal, and – by one calculation – the output of English mines was greater than that of the entire rest of the world combined.[47] In the past, growing fuel requirements had to be met by planting more trees – which in turn reduced the land avail-able for food: coal freed England from this constraint and the poten-tial for growth now seemed limitless.[48]

There seems to have been a notable relaxation of social tension. For reasons that still elude historians, plague never returned after about 1670. There are signs that the English were becoming less violent – at least to each other. Aristocrats were less likely to spend their time duelling or creeping around each other's estates killing deer. People were less likely to carry weapons: the physician William Harvey, for example, had carried a dagger in his youth and frequently pulled it out during heated arguments, but by now this was much less the fashion.[49] Domestic violence was less widely accepted at the end of the seventeenth century than at the start, and the homicide rate was falling: by the end of the century, it was lower than it is in today's United States.[50] The great crime wave that had crested earlier in the century was now on the ebb. Prosecutions for felony, having peaked around the 1620s, were in sustained decline.[51] In Essex, the number of property offences prosecuted around 1700 had fallen to around a tenth of their level a hundred years earlier.[52] There was a dramatic decline, too, in the use of capital punishment: in Cheshire alone there were 160 hangings in the 1620s, but this had dropped to 20 per decade after the Civil War. Even London saw a huge drop in the number of hangings, from around 150 every year under James I, to 20 *per annum* by the early years of the eighteenth century.

Partly this reflected a dramatic fall in the numbers being prosecuted, but it also reflected a greater reluctance to apply capital punishment. New legislation wasn't behind this, although in 1677 heresy was changed from a capital crime by burning to one punished merely by excommunication (the last 'heretics' – both Protestant radicals – had been burned by James I in 1612). Instead, the change permeated through the whole legal process, from arrest to indictment to trial to sentencing and even beyond. In the early seventeenth century, perhaps 25–30 per cent of those indicted for capital offences would be executed; by the century's end, this had fallen to about 10 per cent. The mechanisms for stopping short of hanging had always existed, but now they were used more liberally. Grand juries, who sifted indictments before trial, could return verdicts of *ignoramus* ('we do not know'), meaning the case was dropped. Convicted felons were not generally imprisoned or transported yet (both of these would later offer alternatives to the death penalty), but they could be pardoned or, where applicable, granted 'benefit of clergy'. This was a legal fiction which entailed 'proving' that they were in holy orders, and thus subject to a lesser punishment. They did this by reading a verse from the Bible, and judges could allow them either to learn the skill of reading while in gaol, or could set a well-known 'neck verse' (so-called because it would save your neck):* that could be learned by heart. Women

---

*It was the opening to Psalm 51: 'Have mercy upon me, O God, according to thy lovingkindness: according unto the multitude of thy tender mercies blot out my transgressions.' Those who spoke these words were, of course, hoping that their trial judges would also do some blotting.

could plead the belly, i.e. claim to be pregnant, and while technically this would require proof, that proof could be more or less robust.

Then there was so-called 'pious perjury', whereby juries returned a guilty verdict but for a lesser, non-capital offence even though they knew a more serious one had been committed. The Shropshire yeoman Richard Gough, writing the memoirs of his small village community, Myddle, remembered a classic case of this type of leniency.[53] John Aston was 'a sort of silly fellow, very idle and much given to stealing of poultry and small things', who – Gough noted – walked rather like a pigeon. He was a well-known minor nuisance. Regularly caught in the act, his neighbours would admonish him rather than reporting him to the authorities. Eventually, however, he grew 'insufferable', and began stealing hens in the night, taking them to Shrewsbury and passing them on to 'confederates'. Such organised crime was too much for rural Shropshire, so he was finally arrested for stealing two dozen cocks and hens. Come the trial, the judge, 'seeing him a silly man, told the jury that the matter of fact was so fully proved that they must find the prisoner guilty'. However, he said, 'they would do well to consider of the value'. So the jury duly brought in the guilty verdict, but only to the value of 11 pence (i.e. just below the 12 pence that would have made it a capital felony), 'at which the judge laughed heartily and said he was glad that cocks and hens were so cheap in this country'. Aston was released, though Gough noted that 'he left not his old trade wholly'.

Witch prosecutions, too, were finally dying out in England. The reasons for this were complex. There was a rich tradition of English scepticism, and memories of men like the 'Witchfinder General' Matthew Hopkins helped give witch-hunting a thoroughly bad name, for were not his exploits merely those of a Puritan fanatic? Yet witch beliefs remained strong, including among many members of the Royal Society. Weird phenomena continued to draw popular fascination: publications continued to appear detailing strange ghosts, monstrous births, and even a 'prophetical fish'.[54] Some few unfortunates still admitted to making pacts with the devil, such as the Gravesend man who sold his soul in exchange for the power to live for six years without having to work.[55] In 1663, there was the only known reference to a broomstick in an English witch trial.[56] And local cunning folk and sorcerers still plied their trades: earlier in the century one might not be more than ten miles from a sorcerer, and they had certainly not all disappeared. Some went from place to place, earning money where they could, though not always ingratiating themselves with everyone they met. In 1676, for example, the itinerant wizard Joseph Heynes spent some time fortune-telling at Ware, Hertfordshire. He described his takings as 'five pounds, three maidenheads, and a broken shin'.[57]

But while witch beliefs died only very slowly, there was a growing scepticism among judges and juries as to whether a specific person could legitimately be proved to have committed an actual crime.[58] Such was the scepticism in the legal profession that by 1676, it was said that 'the reverend judges, especially of England now are much wiser, not only than the proletarian rabble, but than they too who profess themselves to be the great philosophers'.[59] By the 1680s, the number of people indicted for witchcraft had slowed to a trickle. Between 1660 and 1701, 48 indictments were filed on the Home Circuit: nine were thrown out by the Grand Jury, the rest (39) resulted in acquittals. In the 1690s, the Lord Chief Justice of the King's Bench Sir John Holt managed to secure 11 witch trial acquittals in a row, and the way he conducted himself in trials led people to suspect he didn't believe in witchcraft at all. There may have been a witch executed in 1716, but aside from that the last known execution was in 1684. In one sensational trial in 1712, that of Jane Wenham of Hertfordshire, the exasperated judge, Justice Powell, was told that the poor woman had flown to a sabbat, but retorted that there was no English law against flying. The jury still convicted her, to Powell's horror, but he made sure the sentence of hanging wasn't carried out, and she was given a home on the estate of a sympathetic local landowner.

It wasn't just the magic arts, for there seems to have been a general decline in most forms of litigation in this period. Civil cases in most courts were plummeting, as was business in the church courts. These, which dealt with misbehaviour in church and other moral lapses, had been abolished during the Revolution, but been brought back at the Restoration. Now, though, they were much less active. The consequence was that you were considerably less likely to be prosecuted for illicit sex at the end of the seventeenth century than you were at the start, even if there was still plenty of room for concerned prurience in some quarters. From the 1690s, for example, the 'Society for the Reformation of Manners' sought to prosecute sex workers and those who engaged in illicit relationships, while further moral panic was touched off by the appearance in London of an organised gay subculture – the beginnings of the world of the Georgian 'molly-houses'.[60]

The focus here was on same-sex relationships between men. Those between women were little recorded, as they were not technically against the law. The most intriguing case was one that emerged not in a criminal trial, but a marital suit that came before the Court of Arches, the highest church court in the land, in 1682.[61] It was launched by the young, beautiful Arabella Hunt. Two years before, she'd married one 'James Howard' at St Martin-in-the-Fields. But James was not quite who they seemed: they had previously gone by another name, which was Amy Poulter, widow of Arthur – a wealthy Hertfordshire man. Amy had dressed in men's clothes to court Arabella, and after their wedding the two lived together for some time. By 1682, though, Arabella had decided she wanted to end the marriage. It seems unlikely that she had been deceived: probably the relationship broke down. But she said she suspected her husband to be 'one of a double gender (being usually called an hermaphrodite)'. So Arabella went to court – her erstwhile spouse was physically examined by a jury of five midwives, who announced them to be a 'perfect woman in all her parts.' The marriage was duly annulled, and soon became the talk of the town. In a play, written the same year, the pioneer female playwright Aphra Behn implied it had all happened because of a shortage of men.

Poor Amy died soon after, buried in Cottered in Hertfordshire. Arabella never remarried, and went on to a glittering career as a lutenist and soprano. It would bring her into the orbit of Mary Stuart, eldest daughter of James, Duke of York. Mary had herself enjoyed an intimate female friendship, with Frances Apsley, Lady Bathurst. They wrote to each other for two decades, pretending that Frances was Mary's husband. Perhaps the most remarkable letter was from 1678. At this point, Mary had become pregnant, but she joked with

Frances that 'though I have played the whore a little, I love you of all things in this world'.[62]

Her marriage at this point was far from idyllic. She'd wept through the ceremony at St James's the previous year, though over time the couple would grow reasonably happy. For now, Mary's personal life had fallen victim to politics. The marriage had been pushed for by her uncle, King Charles II, and his chief minister Lord Danby. It was a marriage that, they insisted, made good political sense, for though the groom was Mary's cousin and though he was a Dutchman, he was also a famous Protestant warrior. Born in 1650, Mary's new husband already had a distinguished political and military career behind him. For he was Charles I's grandson, William of Orange.

19

The Original Sovereign Power
of Mr Multitude

Like many in the Restoration period, John Locke's first memories were of Civil War and revolution. 'I no sooner perceived myself in the world,' he recalled, 'but I found myself in a storm.'[1] Born in 1632, in the small Somerset village of Wrington, on the northern side of the Mendip Hills, his grandfather had been a solid Calvinist and his father had served in the Parliamentarian army, though Locke himself attended Westminster School, where he learned under a noted Royalist headmaster.[2] During the 1650s, Locke was at Oxford, with a 'studentship' (effectively a fellowship for life) at Christ Church, though he admitted to finding the curriculum inadequate, the lectures poor and the teaching of philosophy 'perplexed with obscure terms and stuffed with useless questions'. He was even less impressed by his native county of Somerset ('Zomerzetshire', as he mockingly called it). 'I am in the midst of a company of mortals,' he complained, 'that know nothing but the price of corn and sheep, that can entertain discourse of nothing but fatting of beast and digging of ground.'[3] Clearly he felt his mind was fit for greater things.

Locke was drawn to both the new natural science, including a fascination with medicine, and to theology. He welcomed the Restoration, and although his fellow Oxonian Anthony Wood saw him as 'a man of turbulent spirit, clamorous and never contented',[4] he was in reality becoming something of a moderate, very much at peace with the Anglican establishment. He even suggested that the Civil Wars could have been avoided 'had men been more sparing of their ink'. For, he

said, 'furies, war, cruelty, rapine, confusion' had all been 'conjured up
in private studies'.⁵

In 1665, thanks to the outbreak of the Second Dutch War,
Locke acquired a role as secretary to a diplomatic mission to the
German territory of Cleves on the Rhine, one of the holdings of the
Hohenzollern Elector of Brandenburg. The aim of the mission was
to ensure Brandenburg–Prussia's neutrality, and, although this failed,
here Locke was able to observe the religious toleration practised in the
Elector's territories, in which, as he wrote excitedly to Robert Boyle,
'they quietly permit one another to choose their way to heaven'.⁶

With the mission over, Locke returned to Oxford. Here he came
to the decision to pursue medicine rather than a career in the Church.
But a chance meeting changed Locke's life for ever. In July 1666, he
was asked by a colleague to procure 12 bottles of mineral water from
the nearby village of Astrop, for a wealthy baron who was planning
to be in Oxford visiting his fourteen-year-old son. The baron was
Anthony Ashley Cooper. A Dorset man, he had been elected to serve
the Short Parliament of 1640, aged just eighteen. In the war he had
been a Royalist, but he was able to reconcile himself to the victors and
eventually served on Cromwell's Council of State. Never much of a
republican, he was one of 12 men sent to Holland to acknowledge
Charles II as king in 1660, an act which gained him a noble title and a
place on the Privy Council. By 1661, his vertical rise had continued,
and he was made Chancellor of the Exchequer.

When they first met in 1666, Locke and Ashley Cooper hit it
off famously. Both, it seems, shared views in favour of toleration,
and against royal absolutism. Soon, Locke had moved into Ashley
Cooper's grand mansion at Exeter House, on the northern side of the
Strand in London. One of the earliest projects he worked on here
was related to England's growing colonial empire in the Americas.
Ashley Cooper had been involved in the Barbados sugar plantations
and had owned slaves. Now he devoted his energies to the new colony
of Carolina, and to providing the territory with a new constitution.
The Fundamental Constitutions of Carolina would be adopted in
1669 and contained remarkable provisions for religious liberty for all
Christians, Jews and Native Americans. It also, though, accepted –
and indeed reinforced – the institution of slavery, allowing that 'every
freeman of Carolina shall have absolute power and authority over his

negro slaves, of what opinion or religion soever'.⁷ Locke helped draft
the document and developed – at least for a brief period – his own
investment portfolio that included shares in the slave-trading Royal
African Company.

The biggest service he did his new employer, though, was that he
probably saved his life. In 1668, Ashley Cooper had suffered from a
ruptured cyst on the liver and was in terrible pain. Locke suggested
an operation in which a tube was inserted to drain fluid. Afterwards,
it was decided to leave the tube in, with a copper tap attached to it,
to drain any further build-up. Later that year, Locke was elected to
the Royal Society, and Ashley Cooper's career rose even further. The
fallout from the Dutch War and especially the Medway disaster had
spelled the end of the Earl of Clarendon's long political service, forcing the ageing royal servant into exile (where he could finally finish
a great history of the Civil War). Soon thereafter, a new administration emerged under five leading ministers, known, thanks to a convenient acronym, as the 'Cabal'. Ashley Cooper was one of the 'a's,
and he was joined by two meticulous administrators, Sir Thomas
Clifford and the Earl of Arlington (the one a Catholic, the other on
his way to becoming Catholic), plus the rakish Duke of Buckingham,
and the Scots Presbyterian John Maitland, now Duke of Lauderdale.
The contrast with the Anglican Clarendon was stark, and politically the Cabal represented a spectrum of viewpoints: Ashley Cooper
was an old Cromwellian, but Arlington was an impeccable Royalist.
Buckingham, on the other hand, had been in exile with Charles, but
had also been a friend of John Lilburne, and was now ably assisted
by his secretary and legal adviser John Wildman, the ex-Leveller.
His wife, Mary, was the daughter of Sir Thomas Fairfax. Lauderdale,
meanwhile, had been a Covenanter.

The Cabal's rule was marked by religious controversy: notably
serious riots in London in 1668 arising from anger that the authorities were clamping down on dissenting meetings while doing nothing
about brothels. Then there was a cause célèbre when the Quakers
William Penn and William Mead* were arrested for attending an

---

*Mead would later marry Sarah Fell, daughter of Margaret of Swarthmoor. Sarah's household
accounts survive for the 1670s, and contain some of the earliest references to the growing of potatoes in the north-west of England.

unlawful religious assembly but were found not guilty by a sympathetic London jury. That jury, led by Edward Bushell, was imprisoned by the infuriated judge, but Bushell then petitioned for a writ of habeas corpus, leading to the ruling that judges' coercion of juries was unlawful. It set a critical precedent.

Abroad, Charles was seeking closer alignment with France, despite an unfortunate diplomatic incident in 1669 where Louis XIV sent Charles an astrologer as a special envoy who then failed to predict any of the winners at Newmarket races.[8] Notwithstanding such embarrassments, Louis remained the most powerful king in Europe, and Charles clearly felt it prudent to attach England to France's coattails. So, in 1670, he signed a treaty at Dover which brought him French cash in return for support against the Dutch and a promise both to suspend the old penal laws against Catholics and, eventually, himself to convert. This obviously had to be kept secret from his people, and so a fake treaty was prepared for public consumption, shorn of the explosive religious elements. Two years later, however, Charles publicly moved to improve tolerance of both Catholics and Dissenters, by issuing a Declaration of Indulgence, which would suspend all penal laws.

Unfortunately, Charles was still desperate for money, especially with a third war now beginning against the Dutch (1672), this time in alliance with France. One solution had been simply to stop payments from the exchequer to state creditors, leading to the ruin of several of London's leading bankers, who were emerging as key lenders to the government. But even this only went so far, and Charles was forced to go back to the Cavalier Parliament, by now in its twelfth year. MPs, though, attacked the Declaration of Indulgence, telling the king that – regarding its legality – he had 'been very much misinformed'. They forced him to drop it and, as if to hammer the point home, passed a Test Act (1673), which decreed that all office holders must declare against transubstantiation, something no Catholic could ever do.

It was an act that would bring a stunning revelation, right in the heart of English politics. At some point, perhaps in the late 1660s, James, Duke of York, had converted to Catholicism. The Test Act, which applied to his role as Lord High Admiral, forced this into the open because he would need to take the requisite oath against transubstantiation. Instead, he resigned his commission. The revelation of York's conversion sent shockwaves through the country. To John Evelyn, it 'gave exceeding grief and scandal to the whole nation, that the heir of it, and the son of a martyr for the Protestant religion, should apostatize. What the consequence of this will be, God only knows, and wise men dread.'[9]

That same year, York married a Catholic. Poor Duchess Anne had died back in 1671, and this time James married the fifteen-year-old Italian Mary of Modena. In the meantime, the Cabal was disintegrating – not helped by the fact that Clifford was a Catholic and thus debarred by the Test. For now, though, Ashley Cooper's star was still on the rise. In 1672, he had been raised to the earldom of Shaftesbury, as well as gaining promotion from the role of Chancellor of the Exchequer to the higher office of Lord Chancellor. He had no difficulty with the Test, taking Anglican communion at St Clement Danes, near Exeter House, alongside the king's natural son, James Scot, the Duke of Monmouth, now in his twenties and enjoying a flourishing military career. The communion was witnessed by a dutiful John Locke.

But the controversy over York's failure to take the Test was beginning to push Shaftesbury, as he now was titled, inexorably down a more dangerous path, into opposition to the court. By late 1673, he had fallen far out of favour, so much so that in November the king removed him from the Lord Chancellorship, after just under a year.

As Shaftesbury stumbled, a new politician was on the make. Thomas Osborne was a forty-something Yorkshireman, and one of the age's great survivors. Already in 1638, he had narrowly escaped death at home in York because he was playing with his childhood cat when the chimney collapsed around him, killing his brother. Described even by his one-time friend John Evelyn as 'haughty', Osborne had been appointed Lord Treasurer, one of the great offices of state, in 1673.[10] Thus when the Cabal fell he was able to consolidate his place as Charles's chief minister. An earldom was forthcoming, too, so Thomas Osborne became the Earl of Danby.

In 1674, the Third Dutch War was concluded, much to the relief of the merchant community. It had brought little success and at the cost of considerable ruin for English shipping. Peace also brought a partial diplomatic breach with France, which continued its effort to subdue the Dutch. This in turn allowed Danby's ministry to pursue a more obviously Protestant policy. His aim, as he himself noted, was 'in all things to promote the Protestant interest both at home and abroad'. He was to prove an effective operative, allying with Anglicans and using the royal finances to buy support in Parliament. In order to sell his rule, he tried to align himself to the memory of King Charles I, portraying his enemies as republicans and Dissenters, the heirs of the 1640s. A huge mausoleum was planned for the late martyred king, to be designed by Christopher Wren, and although this ran out of money, a more modest, but equally symbolic, project did come to fruition. In 1675, under Danby's initiative, the Crown purchased an elegant bronze equestrian statue of Charles I, commissioned by the old courtier Richard Weston in 1630, but since gathering dust. It was placed on a pedestal of white Portland stone staring down towards the Banqueting House where its subject had met his death, on the old site of the Charing Cross. It was a triumph of the monarchy over the Puritans who had torn down the old cross in 1647, and just two years later committed the horrid act of treason against their anointed king.

Shaftesbury, meanwhile, was trying to rally opposition to York. Among his associates was the Duke of Buckingham and the aged Denzil Holles, at whose house Shaftesbury's allies would meet to discuss Parliamentary tactics. In 1675, someone in Shaftesbury's circle caused a sensation by publishing an anonymous manifesto: *A Letter from a Person of Quality, to his Friend in the Country*. It attacked Danby, and the 'High Episcopal' and 'Old Cavalier' interests who had been working since the Restoration to bring in 'Government Absolute and Arbitrary', not bounded by human laws.[11] The *Letter* caused an immediate stir. The House of Lords was incensed, and had it burned. The actual authorship remains uncertain, but it seems highly telling that, shortly after its publication, John Locke, who must rank as the most plausible candidate, bolted to France.

Shaftesbury remained, and continued to be an annoyance to the government. Yet, though he narrowly avoided being sent to the Tower, his loss of office meant maintaining Exeter House was impossible. His political career was now stalling badly. After a short period back in Dorset, he returned to London and took up residence in the rather less grand, though Inigo Jones-designed, Thanet House on Aldersgate Street. Meanwhile, by 1677, Danby was basking in one of his greatest triumphs yet: the marriage of Princess Mary, daughter of the Duke of York by his first wife, Anne Hyde, to William of Orange (who, like Mary, was one of Charles I's grandchildren).

Born in 1650, Mary's new husband already had a distinguished political and military career behind him. In William's early life, his family had been frozen out of power by the republican faction in Holland, partly on the insistence of Oliver Cromwell after the First Anglo-Dutch War (1652–4). But in 1672, he enjoyed a complete change in fortunes. That year, as part of an Anglo-French offensive, Louis XIV's troops had invaded the Dutch Republic. Anger was quickly directed at the republican government under Johan de Witt. As a result, De Witt was arrested and eventually lynched in The Hague. William's supporters, meanwhile, were able to take power once more and, late in the year, he had the Dutch 'water line' defences flooded, forcing the French to retreat. His countrymen remembered 1672 as their *Rampjaar*, or 'disaster year', but it brought triumph for William of Orange for his heroic defence against the French menace, and he was installed as Stadtholder. Suddenly he was one Europe's principal figures, and, as such, when he married the second in line to the English, Scottish and Irish thrones, it was a major coup for both sides.

Certainly it tied the Stuart monarchy closer to the European Protestant, anti-French camp. But within a year, any new confidence was shattered. For soon a scandal broke that would, as politics took its twisting path, bring England once more into chaos.

Titus Oates, was, according to his old Cambridge tutor, a 'great dunce'.[12] He had been expelled from school and two Cambridge colleges, before becoming an Anglican minister, having falsely claimed to hold a BA. At Bobbing, Kent, he was ejected for drunkenness, so he became curate to his father at Hastings. Here, he was prosecuted for perjury, having accused the local schoolmaster of sexually abusing the boys. Then Oates fled to the navy from which, in 1676, he was discharged for sodomy. Finally, in 1677, he converted – insincerely, no doubt – to Catholicism, managing to get himself expelled from his Jesuit training school in Spain. Next, twenty-eight-year-old Oates attended the Jesuit school at Saint-Omer, near Calais, where he must have stood out like a sore thumb among his young classmates. For their part, they hated him. One of them once broke a pan over Oates's head 'for recreation'.

By the searing hot summer of 1678, Oates was back in England, where he met up with Israel Tonge, a fanatically anti-papist former academic and schoolmaster. Between them, they invented a plot, by Catholics, to murder the king.

In August, Charles was approached in St James's Park by Christopher Kirkby, a chemist who had helped the king with his amateur experiments, but who was also an acquaintance of Tonge. At first Charles didn't believe the story of the 'Popish Plot', but Danby and York both pushed for an investigation, and in September, Oates presented his evidence before a magistrate, Sir Edmund Berry Godfrey, and a credulous Privy Council chaired by the aged Prince Rupert.

The revelations were kept secret for now, but rumours were already spreading. Oates named dozens of suspects, not just Jesuits and Catholics (including, eventually, Queen Catherine herself), but even rather unlikely accomplices like John Lambert, still alive and imprisoned on Drake's Island.[13] One alleged conspirator was a man called Edward Coleman. A vicar's son from Suffolk, Coleman had been brought up a Puritan but had converted to Catholicism in the early days of the Restoration. A charismatic courtier, he had risen in the service of the king and eventually found a role as secretary to his fellow convert James, Duke of York. He was, therefore, an obvious target for Oates, and so his papers were searched and – as it happened – he had committed some rather rash thoughts to paper. He had hoped that, like him, the English might be enticed to reconvert to Rome. They were statements that would cost him his life.

What really clinched people's willingness to believe in the Popish Plot, though, was the death of the magistrate Godfrey. On 12 October, he disappeared, and five days later was found dead in a ditch on Primrose Hill, struck through with his own sword and – it was later revealed – strangled.

Suddenly the Popish Plot was alive. The City Chamberlain announced that 'He did not know but the next morning they might all rise with their throats cut.'[14] Were not Catholics always plotting the massacre of English Protestants? Had a Catholic massacre not been narrowly averted in 1605? Had not one actually happened in Ireland in '41? Had they not burned the City to the ground in '66? Had not York's conversion encouraged plotting like this? 'I can assign no other cause for this dismal attempt but the hopes the papists have of the Duke's religion,' said one lawyer.[15]

Oates accused five Catholic lords of complicity: Petre, Powis, Stafford, Belassyse and the seventy-year-old Lord Arundel. Charles was unimpressed: Belassyse was gout-ridden and could hardly stand, Stafford and Arundel hated each other. Nonetheless, with a rejuvenated Shaftesbury pushing the agenda in the Lords, they were arrested and sent to the Tower.

Fears only grew. On 1 November, knocking and digging was heard at night-time in the Old Palace Yard. A French Catholic was found to be storing gunpowder next to Parliament, though it turned out he was the king's firework-maker. The militia were ordered to stop funeral processions and search coffins for hidden weapons.[16] There was a bill to exclude Catholics from the Lords (though not York), and Charles was asked to dismiss them from court, paying special attention to guards and cooks (who might be able to poison him). His hand forced, he sent all Catholics away from the capital (except tradesmen who already lived there and anyone else who could get a doctor to attest to their sickness). In the country, they were ordered to stay within five miles of their home, on pain of complete forfeiture of property.

Terror gripped tighter. Strange ships were observed near Chichester. Mysterious lights were seen on the coast. In the Hampshire countryside, officers were sent to investigate a weird knocking sound in Tichborne church, and to search the aisle that still belonged to the Catholic Tichborne family for weapons.[17] Then there were the night riders: 40 nocturnal horsemen near Whitby; in Wiltshire, parties of 20 men each night crossing the Thames bridges and heading north. On 16 November, Sir Edward Dering* told the Commons that something needed to be done, else 'nothing remains but to make our graves and lie down in them'.[18] On 17 November, Queen Elizabeth I's birthday, a huge procession took place in London at which an effigy of the Pope was burned. That day, Charles ordered the constables to draw up lists of local papists and those under suspicion. Three days later, he decreed that all Catholic priests and Jesuits be seized and prosecuted. Already by then the first trial of the panic was under way. A young banker's son called William Staley had got drunk and been overheard giving rash words in the Black Lion Tavern on King Street. In normal times it might have been allowed to slide, but in the heightened tension of November 1678 he found himself, to his considerable shock, arraigned for high treason. The guilty verdict came in and on the 26th, he was hanged, drawn and quartered. His family arranged for requiem masses and a lavish funeral at St Paul's Covent Garden, Inigo Jones's remarkable classical church in what was still then a relatively new square. The Privy Council, outraged by the impertinence, ordered his body exhumed and his head to be stuck on a spike on London Bridge.[19]

In December, rumours spread of a French landing on the Isle of Purbeck in Dorset. The local militia were called out, but could find no trace of it. By then, the Plot had claimed another victim. The Duke of York's Catholic secretary Edward Coleman was brought for trial at Westminster Hall, in front of the Chief Justice of King's Bench, Sir William Scroggs, three more judges and the thirty-three-year-old Recorder of London, a Welshman called Sir George Jeffreys. Coleman was found guilty, despite Oates scuffing his testimony, and went to the gallows on 3 December. Two weeks later, five more Catholics were tried at the Old Bailey. Again Oates was hopeless on the stand, though Scroggs helped the jury along with a haranguing denunciation of the Romish faith: 'They *eat* their God, they *kill* their King, and saint the *murderer!*'[20]

---

*He was the grandson of the Sir Edward Dering who had presented the Kentish Root and Branch petition in 1641 but who had baulked at the Grand Remonstrance later that year.

Later that month, just before Christmas, the order went out to disarm all known Catholics. Meanwhile, at Westminster Danby's position had become untenable. By the end of the year, it was revealed that he'd been secretly negotiating with the French on the king's behalf, for Louis XIV's money, but without the knowledge of the Privy Council. More to the point, he had been working to create a standing army at home, and he'd been sluggish in his response to the Plot. To an unsympathetic observer, it looked like he was taking French gold to set up arbitrary government in England, backed by a standing army.

In Parliament, Shaftesbury and his allies, including the Duke of Buckingham and old Denzil Holles, led the attack, and Danby was impeached. According to the impeachment articles, he was 'popishly affected, and hath traitorously concealed, after he had notice, the late horrid and bloody Plot and conspiracy contrived by the papists against his Majesty's person and government'.[21] It gave Charles no choice. Rather than allow the impeachment to proceed, he was forced to end the Cavalier Parliament. Early in 1679, after 18 years of sitting, it was dissolved.

A new Parliament was called for March, and in the elections Danby's supporters fared badly. But this wasn't all. Three days before Parliament sat, realising that attention was starting to focus again on York, Charles ordered his Catholic brother out of the country, to Brussels. It was York's fate that would divide the nation for the next two years.

The newly elected House went for Danby again, and, reluctantly, Charles was forced to send him to the Tower. Meanwhile, the king's standing army, which he had recently been increasing in size, came under critical scrutiny as, so the Commons would have it, something that was 'illegal, and a great grievance and vexation to the people'.[22] And there were further moves against Catholics. The Lords considered banning them from London, though they shrank back after having been told that this would 'shake the very trade of the City'.[23] In April, impeachment was renewed against the five Catholic Lords allegedly involved in the Plot. They were brought to Westminster by river from the Tower, arriving to a crowd of Londoners who had gathered in boats, jeering at them and waving ropes fashioned into halters and nooses. That month, Titus Oates's evidence, initially kept secret, was finally published, allowing terrified readers to pore over the machinations of the enemy within, rendered in type and ink.

Charles thought Shaftesbury could be bought off, so dismissed his Privy Council and brought the earl in as Lord President with a new salary of £4,000 a year. But it was to no avail, and soon afterwards Shaftesbury was pushing to raise the stakes dramatically. In May, a bill was introduced and passed in the Commons, to exclude York from the throne. It was explosive: the alteration of the succession of the Crown by Parliament, or, to put it another way, the subvention of the divine bloodline of the monarchy by the representatives of the people. Even those who feared Catholics cast around for other, less radical options. Could, perhaps, a successor have their powers so limited by statute that they couldn't present a danger? Indeed, there remained the critical question of, if not York, then who? Could Charles, perhaps, be persuaded to remarry? He wouldn't be the first king to ditch his Iberian wife in the name of getting a male heir. Or could he legitimise the eldest of his many natural sons? James, Duke of Monmouth, was popular, Protestant and principled, even if he maybe wasn't the brightest candle. Could, people wondered, Charles have married Monmouth's mother in secret? Perhaps, as one conspiracy theory put it, the marriage contract had been preserved and hidden in a mysterious black box.

There was significant opposition to the bill: some 128 voted against it on second reading. The Lords, it was clear, would oppose. Suddenly, Charles prorogued Parliament: 'all parted', said one report, 'in a mist of surprise'.[24] Now worrying news came from Scotland. Here an uprising by Covenanters in 1679 led to the assassination of a bishop. Oates's original allegations, indeed, had claimed that trouble would involve a Presbyterian rebellion. Monmouth was sent to quell the insurgency, and he scattered the rebels at Bothwell Bridge. In the aftermath, though, he was to gain much sympathy for the Scottish Presbyterians and their treatment at the hands of government forces. He saw first-hand the brutality with which the Scottish Presbyterians were treated, in a period which came to be known as the 'Killing Time'. It was an experience that helped create a profound sense of alienation in Monmouth.[25] His sympathies increasingly lay with Shaftesbury and those who would exclude the Duke of York from the throne. Not least, of course, because Monmouth himself was the next viable Protestant heir.

There was another great trial, this time of five Jesuits. In summing up the case, Judge Scroggs yielded the floor to Jeffreys, who sternly rebuked the defendants for their audacity in following such a bad religion. 'What a strange sort of religion is that whose doctrine seems to allow them to be the greatest saints in another world, that can be the most impudent sinners in this! Murder, and the blackest of crimes here, are the best means among you to get a man to be canonized a saint hereafter.' The verdict was guilty, the sentence death; 'after which there was a very great acclamation'.[26] As a mercy, they were allowed to die by the hanging, not the drawing and the quartering.

But there were signs the tide was turning. In July, yet another trial began, this time of Sir George Wakeman, a physician accused by Titus Oates of accepting a contract to poison the king, and three Benedictine monks. The outcome was different. The evidence of Oates and his accomplices was forcefully refuted. Summing up, a furious Scroggs ordered the jury to acquit one of the Benedictines, against whom there was only one witness. The evidence against the others, he said, was but 'discourses of doubtful words', while Oates's testimony was 'strange indeed'. The Popish Plot, Scroggs thought, was real enough, but was the evidence against these men convincing? Hardly. 'Let us not be amazed and frightened with the noise of plots,' he warned, 'as to take away any man's life without reasonable evidence.' Scroggs retired, leaving Jeffreys to hear the jury's verdict. After an hour they were back. May we give a verdict of misprision? they asked: the deliberate concealment of knowledge of treason. No, Jeffreys said, they may not: 'you must either convict them of high treason, or acquit them'. And so the foreman came back with the verdict. Not guilty.[27]

The reaction was furious. Leaving on circuit the next day, Scroggs had a dead dog thrown in his coach. Everywhere he was harassed by crowds sarcastically chanting, 'A Wakeman! A Wakeman!' That summer, though, the executions continued throughout the country: some 14 Catholics were killed between June and August. The toll was now 22.

Yet not a single person had confessed to the Plot. It was enough to sow doubts. The diarist John Evelyn still, on balance, believed in it, though he considered Oates a 'vain, insolent man, puffed up with the favour of the Commons'.[28] The government's line, such as it was, was that there had been a plot, but its authors were now safely out of the way. That July, though, Charles had dissolved the new Parliament. Now all talk was of Exclusion.

New elections were called, with the supporters of Exclusion enjoying considerable success (including the return, as MP for Great Bedwyn in Wiltshire, of the old Leveller John Wildman). Then, in August, Charles fell ill. York returned from Brussels and took over the government. He dismissed his nephew Monmouth from the army and sent him to exile. He removed Shaftesbury from the Council, and in October, he prorogued Parliament without it ever having met. The Anglican clergy were pushing back against Exclusion, using their pulpits to support the king and his brother. They warned of a return to civil war and religious anarchy if the Exclusionists got their way. Nothing, wrote one contemporary, 'was so common in their mouths as the year Forty-One'.[29] It was a reflection of how far the Restoration regime had moved in a conservative, Royalist direction. In 1660, many of the reforms of 1641 had been accepted and maintained: Star Chamber remained abolished, for example, Ship Money illegal. By the end of the 1670s, 'Forty-One' had become a byword for anarchy. Far from forgetting the Revolution, the monarchy was now trying to deploy it as a bogeyman. No more was it reaching across political divides; now it was playing to a gallery of its own loyalists.

Charles soon found his health recovering, and in his frustration at his brother for returning from Brussels without his blessing sent him away again, this time to Scotland. Here, in a development not unnoticed in England, a clampdown against the Presbyterians was well under way, with the government deploying a force of Highlanders and using violence and torture. In London, despite Charles's improving health, the political waters remained distinctly troubled. In November, Monmouth, courtier and playboy turned activist, had returned without permission, and so was banished from court. On the 17th, another great Pope-burning procession marched through London: it boasted blazing torches, a bellman shouting, 'Remember Justice Godfrey!', a dead body representing him spattered with blood, plus the Pope himself accompanied by two boys in surplices carrying bloody daggers.[30] Shaftesbury, meanwhile, organised a petitioning campaign aimed at pushing the king into allowing the new Parliament to sit. Charles wasn't cowed, issuing proclamations firstly reminding the country of the 1661 act against tumultuous petitions, and secondly stating that Parliament wouldn't sit until November the next year. In January 1680, a mass ('monster') petition, signed by over 16,000 people, was presented to the king calling for a sitting of the prorogued Parliament. Come the early months of 1680, loyalists were responding by pressing the king to 'abhor' Shaftesbury's petitions. And gradually the 'Abhorrers' and 'Petitioners' took on new names. The Abhorrers were called 'Tories'. The Petitioners were called 'Whigs'. 'Tory' was, of course, an old Irish word for a 'bandit', while 'Whig' came from 'Whiggamore', a term applied to Scottish rebel Presbyterians.

In the summer of 1680, Monmouth toured the West Country, a naked attempt to gauge support. He even touched for the king's evil, a startling show of his confidence in his own royal blood. Charles, meanwhile, shored up his following among the Tories. Publications expounded and clarified the loyalist cause, attacking the idea of the 'Original Sovereign Power of Mr Multitude'.[31] The Whigs, said the Tory press, were the heirs of Pym and Cromwell. Forty-One might come again. Had King Pym not called out crowds of Londoners, as Shaftesbury was doing? Certainly the Whigs were arguing, once more, that the ultimate basis of sovereignty lay in the people. Some, like the thoughtful aristocrat Algernon Sidney, were even talking once more about the Good Old Cause.

Sir Roger L'Estrange, who led the Tory press, mocked Dissenters and invited readers to recall how the Republic had brought heavy taxes, while Puritans had despised 'Comedies, Interludes, Wrestlings, Foot-ball Play, May-Games, Whitsun-Ales, Morris-Dances, Bear-Baitings, etc'.[32] Shaftesbury himself was mocked as 'Tapski', a reference to the copper tap he had attached to his body since his life-saving operation, and to his alleged desire to turn the English monarchy into an elective one like that in Poland. As forceful as anything was a tract by Robert Filmer called *Patriarcha*. Arguing that absolute monarchy was divinely ordained, and that it was 'Unnatural for the people to govern, or choose governors', it had been written in the 1630s but remained in manuscript (partly because it was too close to the bone during Charles I's Personal Rule). Now, in the heightened climate of the Exclusion Crisis, it found an outlet as an exposition of extreme Toryism, even though its author was long dead.[33]

The Whigs naturally gave as good as they got. Along with the petitions and the processions and the arguments for popular sovereignty, they mocked Tories mercilessly. L'Estrange, in particular, came in for regular harpoonings. In an especially effective image, he was portrayed as the loyal lapdog 'Towzer': and all Towzer did was repeatedly bark 'Forty-One'. A dissenter poet, meanwhile, christened him 'Crack-fart', and the name stuck.[34]

Once again politics was being played out in public, based on appeals to the people. It was becoming intensely partisan, and increasingly bad-tempered, focusing on mockery and character assassination as much as reasoned argument.

Parliament finally assembled late in 1680. Another Exclusion Bill was passed by the Commons, but the Lords rejected it. The Lords did pursue the trial of one of the five Catholic peers, though: Stafford. Oates was used again as evidence, even though there were many who, like Evelyn, had now decided that 'such a man's testimony should not be taken against the life of a dog'.[35] In the end, the House of Lords was judge and jury: Stafford was voted guilty by 51 to 31; Charles commuted the sentence to beheading, and the Viscount was duly decapitated shortly after Christmas. It was said, somewhat later, that '[h]e vanished soon out of men's thoughts'.[36]

By now, though, the cause of the Whigs was starting to falter quite seriously. The next year, it collapsed entirely.

Charles summoned Parliament to Oxford, hoping to avoid the tumultuous Whig processions that had become associated with the ever-troublesome capital. The Oxford Parliament now proposed another Exclusion Bill, so Charles dissolved it, again. But this time things were different. Three days before Parliament met, Charles had managed to get more subsidies from France. The revenue from customs and excise was improving. Charles made forceful use of propaganda to push the loyalist cause. Appealing downward to the people went against the absolutist instincts of some of his supporters, but it was the way things were now. The world of print, pamphlets and the public discussion of high policy was here to stay, so Charles might as well use it to his own ends. His enemies were already doing so.

On 8 April 1681, Charles issued a declaration stating why he dissolved the Oxford Parliament, and ordered it to be read in all churches and chapels. It claimed the king was committed to rule through Parliament: 'No irregularities in Parliaments' would 'ever make Us out of love with Parliaments, which we look upon as the best method for healing the distempers of the kingdom'.[37] But it also alleged Parliament was carrying on a path towards the monstrous rule of the Republic: 'Who cannot but remember that religion, liberty and property were all lost when monarchy was shaken off, and could never be revived till that restored.'

The King's Declaration after the Oxford Parliament had a huge impact: it galvanised loyalists and Tories, won over moderates and those who might have been wavering and isolated Whigs and exclusionists. From this point, the Whig cause was dead. Later that year, the Scottish parliament passed a statute guaranteeing their crown – which, of course, was still technically separate, even if currently on the same head – would pass to the Duke of York. Now, if the English wanted to exclude him, they might have to fight the Scots. In England, Charles's government overtly allied itself with the Tories, including the larger part of the Anglican clergy. The Exclusion Crisis was over, the Whigs defeated. Even the coffeehouses were said to be now 'so modest in their discourses, and the City so quiet'.[38] Without Parliament to act as a platform, the Whigs were lost. Some of them, indeed, started to contemplate extreme courses.

In the summer of 1681, Shaftesbury was arrested for treason, his rooms at Thanet House searched. Among the lodgers there, back from France since April 1679, was John Locke, who almost certainly had his papers rifled. Nothing especially incriminating was found, and when

Shaftesbury came to be indicted a London grand jury dominated by Whigs returned an *ignoramus* verdict, meaning the case was thrown out. But the backlash against the Whigs continued. Titus Oates finally had his pension from the government stopped. And that September, Stephen College, a flamboyant Whig poet and activist from Watford, was tried and executed for treason. During the Oxford Parliament, he had been seen around the university town engaging in political arguments while bearing arms. At his trial, it was alleged that he was plotting to seize the king. The real reason was that his vicious satire and anti-Catholic diatribes had been a thorn in the royal side for some time, not least because he linked Charles II's cause to the struggles of the Civil War. The Long Parliament, he said, had 'stood up for the rights of the people'; 'Alas! Poor nation, how art undone by a bad father, and now a worse, his son!'[39]

Then, in May 1682, Charles fell ill again, raising the prospect that York might succeed rather sooner than many had feared. A plot was hatched to rise up against York, but once more the king recovered, so it was abandoned. Others argued for a more radical course: John Wildman suggested assassinating both Charles and York at Newmarket Races. Another plot, again organised around Shaftesbury, aimed for co-ordinated risings on 19 November, under the cover of bonfire celebrations to mark Queen Elizabeth's birthday on the 17th. But there were punch-ups in London on the 6th between Tories and Whigs, so the government heightened security and cancelled the bonfires. Shaftesbury fled to the Netherlands and in January 1683, in Amsterdam, he died, defeated by circumstances, by an increasingly canny and experienced monarch and by popular Tory loyalism.

The more radical Whigs had now organised a committee of six, that planned for a coup. They were Lord Russell, the Earl of Essex,* Lord Howard of Escrick, Algernon Sidney, John Hampden (grandson of the scourge of Ship Money) and the Duke of Monmouth, who was now openly antagonistic to his father's regime. In addition to this, the original assassination plot proceeded as well, the idea being to waylay the royal brothers, on their way back from the races in Newmarket, as

---

*Arthur Capel. This earldom of Essex was a new creation at the Restoration, the previous line having died out for reasons well known to contemporaries who had followed the Overbury scandal of the 1610s, or indeed Royalist propaganda of the 1640s.

they passed near Rye House, a fortified manor in Hertfordshire. But it was thwarted when a fire on 22 March 1683 at Newmarket forced king and York to leave early. The whole web of Whig conspiracy was then betrayed in June. Arrests were made and trials began. In very murky circumstances, Essex was found dead in the Tower, quite possibly assassinated. This allowed the presiding judge, the irascible and now arch-Tory Jeffreys, to allege suicide, and to give an excoriating summing up in the subsequent trial of Lord Russell who, with three co-conspirators, was found guilty. All four were executed.

Monmouth went into rather half-hearted hiding at the house of his mistress in Bedfordshire. In November, he was reconciled with the king in return for confessing (in secret). Sidney, meanwhile, found himself the next up for trial: Lord Escrick – who had turned – was first witness and Sidney's own draft of his political treatise on resistance (*Discourses*) was accepted as second. The treatise, said the Solicitor General Heneage Finch, was 'an argument for the people to rise up in arms against the King', though Sidney said he was being quoted out of context. It didn't save his neck, for he was found guilty and – on a cold December day – he was beheaded on Tower Hill. Before the sentence was carried out, his supporters managed to publish and distribute an excoriating response to his trial, defending his position and his long struggle to uphold Protestantism, the 'common rights of mankind' and the 'laws of this land' against arbitrary rule. On the scaffold, Sidney said he was dying for 'that Old Cause, in which I was from my youth engaged'. He meant the Good Old Cause.[40]

On the day Sidney had been sentenced, Monmouth was pardoned and given £4,000 by Charles. News of the confession was then published in the official newspaper, the *London Gazette*. Furious, Monmouth denied it, but was then persuaded to 'own' the plot, before retracting once again and eventually being banished from court. He was then summoned to appear at the trial of John Hampden, and so he fled the country. Hampden was then tried, but this time there was no second witness and no convenient political tracts to provide the rope, so he was only convicted of disturbing the peace and sedition. That said,

Hampden was fined £40,000 and thrown in gaol until it was paid, which was likely to be never.

Charles and his Tory supporters made the most of what became known as the 'Rye House Plot'. In the summer of 1683, Oxford University, which was now something of a bastion of Toryism, had begun a censorship spree, condemning 'certain pernicious books and damnable principles'.[41] And from the country as a whole there were some 283 'loyal addresses', in which local communities professed their support to the king and the rightful succession, as well as celebratory bonfires.

The two parties were now firmly entrenched. No longer were the terms used simply as insults. In 1681, for example, the mayor of Reading held an event for local loyalists, which he simply called a 'Tory-Feast'. Moderates, on the other hand, and especially those who changed sides, were often derided as 'trimmers'. To hardline Tories and Whigs alike, such people were not to be trusted. Judge Jeffreys was particularly unimpressed by what he called 'snivelling trimmers'; 'for,' he fumed, 'you know what our Saviour Jesus Christ says in the Gospel, that "they that are not for us are against us" '.[42]

Crucially, though, the balance of power between the two parties was tipping decisively, even well before the Rye House Plot. Everywhere the Whigs were losing ground, the Tories winning it. Charles had, unlike his father, played his hand well, though he had been helped by a more robust treasury and by money from France. He had been able to use the Scottish Parliament against the English, and – more than anything – had used the Tory press to appeal to public opinion. This public opinion proved more loyalist than the Whigs expected, not least because there was a real desire to avoid civil war. When propagandists like the consistently angry Roger L'Estrange pushed fears of '41 come again', they hit a raw nerve in a generation of people many of whom still remembered the Civil War and Republic with horror.

Some Exclusionists now actually turned Tory. Back in June 1682, a newsletter had claimed Whigs in London were 'quite down in the mouth. They do not open in coffeehouses as formerly and the thinking men every day desert them.' Now the Crown launched a thorough purge of local government, from deputy lieutenants to magistrates. In fact, this process had begun at the height of the crisis. As early as April 1680, every county had received a new commission of the peace, and over 10 per cent of JPs were removed. The 'Corporations' that governed towns were bigger problem, not least because urban constituencies were responsible for electing around four-fifths of all MPs. In addition, they controlled who sat on juries. London was the worst: it was said to be so Whig that 'the king cannot hope to have justice ... in his own courts', something that Shaftesbury's case in 1681 had shown all too clearly.[43] And so the government went on the attack, using the writ of *quo warranto* ('by what warrant') to bully Whiggish corporations. The writ forced corporations to produce the paperwork that guaranteed their privileges; many couldn't do so (often such documents were lost in the mists of time), and so had to surrender their charter and receive a new one. The new charters were always made favourable to the Tory-Anglican local interest, allowing them to control local government and Parliamentary elections.

This in turn created an opportunity to persecute Dissenters, which the government took up with malevolent zeal. Those who attended Dissenting 'Conventicles' were indicted for riot (technically, three or more people gathering to commit a crime), and officials stepped up their attempt to ensnare Quakers by forcing them to swear the oath of allegiance (Quakers refused to swear all oaths, so their inevitable refusal allowed the authorities to throw them in prison). Tories and Anglicans argued this was bringing them back to communion with the Church, finally ending the schisms that had caused such political chaos throughout the century. But many, many Dissenters – whose only crime was practising their faith – were imprisoned, and, given the wretched conditions in England's prisons, some hundreds died. The so-called 'Tory Reaction' would prove one of the bloodiest periods in the history of English religion.

John Locke, by this point, had left Oxford again, this time for the Netherlands. His association with Shaftesbury meant he was viewed with some suspicion, watched closely by government spies who listened to him at dinner and in the quad. It forced him to become a 'master of taciturnity', though his fellow academics, for sport, would sometimes try to provoke him into venting his true feelings against the government.[44] He had plenty to hide, it seems, for he had evidently been on the periphery, somewhere, of the Rye House Plot. At one point he had visited the conspirator Earl of Essex's house at Cassiobury, near Watford, for reasons unknown.

He had something else to keep secret, too, for by now he had completed two astonishing pieces of political philosophy, thoroughly dangerous at the time of the Tory Reaction. They were untitled as yet, though to friends he referred to them under a code name, *De Morbo Gallico* – the French Disease. It was a common term for syphilis, but this was more than a crude joke, for the other 'French disease', to Whigs, was royal absolutism, and this is what Locke had written against. Framed as a riposte to Robert Filmer, what would become Locke's *Two Treatises of Government* unpicked the logic behind *Patriarcha*, arguing that the people were born free, had the right to choose their own governors and therefore also the liberty to depose those rulers if they transgressed the laws. It was, Locke admitted, a 'doctrine of a power in the people of providing for their safety anew, by a new legislative, when their legislators have acted contrary to their trust by invading their property'. And by 'legislators', in this case, Locke meant rulers: his meaning was that the people could legitimately depose a tyrant. It was an ideology that had underpinned Parliamentarianism in the Civil War and now, in the 1680s, it was to enjoy a rebirth.

With Shaftesbury dead, though, and with the Tory Reaction in full swing, by 1684 there seemed very little chance of any change to the Stuart regime. Charles was now ruling without Parliament, his state was bolstered by burgeoning revenues from international trade and the colonies, not to mention subsidies from Louis XIV. Locke himself settled into exile, spending much of his time shut in his room alone. Even his prized Studentship at Christ Church had been taken away, on request of a vindictive king who complained of how Locke had 'upon several occasions behaved himself very factiously and unduti-fully to the Government'.[45] He had been expelled, noted Anthony Wood not long after, 'for Whiggism'. Nor was Locke alone in his Dutch exile, for many of his fellow Whigs had ended up there in the past few years, including John Wildman the ex-Leveller. But much the most glamorous of the exiles now settling down in William of Orange's Dutch Republic was the Duke of Monmouth. As Charles II's Tory monarchy consolidated its hold, the duke rather than the Stadtholder seemed the most likely source for any potential challenge.

20

The Last Revolution

The night of 1 February 1685 was a restless one for Charles.

He rose early in the morning, and then collapsed. That day, the government put troops on standby and closed the ports. If these were to be the king's last hours, then there were two dissident communities in the Low Countries that needed worrying about. One, mostly comprised of Scots, was around Archibald Campbell, Earl of Argyll, son of one of the great Covenanter aristocrats who had challenged Charles I. In 1681, he had been sentenced to death for opposing an oath of loyalty, but had since escaped from Edinburgh Castle. The other, mostly English, followed the Duke of Monmouth.

The king lasted a few days longer, enough time to call upon a confessor, and finally to be received into the Catholic Church. But on 6 February, aged fifty-four, he died at Whitehall, in his bed, just a few yards away from his place of birth at St James's.

He had been, according to the diarist John Evelyn, 'a prince of many virtues, and many great imperfections', who 'would doubtless have been an excellent prince, had he been less addicted to women'.[1] Charles was a fun-loving dilettante, a spirited raconteur with an easy, personable manner, but equally he was someone happy to while away his time enjoying the pleasures of court and high society while his government became more and more authoritarian. He is remembered for his parties rather than the Quakers who died in his prisons, or the Scots Presbyterians who were tortured by his soldiers, or the slaves who suffered at the hands of the Royal African Company.

Ultimately, the fact that he died in his bed was his greatest achievement, but the main reason behind it wasn't so much his own political skill as the sheer unwillingness of the English political class to challenge him as they had his father, give or take a few diehard Whig radicals. That his reign had lasted so long was as much thanks to memories of Pym and Cromwell as it was to his own efforts. But even so, 25 years of political stability – give or take the Exclusion Crisis – was no mean feat given what had gone before or, indeed, what was about to come.

Charles left a secure England to his brother, who now ruled as James II (VII of Scotland). He had faced down Exclusion and the Whigs and had reinforced royal authority through a drastic purge of local government. He left Ireland at peace and Scotland in the hands of a loyalist, absolutist and Episcopalian regime. His empire was larger than any of his predecessors', with possessions stretching from India to the Americas. More to the point, England's prosperity and the growth of its international trade meant that the royal finances were in a better state than at any time under his father or grandfather. James now had an annual revenue of £2 million, and could keep standing armies in England (nearly 9,000) and Scotland (7,500), without recourse to Parliament.

The trouble was, though, that Exclusion had driven a fracture through English politics. Public opinion had become extremely important, and the royal victory had come through an alliance with only one side of that public: the Tories. The Restoration monarchy of 1660 had become the Tory monarchy of 1685. But Toryism was founded on two pillars: loyalism to the Crown and Anglicanism. Under the new king, those two would run headlong into each other. The question was whether James's monarchy would survive the collision.

James was fifty-one, a ripe age to be taking a throne. His religious conversion defined his life. It had probably happened at some point in the 1660s, in his late twenties or early thirties. Since then, so it was said, James had become 'as very a papist as the pope himself'.[2] He was also very much a military man. Having tasted battle on the field at Edgehill aged just nine, he had fought (bravely) with both the

French and Spanish armies, before becoming Lord High Admiral at
the Restoration. His hero during his exile was not his brother and
certainly not his mother: it was the brilliant French general Turenne
(ironically, as it happens, a Protestant).

With his accession, any previous misgivings about rule by a
Catholic king were quickly forgotten. On 10 February, just four
days after Charles's death, the royal court was said to be full of those
jockeying for James's good grace: 'not a Whig to be heard of'.[3] The
princesses, Mary and Anne, remained next in line, though Mary was
out of the country with her husband, William of Orange. They had
both been brought up as solidly Anglican, thanks to the intervention
of their uncle Charles II, whose Catholicism was never more than
skin-deep, if even that. And, while James's Catholicism was incon-
veniently rather more sincere, he was at least conveniently old. Mary
of Modena, meanwhile, now the queen, had suffered the tragedy of
five children dying desperately young, and a series of miscarriages and
stillbirths. To the informed mind of the age, her difficulties seemed
like a permanent condition and there appeared little likelihood of her
giving birth to an heir. Surely, then, whatever indignities the Anglican
Church would take under James's rule – and they started early, with
James quickly hearing mass at Whitehall – at least they wouldn't last
too long.

There was plenty of enthusiasm for the new king. James, like his
brother, was crowned on St George's Day to general rejoicing. In
Lyme Regis, 300 young girls paraded, fireworks fizzed through the
sky and the conduits which normally supplied the town with water ran
with wine. Loyal addresses from various towns were duly produced, a
task made easier by the recent purges of Whigs. The Nottinghamshire
town of Newark, for example, celebrated the 'great blessing of the
Divine Providence, that in spite of all Democratical spirits, we still
live under the best of Governments, Monarchy, wherein the Crowned
Head is not determinable by plurality of votes'.[4]

James was at pains to stress his willingness to protect the established
Church. After all, it was full of Tories. He told his Privy Council: 'I
know the principles of the Church of England are for monarchy, and

the members of it have showed themselves good and loyal subjects, therefore I shall always take care to defend and support it.'⁵ A new Parliament was called, and the elections went well for the government, though they were helped by a decent dose of sharp practice by their supporters. In the Cheshire election, for example, the Tory sheriff counted Tory votes, and then closed the polls before counting the Whigs. A Whig riot ensued, with chants of 'Down with the clergy, down with the bishops', and this was in turn followed by a Tory bonfire in which a copy of the Exclusion Bill was symbolically burned. But the result stood. Meanwhile, the ongoing *quo warranto* campaign had created a number of safe Tory seats. All told, the elections returned only 57 recognisable Whigs out of 513 MPs, though of course allegiance was never quite clear-cut, nor is it particularly easy for historians to reconstruct such figures at such distance in time.

Parliament met in May, and despite James unlawfully collecting customs before then, it all ran wonderfully smoothly. He told them, rather honestly, that the best way to ensure he met them often was to meet his needs. He expected, he said, to receive the same revenues for life as his brother Charles had, and Parliament agreed. What's more, the Commons passed a declaration stating that, on the question of whether James would protect the Church, they were 'wholly satisfied in his majesties gracious word'.⁶

That month Titus Oates was tried for perjury: revenge, finally, for the chaos he had unleashed with his accusations of a Popish Plot. Already in 1684 he had been prosecuted for *scandalum magnatum* against James, and – after an excoriation from Judge Jeffreys, ordered to pay £100,000 damages, plus £1 costs. Now, again, Jeffreys presided, and Oates had no chance: 'You are a shame to mankind,' the judge informed the defendant. 'My blood does curdle,' Jeffrey noted, for the 'infirmity' of Oates's 'depraved mind'. Moreover, the 'blackness of his soul' and 'the baseness of his actions, ought to be looked upon with such horror and detestation as to think him unworthy any longer to tread upon the face of God's earth'.⁷ The verdict, unsurprisingly, was guilty.

Then Oates faced a second charge – perjury again. Once more, Jeffreys treated the court to some horrified rhetoric and once more the verdict was guilty. Jeffreys would have passed the death sentence had the law allowed him, or at least the cutting out of Oates's tongue as had been possible in what to Jeffreys were the good old days. But instead the irascible judge had to settle for Oates being pilloried and whipped. As the punishment was carried out in London, crowds gathered, shouting 'cut off his ears!' and throwing eggs.

At the same time, two attempts were already under way to topple the new regime.

Argyll made the first landing, at Orkney, early in May, but his attempt to raise Scotland was quixotic and doomed, not least because he set out a hardline Presbyterian stand, rather than seeking support from moderates. On 18 June, he was captured by loyal militiamen, and by the end of the month he was dead, killed on Edinburgh's notorious 'Maiden', an early version of the guillotine.[8]

The more serious uprising took place in England. On 11 June, Monmouth landed at Lyme on the Dorset coast. He, too, set out a radical stall. Governments, he declared, were 'for the peace, happiness and security of the governed', not the 'private interest, and personal greatness of those that rule'. By contrast, England was turning from a 'limited monarchy into an absolute tyranny'.[9] He aimed to overthrow his uncle, and promised liberty of conscience, including for Catholics, plus annual Parliaments, judges chosen by Parliament and the restoration of old corporation charters. Although some of his supporters were republicans, on 20 June he announced that he'd decided to take upon himself the title of king. Gathering followers from the Whig heartlands of the West Country, he swung north. On Sunday 5 July, he was at Bridgwater in Somerset with roughly 4,000 men, mostly recruits from the local towns and villages with little military training. Late that evening, he addressed them. The king's men, he informed his supporters, were just three miles away, on Sedgemoor.

The royal army, under the French Earl of Feversham, comprised around 2,500 men, though they had the Wiltshire militia in reserve. They were a fearsome enemy, but if they could be approached under cover of night, perhaps they could be surprised. Monmouth told his men they must 'make no noise in their march, neither by talking nor otherwise', nor were they to shoot until ordered.[10] There was a full moon, and it was the height of summer, but still the half-lit night and difficult terrain made it a difficult operation, especially for

Monmouth's raw recruits. The path they took got narrower as they passed silently along it, and as morning approached a mist rose off the flat expanse of the moor. Their guide at times seemed lost, but eventually the shuffling nocturnal column approached the royal camp.

Then they blew it. A trooper, it seems, saw a moving shadow, panicked and fired his pistol. The loyalist camp heard and the alarm was raised. Now Monmouth had to act. He sent in his cavalry, hoping to maintain some level of surprise. Meanwhile, Feversham was late to the field. As battle began, he was still looking for his wig. But it didn't matter. When he arrived, he found his troops in good order, under the direction of John Churchill, a skilled soldier from an old West Country family – and ironically a former captain under Monmouth what seemed like a lifetime ago.

It was Churchill's leadership that ensured Monmouth's defeat. As the sun rose, the duke's men turned and ran. Many hundreds were killed while fleeing: more than on the field of battle itself. Monmouth was found, a few days later, hiding in a ditch. He had somehow made it all the way to Hampshire.

The reprisals were severe. The 26th was set aside as a day of thanksgiving, but gratitude was seasoned with retribution. In Scotland, there were executions, a massacre of members of clan Campbell (of which Argyll was the head), and some 177 rebels were transported to New Jersey. In England, around a hundred rebels were summarily killed. Monmouth was taken back to London and beheaded – ominously for the king, the execution was botched and the crowd reacted with some anger. Then came the trials. Under Judge Jeffreys, some 250 were convicted and executed – many suffering the terrible brutality of hanging, drawing and quartering – in public squares in Winchester, Salisbury, Dorchester, Exeter and Taunton. Another 850 were transported to the West Indies, a grim fate in which the chances of dying en route were about one in six.[11] It was important, said Jeffreys, that the 'Whigs' had 'the utmost vengeance of the law taken upon them'.[12] One of those who suffered was Alice Lisle, sixty-seven-year-old widow of a regicide. She had sheltered a fleeing nonconformist minister, John Hickes (also later executed), at her house near Ringwood on the edge of the New Forest.

Jeffreys repeatedly reminded the jury that Alice's dead husband was a king-killer and, once the guilty verdict was in, he sentenced her to be burned at the stake. The king's only mercy was to allow her to die by beheading – the last woman in English legal history to suffer this fate – in a market square in Winchester.

On 14 October, there were lavish celebrations for the king's birthday, including a bonfire at Drury Lane with Oates and various nonconformist preachers burned in effigy. But another side was shown when celebrations for 5 November were cancelled, and aggrieved Londoners put candles in their windows to replace the usual bonfires.[13] Rumours persisted that Monmouth hadn't died. A man claiming to be Monmouth was found in a house just beyond Hampstead, and treated to a whipping and pillorying. Some said over the coming years that he was wandering around the West Country in women's clothes.

More than anything, Monmouth's rebellion had convinced James that he needed to improve and expand his army. From now on he would rely on the royal army for defence, not the local militia. It was a significant step, and one that took real power out of the hands of the local gentry. '[N]othing but a good force of well disciplined troops, in constant pay,' he thought, could do the job of defending the country. By December, his army had reached a size of nearly 20,000, the largest peacetime force since Cromwell.[14] The government even began a detailed central survey of inns, so that they knew where their soldiers could find accommodation outside of their garrisons. It was a remarkable piece of data collection by the central government, in the name of military control.

Most controversial of all was the fact that some commissions were given to Catholics, in defiance of the Test Act of 1673. James was not just building up a standing army, he was putting Catholics in charge of it. This brought inevitable trouble in Parliament, meeting for its second session in November. The Commons presented an address to the king, telling him that he could not simply ignore the Test Act. He was incandescent, and sent a stinging rebuke. They set aside Friday the 20th to consider a reply; John Coke, MP for Derby, was defiant: 'I hope we are all Englishmen, and are not frighted out of our duty by a few high words.'[15] He was sent to the Tower for his pains, and James prorogued the Parliament, even though it meant losing a grant of £700,000 from the House. The Bishop of London, Henry Compton – who had not only opposed the king's promotion of Catholics in Parliament but had made the grave error of doing it calmly and rationally – was removed from the Privy Council. Meanwhile, several Protestant officers in the army resigned in protest at the new Catholic officers, including Christopher Monck, 2nd Duke of Albermarle, whose late father George had brought about the Restoration.

The clash with Compton got worse in 1686. Whatever loyalty to the rightful king existed, there was still considerable disquiet about the rising fortunes of Catholics. These were not just evident in the army: as early as May 1685, James had ordered a stop to all recusancy processes against any Catholics whose families had been Civil War Royalists (essentially this was all of them). He reopened diplomatic ties with Rome, brought in a Jesuit, Edward Petre, as an adviser, and even started poking around people's titles to ex-monastic land.

Anglicans pushed back. A group in London undertook to publish 'a great variety of small books, that were easily purchased and soon read', against Catholicism.[16] There was popular resistance, too: 'they would have no wooden gods worshipped there,' said a London crowd attacking Catholics at a new chapel in Lime Street in April 1686.[17] In May, in Bristol, the 'lower orders' staged a procession in which a piece of bread was carried about 'with much ceremony' and where two people dressed as a monk and the Virgin Mary canoodled 'very rudely and immoderately'. It was all done 'in scoff of popery'.[18]

Anglican ministers joined in. Those of London were especially vitriolic, and this was Bishop Compton's patch. In June, Compton was ordered to silence one particularly outspoken preacher, but he refused. James, by this point, had created a new body, a Commission for Ecclesiastical Causes, to discipline the clergy – a rather worrying turn and one that ominously highlighted the problem of having a Catholic as the head of the Anglican Church. Even the Archbishop of Canterbury, William Sancroft – a notably loyal Tory – refused to be part of it. It met, nonetheless, presided over by Jeffreys, now

Lord Chancellor, and Compton was duly summoned before it, and suspended from duties.

Ideally James needed legal backing for his appointment of Catholics to the army. With each commission, he had to dispense the recipient from the Test Act, but his power to do this was questionable. Thus, a collusive* action was brought against Sir Edward Hales, a Catholic officer, by his coachman, Arthur Godden.

Born into the wealthy Kentish gentry, Hales had an impeccably loyal pedigree. His great-grandfather had been a Royalist in the Long Parliament, his father among the leaders of the Kent uprising of 1648. In 1657, he had left Cromwell's England to seek education in Italy, where – at some point before he returned in 1664 – he converted to Catholicism. Come the reign of his co-religionist James II, Hales was a prominent man in the county where, as the new king expanded his armed forces, Hales raised his own regiment of infantry.

It was this that allowed Hales to become a critical test case. With his support, his coachman Godden had Hales prosecuted at Rochester assizes for holding a commission without taking the Test, and he was duly convicted and fined £500. This allowed Hales to plead dispensation, i.e. that the king had the right to 'dispense' with the penalties of a statute – in this case the Test Act – and that James had duly 'dispensed' with any fines that Hales owed. The case therefore went up to Westminster, to the King's Bench – the highest common-law court of the land, where it was heard in the spring. Happily, James had already consulted the judges for their views on the dispensing power and made sure to remove six he knew would come to the wrong conclusion, so the ruling was never in much doubt. James now had confirmation of the legality of his dispensing power, Catholics could now be appointed with ease to various offices, and James added a few to the Privy Council. Notable among them was Richard Talbot, an Irish Catholic veteran who had fought against Cromwell at Drogheda and who had recently been created Earl of Tyrconnell. Meanwhile, Hales

---

*This was a relatively common legal practice in which someone deliberately sued an ally in order to bring a test case and hopefully obtain a useful judgement

himself was lavished with promotions, becoming governor of Dover Castle and Admiralty judge of the Cinque Ports, the defensive line of fortified towns on the south-east coast, which also had an extensive role in policing smuggling. It was to be a significant appointment, for reasons that no one could suspect in 1686.

A judgement in the courts in favour of the dispensing power was one thing, but ultimately James wanted the total suspension of the Test Acts, and so this now became his key policy goal.

On 4 April 1687, James issued a Declaration of Indulgence, offering toleration for both Catholics and Dissenters, with a preamble that specifically wished that English people would become Catholics. The religious affront was obvious, but it was also a constitutional issue: he was suspending a Parliamentary statute using the royal prerogative. Roger L'Estrange, ever loyal, was brought out to support it in print. Tory Anglicans were appalled though, even if not everyone was entirely sympathetic to their new predicament. Some thought they'd brought this on themselves. 'You have made a turd pie, seasoned it with passive obedience,' Elizabeth, Lady Harvey, was reported as telling several bishops (to their faces), 'and now you must eat it yourselves'.[19]

Cautiously, Protestant Dissenters began meeting in the open again, despite their suspicion of the king. The biggest winners, though, were Catholics, who were now freely and rapidly ascending. Sir Edward Hales, for example, was appointed to the strategically vital position of Lieutenant of the Tower of London in June 1687, and he was able to move to a lavish and fashionable new house in Mayfair. At the same time, James was making aggressive moves to bring Catholics back into the universities. Late in 1687, he ended up in a fierce fight with Magdalen College, Oxford. First James tried to impose, as college president, one Anthony Farmer, who was both a drunk and a suspected Catholic; a man known to get women to 'dance naked before him' and who had on at least one occasion 'put his hands under a Fair Lady's coats'.[20] The fellows couldn't have this, so they elected a president of their own choosing, leading a furious James to use his Ecclesiastical Commission to bring them into line. The Commissioners declared the fellows' choice to be invalid, but did, to be fair, also find Farmer to be 'a very bad man'. So instead James put forward the Bishop of Oxford, Samuel Parker, even though he didn't technically qualify because he hadn't ever had a fellowship at Magdalen or New College (which the rules said he needed to). James visited Oxford, but the fellows insisted that electing the bishop would go against their fellowship oaths: no small matter for the conscience, even at Oxford University. A formal 'visitation' was arranged by the Bishop of Chester, which resulted in the removal of all the fellows bar three. Many of them, naturally, were replaced by Catholics and James's choice of president was duly elected. That winter, the new fellows were arranging for mass to be heard in the college chapel. This was too much even for Bishop Parker, but it didn't matter for, in March 1688, he died and was replaced by a Catholic.

Another bitter issue was James's standing army. He could afford it because of customs and excise revenue: England's increasingly busy trade – including that of sugar and tobacco underpinned by slavery – was paying for men, muskets, red coats and the newfangled plug 'bayonets' (an early form of bayonet, in which the knife was plugged into the muzzle, blocking it*), all without any need for Parliament. Still, James's army was so large that it increasingly had to be quartered in private houses, in defiance – as it happens – of the 1628 Petition of Right. Even nonconformist meeting houses were used. In London, meanwhile, a dispute broke out when troops sought to quarter there. The City authorities resisted, so the troops, with traditional military tact, informed the citizens that they were 'not worthy to kiss their arses' and were, in addition, cuckolds.[21]

James, though, still needed a new Parliament, for he wanted to make sure his policy of Indulgence became permanent. The fact that he considered Parliament so important shows the changed circumstances in the later seventeenth century. Although Charles II had briefly ruled without Parliament, few believed that personal rule was a viable long-term strategy, as Charles I had. Rather, James II's authoritarianism was, ironically, closer to that of Oliver Cromwell's than it was to his father's, though of course he would never admit as such. Like Cromwell, James rested his power on his army, and his willingness to

---

*The obvious flaw was finally circumvented with the invention of the socket bayonet, which could be fixed at the same time as the musket being fired. Ultimately, the bayonet would see the end to the use of pikes on the battlefield.

tolerate Dissenters – although in James's case, this included Catholics. Nearly all of James's revenue, unlike that of his father Charles I, had been granted to him by Parliament (even if, as life grants, the customs and excise didn't require regular *meetings* of the legislature). More to the point, as Cromwell had, James dealt with Parliament not by ruling without it, but by trying to ensure it had the right people in it.

The plan, then, was to create an assembly packed with supporters, so in July 1687 James formally dissolved the old Parliament. His government issued three questions to key office holders, including magistrates, deputy lieutenants, officers in urban corporations and members of the London livery companies. One: would you vote to repeal the Test and Penal laws? Two: will you work for the election of men who would vote this way? Three: will you support the Declaration of Indulgence by living in peace with your neighbours, be they of different religious persuasions? Most people had no difficulty with the last, but questions one and two were another matter. Many office holders tried desperately to avoid answering. More to the point, the Three Questions were used to force Anglicans out of borough corporations. Most counties, meanwhile, got a new Commission of the Peace. By 1688, a third of all deputy lieutenants and a fifth of all magistrates were Catholic, and there had been major purges in London as elsewhere. James was trying to create a very different local government personnel from that of his brother, more Catholic than Tory. One loser from all this was Danby (who had been released from the Tower in 1684), many of whose relatives had found themselves removed from office. Such was the old politician's disquiet that in 1687, he had been visited by agents of William of Orange. And Danby had promised to give him service.

William was keeping a close eye on developments, for, with James and the queen remaining childless, he still expected his wife Mary to succeed to the throne in due course. The exiled Whigs in the Netherlands hoped for better times. James had offered a general pardon in March 1686, though some, like the old Leveller John Wildman, were excluded. John Locke, meanwhile, was by early 1687 in Rotterdam, focusing on his writing, while his Quaker host's children drove him to distraction.

In England, James was desperate to protect his co-religionists. He knew the anger this was drawing from Tories and Anglicans – or, perhaps to put it another way, he had overestimated the limits of their loyalty. Instead, he was now trying to build an alliance of convenience with the Dissenters. It was a bold strategy, to say the least. Catholics represented perhaps 1 per cent of the population, Dissenters probably no more than 10–15 per cent. The proportion of Catholics was higher further up the social scale, as it had been since the Reformation. This helped with filling army commissions, for those of the officer class were more likely to be Catholics than the ranks. But in society in general, James was in effect alienating a vast Anglican majority to protect the tiny Catholic population, while relying on a new relationship with a somewhat larger minority of Dissenters, who already greatly distrusted him.

There were sustained attempts by Whigs and their allies to make sure England's Dissenters didn't fall into the snare. The witty Marquess of Halifax, in his bestselling (though anonymous) *Letter to a Dissenter*, told them they were being 'hugged now, only that you may be the better squeezed at another time'.[22] Gilbert Burnet, a Scottish churchman now in exile with William of Orange, even suggested that James, 'by transgressing against the laws of the Constitution, hath abdicated himself from the Government, and stands virtually deposed'.[23] Perhaps most effective, though, was a tract written by the Dutch Grand Pensionary Gaspar Fagel but containing the views of William and Mary themselves. It showed their willingness, should they come to the throne, to repeal the penal acts, so long as the Test remained in place. Catholics would still be debarred from office, but they would live in peace and no longer have their lands forfeit for recusancy, thus righting a great wrong that had been done to them since the Gunpowder Plot of 1605.

There was trouble in James's other kingdoms, too. In Ireland, Tyrconnell had been installed as viceroy, and he was busy promoting Catholic interests, notably in the army. Soon it would be 90 per cent Catholic: full, thought Irish Protestants, of the 'bloody Murtherers of Forty-One' and their offspring.[24] Some Protestants fled the country for

England. The earl's main aim, though, was to overturn the land settlement by which Cromwell's soldiers had taken the lands of the Irish
and – at the Restoration – been allowed to keep them. James, in fact, was
a major beneficiary of the Settlement, for he had gained vast Irish estates
after his brother took the throne in 1660, but Tyrconnell managed to
persuade James that most of the Protestant landowners in Ireland were
old Cromwellian soldiers and that the question should be reopened. By
early 1688, Tyrconnell had sent a delegation to England with proposals
for land reform. It was a difficult business. The delegation was followed
around London by crowds of youths mocking them by brandishing
potatoes on sticks, apparently encouraged by English Catholics (within
the government, no less), so as to impress on James the hornet's nest
he was poking. They knew that land reform in Catholicism's favour in
Ireland would only reinforce the prejudice of English Protestants.

In Scotland, meanwhile, James tried to improve the lot of Catholics,
while cosying up to Presbyterians, thereby alienating Episcopalians.
Catholics – only a tiny minority in Scotland – were brought into the
administration, and by late 1686, there was a Catholic chapel and a
group of Jesuits residing at Holyrood. James hoped to use Parliament
to give similar relief to Catholics as in England, but the 'Black Rainy
Parliament' of 1686 – so-called because of the foul weather during its
sitting – refused to comply, so he prorogued it. Later that year, James
admitted to the French ambassador that 'the affairs of Scotland had not
taken the turn he at first expected', and so he resorted to the prerogative
power.[25] In February 1687, in advance of that for England, he issued
a Declaration of Indulgence for Scotland. It offered limited toleration
for 'Moderate Presbyterians', and much wider indulgence for Quakers.
Then, in June, Indulgence was extended to allow all Presbyterians
similar liberties to Catholics, breaking further with the Episcopalians.

Two days before Christmas 1687, an official announcement was made.
The queen was pregnant again.

A day of thanksgiving was appointed for 15 January 1688 in
London (later elsewhere), but the reaction was muted. Notably so.
When Henry Hyde, 2nd Earl of Clarendon, attended the service at the
elegant new Christopher Wren church of St James, Westminster, he

found that the pregnancy was mocked 'as if scarce anybody believed it to be true'.[26]

In the spring, James pressed on with his plan to bring respite to Catholics in England. On 27 April, he reissued his 1687 Declaration of Indulgence.

Then, he raised the stakes.

On 4 May, the bishops were ordered to ensure that the Declaration was read, on two separate Sundays. This was provocation. Most of the Anglican clergy believed the Declaration to be illegal, and in any case, how could they read from their own pulpits a document that wished the English were Catholics? Most clergy refused.

In response, seven bishops, including the Tory Archbishop of Canterbury, William Sancroft, wrote a petition. Six of them presented it to James in person (Sancroft, who had physically penned the petition, was missing as he was sick). It asked to be excused from reading the Indulgence. James was furious. The petition, he spat, was nothing but a 'standard of rebellion'. The bishops were summoned to Whitehall on 8 June, where James demanded an explanation, but they refused, saying that 'no Subject was bound to accuse himself'.[27] So they were sent to the Tower, guarded by Edward Hales, whom they positively despised.

A week later, the bishops appeared at Westminster Hall, along with 21 nobles, including Halifax, Danby and Clarendon, who offered to post their bail (it wasn't needed for the bishops were released on their own recognisance). More to the point, Westminster was filled with a supportive crowd. If the bishops had been public enemies in 1641, now, in 1688, they were heroes. The trial was set for two weeks' hence, on a charge of seditious libel.

The main defence argument was that the petition couldn't have been seditious, because the Declaration itself was unlawful, since the king didn't possess the power to suspend statutes. Justice Wright, presiding, summed up. His belief was, he said, that since seditious libel encompassed anything 'that shall disturb the government, or make mischief and a stir among the people', the petition was indeed libellous. But the case involved a question of law, so the other three judges were permitted to give comments, and these were rather mixed. One of them, Justice Powell, told jurors that he believed 'if there be no such dispensing power in the king', then the petition wasn't libel.[28] The jury should base their finding on whether they considered the King's Declaration was legal.

Next morning, jury brought in their verdict. Not guilty.

The celebrations were ecstatic. The seven bishops basked in the acclaim. Londoners made bonfires outside the homes of known Catholics. News filtered to the army camp on Hounslow Heath, and even James's soldiers, the majority of whom remained Protestant, met it with loud huzzas and toasts.[29]

While all this was going on, though, the new royal baby was born. It was a boy.

James Francis Edward Stuart was born on 10 June. So long as he lived, he was heir apparent. Old Clarendon's grandchildren, Mary and Anne, were no longer next in line for the throne; and there was no doubt, of course, that young Prince James would be raised a Catholic. Now, what had hopefully been the temporary inconvenience of a bad papist king was transformed into a vision for England's future over several generations. It would be a hereditary Catholic monarchy, presiding over a nation of Protestants.

Some reacted in disbelief. Surely, it was said, 'the Queen lay under such circumstances at the time of the report of her Conception, that not all the Stallions in Europe could have got her with child'.[30] Others suggested the baby had been smuggled into the birthing room in a warming pan.

But what could be done?

The answer lay on the Continent, for the birth of Prince James was not just of English, Scottish and Irish significance. It was critical to the balance of power in Europe.

Europe in the 1680s was dominated by the decline of two empires and the rise of another. In the east, the Ottoman Empire had failed in 1683 to take Vienna and was now being pushed back. In the west, the vast Spanish Empire was in decline, particularly under their sickly and childless king, Carlos II. In the middle was France, rising to greatness under their absolutist 'Sun-King', Louis XIV, and with a vast army to match. The fortunes of the three empires were intertwined, and in turn they pulled in everyone else. Louis had been engaged in a policy of aggressive diplomacy on his eastern frontier, gradually and forcefully annexing territories, like Strasbourg and Luxembourg. But now, with the Turkish threat on the wane, the Holy Roman Emperor Leopold could turn his attention more fully to confronting the French. In Spain, meanwhile, the anticipated death of Carlos II would throw up the tricky question as to who should succeed him, for there was no chance of a direct heir. A fellow Habsburg, like Leopold, was one possibility, but so, too, was a Bourbon, like Louis XIV. Either way threatened a drastic realignment of the balance of power between the two rival dynasties: win the Spanish Succession, win the Spanish Empire, win the world.

Both Leopold and Louis were Catholics, but the former also counted among his allies a cluster of northern Protestant states, notably the Dutch Republic, under William of Orange. William bore particular animus towards Louis, not least after the 'Disaster Year' of 1672. Crucially, though, with William's marriage to Mary, he expected to gain control of the British Isles, their growing empire and their increasingly large navy. The Channel – and indeed the Atlantic – would be made very hostile territory for Louis, in any upcoming war.

The birth of Prince James changed the picture overnight. Now, with William kept out, there seemed every possibility of a neutral or even pro-French regime in London. At the sound of a screaming newborn, the European balance of power was overturned.

On 30 June, William was given the pretext he needed. Not for the first time this century, dissident members of England's social elite turned abroad for help against their monarch. That day, the same day the bishops were acquitted at Westminster Hall, William was sent a letter from seven Englishmen, inviting him to intervene. The people, they said, were 'so generally dissatisfied with the present conduct of the government' that 'nineteen parts out of twenty' wanted change.[31] It was a cry for help, evoking the discontent of the people, coming from key political figures: not just Whigs, who had always been suspicious of James, but Tory Anglicans, too. There were the earls of Devonshire and Danby, both large northern landowners – one Whig, one Tory. There was the Earl of Shrewsbury and Viscount Lumley, both of whom had been forced out of James's army for opposing its Catholicisation. There was Edward Russell and Henry Sidney (brother of Algernon), representatives of the navy. And there was Bishop Compton, who represented the Church. James's singular achievement had been to close the fracture opened during the Exclusion Crisis, to unite Whig and Tory once more. The problem was that he had united them against himself.

James knew that William was preparing a major naval operation – but he initially thought it would be directed against France. As late as September, he was still planning to call a new Parliament which, he hoped, would finally overturn the Test and Penal Laws. On 18 September, the writs for elections went out as expected.

Suddenly, James seems to have realised the danger he was in. Finally, he responded. Army recruitment was stepped up in England, and the Irish and Scottish armies were ordered to reinforce the English. Panicked, he started to drop concessions: 'to still the people, like plums to children,' said one detractor.[32] Anglicans were cosied up to once more; Compton was restored, as were the fellows of Magdalen, as were old Corporation charters. The Ecclesiastical Commission was disbanded, and the writs to the new Parliament recalled. The dispensing power, James conceded, could be settled by a future Parliament.

William's preparations were now proceeding quickly. He'd amassed £200,000 in donations from dissident English merchants, who wanted the Dutch as allies rather than potential belligerents. Meanwhile, William needed to appeal to English public opinion, so the decision was made to put out a Declaration of his intent. Gilbert Burnet, who was with William, recorded how a 'great many drafts' were sent from various people in England, consolidated into a single text in Dutch by the Grand Pensionary Fagel, and then translated back to English by Burnet himself. It insisted that all William wanted was a free Parliament and claimed that evil counsellors had corrupted James's rule, bringing disorder to the commonwealth: Roman Catholicism was ascendant, and ancient rights and liberties were being destroyed. It created no little debate, for it was a pointedly moderate manifesto. John Wildman in particular 'took great exceptions to it', and argued for a far less compromising statement, listing grievances going back to Charles II's reign and therefore implicating Tory Anglicans. But the moderates held firm.[33]

The most important thing now was to gain approval for a military operation from the Dutch States General and by the end of September, William had it. For now, though, the weather remained James's first line of defence. For three weeks, adverse south-westerlies held William's fleet of 500 ships – four times the size of the Spanish Armada of 1588 – in port. Then, on 14 October, James's birthday, the winds changed and blew from the east, but as William's fleet set out, it was buffeted and forced to pull back. On 1 November, the fleet set out again, heading north as planned, but again the wind intervened, forcing the fleet south, past the English fleet, into the English Channel. Sailing in a huge square formation, with colours flying and military bands playing, William's fleet sailed west along the Channel. Those same winds – and the tides – meant all James's fleet could do was look on.

On 5 November, the anniversary of the Gunpowder Plot, William made his landfall, at Torbay, in Devon, and began offloading the 5,000 horses and 20,000 soldiers, mostly Dutch. Soon, his force was at Exeter, where he established a headquarters.

All was not lost for James, though, for he had much the larger army. His land forces were gathering west of London, while the capital itself lay under the shadow of the Tower, on which Edward Hales was busily placing mortars to fire on the people should they rebel. The king had a formidable military apparatus to challenge William in the field and to quell any nascent uprising from the capital.

But in November, his government collapsed. There had been anti-Catholic rioting through the autumn. There were rumours that gridirons, spits and cauldrons and other 'very strange and unusual instruments of cruelty' were being hoarded at the new Benedictine priory at Clerkenwell, for future use on Protestants. Youths attacked the building, so the authorities fired on them, killing four. James, in response, ordered all Catholic chapels to close (save those belonging to foreign ambassadors or the royal family). The same month, there were uprisings across the country led by dissident aristocrats. At Nottingham, northern landowners issued a declaration to the effect that since James was a 'tyrant', it was not rebellion to resist him, 'but a necessary defence'.[34] The Duke of Norfolk entered King's Lynn and Norwich, while the gentry of the Welsh Marches, led by Lord Herbert and Sir Edward Harley, took Ludlow Castle. On 22 November, Danby took control of York for William, leading horsemen through the town to cries for 'a free Parliament and the Protestant religion and no popery'.

James was visibly anxious, taking opium to help him sleep, and now suffering recurrent nosebleeds. On 23 November, after a skirmish at Wincanton, he was with his army was on Salisbury Plain, but a Council of War advised him to retire to Reading. Among those arguing the opposite case – for an advance – was John Churchill. Later that evening, Churchill defected to William. He wasn't alone. No one could be sure James's army would fight for him, nor could he even be sure of the loyalty of his own family. On the 24th, the day after the skirmish at Wincanton, Prince George of Denmark, husband to Princess Anne, defected. Then came Anne herself – slipping out of Whitehall with Sarah Churchill (John's wife) – into the care of Bishop Compton, and north to Nottingham.

Anti-Catholic rioting continued. On 4 December, a crowd in Oxford of 200, mostly lads, smashed the windows of Catholics, starting at the Mitre Inn, whose owner had publicly disparaged those who had gone over to William. That day, a fake declaration – purportedly from William – called on magistrates to disarm Catholics. In the countryside, crowds of people gathered and stormed the houses of

Catholic aristocrats, looking for weapons, damaging furniture, raiding deer parks and pulling down chapels. On 8 December, Edward Hales's country mansion in Kent was attacked, his deer park ransacked and the animals killed. Now Catholic office holders were resigning in droves. '[I]t looks like a revolution,' wrote John Evelyn.[35] On the 9th, after another bloody skirmish, William's forces took Reading.

James was now back in the capital, but his authority was collapsing around him, and William's army was just a few miles away up the Thames. On the 10th, the queen was evacuated to safety, dressed as a laundrywoman, taking the baby prince with her to France. The next day, at 3 a.m., James left Whitehall, hurried down to the river at Westminster and stepped into a small boat, accompanied by his loyal Kentish servant, Edward Hales. As his men pulled their oars against the pitch-dark water, somewhere near Vauxhall, James tossed his Great Seal into the Thames.

That morning all was chaos. As news spread of the king's flight, Catholic chapels were attacked once more. Furnishings were taken and brought through the City in mock processions, with people brandishing oranges on the tops of their swords. Desperate to maintain control, members of the House of Lords who were present in the capital hastily organised themselves into a provisional government.

Soon, though, James had been captured.

He had accompanied the trusty Hales to a corner of the latter's large Kentish estate, on the Isle of Sheppey by the coast, where he hoped to slip out to sea. They had boarded a customs hoy, a small sail barge used for coasting. But they needed to wait to take on ballast. Around eleven o'clock at night, as they waited, they attracted the attention of the local fishermen, sailors and smugglers, some of whom undoubtedly recognised Hales as the notorious Catholic judge of the Cinque Ports, and assumed he was moving a spy, or – in the words of one of the searchers – an 'ugly, lean-jawed, hatchet-faced Jesuit'.[36] The curious-looking party were hastily brought to the breezy local market town of Faversham, and the suspicious Jesuit man was subject to a search of his undergarments for the treasure people were sure he was hiding, at which point his shocking real identity was realised.

Quickly, and quite against his will, King James II was heading back to London, escorted by a force sent by the provisional government there. Edward Hales was left to stew in Maidstone gaol.

In the country, James's Irish troops, now disbanded, were heading back towards the west coast ports, causing panic as they went. Amid the chaos, James arrived back in London on the 16th, where he was met by a huge show of support from the population. The expressions of joy took Williamites by surprise, and some tried to downplay it. '[T]here was some shouting, by boys,' one wrote dismissively.[37] Certainly London was more divided than William would have liked, but more generally, there was still a belief among most observers that once the evil counsellors had been dismissed, James could return as legitimate king. By this point, though, William had other ideas, as did James.

William knew he had to act fast, else he fall victim to 'the unsettled genius of the people'.[38] On the 17th, he sent troops to take control of Whitehall Palace, where James was lodged. Meanwhile, he worked on James himself, sending the Earl of Middleton as an emissary. Middleton woke James up shortly after midnight, bearing a message from William. Perhaps it was time for James to leave London, the message suggested, for it was going to be hard to ensure James's safety. Perhaps it was better for him to repair to Ham House, out to the west, for his own good. But James said he wanted to try Kent again: to head for the old cathedral city of Rochester on the Medway. William agreed, and offered a military escort – protection, of sorts. On the 18th, James left for the east. The same day, as rain pelted down on the new brick buildings of London, William entered from the west. He was met by a parade of Londoners, wearing ribbons and carrying oranges. '[O]rdinary women,' it was noted, 'shook his soldiers by the hand as they came by and cried "Welcome, welcome, God bless you, you come to redeem our religion, laws, liberties, and lives. God reward you."'[39]

On 21 December, William called together an assembly of the peers who were available in London. Two days later at Rochester, finding his guard had relaxed, James fled to sea. By Christmas morning, he was in France.

In London, the peers presented two appeals to William. The first invited him to issue writs for a convention* Parliament. The second asked him, in the meantime, to assume control of the government. This was a revolution. Excitedly, one of John Locke's friends in London wrote to him in the Netherlands, praising the 'wonderful success which the Almighty has given to the Prince of Orange', allowing him 'to deliver our miserable and distressed kingdoms from popery and slavery, which mercy we in England esteem no less than the Israelites' deliverance from Egypt by the hands of Moses'.[40]

The elections to the new Convention in January 1689 – England's second in less than 30 years – were relatively peaceful. The results showed a dramatic swing away from those of 1685. Now there were some 174 known Whigs, against 156 Tories (the remaining 200 or so were less obviously aligned). In the press, though, the debate about what to do next was heated. Whigs and Tories had been united in their desire to reform James's government, and even many Tories accepted the intervention of William. But beyond that, there was still huge disagreement on the constitutional future. Once again, the English were treated to a series of discourses, some thoughtful, some less so. Some radicals, like John Hampden and John Wildman, argued for a republic. *Now is the Time*, went the stirring title of one influential pamphlet calling for a republican regency while James was still alive.[41] Wildman argued for elected judges and a redistribution of seats to better reflect the population, one of the original Putney projects, though this time with a rather un-Leveller reform of the franchise to make the property qualification much higher (£40 vs 40 shillings), so as to make voters less susceptible to bribery.[42]

---

*Technically, a Parliament summoned without the usual royal writs.

Not everyone was convinced. The Scot Robert Ferguson, for example, didn't think a 'democratical republic' would suit the temper of England, for – he felt – 'the Mercurial and Masculine Temper of the English people, is not to be moulded and accommodated to a Democracy'.[43] Tories, meanwhile, were in a bind. Whatever the facts on the ground, and whatever they had done to ease William's take-over, many found it very difficult to countenance an actual change in the succession; at most, they felt they might possibly accept Mary as sole queen with William as a mere consort.

The Convention began sitting on 22 January 1689. That day a letter from William was read. The future of the kingdom needed settling quickly, it said, given the 'dangerous condition of the Protestant interest in Ireland' and 'the present State of Things Abroad'.[44] Clouds were darkening on the Continent, with a full-scale French invasion of the Rhineland now in motion. And with James still likely to enjoy support in Ireland, the uncertainty at Westminster was starting to look like a dangerous indulgence.

In the Commons, the Whig Sir Robert Howard argued that James had abdicated, even comparing him to Richard II. It was, Howard argued, a maxim of law that the king could do no wrong. If – then – he knowingly did wrong, then he ceased to be king. The 'Original of power,' he said, was 'by Pact and Agreement from the People'. The 'Office of the King,' said another Whig, was 'originally from the People'.[45] On the 28th, the Commons passed a remarkable reso-lution: James, had endeavoured 'to subvert the Constitution of the Kingdom, by breaking the Original Contract between King and People'. Having, 'by the advice of Jesuits, and other wicked Persons' violated England's fundamental laws, and having left the kingdom, he had now abdicated, and 'the Throne is thereby vacant'.[46]

But progress was held up in the Lords. One proposal, put forward by the Bishop of Ely and supported by many Tories and all of the bishops bar Compton, was that James's Catholicism made him unfit to rule, so his power would be administered by a regency while he was alive. It was defeated, but only narrowly. Then, on the 30th, the Lords debated the Commons resolution on the vacancy of the throne. On a cold winter's night, the candlelit house argued until 10 p.m. They agreed, eventually, to most of the resolution; but they didn't like the word 'abdicated', so they changed it to 'deserted'. And they voted down the clause about vacancy.

Things were stalling, so on 2 February, William's allies launched a petition, asking for the throne to be settled on William and Mary. The plan was for a large crowd to come down to Westminster and present it on the 4th. William agreed to have the petition suppressed, but on the 3rd, he made it clear that if Mary was made sole queen, an idea that appealed to those who wanted minimal damage to the line of succession, then he would return home to the Netherlands. This finally swung the Lords. On the 6th, a majority agreed in full to the Commons resolution. Church bells rang, and bonfires were lit, to celebrate the breaking of the impasse.

The Convention had not deposed James. They had merely decided that he had deposed himself. What this finer point meant in practice, though, was somewhat debatable, not least because James was soon trying to win the throne back. They also, meanwhile, decided that the country needed a public statement of 'such things ... absolutely necessary' to secure 'our Religion, Laws, and Liberties'. A committee was appointed, which came up with 23 'Publick Grievances of the Nation'. These in turn evolved into a Declaration of Rights, which the Convention approved on the 12th. Little of the content was especially radical, though it did commit one novel restriction of monarchical power to law – namely that keeping a standing army in peacetime was illegal without Parliament. The suspending and dispensing powers were declared illegal, as was raising taxes without Parliament. Petitioning the king was declared to be a right, and excessive bail, excessive fines and cruel and unusual punishments were banned. The Declaration of Rights wasn't to be a condition of William and Mary's accession, but it did neatly set out some of the ways a monarch might break the law, thus – perhaps – invalidating their claim. All told, while people obfuscated and tried to wriggle out of the obvious conclusion, the monarchy was now accountable to the law and to the people's representatives in Parliament. The 'Glorious' Revolution of 1688–9, as it would come to be called, had a softer edge than the regicide of 1649, but it was forged from the same steel.

The same day, 12 February, Princess Mary arrived in London from the Netherlands. She was greeted with 'the lofty shouts and acclamations of huzzaing throngs and multitudes'. Two days earlier, John Locke had boarded a boat at Brill, packed up 20 boxes of possessions, mostly books, and sailed for England. He, too, was in London on the 12th, the very day it became quite clear that the English people were about to oust their ruler.

On the 13th, a Wednesday, William and Mary were proclaimed king and queen. That cold February night, London glowed to the blazing embers of the 'very great and universal bonfires in every street'.[47]

Epilogue

In the seventeenth century the word 'revolution' was used more literally than it is today. Instead of a drastic change, it usually meant a cycling back, a turning of the wheel of power. It could be restorative as much as transforming, conservative rather than radical. It was an idea cut from the same cloth of that of the skimmington. The world could cycle between order and disorder, a revolution could set it back the right way up as well as turn it upside down.

On these terms, the period had seen many revolutions: 1640, 1647, 1649, 1653, 1660, even the restoration of royal control after the Exclusion Crisis could be viewed in this way. And the latest revolution, that of 1689, could easily be seen as a tracking back, too. James had upset the natural order, William was merely restoring the ancient constitution. In fact the 'Glorious' Revolution could be emblematic of the whole century: the Stuarts, from James I onwards, had embraced a forward-looking political ideology – absolutism – and tried to reform and override England's ancient constitution. They had been challenged during the 1640s and 1650s, only for that challenge to go too far for the political classes. The result was a Restoration in 1660 that cast out the upstart Republicans who had turned the world upside down. This, though, was then followed by a swing in the other direction, towards monarchical absolutism. Reaching its apogee under James II, this was in many ways more troubling than the absolutism under Charles I, because it was explicitly Catholic and because it was backed by a well-funded military. The Revolution of 1689 challenged that, cast out James as an agent of disorder and restored balance.

But there is another way of looking at the century, and that is to see a deeper, further-reaching change. Revolutionary in our sense of representing fundamental alterations. In the political sphere, the key principle that monarchs were accountable to the law, and to their people, were now firmly established. The regicide, often seen as a misstep, was based on this idea. The Revolution of 1689 gave a more acceptable face, associating it not with republicanism or Puritanism or with the military, but with a moderate Anglicanism.

And this is not all. At a deeper level, society was undergoing profound, if gradual, changes, that were ushering in a more modern landscape: everything from the establishment of a robust system of welfare to the poor, to the gradual reduction of interpersonal violence, to the disappearance of witchcraft prosecutions, to the slow decline of capital punishment. The economy, meanwhile, was evolving as a sophisticated market system based on efficient farming and international trade. It meant that some of the markers of pre-modern life were ebbing away: famine, plague, even regular urban fires (as towns were rebuilt in brick). In the vogue for 'improvement' lay the seeds of agricultural revolution, and in the increased use of coal lay the foundations of an industrial one. All this was also accompanied by the beginnings of a vast imperial project that would bring violence around the world, and misery to millions of enslaved people.

The Church had been through a traumatic century, but what came out was an Anglicanism more confident in itself and rooted in the words and idioms of the Book of Common Prayer and the King James Bible. After the Revolution of 1689, a modicum of toleration was added, too: Protestant Dissenters found themselves allowed to worship publicly, although moves to comprehend Dissenters within the Anglican communion – what John Locke called 'the enlargement of the boundaries of the Church' – failed. Even Quakers were increasingly accepted. Seen as less of a threat, they had become a sect of shopkeepers rather than revolutionaries: 'nothing like what they were formerly,' one Yorkshire clergyman observed. 'They do not quake, howl, and foam with their mouths', but instead they 'modestly and devoutly behave themselves'.[1]

To some, tolerance was to be England's strength. A generation later, the French philosopher Voltaire quipped, 'If there were only one religion in England, there would be danger of despotism, if there were two they would cut each other's throats, but there are thirty, and they live in peace and happiness.' (Though this didn't prevent him joking that England had 42 religions, but only two sauces: his Anglophilia didn't stretch to cuisine.)

Not everyone at the time was so sure. Toleration, raged an angry preacher in Dorchester, gave 'every man liberty to spit in the face of the Church'.[2] The fact was that religion was now enjoying less of a stranglehold on everyday life. The church courts, which had been used to control people's sexualities, were in decline. So, after the first decade of the eighteenth century, were the printed sermons which had formed such a central role in public culture under the Stuarts. And while people still looked for God's providence in natural events – fearing the implications, for example, of a great salmon washed up outside Whitehall in 1717, now the Newtonian universe existed as a mathematically satisfying challenge to this.[3] If God was just a divine watchmaker, setting the whole thing in motion, then Providence held no power.

Some of those who witnessed England's seventeenth-century upheavals saw their lives come full circle. Charles II had, for everything that had happened, died just a few yards away from his birthplace: a first son of a king who died on the throne he was born to inherit. His brother, by contrast, died in exile in France.

The most revolutionary thing about this century, though, was that politics was really no longer about monarchs. Certainly the personalities of the kings and queens still mattered, and the role of the aristocracy – and the House of Lords – remained important. But so much of the political story was now being driven by those outside the top echelons of the elite. The House of Commons now dominated at Westminster and the whole structure depended on the magistracy in the localities, and the yeomen, tradesmen and shopkeepers who held the smaller offices. The lower gentry and the middle sort of people had emerged as readers, political actors, voters, officeholders. In a cacophonous century, it was their voices which were new and most remarkable.

People of all classes rose and fell. Oliver Cromwell was born a minor gentleman's son from Cambridgeshire, but he died head of state. His son Richard began and ended his life as a modest countryman, eventually returning from exile (which he undertook to escape his creditors more than the Royalists who actually rather liked him) to life in rustic retirement in Hertfordshire. John Lambert had risen from a small manor house in the Yorkshire Dales to become the most important soldier in England, but ended his days imprisoned on a tiny island in the Channel. George Fox started off a Leicestershire yeoman but died a visionary who had founded a faith. William Petty was born and buried in Romsey, yet a clothier's son had become one of the foremost intellectuals of the day. Margaret Lucas began life in a thoroughly unpopular Essex gentry family, and ended it married to a duke. She was buried, when her time came, in Westminster Abbey, a stone's throw, but a million miles, away from the unmarked graves that now housed her republican enemies in the grounds of the adjacent St Margaret's. Jane Thornborough of Cartmel died in complete obscurity: her family eventually sold up and moved to Westmorland.

The 'Glorious' Revolution, as it came to be known, brought a late flowering in the career of John Locke. Within a couple of weeks of William taking the throne, Locke was offered a government position, though he felt compelled to refuse on grounds of ill health. Instead, it was his writing that was to flourish, now that it was in step with the political realities of the time. His works were freely published, not just the *Two Treatises*, but also his hugely influential tract on the nature of knowledge: *An Essay Concerning Human Understanding*. He wrote on toleration and on childhood. He devoted a short tract to the benefits of immigration, for '[i]t is the number of people that makes the riches of any country', and he turned his mind to the growing problems England was having with her coins, which were being 'clipped' for their precious metal content, and thus suffering serious declines in value.[4]

Locke still hated the foul stench of London, so reposed at Oates in Essex, with his great friend and fellow philosopher Lady Masham. Oates was close enough to the capital to be visited regularly by public coach, yet far enough away to have much clearer air. Here, in the verdant Essex countryside, Locke could enjoy the charms of country life, watching the seasons change and the swallows migrate. In theory

Locke was a paying guest, but in reality the Mashams let him get by for months on end without handing over a penny. It was an intellectually satisfying arrangement for everyone. Isaac Newton was an occasional visitor, and while Lady Masham would expound her views on the importance of a female education, Newton would discuss his theories on the books of Daniel and Revelation. Locke was fascinated by both, and he grasped the notion that Newton's gravity was actually an argument in favour of a divine Creation, for it was only explicable by the 'positive will of a superior being'.[5] He was in touch with Boyle, too, taking inspiration from the scientist – whom he occasionally met in London – to record the weather at Oates, using a hygroscope, thermometer and a barometer.

By late 1690s, the old philosopher was increasingly infirm. He still occasionally got the public coach down to London, braving the terrible smog there and the occasional highwayman in Epping Forest on the journey down. And he stayed in touch with the luminaries of the Royal Society. On one occasion Locke sought out the Society's secretary Hans Sloane in order to tell him about a man he had met in Paris some 20 years earlier with remarkably long fingernails. Rifling his papers before the journey, Locke found he had misplaced the written account he had made of the man, so instead he took something else to show Sloane: clippings of the 'monstrous nails' themselves. Sloane was duly impressed, and brought them before a meeting of the Society, who in turn ordered the 20-year-old 'pieces of horny substance' to be placed in their museum.[6]

Locke's mind was active to the end, and he remained a persuasive, earnest presence. To anyone who would listen, he would advocate for the health properties of drinking water, and he himself stayed away from wine and malt liquors. He considered the recent rises in the cost of poor relief, concluding that around half of those in receipt of relief didn't really need it. Pauperism was not caused by real hardship, he thought, but by a lack of discipline, idleness and the 'corruption of manners'. Those who forged passes allowing them to beg, Locke argued, should have their ears cut off for a first offence and be transported to the colonies for a second. It was a harsh way of seeing things, though Lady Masham defended him from claims of miserliness: he was, she said, compassionate to 'working, laborious, industrious people'.[7]

The 1690s were a hard decade for everyone, 'working', 'laborious' or otherwise. Harvests failed and prices were high. There was also a world war to fight, for the Revolution of 1689 had brought England into William's great coalition against Louis XIV, and the next nine years were spent fighting him. Before this, William had to defeat James Stuart once again, this time in Ireland in a conflict that culminated (though didn't quite end) in the Battle of the Boyne.

The European conflict brought great political change at home. William was regularly absent from England, leading the war effort on the Continent. Even when he was in London the foul air kept him away from Whitehall Palace and holed up in the fresher climes of Kensington, away from the centre of government. More to the point, with the cost of war ballooning, new forms of finance and government were necessary: a land tax, overseen by Parliament, frequent elections backed by a new Triennial Act, the foundation of the Bank of England and a national (as opposed to a royal) debt. All of these consolidated the control that the legislature had over the government and marginalised the Crown. It was a situation unthinkable to James I, and a much closer approximation to the political system under Queen Elizabeth II than to that of Queen Elizabeth I.

In early 1698, Whitehall Palace caught fire, in a blaze caused by a Dutch washerwoman. The flames tore through the old buildings, gutting the palace that been such a central part of the monarchy's life since the 1530s. Little was left beside the Banqueting House, the building that had been built to show off the absolute power of James I, but which had ended up witnessing the execution of his son in the name of the people. It was a fitting epitaph for a turbulent century. The monarchy never returned to Whitehall: it now based itself at St James's and Kensington Palaces. When the area was rebuilt over the coming century, it was not as the seat of the monarchy, but rather the government, as it remains today. Again, it was a distinction unthinkable in 1603.

John Locke died in October 1704, at Oates, with Lady Masham by his side, reading him Psalms until the end. He had felt like death was coming for some time. His stomach was bad, his lungs worse. Everything told him, he said, that 'the dissolution of this cottage is not far off'. Friends brought pamphlets, oranges and chocolate, and he was able to pick up his pen again, but come autumn his legs were swollen and he decided to sell his horse. On sunny afternoons he would ask friends to draw his chair out into the light of the sun as it set.

The country was at war with France once more, this time over the Spanish Succession, and had just scored a major victory, at Blenheim on the Danube. King William was now dead, and with his wife Mary having died in 1694 her sister Anne became the latest, and as it would prove the last, Stuart monarch. War would define her reign as it had her predecessor. England's army, led by John Churchill, now Duke of Marlborough and funded by a well-oiled system of tax and state finance, swept through Europe, winning a series of victories of which none were more dramatic than that of Blenheim in 1704. The peace of 1713 came at the cost of some concessions to Louis: the Bourbon Philip IV, grandson to Louis XIV, would now sit on the Spanish throne, but the two empires of France and Spain would be barred from ever merging. For Britain it was a qualified victory in a great world conflict which had seen fighting in Europe, in India, in the Americas and on the high seas.

By this point, England was joined, at last, into a new kingdom of Great Britain. With William, Mary and Anne all childless, there was a serious question of who would come next. In keeping with a world in which Parliament was effectively supreme over the monarchy, the decision was made by statute, the Act of Succession of 1701. It overturned any vestiges of the hereditary principle, barred Catholics from the throne and placed the crown on the head of the Hanoverian line, the descendants of James I's Protestant heroine daughter, and one-time Queen of Bohemia, Elizabeth.

But one critical issue was what the Scots would think. The 'Glorious' Revolution had been a rougher experience there than it had in England. Violence had culminated in the notorious massacre at Glencoe in 1692, in which government troops had fired on clan members who had been slow to pledge allegiance to William. James still had supporters there, and the movement in his name, and eventually that of his son (the 'Old Pretender' James) and grandson ('Bonnie' Prince Charlie), would take deep hold. So when the English Parliament told the Scots in 1701 to accept an obscure German – albeit one of James I's grandchildren, Sophie of Hanover – as their monarch rather than a Stuart, their political class began to contemplate going their own way. In the end, the answer was found in the other direction – a political union that would give the Scots representation at Westminster, much needed trading rights in England and see them keep their own law and Church. But the Act of Union of 1707 came at the cost of Scottish independence, and it was bitterly divisive.

Sophie of Hanover died, just months before Queen Anne, in 1714, meaning that the succession fell on her eldest son, George. Born at the time of Charles II's Restoration, George was Lutheran, spoke German and had little understanding of his new country. He should have been so far down the succession that his only claim, in reality, rested only on Parliamentary sanction. If the 'Glorious' Revolution had established the principle that monarchs could be cashiered if they broke the law, the Hanoverian succession finally confirmed the supremacy of Parliament.

Both of these were preconditions of democracy, but they were only steps on a longer journey. In 1716, the role of regular elections was scaled back somewhat, with a Septennial Act for elections every seven years replacing the Triennial. It was necessary – so it was argued – in order that Parliament would not be such 'slaves to the populace'.[8] Meanwhile, reform of the franchise, even of the old constituency boundaries, lay well in the future. In 1701, there were around 200,000 voters out of an English population of about five million (to put it another way, about one out of every six adult males could vote). The hopes of the Levellers in these regards were not to be realised until the Victorian age. And, of course, it would only be in the twentieth century that women gained the vote.

It was, in effect, a democracy of property owners: John Locke's commonwealth not John Lilburne's or John Wildman's. It wasn't even John Lambert's, for his written constitution had included both franchise and constituency reform, each of which would have to wait until the nineteenth century. If there had been a moment when a more wide-ranging revolution could have taken hold then it was in 1647, when Levellers and radicals had a brief chance of taking control of the New Model Army. Had, say, a Henry Marten or a Thomas Rainborough risen to political prominence in the way that Oliver Cromwell had, then a more thorough step towards democracy could have taken place, though we can never know whether it would have stuck. In any case, the moment passed. The Levellers were defeated, the Republic gradually moved back towards a conservative, even monarchical constitution, and the energies of English radicals were poured into religious movements. In a world where faith lay at the heart of everything, where human existence for many was but preparation for the afterlife, it all made perfect sense, as regrettable as it looks to us in our more secular age.

There is so much that is alien about the seventeenth century. Historians always must remember that the past is its own being, not ours. Like the Cheshire Cat, it can tempt us with a familiar smile, but fades away before we can gain the measure of it.

In the seventeenth century we might see a society grappling with new forms of media, with a divisive culture war and with questions about who holds power, and the degree to which Parliament is accountable to the people. Yet the people who lived in the seventeenth century were their own. The Stuart monarchs, Oliver Cromwell, John Lambert, the Levellers, the Quakers, Margaret Cavendish, John Locke, Jane Thornborough: all of these were of their time. None of them could have been from any other century.

We still have remnants from that past age – the Banqueting House is still there, as is the equestrian statue of Charles I. Across the country the people of the century are survived by thousands of buildings – from great houses to ordinary peasant dwellings – not to mention the great cascade of print and manuscript. Some of their traditions survive, too – Oak Apple Day is hardly noticed, but 5 November remains part of the national consciousness in England at least. There is still a tradition that the monarch cannot enter the House of Commons, and on state openings of Parliament they are ceremoniously refused entry, a reference to the notorious attempt by Charles I to arrest the Five Members in 1642.

Rushbearings, on the other hand, have changed beyond all recognition. They were long forgotten in Cartmel, at least. The chaotic skimmington of 1604 finds no mention in any local history, only surviving in the records of a lawsuit in the crumpled papers of the court of Star Chamber. People wrote about George Preston, who was probably there that day and who went on to pay for new carvings that still decorate the church. But they didn't write about Jane Thornborough, let alone Oliver Staines, the lad in the gown. By the later seventeenth century, a local antiquarian would comment on how rushbearings had 'formerly' been widely seen in the north-west, but were now mostly gone.[9]

The tradition of bearing rushes to the church would resurface in the region in the nineteenth century, but as a rather genteel affair. Children would dress in fine bonnets and country costumes, and there would be no place for raucous topsy-turvy weddings in the church. Today, there are annual rushbearings at a handful of churches in England's north-west. The closest to Cartmel is at Urswick, taking place in September, but the most famous is that at Grasmere, which has recently moved to the middle of July.

Here, in an ancient country church by a gently winding river, a distant echo of that old tradition takes place. The children wear fine green clothes, they do not put on masks. Teenaged boys do not put on wedding gowns and they do not pretend to marry other boys their age. There is no lord of misrule, and no one is chased from the pulpit. In fact, no members of the clergy are harmed in any way.

Acknowledgements

Every book like this is a collaborative effort, and *The Blazing World* has benefited from the professional input of so many brilliant people. More than this, I've also really enjoyed working with all of them.

My agent Charlotte Merritt has been absolutely terrific as a critical friend to the text and its author, always willing to advise and support, including – most importantly – giving advice that the author didn't always want to hear. It takes, for example, dedication to inform a budding writer that their book, in its early draft stage, needed 'about 20 per cent less bottoms and farts' (it still has a few, though). The team at Bloomsbury have been wonderfully supportive of the book from inception to completion: Michael Fishwick was an enthusiastic, inspiring and extremely supportive editor, taking a punt on a new(ish) writer and an ambitious project. More recently, Jasmine Horsey has taken on the book and got behind it with great energy and thought. The managing editor Francisco Vilhena and the copyeditor Richard Collins have worked wonders, excising countless howlers. I'm also not sure where things would be without the work of Molly McCarthy and Jonny Coward. Meanwhile at Knopf in the US, my editor Keith Goldsmith has been incredible, showing deep dedication to the text and saving me from many a stylistic sin.

My colleagues at Oxford University's Department for Continuing Education have been supportive, and – in particular – the many history and local history students at OUDCE, some taking diplomas, some Master's degrees and doctorates, have inspired and challenged in equal measure. Hopefully they will forgive my love of a good story, and my occasional testing out of the narrative on them in classes on seventeenth-century England.

Writing accessible history and teaching students are related endeavours, and whenever I write I always think about the great teachers I've been so lucky to have. At school, Jonathan Hopkins, Hugh Castle, and the late Alan Petford (who first taught me, in his inimitable old-fashioned way, about seventeenth-century England) all helped me to love the subject. At university, Emily Cockayne first got me into social history, while Laurence Brockliss did so much to support a wavering young historian taking his first steps into the profession. So, too, did my doctoral supervisor Martin Ingram, whose ability to root history in both precision and good sense have helped define my own approach, at least as an aspiration. Finally, the late Clive Holmes was a brilliant and galvanising tutor of all things seventeenth-century politics. His eye for the personalities and the action of history is something that has never left me. To him, the political machinations of Cromwell, the New Model Army, the Rumpers, and so forth were never dry, always fascinating, and – most of all – always thoroughly *dramatic*. Because that's how things were.

No history book like this is possible without the custodianship of the documentary remnants of our past by the very many dedicated archivists. The county archive staff, working in small operations with even smaller budgets, keeping watch over priceless fragments of history while patiently balancing the needs of preservation, history and genealogy, deserve special mention. Without them, seventeenth-century history as we know it would not be possible. I've also benefited from the care and dedication of larger repositories, such as the British Library and especially the National Archives at Kew. The latter in particular is an underrated national treasure and should be protected and cherished at all costs.

I hope readers of *The Blazing World* will get a sense of place, and of the richness and history that saturates the English landscape – rural and urban. In some ways this is a London book, for much of the action takes place in the animated urban environment of the City and Westminster. But I hope I've also found space for some of the sweeping drama of the countryside too: the battles on boggy moors, the riots in knotty western forests, the Quaker meetings on the wind-swept hillsides of the north, and the sheer intricate variety of the peasant cottages and country churches everywhere. My love for all this came from my parents, who helped me see and appreciate the world around me.

My friends, meanwhile, have shown great enthusiasm for the project as it matured. Rachel Antony-Roberts, Katy Pullen, Liz Kashyap, Vach Kashyap, Rebecca Rideal, Phil Abraham and Sarah Crook either read and commented on parts of the text, or gave the author many a good laugh while talking about it. Some even did both. Not inconsiderable sections of the actual writing, meanwhile, were done while I was enjoying the wonderful hospitality of my parents-in-law, John and Christine, especially in the fresh sea air and gentle pace of life in Les Moutiers-en-Retz in Brittany.

Most of all, my wife Sophie has been a constant source of love and inspiration. Her enthusiasm for this project has been unbounded, her support in times of challenge unstinting. Every word was written with her in mind, and if only one person in the world likes the book and it is her then I will be happy with it.

Between the first idea for the book and – finally – its eventual release, we were joined by Alice, our wonderful and effervescent daughter. She's now four years old and just starting to get interested in castles and historic places (though like her Dad she prefers those with things she can climb). In years to come, she may well grow tired of her parents droning on about history, but for now I'm just going to enjoy the fact she asks me questions like 'Daddy, what was different in the past?' and trying to think of a better response than 'Errrrrr'. If *The Blazing World* is me trying to pass on my enthusiasm for seventeenth-century history to the wider world, then hopefully one day I can also pass on my love of exploring the past to Alice. She has been like a whirlwind of fun for most of the writing of this book, and it is to her that I dedicate it.

Further Reading

There are some excellent general readership books on seventeenth-century England, and you can't go too far wrong just going to your local bookshop and picking up what interests you. The following books, rather, are aimed at those who want to take the plunge into more academic work.

As befits a period of constitutional, religious, social and economic turmoil, the scholarly literature presents an embarrassment of riches. But it can be daunting for those new to the field, and not every academic writer has the gift of pacey prose. These suggestions are not university textbooks or intricate and esoteric monographs with little appeal to those outside the profession, but well-written books that combine erudition of scholarship with effective and engaging style.

Starting with society, because that's always the best place to begin, the classic introduction remains Keith Wrightson's *English Society 1580–1680*. Based on a wide reading of diaries, autobiographies, legal records and so much more, it is a riveting and myth-busting discussion of social change. Its central theme, that the rise of the 'middling sort' defined so much of the age, was hugely influential to *The Blazing World*. In addition, James Sharpe's *Early Modern England: A Social History, 1550–1760* is also very fine, as is the recent collection of essays edited by Keith Wrightson, *A Social History of England, 1550–1750*. Wrightson has also given us the best introduction to the economic history of the period, in *Earthly Necessities: Economic Lives in Early Modern Britain*.

The social history of the seventeenth century remains an extraordinarily rich field: the profusion of documentation that underpins my book has made this one of the most picked-over periods. There is really so much to choose from: Alexandra Walsham's *The Reformation of the Landscape: Religion, Identity and Memory in Early Modern Britain and Ireland* gives a sense of how cultural understandings of the very land itself saw dramatic upheaval, Sara Mendelson and Patricia Crawford's book on *Women in Early Modern England, 1550–1720* is vivid and engrossing. Steve Hindle's *The State and Social Change in Early Modern England, c. 1550–1640* and *On the Parish? The Micro-Politics of Poor Relief in Rural England* are a great way of understanding social policy, and James Sharpe's *Instruments of Darkness: Witchcraft in Early Modern England* remains the best overview of the witch trials. Sharpe has also given us a great introduction to crime in the period, with his *Crime in Early Modern England, 1550–1750* although another way into this perennially gripping topic is Alan Macfarlane's *The Justice and the Mare's Ale: Law and Disorder in Seventeenth-Century England* on a specific gang of violent criminals operating near the Lake District in the later century.

For the intersection between society and politics, Susan Amussen and David Underdown's *Gender, Culture and Politics in England, 1560–1640: Turning the World Upside Down* is a fascinating recent addition to the literature, showing the deep levels of conflict in the early Stuart period. Scientific culture, meanwhile, is gloriously explored by Michael Hunter in *Science and Society in Restoration England*, while the same author's *John Aubrey and the Realm of Learning* is an endlessly fascinating account of an absorbing character. Finally, some wonderful primary sources are available to the general reader. Samuel Pepys's diary is well known and, frankly, entirely deserving of the hype, but Richard Gough's 'History of Myddle' (two modern editions are easily found via second-hand retailers), which consists of his memoirs of life in a small rural village in Shropshire, is just as illuminating. Readers will also find key constitutional documents, diaries and autobiographies, newspapers and so much more all easily available in print.

High politics has, naturally, brought some wonderful historical writing. Some readers will have noted my preference for J. P. Sommerville's *Royalists and Patriots: Political Ideology in England, 1603–1640* as an introduction to the constitutional conflicts of the age. And, for all his idiosyncrasies, I don't think that Patrick Collinson's work on Puritanism has ever been surpassed, and his prose was always crisp and engaging, which helps a lot: try his *The Birthpangs of Protestant England: Religious and Cultural Change in the Sixteenth and Seventeenth Centuries* as a starting point. Nonetheless the reader could do a lot worse than immerse themselves in the work of, say, Peter Lake for more recent discussions of faith and conflict.

The political narrative itself is confusing and complicated. To get an overview, Tim Harris's three great narrative books are superb. They cover the period up to 1642 (*Rebellion: Britain's First Stuart Kings, 1567–1642*), the reign of Charles II (*Restoration: Charles II and his Kingdoms, 1660–1865*), and the reign and fall of James II (*Revolution: The Great Crisis of the British Monarchy, 1685–1720*). The three books are especially successful at integrating Scotland and Ireland, and Harris is also unusually good on the social depth of politics. To Harris, as to me, the people mattered. To fill in the chronological gap, Austin Woolrych's *Britain in Revolution, 1625–1660* is a bit of a door-stopper, but it's judicious, clear, and reads well.

Rulers themselves are well served, of course: Pauline Croft's study of James VI and I, *King James* is judicious and accessible, Richard Cust's political biography *Charles I: A Political Life* not only gets the measure of this elusive man but also sets him in the context of his times. For Cromwell, Antonia Frasier's *Oliver Cromwell: Our Chief of Men* remains a great starting point, as is the collection of essays *Oliver Cromwell and the English Revolution*, edited by John Morrill. Charles II is the subject of a fine biography, *Charles the Second: King of England, Scotland and Ireland* by Ronald Hutton (whose study of the Restoration – *The Restoration: A Political and Religious History of England and Wales, 1658–1667* itself remains indispensable).

On the origins of the mid-century crisis, Ann Hughes's book on the causes of the Civil War, called *The Causes of the English Civil War*, is indispensable, and Clive Holmes's *Why Was Charles I Executed?* is snappy and elegantly argued, covering some of the major questions of the period. On the mid-century upheavals themselves, Christopher Hill's *The World Turned Upside Down: Radical Ideas during the English Revolution*, for all its arguable over-enthusiasm, remains essential reading. Michael Braddick has given us a very fine and hap-pily readable narrative of the course of events, including the war itself, in *God's Fury, England's Fire: A New History of the English Civil*

Wars while Dianne Purkiss's book *The English Civil War: A People's History* is rich with character and full of fascinating social history.

Special mention, finally, should be made to three riveting books which detail three especially revolutionary moments. John Adamson's *The Noble Revolt: The Overthrow of Charles I* is a remarkable narrative of the early months of the Long Parliament, written in elegant and atmospheric prose. Meanwhile, Veronica Wedgwood's telling of the king's execution and the events that led up to it, *The Trial of Charles I*, remains unsurpassed not least in pace and pathos. In between these, covering the great political breakdown of 1647, the rise to power of the New Model Army, and the endlessly fascinating 'Putney Debates', is perhaps my favourite book on the whole period: Austin Woolrych's *Soldiers and Statesmen: The General Council of the Army and its Debates, 1647–1648*. It's not only meticulously researched and analytically clear, but also compulsive and – dare it be said for a genuine academic text – even exciting. It's one of those books that every student of Stuart England should read, if they haven't already.

Notes

INTRODUCTION

1 P. Seaward (ed.), *The Clarendon Edition of the Works of Thomas Hobbes, vol. 10: Behemoth, or the Long Parliament* (Oxford, 2010), p. 128.
2 R. Dallington, *Aphorismes Civill and Militarie* (London, 1613), p. 211.

1. ST JAMES'S DAY

1 F. Bacon, *The Essayes or Counsels, Civill and Moral, of Francis Lord Verulam, Viscount St Albans*, London, 1625, p. 214.
2 J. Healey, 'The Curious Case of the Cartmel Cross-Dresser: Recusants, Revelry and Resistance in Lancashire, 1604', in N. Hodgson, A. Fuller, J. McCallum and N. Morton (eds.), *Religion and Conflict in Medieval and Early Modern Worlds*, London, 2020, pp. 79–95.
3 K. Thomas, *Religion and the Decline of Magic: Studies in Popular Beliefs in Sixteenth and Seventeenth Century England*, London, 1972, pp. 541–2.
4 D. Cressy, *Travesties and Transgressions in Tudor and Stuart England*, Oxford, 1999, pp. 29–50.
5 Thomas, *Religion and the Decline of Magic*, p. 104.
6 M. Ingram, 'Ridings, Rough Music and the "Reform of Popular Culture", in Early Modern England', *Past and Present*, 105 (1984), pp. 79–113.
7 Thomas, *Religion and the Decline of Magic*, p. 195.
8 'The Life of Master John Shaw', in *Yorkshire Diaries and Autobiographies of the Seventeenth and Eighteenth Centuries*, Surtees Society, 65 (1877), pp. 138–9.

9 N. Tyacke, 'Puritanism, Arminianism and Counter-Revolution', in C. Russell (ed.), *The Origins of the English Civil War*, London, 1973, pp. 119–43.

10 Healey, 'Curious Case', p. 91.

11 P. Collinson, 'Elizabethan and Jacobean Puritanism as Forms of Popular Religious Culture', in C. Durston and J. Eales (eds.), *The Culture of English Puritanism*, London, 1996, pp. 32–57.

12 J. Aubrey, *Brief Lives*, ed. K. Bennett, Oxford, 2015, p. 649.

13 W. Abbot (ed.), *The Writings and Speeches of Oliver Cromwell*, 4 vols, Oxford, 1988, I, 96–7.

14 P. Lake, ' "A Charitable Christian Hatred": the Godly and their Enemies in the 1630s', in Durston and Eales (eds.), *Culture of English Puritanism*, pp. 145–83.

15 W. Stoughton, *An Assertion for True and Christian Church-Policie*, Middelburg, 1604, pp. 246–7.

16 W. Barlow, *One of the Four Sermons Preached Before the Kings Majestie, at Hampton Court in September last*, London, 1606, unpaginated.

17 D. Underdown, *Revel, Riot and Rebellion: Popular Culture in England, 1603–1660*, Oxford, 1985, p. 48.

18 G. Gifford, *A Brief Discourse of Certaine Points of the Religion which is among the Common Sort of Christians*, London, 1581, f. 3r. This was a pro-Puritan book, though the line ventriloquised a common complaint about the Godly.

19 J. Bruce (ed.), *The Diary of John Manningham of the Middle Temple, and of Bradbourne, Kent, Barrister-at-Law, 1602–1603*, London, 1868, p. 156.

20 The National Archives [TNA], STAC 8/252/2.

21 H. Alford (ed.), *The Works of John Donne, DD, Dean of St Paul's, 1622–31*, 6 vols, London, 1839, III, 344.

22 *Stuart Royal Proclamations*, vol. I, *Royal Proclamations of King James I, 1603– 1625*, ed. James F. Larkin and Paul L. Hughes, Oxford, 1973, no. 6, p. 14.

23 T. Harris, *Rebellion: Britain's First Stuart Kings, 1567–1642*, Oxford, 2014, p. 71.

24 Ibid., pp. 80–84.

25 D. Cressy, *Charles I and the People of England*, Oxford, 2015, p. 246.

26 M. Ingram, *Church Courts, Sex and Marriage in England, 1570–1640*, Cambridge, 1986; L. Gowing, *Domestic Dangers: Women, Words and Sex in Early Modern London*, Oxford, 1996.

27 TNA, STAC 8/252/2; also STAC 5/R26/20.

28 TNA, SP 14/17 f. 15.

29 TNA, SP 14/2/51.
30 A. Fraser, *The Gunpowder Plot: Terror and Faith in 1605*, London, 1996, p. 150.
31 C. Jackson, *Devil-Land: England Under Siege, 1588–1688*, London, 2021, p. xxxviii.
32 3 James I, c. 4.

2. THE SMART OF THESE ENCROACHING TYRANTS

1 J. Walter, 'John Reynolds (c. 1607)', *Oxford Dictionary of National Biography [ODNB]* (2008).
2 I. Habib, *Black Lives in the English Archives, 1500–1677*, London, 2008.
3 A. Appleby, *Famine in Tudor and Stuart England*, Liverpool, 1978.
4 S. Hindle, *The State and Social Change in Early Modern England, c. 1550-1640*, Basingstoke, 2002.
5 TNA, STAC 8/123/16.
6 A. Shepard, *Meanings of Manhood in Early Modern England*, Oxford, 2003.
7 J. Walter, 'A "Rising of the People"? The Oxfordshire Rising of 1596', *Past and Present*, 107 (1985), pp. 90–143.
8 Walter, '"Rising of the People", p. 108.
9 E. Gay, 'The Midland Revolt and the Inquisitions of Depopulation of 1607', *Transactions of the Royal Historical Society*, 18 (1904), p. 212.
10 Ibid., p. 215.
11 Thomas, *Religion and the Decline of Magic*, p. 97.
12 J. Walter, '"The Pooremans Joy and the Gentlemans Plague": A Lincolnshire Libel and the Politics of Sedition in Early Modern England', *Past and Present*, 203 (2009), pp. 29–67.
13 J. Stow, *Annales, or a General Chronicle of England*, London, 1631, p. 890.
14 J. Martin, *Feudalism to Capitalism: Peasant and Landlord in English Agrarian Development*, London, 1986, p. 169.
15 Ibid., p. 171.
16 Walter, 'John Reynolds'.
17 R. Page, 'New Insights into the Newton Riot of 1607', *Northamptonshire Past and Present*, 71 (2018), p. 22.
18 J. Stow and E. Howes, *The Annales, or A Generall Chronicle of England*, London, 1615, p. 889.
19 Ibid.

20 T. Fuller, *The Holy State*, London, 1642, p. 117.

21 A. Shepard, *Accounting for Oneself: Worth, Status and the Social Order in Early Modern England*, Oxford, 2015, p. 69.

22 M. Campbell, *The English Yeoman under Elizabeth and the Early Stuarts*, London, 1942.

23 Aubrey, *Brief Lives*, p. 351.

24 J. Aubrey, *The Natural History and Antiquities of the County of Surrey*, 5 vols, London, 1718, III, pp. 280–81.

25 C. Muldrew, 'The "Middling Sort": An Emergent Cultural Identity', in K. Wrightson (ed.), *English Social History, 1500–1750*, Cambridge, 2017, p. 294.

26 K. Wrightson, '"Sorts of People" in Tudor and Stuart England', in J. Barry and C. Brooks (eds.), *The Middle Sort of People: Culture, Society and Politics in England, 1550–1800*, London, 1994, pp. 28–51.

27 A. Fox, *Oral and Literate Culture in England, 1500–1700*, Oxford, 2000, p. 46.

28 D. Underdown, *A Freeborn People: Politics and the Nation in Seventeenth-Century England*, Oxford, 1996, p. 46.

29 J. Howell, *Paroimiographia Proverbs, or Old Sayed Sawes & Adages in English*, London, 1659, p. 13.

30 J. Sommerville, *Royalists and Patriots: Politics and Ideology in England, 1603–1640*, Oxford, 2014, p. 70.

31 Ibid., p. 109.

32 Ibid., p. 44.

33 C. Muldrew, *The Economy of Obligation: The Culture of Credit and Social Relations in Early Modern England*, Basingstoke, 1998.

34 R. B. Manning, *Hunter and Poachers: A Social and Cultural History of Unlawful Hunting in England, 1485–1640*, Oxford, 1993, p. 203.

35 Sommerville, *Royalists and Patriots*, p. 141.

36 Ibid., p. 240.

37 J. Wormald, *James VI and I: Collected Essays*, Edinburgh, 2021, p. 59.

38 Thomas, *Religion and the Decline of Magic*, p. 506.

39 S. Amussen and D. Underdown, *Gender, Culture and Politics in England, 1560–1640*, London, 2017, pp. 31–50.

40 V. Gregory, 'William Bradshaw (1570–1618)', *ODNB* (2008).

41 D. Como, 'Bartholomew Legate (c. 1612)', *ODNB* (2004).

42 S. Wright, 'Edward Wightman (c. 1580–1612)', *ODNB* (2004).

43 Underdown, *Freeborn People*, p. 28.

44 T. Sutton, *Englands First and Second Summons. Two Sermons preached at St Pauls Crosse*, London, 1616, p. 58.

45 J. Day, *Day's Festivals, or Twelve of his Sermons*, Oxford, 1615, p. 346.

46 Cressy, *Travesties and Transgressions*, p. 43.

47 King James I, *His Majesties Speech in the Starre-Chamber, the xx of June Anno 1616*, London, 1616.

48 Thomas, *Religion and the Decline of Magic*, p. 21.

49 M. Dalton, *The Countrey Justice*, revised edn, London, 1670, p. 27.

50 Cambridge University Library, Ely Diocesan Records, B2/35, fol. 85r.

51 J. Kent, ' "Folk Justice" and Royal Justice in Early Seventeenth-Century England: a "Charivari" in the Midlands', *Midland History*, 8 (1983), pp. 70–85; M. Ingram, 'Juridical Folklore in England Illustrated by Rough Music', in C. Brooks and M. Lobban (eds.), *Communities and Courts in Britain, 1150–1900*, London, 1997, pp. 72–3.

52 D. Underdown, ' "But the Shows of their Street": Civic Pageantry and Charivari in a Somerset Town, 1607', *Journal of British Studies*, 50 (2011), pp. 4–23.

53 J. Tait, 'The Declaration of Sports for Lancashire (1617)', *English Historical Review*, 32 (1917), pp. 561–8.

54 T. Beard, *The Theatre of Gods Judgements*, London, 1597, p. 211.

55 Rev'd Cooper, 'George Preston and Cartmel Priory Church', *Transactions of the Historic Society of Lancashire and Cheshire*, 51 (1899), pp. 221–7.

3. A STRANGE HUMMING OR BUZZ

1 TNA, SP 14/118/37, SP 14/118/38.

2 T. Cogswell, 'England and the Spanish Match', in R. Cust and A. Hughes (eds.), *Conflict in Early Stuart England: Studies in Religion and Politics, 1603–1642*, London, 1989, p. 120.

3 Underdown, *Freeborn People*, p. 29.

4 *King James Bible, Authorized Version*, Joshua 5:13, Mark 12:30.

5 D. Cressy, *Literacy and the Social Order: Reading and Writing in Tudor and Stuart England*, Cambridge, 1980.

6 J. Earle, *Micro-Cosmography. Or, a Peece of the World Discovered in Essayes and Characters*, London, 1628, ch. 53.

7 J. Raymond, *The Invention of the Newspaper: English Newsbooks, 1641–1649*, Oxford, 1996, p. 7.

8 British Library, Additional MS 35331, The Diary of Walter Yonge.

9 A. Fox, 'Rumour, News and Popular Political Opinion in Elizabethan and Early Stuart England', *Historical Journal*, 40 (1997), p. 599.

10   A. Bellany, ' "Raylinge Rymes and Vaunting Verse": Libellous Politics in Early Stuart England, 1603–1628', in K. Sharpe and P. Lake (eds.), *Culture and Politics in Early Stuart England*, London, 1994, p. 293; Underdown, *Freeborn People*, p. 57.

11   Fox, 'Rumour', p. 611.

12   Ibid., p. 612.

13   Cogswell, 'England and the Spanish Match', p. 117.

14   M. Young, *King James VI and I and the History of Homosexuality*, New York, 2000, pp. 75, 138.

15   Harris, *Rebellion*, p. 195.

16   Ibid.

17   Ibid.

18   J. Ingram, 'The Conscience of the Community: the Character and Development of Clerical Complaint in Early Modern England' (Univ. of Warwick, PhD Thesis, 2004), p. 236.

19   Harris, *Rebellion*, p. 197.

20   Ibid., p. 200.

21   Ibid., pp. 206–7.

22   Ibid., p. 207.

23   Young, *King James VI and I*, p. 75.

24   A. Bellany and T. Cogswell, *The Murder of King James I*, London, 2015, p. 8.

25   A. McRae, *Literature, Satire, and the Early Stuart State*, Cambridge, 2004, p. 170.

26   Bellany, ' "Raylinge Rymes" ', p. 298.

27   R. Lockyer, 'George Villiers, first Duke of Buckingham (1592–1628)', *ODNB* (2011).

28   Bellany and Cogswell, *Murder of King James I*, p. 12.

29   Young, *James VI and I*, p. 47. The word 'dog' carried connotations of loyalty, as it does today, but it could also refer to a male sex worker or a sodomite.

30   E. Bourcier, *Diary of Sir Simonds D'Ewes (1622–24)*, Paris, 1974, pp. 92–3.

31   Amussen and Underdown, *Gender, Culture and Politics*, p. 41.

32   K. Rolfe, 'Probable Past and Possible Futures: Contemporaneity and the Consumption of News in the 1620s', *Media History*, 23 (2017), p. 163.

33   Cogswell, 'England and the Spanish Match', p. 129.

34   Ibid., p. 119.

35   R. Hoyle, 'Famine as Agricultural Catastrophe: The Crisis of 1622–4 in east Lancashire', *Economic History Review*, 63 (2010), p. 978.

36 J. Thirsk and J. Cooper (eds.), *Seventeenth-century Economic Documents*, Oxford, 1972, p. 24.

37 Appleby, *Famine*; J. Healey, 'Land, Population and Famine in the English Uplands: a Westmorland Case Study, c. 1370–1650', *Agricultural History Review*, 59 (2011), pp. 151–75.

38 H. Brierley (ed.), *The registers of the parish church of Cartmel in the county of Lancaster, 1559–1661*, Lancashire Parish Register Society, 28, Rochdale, 1907, pp. 28, 178.

39 A. Maclean, *The Registers of the Parish of Greystoke in the County of Cumberland, baptisms, marriages and burials, 1559–1757*, Kendal, 1911.

40 J. Healey, 'The Northern Manor and the Politics of Neighbourhood: Dilston, Northumberland, 1558–1640', *Northern History*, 51 (2014), p. 233.

41 A. Winchester, 'Response to the 1623 Famine in Two Lancashire Manors', *Local Population Studies*, 36 (1986), pp. 47–8.

42 Cogswell, 'England and the Spanish Match', p. 125.

43 Ibid., p. 120.

44 Ibid.

45 R. Lockyer, *Buckingham: The Life and Career of George Villiers, first Duke of Buckingham, 1592–1628*, London, 1981, p. 116.

46 R. Cust, *Charles I: A Political Life*, London, 2005, p. 36.

47 Cogswell, 'England and the Spanish Match', pp. 108–9.

48 Bellany and Cogswell, *Murder of King James I*, p. 6.

4. IF PARLIAMENTS LIVE OR DIE

1 Cust, *Charles I*, p. 150.

2 Harris, *Rebellion*, p. 235.

3 Cust, *Charles I*, pp. 6–7.

4 Ibid., p. 44.

5 K. Fincham, 'George Abbot (1562–1633)', *ODNB* (2011).

6 R. Montague, *A Gagg for the New Gospel? No: A New Gagg for an Old Goose*, London, 1624.

7 Harris, *Rebellion*, p. 222.

8 Cust, *Charles I*, p. 95.

9 *House of Lords Journal*, 6 February 1626.

10 Underdown, *Freeborn People*, p. 35.

11 S. R. Gardiner (ed.), *Constitutional Documents of the Puritan Revolution*, London, 1889, pp. 4–6. (Hereafter *Constitutional Documents*.)

12 Harris, *Rebellion*, p. 250; Underdown, *Freeborn People*, p. 19.

13 Harris, *Rebellion*, p. 250.

14 Underdown, *Freeborn People*, p. 19.

15 Amussen and Underdown, *Gender, Culture and Politics*, p. 152.

16 J. Rushworth, *Historical Collections of Private Passages of State*, 8 vols, London, 1721, I, 374–422.

17 R. Cust, *The Forced Loan and English Politics, 1626–1628*, Oxford, 1987, p. 175.

18 Harris, *Rebellion*, p. 255.

19 Cust, *Charles I*, p. 66.

20 *Proceedings in Parliament, 1628*, 6, London, 1983, pp. 222–3.

21 Sommerville, *Royalists and Patriots*, p. 122.

22 Harris, *Rebellion*, p. 257.

23 Sommerville, *Royalists and Patriots*, p. 121.

24 P. Gregg, *Charles I*, London, 1981, p. 168.

25 C. Carlton, *Charles I: The Personal Monarch*, London, 1995, p. 98.

26 Harris, *Rebellion*, p. 262.

27 *Proceedings in Parliament, 1628*, 2, London, 1977, p. 325.

28 Harris, *Rebellion*, p. 263.

29 Ibid.

30 Ibid., p. 265.

31 A. Bellany, 'The Murder of John Lambe: Crowd Violence, Court Scandal and Popular Politics in Early Seventeenth Century England', *Past and Present*, 200 (2008), pp. 37–76.

32 J. Holstun, *Ehud's Dagger: Class Struggle in the English Revolution*, London, 2000, pp. 160–63; Bellany, '"Raylinge Rymes"', p. 304.

33 Cust, *Charles I*, p. 75.

34 Underdown, *Freeborn People*, p. 51.

35 Holstun, *Ehud's Dagger*, p. 166.

36 Cust, *Charles I*, pp. 95–6.

37 Bellany, '"Raylinge Rymes"', p. 305.

38 Harris, *Rebellion*, p. 269.

39 G. Hammond, *Fleeting Things: English Poets and Poems, 1616–1660*, London, 1990, p. 61.

40 Harris, *Rebellion*, p. 273.

41 Ibid., p. 274.

42 Rushworth, *Historical Collections*, I, pp. 662–91.

43 Harris, *Rebellion*, p. 275.

44 Rushworth, *Historical Collections*, I, Appendix, 1–11.

45 Fox, 'Rumour', p. 618.

46 Ibid.

5. THE ARCH OF ORDER AND GOVERNMENT

1 J. Walter, 'Grain Riots and Popular Attitudes to the Law: Maldon and the crisis of 1629', in J. Brewer and J. Styles (eds), *An Ungovernable People? The English and their Law in the Seventeenth and Eighteenth Centuries*, London, 1980, pp. 47–84; J. Walter, 'Ann Carter [formerly Barrington] (d. 1629)', *ODNB* (2008).

2 TNA, SP 16/175/81.

3 TNA, SP 16/185/55.

4 D. Pennington, *Going to Market: Women, Trade and Social Relations in Early Modern English Towns, c. 1550–1650*, Farnham, 2015, p. 151.

5 B. Sharp, *In Contempt of All Authority: Rural Artisans and Riot in the West of England, 1586–1660*, London, 1980.

6 K. Sharpe, *The Personal Rule of Charles I*, London, 1992, p. 56.

7 E.g. Cressy, *Charles I*, p. 19.

8 D. Purkiss, *The English Civil War: A People's History*, London, 2007, p. 246.

9 Sharpe, *Personal Rule*, p. 212.

10 Cressy, *Charles I*, p. 35.

11 Cust, *Charles I*, p. 157.

12 Ibid., p. 149.

13 Cressy, *Charles I*, p. 155.

14 Ibid., p. 157.

15 V. Wedgwood, *The King's Peace, 1637–41*, London, 1955, p. 65.

16 Sharpe, *Personal Rule*, p. 211; Cressy, *Charles I*, p. 156.

17 C. Herrup, *A House in Gross Disorder: Sex, Law and the 2nd Earl of Castlehaven*, Oxford, 2001, p. 50.

18 Sharpe, *Personal Rule*, p. 172.

19 Cust, *Charles I*, p. 26.

20 Ibid., p. 215.

21 Sharpe, *Personal Rule*, p. 404.

22 Ibid., p. 414.

23 Ibid., p. 473.

24 Sharpe, *Personal Rule*, p. 417.

25 Ibid., p. 208.

26 Ibid., p. 138.

27 Ibid.

28 Ibid., p. 135.

29 Cressy, *Charles I*, p. 41.

30 Sharpe, *Personal Rule*, p. 646.

31 Ibid., p. 682.

32 F. Condick, 'Alexander Leighton (c. 1570–1649)', *ODNB* (2008). In prison, he picked up the medical trade again.

33 W. Prynne, *Histrio-Mastix, the Players Scourge, or Actors Tragaedie*, London, 1633.

34 Cressy, *Travesties and Transgressions*, p. 221.

35 K. Fincham, 'Introduction', in K. Fincham (ed.), *The Early Stuart Church, 1603–1642*, London, 1993, p. 16.

36 Cressy, *Charles I*, p. 38.

37 Ibid., p. 39.

38 P. Slack, 'Books of Orders: the Making of English Social Policy', *Transactions of the Royal Historical Society* 5th Ser., 30 (1980), pp. 1–22.

39 Lancashire Record Office, QSB 1/114/58; there is another similar note, made slightly earlier, on QSB 1/126/76.

40 TNA, SP 16/250, f. 17.

41 Cressy, *Charles I*, p. 104.

42 British Library, Additional MS 34324, f. 281v.

43 M. Braddick, *The Nerves of State: Taxation and the Financing of the English State*, Manchester, 1996, p. 71.

44 Harris, *Rebellion*, p. 294.

45 Cressy, *Charles I*, p. 149.

46 Sharpe, *Personal Rule*, p. 692.

47 J. S. Hart, *The Rule of Law, 1603–1660: Crowns, Courts and Judges*, London, 2003, p. 150.

48 Sharpe, *Personal Rule*, p. 581; Wrightson, '"Sorts of People"', p. 45.

49 Sharpe, *Personal Rule*, p. 598.

50 Cressy, *Charles I*, p. 213.

51 Ibid., p. 214.

52 R. Griswold (ed.), *The Prose Works of John Milton*, I, Pennsylvania, 1848, p. 11. Milton was describing changes to the early Christian Church wrought by Constantine, but he was equally passing comment on Charles.

53 [J. Milton], *Of Reformation Touching Church-Discipline in England*, London, 1641, p. 28.

54 Thomas, *Religion and the Decline of Magic*, p. 43.

55 W. Laud, *The Works of the Most Reverend Father in God, William Laud, DD, sometime Lord Archbishop of Canterbury*, ed. W. Scott and J. Bliss (7 vols, 1847–60), VI, 57.

56 Bodleian Library, Tanner MS 68, f. 104.

57 Cressy, *Charles I*, p. 229.

58 Laud, *Works*, VI, 574.

59 Sharpe, *Personal Rule*, p. 142.

60 Cressy, *Charles I*, p. 226.

61 E. Boughen, *A Sermon Concerning Decencie and Order in the Church*, London, 1638, p. 12.

62 S. R. Gardiner, *Reports of Cases in the Courts of Star Chamber and High Commission*, London, 1886, p, 305.

63 J. Adamson, *The Noble Revolt: The Overthrow of Charles I*, London, 2007, p. 118.

64 D. Cressy, *England on Edge: Crisis and Revolution, 1640–1642*, Oxford, 2006, p. 179.

65 Sharpe, *Personal Rule*, p. 324.

66 D. George, 'Rushbearing: a forgotten British custom', in A. F. Johnston and W. N. M. Hüsken (eds.), *English Parish Drama*, Amsterdam: Rodopi, 1996, pp. 17–29; E. Baldwin, 'Rushbearings and Maygames in the Diocese of Chester before 1642', in Johnston and Hüsken (eds.), *English Parish Drama*, pp. 31–40.

67 A. Dougall, *The Devil's Book: Charles I, The Book of Sports and Puritanism in Tudor and Early Stuart England*, Exeter, 2011.

68 W. Knowler (ed.), *The Earl of Strafforde's Letters and Dispatches*, V. I, London, 1739, p. 166.

69 J. Turner, 'The Clergy of Buckinghamshire, 1630–1665' (Univ. of Oxford, MSc Thesis, 2022), p. 45.

6. BLACK RIBBONS

1 Harris, *Rebellion*, p. 365.

2 Sharpe, *Personal Rule*, p. 784.

3 Purkiss, *English Civil War*, p. 76.

4 Cressy, *Charles I*, p. 282.

5 A. Woolrych, *Britain in Revolution, 1625–1660*, Oxford, 2002, p. 99.

6 J. Lawson, *The Episcopal Church of Scotland from the Reformation to the Revolution*, Edinburgh, 1844, pp. 546–7.

7 TNA, SP 16/387/64.

8 A. Gill, 'Ship Money during the Personal Rule of Charles I: Politics, Ideology and the Law, 1634–1640' (Univ. of Sheffield, PhD Thesis, 1990), pp. 452–72.

9 Cust, *Charles I*, p. 230.

10 Sharpe, *Personal Rule*, p. 793.

11 Purkiss, *English Civil War*, p. 146.

12 A. Tinniswood, *The Verneys: Love, War and Madness in Seventeenth-Century England*, London, 2008, p. 90.

13 Sharpe, *Personal Rule,* p. 194.

14 Underdown, *Revel, Riot and Rebellion*, p. 135.

15 Adamson, *Noble Revolt*, p. 3.

16 Rushworth, *Historical Collections*, III, 1128.

17 C. Russell, 'John Pym (1584–1643)', *ODNB* (2009).

18 Cust, *Charles I*, p. 254.

19 *House of Lords Journal*, 24 April 1640.

20 Sharpe, *Personal Rule*, p. 871.

21 Historical Manuscripts Commission, *Third Report of the Royal Commission on Historical Manuscripts*, London, 1873, p. 3.

22 Cressy, *England on Edge*, p. 36.

23 Ibid., p. 115.

24 J. Rees, *The Leveller Revolution: Radical Political Organisation in England, 1640–1650*, London, 2016, p. 33.

25 K. Lindley, *Popular Politics and Religion in Civil War London*, Aldershot, 1997, p. 9.

26 TNA, SP 16/455, f. 78.

27 Cressy, *England on Edge*, p. 150.

28 Quoted in P. Seaver, *Wallington's World: A Puritan Artisan in Seventeenth-Century London*, London, 1985, p. 162.

29 Cressy, *England on Edge*, p. 32.

30 Ibid., p. 78.

31 Ibid., p. 80.

32 TNA, SP 16/456, ff. 83–85.

33 Cressy, *England on Edge*, pp. 236–7.

34 TNA, SP 16/457, ff. 242–3.

35 TNA, SP 16/461/57/1.

36 M. Stoyle, 'The Cannibal Cavalier: Sir Thomas Lunsford and the Fashioning of the Royalist Archetype', *Historical Journal*, 59 (2016), pp. 293–317.

37 Adamson, *Noble Revolt*, p. 54.

38 Ibid., pp. 67–70; I. Pells, *Philip Skippon and the British Civil Wars: The 'Christian Centurion'*, Abingdon, 2020, pp. 80–84; Harris, *Rebellion*, p. 397.

39 Adamson, *Noble Revolt*, p. 71.

40 P. Donald, 'New Light on the Anglo-Scottish Contacts of 1640', *Historical Research*, 62 (1989), p. 228.

41 Ibid., p. 221–9.

42 Adamson, *Noble Revolt*, p. 62.

43 TNA, SP 16/467/9.

44 Donald, 'New Light', 1989, pp. 226–7; Lindley, *Popular Politics*, p. 10.

45 Adamson, *Noble Revolt*, p. 81.

7. TO KNOCK FOXES AND WOLVES ON THE HEAD

1   E. Hyde, Earl of Clarendon, *The History of the Rebellion and Civil Wars in England*, 3 vols, London, 1702, I, 295.

2   A. Fletcher, *The Outbreak of the English Civil War*, London, 1985, p. 1.

3   C. Russell, *The Fall of the British Monarchies, 1637–1642*, Oxford, 1991, p. 177.

4   *Proceedings of the Long Parliament*, I, 100.

5   Ibid., I, 103.

6   Cressy, *England on Edge*, p. 41.

7   H. Gee and W. J. Hardy (eds.), *Documents Illustrative of English Church History*, London, 1896, pp. 537–45.

8   Adamson, *Noble Revolt*, p. 158 and footnote.

9   Ibid., p. 168.

10 Cust, *Charles I*, p. 279.

11 Cressy, *England on Edge*, p. 201. She was the sister of Lord Saye.

12 Ibid., p. 216.

13 P. Christianson, 'The Peers, the People and Parliamentary Management in the First Six Months of the Long Parliament', *Journal of Modern History*, 49 (1977), p. 591.

14 Fletcher, *Outbreak*, p. 7.

15 Clarendon, *History*, I, 423.

16 Adamson, *Noble Revolt*, p. 228.

17 HMC, Various, II, 261.

18 Adamson, *Noble Revolt*, p. 231.

19 Ibid., p. 237.

20 Ibid., p. 244.

21 Clarendon, *History*, I, 496.

22 *A Briefe and Perfect Relation: of the Answers and replies of Thomas Earle of Strafford; to the articles exhibited against him*, London, 1647, p. 78.

23 Adamson, *Noble Revolt*, p. 272.

24 Ibid., p. 276. Adamson incorrectly glosses this as meaning a 'village' constable. In fact, the 'high' constable operated at the level of the hundred; village constables were known as 'petty'.

25 V. Wedgwood, *Thomas Wentworth, first Earl of Strafford, 1593–1641: A Revaluation*, London, 1961, p. 372.

26 J. Nalson, *An Impartial Collection of the Great Affairs of State from the Beginning of the Scotch Rebellion in the year MDCXXXIX to the Murther of King Charles I*, 2 vols, London, 1682–3, II, 188.

27 J. Walter, *Covenanting Citizens: The Protestation Oath and Popular Political Culture in the English Revolution*, Oxford, 2017, p. 16.

28 Adamson, *Noble Revolt*, p. 296.

29 Ibid., p. 300.

8. THIS IS A REMONSTRANCE TO THE PEOPLE

1 T. Kilburn and A. Milton, 'The Public Context of the Trial and Execution of Strafford', in J. Merritt (ed.), *The Political World of Thomas Wentworth, Earl of Strafford, 1621–1641*, Cambridge, 1996, p. 242.

2 Seaver, *Wallington's World*, p. 164.

3 Russell, *Fall of the British Monarchies*, p. 291.

4 Fletcher, *Outbreak*, p. 16.

5 Ibid., p. 24.

6 Cressy, *England on Edge*, p. 171.

7 Ibid., p. 292.

8 Ibid., p. 217.

9 Fletcher, *Outbreak*, p. 111.

10 Cressy, *England on Edge*, p. 226.

11 Adamson, *Noble Revolt*, p. 388; Thomas, *Religion and the Decline of Magic*, p. 457.

12 Fletcher, *Outbreak*, pp. 112–13.

13 Ibid., p. 43.

14 *House of Commons Journal*, 1 September 1641.

15 Cressy, *England on Edge*, p. 173.

16 Purkiss, *English Civil War*, p. 147.

17 Fletcher, *Outbreak*, p. 119.

18 *An Honourable and Worthy Speech: Spoken in the High Court of Parliament by Mr Smith of the Middle Temple, 28 October 1641*, London, 1641.

19 Cust, *Charles I*, p. 356.

20 W. Coates (ed.), *The Diary of Sir Simonds D'Ewes*, New Haven, 1942, p. 37.

21 Anon., *A Damnable Treason, by a Contagious Plaster of a Plague-Sore wrapt up in a letter, and sent to Mr Pym*, London, 1641.

22 Adamson, *Noble Revolt*, pp. 426–7; *House of Commons Journal*, 5 November 1641.

23 *Constitutional Documents*, p. 229.

24 Adamson, *Noble Revolt*, pp. 434–5.

9. DARK, EQUAL CHAOS

1 Fletcher, *Outbreak*, p. 161.

2 Adamson, *Noble Revolt*, p. 445.

3 W. Lilly, *Monarchy or No Monarchy in England*, London, 1651, pp. 106–7.

4 Cust, *Charles I*, p. 315.

5 Fletcher, *Outbreak*, p. 171.

6 Ibid., p. 173.

7 B. Manning, *The English People and the English Revolution*, Harmondsworth, 1976, p. 89.

8 Ibid., p. 89.

9 Ibid.

10 Ibid., p. 90.

11 TNA, SP 16/486, f. 208; *Diurnall Occurrences: or, the Heads of Several Proceedings in both Houses of Parliament* (27 Dec 1641–3 Jan 1642).

12 Adamson, *Noble Revolt*, p. 480.

13 Ibid., p. 496.

14 Ibid., p. 497.

15 J. Forster, *Arrest of the Five Members by Charles the First*, London, 1860, pp. 191–2.

16 Manning, *English People*, p. 111.

17 Fletcher, *Outbreak*, p. 178.

18 Ibid., p. 186.

19 J. Childs, *The Siege of Loyalty House: A Civil War Story*, London, 2022, p. 45.

20 Fletcher, *Outbreak*, p. 185.

21 Seaver, *Wallington's World*, p. 151.

22 Fletcher, *Outbreak*, p. 198.

23 Ibid., p. 188.

24 Cust, *Charles I*, p. 337.

25 *His Majesties Answer to the Nineteen Propositions of both Houses of Parliament*, Cambridge, 1642.

26 Cressy, *England on Edge*, p. 208.

27 Fletcher, *Outbreak*, p. 378.

28 Ibid., p. 340.

29 Harris, *Rebellion*, pp. 481–4.

30 Fletcher, *Outbreak*, p. 365.

31 Ibid., p. 319.

32 Harris, *Rebellion*, p. 489.

33 Fletcher, *Outbreak*, p. 324.

34 Ibid., p. 413.

35 Ibid., p. 378.

36 S. Porter, *The Battle for London*, Stroud, 2011, p. 86.

37 A. Woolrych, *Battles of the English Civil War*, London, 1966, p. 16.

38 Porter, *Battle*, p. 90.

39 Ibid., p. 90.

40 Ibid., p. 97.

10. THE SWORD OF HIS VENGEANCE

1 *A great vvonder in heaven: shewing the late apparitions and prodigious noyses of war and battels, seen on Edge-Hill neere Keinton in Northampton-shire*, London, 1643.

2 Purkiss, *English Civil War*, p. 169.

3 Cust, *Charles I*, p. 183.

4 E. Ludlow, *Memoirs of Edward Ludlow Esquire*, 2 vols, Vevey, 1698, I, 121.

5 Wrightson, '"Sorts of People"', p. 46.

6 Purkiss, *English Civil War*, p. 194.

7 M. Hunter, *John Aubrey and the Realm of Learning*, London, 1975, p. 127.

8 Aubrey, *Brief Lives*, p. 340.

9 R. Baxter, *Reliquiae Baxterianae, or Mr Baxters Narrative of the most Memorable Passages of his Life and Times*, London, 1696, p. 177.

10 S. Mendelson and P. Crawford, *Women in Early Modern England, 1550–1720*, Oxford, 1998, p. 415.

11 F. Bickley, *The Cavendish Family*, London, 1911, p. 73.

12 Woolrych, *Britain in Revolution*, p. 247.

13 Purkiss, *English Civil War*, p. 248.

14 Aubrey, *Brief Lives*, p. 340.

15 P. Higgins, 'The Reactions of Women, with Special Reference to Women Petitioners', in B. Manning (ed.), *Politics, Religion and the English Civil War*, London, 1973, pp. 189–99.

16 Anon., *A Narrative of the Disease and Death of that Noble Gentleman John Pym Esquire*, London, 1643.

17 D. Underdown, *Pride's Purge: Politics in the Puritan Revolution*, Oxford, 1971, p. 77; R. Ashton, *Counter Revolution: The Second Civil War and its Origins, 1646–8*, London, 1994, p. 95.

18 Purkiss, *English Civil War*, p. 267.

19 Aubrey, *Brief Lives*, pp. 174–83.

20 B. Morgan, 'Sir Arthur Aston (1590x93–1649)', *ODNB* (2004).

21 Purkiss, *English Civil War*, p. 365.

22 Cust, *Charles I*, p. 398.

23 Calendar of State Papers, Venetian, XXVII, pp. 156–67.

24 C. Hill, *The World Turned Upside Down: Radical Ideas During the English Revolution*, Oxford, 1972, p. 64.

25 Cromwell, *Writings and Speeches*, I, 256.

26 Ibid., III, 452.

27 Underdown, *Pride's Purge*, p. 67.

11. GANGRENE

1 M. Evans, *Naseby 1645: The Triumph of the New Model Army*, Oxford, 2007, p. 59.

2 Raymond, *Invention of the Newspaper*, pp. 20–79.

3 Aubrey, *Brief Lives*, p. 268.

4 Underdown, *Freeborn People*, p. 87.

5 J. Macadam, '*Mercurius Britanicus* on Charles I: An Exercise in Civil War Journalism and High Politics, August 1643 to May 1646', *Historical Research*, 84 (2011), p. 476.

6 *The Kings Cabinet Opened, or Certain Packets of Secret Letters & Papers, Written with the Kings own Hand, and taken in his Cabinet at Nasby-Field*, London, 1645.

7 Baxter, *Reliquiae Baxterianae*, p. 54.

8 S. Gardiner, *History of the Great Civil War*, 4 vols, London, 1886–1901, III, 209.

9 https://www.civilwarpetitions.ac.uk/petition/the-petition-of-william-summer-of-leicester-leicestershire-1645-to-1647/.

10 C. Carlton, *Going to the Wars: The Experience of the British Civil Wars, 1638–1651*, London, 1992, p. 273.

11 I. Beckett, *Wanton Troopers: Buckinghamshire in the Civil Wars, 1640–1660*, Barnsley, 2015, p. 125.

12 E. Hyde, Lord Clarendon, *The Life of Edward, Earl of Clarendon*, 3 vols, Oxford, 1827, I, 39.

13 Underdown, *Revel, Riot and Rebellion*, p. 180.

14 Ibid., pp. 177–8.

15 Purkiss, *English Civil War*, pp. 244–5.

16 M. Gaskill, *Witchfinders: A Seventeenth-Century English Tragedy*, London, 2007, p. 101.

17 Ibid., p. 113; J. Sharpe, *Instruments of Darkness: Witchcraft in Early Modern England*, London, 1997, pp. 136–7.

18 M. Gaskill, 'Witchcraft and Evidence in Early Modern England', *Past and Present*, 198 (2008), p. 55.

19 Sharpe, *Instruments of Darkness*, p. 182.

20 J. Stearne, *A Confirmation and Discovery of Witchcraft*, London, 1648.

21 Underdown, *Pride's Purge*, p. 54.

22 Ibid., p. 69; H. Lancaster, 'Sir Walter Long (c. 1591–1672)', *ODNB* (2010).

23 S. Hindle, 'Dearth and the English Revolution: the Harvest Crisis of 1647–50', *Economic History Review*, 61 Supplement 1 (2008), p. 68; R. Josselin, *The Diary of Ralph Josselin, 1616–1683*, ed. A. Macfarlane, Oxford, 1976.

24 *Jacob Raised: Or, The Means of making a nation happy both in spiritual and temporal privileges*, London, 1647.

25 Cromwell, *Writings and Speeches*, IV, 471.

26 A. Woolrych, *Soldiers and Statesmen: the General Council of the Army and its Debates, 1647–1648*, Oxford, 1987, pp. 21–2.

27 R. Williams, *The Bloudy Tenet, of Persecution, for Cause of Concience*, London, 1644.

28 J. Milton, *Areopagitica: A Speech of Mr John Milton for the Liberty of Unlicensed Printing, to the Parliament of England*, London, 1644, p. 12.

29 R. Foxley, *The Levellers: Radical Political Thought in the English Revolution*, Manchester, 2013, p. 99.

30 Ibid., p. 9.

31 G. Aylmer, *The Levellers in the English Revolution*, London, 1975, p. 58.

32 Ibid., p. 70.

33 R. Overton, *The Arraignment of Mr Persecution: Presented to the Consideration of the House of Commons, and to all the Common People of England*, London, 1645, p. 22.

34 W. Walwyn, *The Fountain of Slaunder Discovered*, London, 1649, p. 22.

35 Foxley, *Levellers,* p. 9.

36 Rees, *Leveller Revolution,* pp. 54–5.

37 *Remonstrance of Many Thousand Citizens, and other Free-born people of England to their own House of Commons,* London, 1646.

38 Foxley, *Levellers,* p. 103.

39 H. Parker, *Jus Populi, or a Discourse wherein Clear Satisfaction is given as well concerning the right of princes,* London, 1644, p. 18.

40 Foxley, *Levellers,* p. 12.

12. TO SATISFY ALL MEN

1 Rees, *Leveller Revolution,* pp. 164–71.

2 Woolrych, *Soldiers and Statesmen,* p. 38.

3 Ibid., p. 55.

4 Ibid., p. 59.

5 Ibid., p. 98.

6 C. Firth, *The Clarke Papers: Selections from the Papers of William Clarke,* 4 vols, London, 1891–1901, I, 111–13.

7 Ibid., I, 118–19.

8 Woolrych, *Britain in Revolution,* p. 364; Rushworth, *Historical Collections,* VI, 513–19.

9 *Clarke Papers,* I, 119–20.

10 *A Solemn Engagement of the Army under the Command of his Excellency Sir Thomas Fairfax,* London, 1647.

11 S. Mortimer, 'Henry Ireton and the Limits of Radicalism, 1647–9', in G. Southcombe and G. Tapsell (eds), *Revolutionary England, c. 1630–c. 1660: Essays for Clive Holmes,* London, 2017, pp. 55–72.

12 *Clarke Papers,* I, 132–3.

13 Woolrych, *Soldiers and Statesmen,* p. 126.

14 *House of Commons Journal,* 26 June 1647.

15 *Clarke Papers,* I, 216.

16 Ibid., I, 213.

17 Woolrych, *Britain in Revolution,* p. 374.

18 Rees, *Leveller Revolution,* p. 194.

19 *The Journal of Thomas Juxon, 1644–1647,* ed. K. Lindley and D. Scott, London, 2000, p. 165.

20 Woolrych, *Soldiers and Statesmen,* p. 175.

21 Ibid., pp. 177–8.

22 *Clarke Papers,* I, 220.

23 Rees, *Leveller Revolution*, p. 194.

24 D. Scott, 'Party Politics in the Long Parliament, 1640–8', in Southcombe and Tapsell (eds), *Revolutionary England*, p. 46.

25 Woolrych, *Soldiers and Statesmen*, p. 192.

26 *The Case of the Armie Truly Stated*, London, 1647.

27 Woolrych, *Soldiers and Statesmen*, p. 214.

28 *An Agreement of the People for a Firme and Present Peace, upon Grounds of Common Right and Freedom*, London, 1647.

29 A. Keay, *The Restless Republic: Britain without a Crown*, London, 2022, p. 76.

30 *Clarke Papers*, I, 227–8.

31 Ibid., I, 236–8.

32 Ibid., I, 246.

33 Ibid., I, 286.

34 J. Lawmind [Wildman], *Putney Projects: Or, the Old Serpent in a New Form*, London, 1647.

35 Underdown, *Pride's Purge*, p. 78.

36 P. Gregg, *Free-Born John: A Biography of John Lilburne*, London, 1961, p. 385.

13. BLOOD DEFILETH THE LAND

1 M. Braddick, *God's Fury, England's Fire: A New History of the English Civil Wars*, London, 2009, p. 531.

2 Mortimer, 'Henry Ireton', p. 66.

3 Hindle, 'Dearth and the English Revolution', p. 84.

4 D. Wolfe, *Leveller Manifestoes of the Puritan Revolution*, London, 1944, p. 278.

5 C. H. Firth and R. S. Rait (ed.), *Acts and Ordinances of the Interregnum, 1642–1660*, London, 1911, pp. 1133–6.

6 Underdown, *Freeborn People*, p. 72.

7 P. Crawford, 'Charles Stuart, that Man of Blood', *Parergon*, 32 (2015), p. 56.

8 Rees, *Leveller Revolution*, p. 250.

9 Woolrych, *Battles*, p. 169.

10 Hindle, 'Dearth and the English Revolution', p. 90.

11 Rees, *Leveller Revolution*, pp. 238–44.

12 Underdown, *Pride's Purge*, p. 109.

13 N. Carlin, *Regicide or Revolution? What petitioners wanted, September 1648–February 1649*, London, 2020, p. 70.

14 C. Holmes, 'The Trial and Execution of Charles I', *Historical Journal*, 53 (2010), p. 302.

15 Thomas, *Religion and the Decline of Magic*, p. 442.

16 Rees, *Leveller Revolution*, p. 267.

17 *House of Commons Journal*, 15 November 1648.

18 Underdown, *Pride's Purge*, p. 120.

19 C. Holmes, 'The Remonstrance of the Army and the Execution of Charles I', *History*, 104 (2019), p. 585.

20 Holmes, 'Trial and Execution', p. 305; V. Wedgwood, *The Trial of Charles I* (1964), p. 29.

21 *Mercurius Pragmaticus*, 21–28 November 1648; Wedgwood, *Trial of Charles I*, p. 30.

22 Cromwell, *Writings and Speeches*, I, 696–9.

23 Holmes, 'Remonstrance', p. 597.

24 Underdown, *Pride's Purge*, p. 132.

25 G. Stevenson, *Charles I in Captivity, from Contemporary Sources*, New York, 1927, p. 143.

26 Ibid., p. 165.

27 Underdown, *Pride's Purge*, p. 134.

28 Ludlow, *Memoirs*, I, 269.

29 Underdown, *Pride's Purge*, p. 157.

30 J. Evelyn, *The Diary of John Evelyn*, ed. A. Dobson, 3 vols, London, 1906, II, 7.

31 *Clarke Papers*, II, 132.

32 *An Abridgement of the Late Remonstrance of the Army*, London, 1648, p. 10.

33 Holmes, 'Trial and Execution', p. 305.

34 *Acts and Ordinances*, p. 1253.

35 J. Fitzgibbons, 'Rethinking the English Revolution of 1649', *Historical Journal*, 60 (2017), p. 900.

36 B. Taft, 'The Council of Officers' *Agreement of the People*, 1648/9', *Historical Journal*, 28 (1985), p. 169.

37 *Constitutional Documents*, pp. 371–4.

38 E. Vallance, 'Testimony, Tyranny and Treason: the Witnesses at Charles I's Trial', *English Historical Review*, 136 (2021), p. 893.

39 Wedgwood, *Trial of Charles I*, pp. 119–45.

40 Vallance, 'Testimony, Tyranny and Treason', p. 880.

41 *Constitutional Documents*, p. 380.

42 Wedgwood, *Trial of Charles I*, pp. 177–9.

43 J. Forster, *The Statesmen of the Commonwealth of England*, New York, 1846, p. 377.
44 Mendelson and Crawford, *Women in Early Modern England*, p. 416.
45 Keay, *Restless Republic*, p. 71.
46 *Letters and Speeches*, II, p. 147; J. Coffey, 'Religious Thought', in M. Braddick (ed.), *The Oxford Handbook of the English Revolution*, Oxford, 2015, p. 447.
47 Fitzgibbons, 'Rethinking the English Revolution', p. 910.
48 J. Lilburne, *England's New Chains Discovered*, London, 1649.
49 W. Chernaik, *Milton and the Burden of Freedom*, Cambridge, 2017, p. 109.
50 Rees, *Leveller Revolution*, pp. 288–9.
51 Ibid., p. 290.
52 Ibid., p. 291.

14. TO TRANSLATE THE NATION FROM OPPRESSION TO LIBERTY

1   F. Thorpe, *Serjeant Thorpe Judge of Assize for the Northern Circuit his Charge*, London, 1649.
2   *Light Shining in Buckinghamshire, Or, A Discovery of the Main Grounds; original cause of all the Slavery in the World, but chiefly in England*, London, 1648.
3   Hill, *World Turned Upside Down*, p. 129.
4   Ibid., p. 136.
5   Ibid., p. 14.
6   Thomas, *Religion and the Decline of Magic*, p. 177.
7   G. Winstanley, *Winstanley: 'The Law of Freedom' and other Writings*, ed. C. Hill, Cambridge, 1983, p. 198.
8   P. Slack, *The Invention of Improvement: Information and Material Progress in Seventeenth-Century England*, Oxford, 2014, p. 93.
9   Slack, *Invention of Improvement*, p. 231.
10 W. Blith, *The English Improver Improved*, London, 1653.
11 Ibid., p. 93.
12 Ibid., p. 118.
13 Ibid., p. 117.
14 Ibid., p. 103.
15 Hill, *World Turned Upside Down*, p. 223.
16 J. Nickolls (ed.), *Original Letters and Papers of State Addressed to Oliver Cromwell*, London, 1743, pp. 99–102.

17 T. Hobbes, *Leviathan, or, The Matter, forme, & Power of a Common-wealth Ecclesiasticall and Civill*, London, 1651.

18 Hill, *World Turned Upside Down*, p. 96.

19 Woolrych, *Britain in Revolution*, p. 451.

20 A. Coleby, *Central Government and the Localities: Hampshire 1649–1689*, Cambridge, 1987, p. 59. The church was St Michael's Kingsgate.

21 J. Coffey, 'Puritanism and Liberty Revisited: The Case for Toleration in the English Revolution', *Historical Journal*, 41 (1998), p. 966.

22 Thomas, *Religion and the Decline of Magic*, p. 457.

23 Keay, *Restless Republic*, p. 81.

24 Hill, *World Turned Upside Down*, p. 157.

25 L. Clarkson, *A Single Eye all Light No Darkness; or, light and darkness one*, London, 1650.

26 Thomas, *Religion and the Decline of Magic*, p. 162.

27 Hill, *World Turned Upside Down*, pp. 226–7.

28 Ibid., p. 211.

29 R. Moore, *The Light in their Consciences: Early Quakers in Britain, 1646–1666*, Philadelphia, PA, 2020, p. 6.

30 Mendelson and Crawford, *Women in Early Modern England*, p. 408.

31 G. Fox, *A Journal or Historical Account Journal*, London, 1694, p. 72.

32 *The Moderate*, 48 (5–12 June 1649).

33 Charles I, *Eikon Basilike: The Pourtraicture of His Sacred Majestie in his Solitude and Sufferings*, London, 1649.

34 J. Milton, *Eikonoklastes in Answer to a Book intitl'd Eikon Basilike*, London, 1649.

35 D. Washbrook, *Writing the English Republic: Poetry, Rhetoric and Politics, 1627–1660*, Cambridge, 1999, p. 223.

36 Wedgwood, *Trial of Charles I*, p. 199.

37 Cromwell, *Writings and Speeches*, II, 127.

38 Slack, *Invention of Improvement*, p. 26.

39 Cromwell, *Writings and Speeches*, II, 325.

40 Ibid., II, 463.

41 Woolrych, *Britain in Revolution*, p. 525.

42 B. Worden, *The Rump Parliament*, Cambridge, 1974, p. 269.

43 M. Brod, 'The Uses of Intelligence: the Case of Lord Craven', in Southcombe and Tapsell (eds.), *Revolutionary England*, p. 117.

44 B. Worden, *Literature and Politics in Cromwellian England*, Oxford, 2009, p. 291.

45 Cromwell, *Writings and Speeches*, III, 52–67.

46 M. Braddick, *The Common Freedom of the People: John Lilburne and the English Revolution*, Oxford, 2018, p. 255.

47 Woolrych, *Britain in Revolution*, p. 550.

48 L. Hutchinson, *Memoirs of the Life of Colonel Hutchinson*, ed. J. Hutchinson and C. Firth, London, 1906, p. 299.

15. A GOOD CONSTABLE TO KEEP THE PEACE OF THE PARISH

1 *Constitutional Documents*, pp. 405–17.

2 Worden, *Rump*, p. 360.

3 Cromwell, *Writings and Speeches*, III, 434–43.

4 J. Rutt (ed.), *Diary of Thomas Burton, Member in the Parliaments of Oliver and Richard Cromwell, from 1656 to 1659, with an Account of the Parliament of 1654 from the Journal of Guibbon Goddard*, 4 vols, London, 1828, I, lxiv.

5 J. Fitzgibbons, 'The Definition of Treason and the Offer of the Crown', in Southcombe and Tapsell (eds.), *Revolutionary England*, p. 130.

6 TNA, SP 18/95 f. 88.

7 Fitzgibbons, 'Definition of Treason'.

8 Keay, *Restless Republic*, p. 210.

9 Underdown, *Freeborn People*, p. 97.

10 Ibid., p. 101.

11 B. Capp, *England's Culture Wars: Puritan Reformation and its Enemies in the Interregnum, 1649–1660*, Oxford, 2012, p. 72.

12 Ibid., p. 92.

13 Ibid., p. 153.

14 Ibid., p. 180.

15 Ibid., p. 189.

16 Ibid., p. 177.

17 Ibid., p. 120.

18 Ibid., p. 2.

19 Ibid., p. 23.

20 G. Southcombe, 'Thomas Ady and the Politics of Scepticism in Cromwellian England', in Southcombe and Tapsell (eds.), *Revolutionary England*, pp. 163–75.

21 Sharpe, *Instruments of Darkness*, p. 221.

22 Southcombe, 'Thomas Ady', p. 168.

23 *Diary of Thomas Burton*, pp. 53–208; L. Damrosch, *The Sorrows of the Quaker Jesus: James Nayler and the Puritan Crackdown on the Free Spirit*, London, 1996, pp. 177–229.

24 *Diary of Thomas Burton*, p. 317.

25 *Constitutional Documents*, pp. 447–59.

26 C. H. Firth, 'Cromwell and the Crown II', *English Historical Review*, 69 (1903), p. 55.

27 Fitzgibbons, 'Definition of Treason', p. 141.

28 Woolrych, *Britain in Revolution*, p. 653.

29 B. Worden, *God's Instruments: Political Conduct in the England of Oliver Cromwell*, Oxford, 2012, pp. 13–32.

30 Fox, *Journal*, p. 188.

31 Cromwell, *Writings and Speeches*, IV, 512–14.

32 Capp, *England's Culture Wars*, p. 154.

33 K. Thomas, *The Ends of Life: Roads to Fulfilment in Early Modern England*, Oxford, 2009, p. 120.

34 *Acts and Ordinances*, pp. 1162–70.

16. PROVIDENCE AND POWER

1 Fox, *Journal*, p. 195.

2 R. Hutton, *The Restoration: A Political and Religious History of England and Wales, 1658–1667*, Oxford, 1985, p. 21.

3 Ibid., p. 68.

4 Keay, *Restless Republic*, p. 317.

5 G. Smith, *The Cavaliers in Exile, 1640–1660*, London, 2003, p. 166.

6 Woolrych, *Britain in Revolution*, p. 707.

7 Coleby, *Central Government and the Localities*, p. 77.

8 Thomas, *Religion and the Decline of Magic*, p. 399.

9 F. Maseres (ed.), *Select Tracts Relating to the Civil Wars in England in the Reign of Charles the First*, London, 1815, pp. 703, 770.

10 C. Hill, 'God and the English Revolution', *History Workshop Journal*, 17 (1984), p. 26.

11 R. Latham and W. Matthews, *The Diary of Samuel Pepys*, 11 vols, London, 1970–1983), I, 7 February 1660.

12 Ibid., I, 15 February 1660.

13 Ibid., I, 22 February 1660.

14 Ibid., I, 27 February 1660.

15 Ibid., I, 15 March 1660.

16 M. Nedham, *News from Brussels*, London, 1660.

17 Anon., *Arsy Versy: Or, the Second Martyrdom of the Rump*, London, 1660.

18 These, together with many other scurrilous, bottom-featuring anti-Rump tracts, were collected and published in November 1659 in: *Ratts Rhimed to Death, or, the Rump Parliament Hang'd Up in the Shambles*, London, 1659, pp. 73–9. Anon., *The Four Legg'd Quaker*, London, 1664, but on the Bodleian Library's copy, there is a handwritten note attributing the verse to Birkenhead. J. Denham (attrib.), *A Relation of a Quaker, that to the shame of his profession, attempted to Bugger a Mare near Colchester*, London, 1659.

19 D. Farr, *John Lambert: Parliamentary Soldier and Cromwellian Major-General, 1619–1684*, Woodbridge, 2003, p. 212.

20 *House of Commons Journal*, 1 May 1660.

21 Underdown, *Freeborn People*, p. 89.

22 A. Ailes, ' "A Pair of *Garters*": Heralds and Heraldry at the Restoration', in Southcombe and Tapsell (eds.), *Revolutionary England*, p. 223.

23 *Diary of Samuel Pepys*, I, 31 May 1660.

24 T. Harris, *Restoration: Charles II and his Kingdoms, 1660–1685*, London, 2006, p. 4.

25 N. Jose, *Ideas of the Restoration in English Literature, 1660–71*, London, 1984, p. 32.

26 TNA, SP 29/1 f. 16.

27 E. Ludlow, *A Voyce from the Watch Tower: Part Five, 1662*, ed. A. B. Worden, Camden Society, 4th ser., 21, 1978, 215.

28 G. Southcombe and G. Tapsell, *Restoration Politics, Religion and Culture: Britain and Ireland, 1660–1714*, London, 2009, p. 10.

29 *Diary of John Evelyn*, II, 158.

30 Harris, *Restoration*, p. 49.

31 12 Charles II, c. 14.

32 T. P. Slaughter (ed.), *Ideology and Politics on the Eve of the Restoration: Newcastle's Advice to Charles II*, Philadelphia, PA, 1984.

33 S. Johnson, 'Waller', *The Lives of the English Poets*, ed. G. Hill, 3 vols, Oxford, 1905, I, 271.

34 *Diary of Samuel Pepys*, II, 10 January 1661.

35 T. Harris, *Politics under the Late Stuarts: Party Conflict in a Divided Society, 1660–1715*, London, 1993, p. 37.

36 A. Bryant (ed.), *The Letters, Speeches and Declarations of King Charles II*, London, 1935, p. 128.

37 B. Cowan, 'The Rise of the Coffeehouse Reconsidered', *Historical Journal*, 47 (2004), pp. 28–9.

38 Southcombe and Tapsell, *Restoration Politics, Religion and Culture*, p. 13.

39 Hutton, *Restoration*, p. 186.

40 S. Butler, *Hudibras: Written in the Time of the Late Wars*, London, 1663.

41 Quoted in Higgins, 'Reactions of Women', p. 184.

42 Aubrey, *Brief Lives*, pp. 386–7.

43 *Diary of Samuel Pepys*, III, 26 December 1662.

17. THE BLAZING WORLD

1   R. Rideal, *1666: Plague, War and Hellfire*, London, 2017, p. 36.

2   T. Sprat, *The History of the Royal-Society of London for the Improving of Natural Knowledge*, London, 1667, p. 362.

3   Hunter, *John Aubrey*, p. 45.

4   R. Filmer, *An Advertisement to the Jury-men of England, touching Witches*, London, 1653, p. 8.

5   Sprat, *History*, p. 53.

6   Hunter, *John Aubrey*, pp. 15–16.

7   M. Hunter, *Science and Society in Restoration England*, Cambridge, 1981, p. 29.

8   M. Feingold, 'The Origins of the Royal Society Revisited', in S. Mandelbrote and M. Pelling (eds.), *The Practice of Reform in Health, Medicine, and Science, 1500–2000: Essays for Charles Webster*, London, 2005, p. 181.

9   Hunter, *John Aubrey*, p. 16.

10 Hunter, *Science and Society*, p. 5.

11 Ibid., p. 130.

12 D. Wootton, *The Invention of Science: A New History of the Scientific Revolution*, London, 2015, p. 282.

13 R. Hooke, *Micrographia, or, Some Physiological Descriptions of Minute Bodies made by Magnifying Glasses*, London, 1665.

14 D. A. Kronick, *'Devant le deluge' and Other Essays on Early Modern Scientific Communication*, Oxford, 2004, p. 164.

15 S. Danforth, *An Astronomical Description of the Late Comet or Blazing-Star as it Appeared in New-England*, Cambridge, 1665.

16 Thomas, *Religion and the Decline of Magic*, p. 11.

17 Rideal, *1666*, p. 29.

18 *Diary of Samuel Pepys*, VI, 30 August 1665.

19 Rideal, *1666*, pp. 46–7.

20 Thomas, *Religion and the Decline of Magic*, p. 667.

21 Rideal, *1666*, p. 68.

22 Ibid., pp. 84–5.

23 P. Slack, *The Impact of Plague in Tudor and Stuart England*, Oxford, 1991, p. 133.

24 S. Porter, *The Great Fire of London*, Stroud, 2009, p. 25.

25 Ibid., p. 27.

26 Ibid., p. 2.

27 *Diary of Samuel Pepys*, VI, 2 September 1665.

28 *Diary of John Evelyn*, II, 253.

29 Porter, *Great Fire*, p. 36.

30 Ibid., p. 34.

31 TNA, SP 29/170 f. 69.

32 Porter, *Great Fire*, pp. 68–9.

33 M. A. Kingsley, *Transforming the Word: Prophecy, Poetry and Politics in England, 1650–1742*, London, 2001, p. 91.

34 K. Whitaker, *Mad Madge: Margaret Cavendish, Duchess of Newcastle. Royalist, Writer and Romantic*, London, 2003, p. 15.

35 Ibid., p. 20.

36 Ibid., p. 24.

37 Ibid., p. 22.

38 Ibid., p. 160.

39 Ibid., p. 1.

40 Ibid., p. 192.

41 Ibid., p. 286.

42 Duchess of Newcastle, *Observations upon Experimental Philosophy, to which is Added The Description of a New Blazing World*, London, 1666.

43 *Diary of Samuel Pepys*, VIII, 30 March 1667.

44 *Diary of John Evelyn*, II, 269.

45 Whitaker, *Mad Madge*, pp. 296–7.

46 M. Narain, 'Notorious Celebrity: Margaret Cavendish and the Spectacle of Fame', *Journal of the Midwest Modern Language Association*, 42 (2009), p. 84.

47 *Diary of Samuel Pepys*, VIII, 11 April 1667.

48 Whitaker, *Mad Madge*, p. 16.

49 Narain, 'Notorious Celebrity', p. 89.

50 *Diary of Samuel Pepys*, IX, 18 March 1668.

18. ALL THE BLESSINGS OF HEAVEN AND EARTH

1 *Diary of Samuel Pepys*, VIII, 19 July 1667.

2 E. Chamberlayne, *Angliae notitiae, or, The Present State of England*, London, 1669.

3 R. Gair, 'Edward Chamberlayne (1616–1703)', *ODNB* (2004).

4 Hunter, *Science and Society*, pp. 95–6.

5 E. Forbes, L. Murdin and M. Forbes (eds.), *The Correspondence of John Flamsteed, the first Astronomer Royal*, 3 vols, Bristol, 1995–2002, I, p. 13.

6 Thomas, *Religion and the Decline of Magic*, p. 270.

7 Hunter, *John Aubrey*, p. 135.

8 J. Aubrey, *Miscellanies*, London, 1696, p. 67.

9 Hunter, *Science and Society*, p. 174.

10 M. Hunter, 'Robert Boyle (1627–1691)', *ODNB* (2015).

11 J. Ray, *The Wisdom of God manifested in the Works of Creation*, London, 1691, p. 11.

12 I. Newton, *Philosophiae Naturalis Principia Mathematica* (1687).

13 Aubrey, *Brief Lives*, pp. 100–104.

14 Hunter, *John Aubrey*, p. 48.

15 Ibid., pp. 54–5.

16 Ibid., p. 113.

17 Ibid., p. 220.

18 Ibid., p. 115.

19 J. Aubrey, *The Natural History of Wiltshire: written between 1656 and 1691*, ed. J. Britton, London, 1847, p. 11.

20 Aubrey, *Natural History and Antiquities of the County of Surrey*, IV, 147–8.

21 Slack, *Invention of Improvement*, p. 116.

22 Ibid., p. 119.

23 Ibid., p. 28.

24 Ibid.

25 Ibid., p. 163.

26 Ibid., p. 28.

27 J. Hoppit, *A Land of Liberty? England, 1689–1727*, Oxford, 2002, p. 364.

28 Slack, *Invention of Improvement*, p. 108.

29 Ibid., p. 133.

30 M. Overton, *Agricultural Revolution in England: The Transformation of the Agrarian Economy, 1500–1850*, Cambridge, 1996, p. 87.

31 Underdown, *Freeborn People*, p. 122.

32 S. Macfarlane, 'Social Policy and the Poor in the Later 17th Century', in A. L. Beier and R. Finlay (eds.), *London, 1500–1700: The Making of the Metropolis*, London, 1986, p. 253.

33 S. Amussen, *Caribbean Exchanges: Slavery and the Transformation of English Society, 1640–1700*, Chapel Hill, NC, 2007, pp. 177–226.

34 Hoppit, *Land of Liberty?*, p. 448.

35 F. Kirkman, *The Wits, or Sport upon Sport*, London, 1662.

36 J. Sharpe and J. Dickinson, 'Revisiting the "Violence we have Lost": Homicide in Seventeenth-Century Cheshire', *English Historical Review*, 131 (2016), p. 321.

37 J. Ogilby, *Britannia*, London, 1675.

38 Slack, *Invention of Improvement*, p. 173; Hoppit, *Land of Liberty?*, p. 333.

39 Slack, *Invention of Improvement*, p. 174.

40 Hoppit, *Land of Liberty?*, p. 430.

41 C. Fiennes, *The Journeys of Celia Fiennes*, ed. C. Morris, London 1947, pp. 132–7.

42 Hoppit, *Land of Liberty?*, p. 320.

43 Slack, *Invention of Improvement*, p. 143.

44 Ibid., p. 146.

45 Ibid., p. 145.

46 Ibid., p. 156.

47 J. Hatcher, *The History of the British Coal Industry*, vol. I: *Before 1700, towards the Age of Coal*, Oxford, 1993, p. 55; Hoppit, *Land of Liberty?*, p. 324.

48 E. A. Wrigley, *Continuity, Chance, and Change: The Character of the Industrial Revolution in England*, Cambridge, 1990.

49 Aubrey, *Brief Lives*, p. 200.

50 Mendelson and Crawford, *Women in Early Modern England*, pp. 37–8; Sharpe and Dickinson, 'Revisiting the "Violence we have Lost"'; Hoppit, *Land of Liberty?*, p. 482.

51 Hindle, *State and Social Change*, pp. 116–45.

52 J. Sharpe, *Crime in Seventeenth-Century England: A County Study*, Cambridge, 1983, pp. 198–200.

53 R. Gough, *The History of Myddle*, ed. D. Hey, Harmondsworth, 1981, pp. 145–6.

54 Sharpe, *Instruments of Darkness*, p. 251.

55 Underdown, *Freeborn People*, p. 119.

56 Thomas, *Religion and the Decline of Magic*, p. 529.

57 Ibid., p. 297.

58 Sharpe, *Instruments of Darkness*, pp. 213–34.

59 Thomas, *Religion and the Decline of Magic*, pp. 546–7.

60 Hoppit, *Land of Liberty?*, p. 66.

61 P. Crawford and S. Mendelson, 'Sexual identities in early modern England: the marriage of two women in 1680', *Gender and History*, 7 (1995), pp. 362–77.

62 M. McClain, 'Love, Friendship, and Power: Queen Mary II's Letters to Frances Apsley', *Journal of British Studies*, 47 (2008), pp. 505–27.

19. THE ORIGINAL SOVEREIGN POWER OF MR MULTITUDE

1　R. S. Woolhouse, *John Locke: A Biography*, Cambridge, 2009, p. 9.

2　Ibid., p. 11.

3　Ibid., p. 23.

4　Ibid., p. 52.

5　Ibid., p. 45.

6　Ibid., p. 63.

7　*The Fundamental Constitutions of Carolina*, London, 1669, p. 23.

8　Thomas, *Religion and the Decline of Magic*, p. 345.

9　*Diary of John Evelyn*, II, 356.

10　M. Knights, 'Thomas Osborne, first duke of Leeds (1632–1712)', *ODNB* (2008).

11　Anon., *A Letter from a Person of Quality, to his Friend in the Country*, London, 1675.

12　J. Kenyon, *The Popish Plot*, London, 2000, p. 54.

13　Ibid., pp. 94–5.

14　Ibid., p. 92.

15　A. Grey, *Debates of the House of Commons*, VI, London, 1769, 4 November 1678.

16　Kenyon, *Popish Plot*, pp. 95–6.

17　Coleby, *Central Government and the Localities*, p. 180.

18　Kenyon, *Popish Plot*, p. 116.

19　Ibid., p. 113.

20　Ibid., p. 146.

21　Ibid., p. 149.

22　*Grey's Debates*, VII, 1 April 1679.

23　Kenyon, *Popish Plot*, p. 266.

24　Ibid., p. 179.

25　A. Keay, *The Last Royal Rebel: The Life and Death of James, Duke of Monmouth*, London, 2017, pp. 207–8.

26　Kenyon, *Popish Plot*, pp. 188–9.

27　Ibid., p. 201.

28　*Diary of John Evelyn*, III, 33.

29　Kenyon, *Popish Plot*, p. 210.

30　Ibid., pp. 214–15.

31　Harris, *Restoration*, p. 224.

32　Ibid., p. 246.

33　R. Filmer, *Patriarcha: or the Natural Power of Kings*, London, 1680.

34　H. Love, 'Sir Roger L'Estrange (1616–1704)', *ODNB* (2007).

35 Kenyon, *Popish Plot*, p. 232.

36 Ibid.

37 Harris, *Restoration*, p. 255.

38 Ibid., p. 268.

39 G. S. De Krey, 'Stephen College (c. 1635–1681)', *ODNB* (2008).

40 *Colonel Sidney's Speech delivered to the Sheriff on the Scaffold, December 7th 1683*, London, 1683, p. 7.

41 *The Judgement and Decree of the University of Oxford passed in their Convocation July 21 1683 against certain pernicious books and damnable doctrines destructive to the sacred persons of princes, their state and government, and of all humane society*, Oxford, 1683.

42 Harris, *Restoration*, p. 326.

43 Ibid., p. 195.

44 Woolhouse, *John Locke*, p. 211.

45 Ibid., p. 207.

20. THE LAST REVOLUTION

1 *Diary of John Evelyn*, III, 140–42.

2 T. Harris, *Revolution: The Great Crisis of the British Monarchy, 1685–1720*, London, 2006, p. 8.

3 Southcombe and Tapsell, *Restoration Politics, Religion and Culture*, p. 77.

4 Harris, *Revolution*, p. 49.

5 *An Account of what His Majesty Said at his First Coming to Council*, London, 1685.

6 Harris, *Revolution*, p. 73.

7 Kenyon, *Popish Plot*, pp. 288–9.

8 As his father had been.

9 Harris, *Revolution*, p. 83.

10 Ibid., p. 80.

11 Hoppit, *Land of Liberty?*, p. 268.

12 Harris, *Revolution*, p. 89.

13 J. Miller, *Popery and Politics in England, 1660–1688*, Cambridge, 1973, p. 186.

14 *Grey's Debates*, VIII, 9 November 1685.

15 Harris, *Revolution*, p. 98.

16 Ibid., p. 199.

17 Ibid., p. 201.

18 Ibid.

19 Ibid., p. 239.

20 Ibid., p. 226.

21 Ibid., p. 189.

22 Ibid., pp. 253–6.

23 Ibid., p. 250.

24 Ibid., p. 121.

25 Ibid., p. 163.

26 Ibid., p. 258.

27 Ibid., p. 264.

28 Ibid., p. 267.

29 Ibid.

30 Ibid., p. 271.

31 Ibid., pp. 271–2.

32 M. Kishlansky, *A Monarchy Transformed: Britain, 1603–1714*, London, 1997, p. 279.

33 G. Burnet, *History of His Own Time: From the Restoration of King Charles the Second to the Treaty of Peace at Utrecht*, 2 vols, London, 1724–34, I, 780.

34 Hoppit, *Land of Liberty?*, p. 18.

35 *Diary of John Evelyn*, III, 247.

36 Harris, *Revolution*, p. 303.

37 Ibid., p. 304.

38 Ibid., p. 305.

39 Ibid., p. 306.

40 Woolhouse, *John Locke*, p. 262.

41 Anon., *Now is the Time*, London, 1689.

42 Harris, *Revolution*, pp. 317–18.

43 [Robert Ferguson], *A brief justification of the Prince of Orange's Descent into England*, London, 1689, p. 23.

44 Harris, *Revolution*, p. 321.

45 Ibid., p. 323.

46 Ibid., p. 324.

47 Ibid., p. 355.

EPILOGUE

1 Hoppit, *Land of Liberty?*, p. 218.

2 Ibid., p. 470.

3 Ibid., p. 204.

4 Woolhouse, *John Locke*, p. 385.
5 Ibid., p. 415.
6 Ibid., pp. 375–6.
7 Ibid., pp. 396–7.
8 Hoppit, *Land of Liberty?*, pp. 28–9.
9 A. Fox, 'Vernacular culture and popular customs in early modern England: evidence from Thomas Machell's Westmorland', *Cultural and Social History*, 9 (2012), p. 342.

A Note on the Engraving

The upturned church motif is taken from a cheap publication, *The World Turn'd Upside Down*, dating to 1647. It satirises a world in which the normal order of things has been upended by war and revolution: rabbits chase dogs, carts pull horses, and men's trousers come out of their armpits. In the topsy-turvy 'carnival' tradition of the age, the old order would eventually return, though it was far from clear in 1647 that this would happen any time soon. The author, 'T.J.', is John Taylor, the famous 'Water Poet' (whose own initials have been upturned). A dedicated royalist, Taylor would live to see the monarchy abolished in 1649, but died before it returned in 1660.

Image Credits

Plate section: Cartmel Priory: Museum of Lakeland Life and Industry, Kendal, Cumbria, UK © Abbot Hall Art Gallery/Bridgeman Images; View of London, by Wenceslaus Hollar, 1647: Private Collection © Look and Learn/Peter Jackson Collection/Bridgeman Images; Plan of Whitehall Palace: Private Collection © Look and Learn/Peter Jackson Collection/Bridgeman Images; Two views of Westminster, by Wenceslaus Hollar, 1647: Private Collection © Look and Learn/Bridgeman Images; Records of the Star Chamber: courtesy of the author; James I: Musée des Beaux-Arts, Caen, France/Bridgeman Images; Hoghton Tower: Private Collection © Look and Learn/Bridgeman Images; Cotswold Games: Granger/Bridgeman Images; George Villiers: Art Gallery and Museum, Kelvingrove, Glasgow, Scotland © CSG CIC Glasgow Museums Collection/Bridgeman Images; William Laud: National Portrait Gallery, London, UK. Photo © Stefano Baldini/Bridgeman Images; Charles I: Royal Collection Trust © His Majesty King Charles III, 2022/Bridgeman Images; *Sovereign of the Seas*: Parham House, West Sussex, UK © Parham House/Nick McCann/Bridgeman Images; Strafford's trial, by Wenceslaus Hollar, 1641: Private Collection © Look and Learn/Bridgeman Images; Charles's rule unravels: Private Collection/Bridgeman Images; John Pym: Private Collection/Bridgeman Images; Oliver Cromwell after the Battle of Marston Moor: Towneley Hall Art Gallery and Museum, Barnley, Lancashire © Towneley Hall Art Gallery and Museum/Bridgeman Images; Battle of Naseby: Private Collection/Bridgeman Images; The Parliament of Women: Private Collection/Bridgeman Images; Matthew Hopkins, the Witchfinder

Index

A Note About the Author

Jonathan Healey is a historian of the sixteenth and seventeenth centuries and author of *The First Century of Welfare: Poverty and Poor Relief in Lancashire, 1620–1730.* He is associate professor in social history at Oxford University, where he earned his doctorate in 2008. He lives in Oxford.

A Note on the Type

This book was set in Garamond, a typeface originally designed by the famous Parisian type cutter Claude Garamond (ca. 1480–1561). This version of Garamond was modeled on a 1592 specimen sheet from the Egenolff-Berner foundry, which was produced from types thought to have been brought to Frankfurt by Jacques Sabon (d. 1580).

Claude Garamond is one of the most famous type designers in printing history. His distinguished romans and italics first appeared in *Opera Ciceronis* in 1543–44. While delightfully unconventional in design, the Garamond types are clear and open, yet maintain an elegance and precision of line that mark them as French.

Composed by North Market Street Graphics,
Lancaster, Pennsylvania

Printed and bound by Berryville Graphics,
Berryville, Virginia